TRAGEDY:

Plays, Theory, and Criticism

Richard Levin

STATE UNIVERSITY COLLEGE ON LONG ISLAND

HARBRACE SOURCEBOOKS

HARCOURT, BRACE & WORLD

NEW YORK   BURLINGAME

LIBRARY OF CONGRESS CATALOG CARD NUMBER: 60–10391

PRINTED IN THE UNITED STATES OF AMERICA

[d · 3 · 61]

The cover illustration shows James Mason as Oedipus in the production of
Oedipus Rex *at the Stratford Shakespearean Festival in Ontario during
the Festival's second season, 1954. The use of masks derives from the
ancient Greek tradition of performance and typifies the highly stylized
character of the Stratford production. Photo courtesy of Peter Smith
Studio, Stratford, Ontario.*

ACKNOWLEDGMENTS

The editor wishes to thank the following for their permission to reproduce material in this book:

AMERICAN SCANDINAVIAN FOUNDATION: For the selections from
Halvdan Koht, *The Life of Ibsen,* translated by Ruth L.
McMahon and Hanna A. Larsen, Vol. II.

BASIL BLACKWELL: For "The Tragic Form," by Richard B.
Sewall, *Essays in Criticism,* Vol. IV, No. 4 (October 1954).

BOWES & BOWES PUBLISHERS LTD.: For the selection from
Peter F. D. Tennant, *Ibsen's Dramatic Technique.*

CLARENDON PRESS: For excerpts from Ingram Bywater's
translation of Aristotle's *Poetics.* For the selections from
C. M. Bowra, *Sophoclean Tragedy.*

CLASSICAL ASSOCIATION OF THE ATLANTIC STATES: For
"Oedipus Rex as the Ideal Tragic Hero of Aristotle," by
Marjorie Barstow, *Classical Weekly* (since October 1957
Classical World), Vol. VI, No. 1 (October 5, 1912).

CROWELL-COLLIER PUBLISHING CO.: For the excerpt from
Mary B. Mullett, "The Extraordinary Story of Eugene
O'Neill," *American Magazine,* Vol. XCIV, No. 5 (November 1922).

HARCOURT, BRACE & WORLD, INC.: For *The Oedipus Rex of
Sophocles: An English Version* by Dudley Fitts and Robert
Fitzgerald, copyright, 1949, by Harcourt, Brace & World,
Inc. For *Othello* from *Shakespeare: The Complete Works,*
edited by G. B. Harrison, copyright, 1948, by Harcourt,
Brace & World, Inc. For "The Tragic Fallacy" from
The Modern Temper by Joseph Wood Krutch, copyright,
1929, by Harcourt, Brace & World, Inc.; renewed, 1956,
by Joseph Wood Krutch. Reprinted by permission of the
publishers.

HARVARD UNIVERSITY PRESS: For the selection from Cedric H.
Whitman, *Sophocles: A Study of Heroic Humanism,*
Cambridge, Mass.: Harvard University Press, copyright,
1951, by The President and Fellows of Harvard College.
Reprinted by permission of the publishers.

HENRY HOLT AND COMPANY, INC.: For the selection from
Cleanth Brooks and Robert B. Heilman, *Understanding
Drama.*

NEW YORK HERALD TRIBUNE: For the excerpt from "Eugene
O'Neill Talks of His Own and the Plays of Others," New
York *Herald Tribune,* November 16, 1924.

NEW YORK TIMES AND MCA ARTISTS, LTD.: For "Tragedy and
the Common Man," by Arthur Miller, New York *Times,*
February 27, 1949. Copyright, 1949, New York *Times.*

PRINCETON UNIVERSITY PRESS: For the selections from Francis Fergusson, *The Idea of a Theater.*

RANDOM HOUSE, INC.: For *Ghosts* from *Six Plays by Henrik
Ibsen.* Copyright 1951 by Eva Le Gallienne. Reprinted
by permission of Random House, Inc. For *The Hairy Ape,*
copyright, 1922, 1949, by Eugene O'Neill. Reprinted
from *The Plays of Eugene O'Neill,* 3 vols., Vol. III, by
permission of Random House, Inc. For the selection from
"A Note to this Edition," reprinted from *The Plays of
Eugene O'Neill* by permission of Random House, Inc.

ST MARTIN'S PRESS, INC.: For Lecture I, "The Substance of
Shakespearean Tragedy" from Andrew Cecil Bradley,
Shakespearean Tragedy. Used by permission of Macmillan & Company and St Martin's Press.

CHARLES SCRIBNER'S SONS: For excerpts from William Archer,
Introduction to *Ghosts* in *The Works of Henrik Ibsen,*
Vol. VII, Viking Edition. For the selections from *From
Ibsen's Workshop* in *The Works of Henrik Ibsen,* Vol.
XII, Viking Edition.

THE SOCIETY OF AUTHORS AND THE PUBLIC TRUSTEE: For excerpts from George Bernard Shaw, *The Quintessence of
Ibsenism.*

YALE UNIVERSITY PRESS: For *Oedipus,* translated by Clarence W. Mendell, from *Our Seneca.*

Introduction

Tragedy occupies a special place of honor among the arts of Western man. Probably no other mode of esthetic expression has so compellingly engaged his attention over so long a span of history, from its emergence out of the religious rituals of ancient Greece, through two great periods of artistic achievement—the Athens of the fifth century B.C. and the Renaissance, which produced some of the most treasured monuments of our civilization—on down to the present day, when its great vitality and power still inspire playwrights and move audiences. The theoretical discussion of tragedy has had almost as long a history as tragedy itself, going back to the oldest document of literary criticism known to us; in the work of recent scholars and critics we see a resurgence of interest in this intriguing subject. There is no simple or generally accepted explanation for this fascination that tragedy has held for Western man, any more than there is for the closely related problem of why we can take pleasure in the contemplation of the painful events that tragedies portray. However, there can be no dispute over the fact that the tragic form has, over long periods of our history, seemed to authors, audiences, and critics alike to be suited to the most exalted, significant, and beautiful of man's artistic creations.

This book attempts to provide an introduction to the study of tragedy by bringing together some plays which have been considered superior or interesting examples of this literary genre, and some of the more stimulating discussions of these plays and of the nature of tragedy itself. It is designed for possible use in composition courses as controlled source material for written assignments leading up to and including the long research paper, and in courses dealing with world literature, the drama, or literary criticism as a primary or supplementary text; it should be especially appropriate for those courses which combine the teaching of composition and of literature. To serve these purposes, four different kinds of materials have been assembled:

Part One contains four tragedies carefully selected in terms of their special function here.

An attempt was made to choose plays which not only are valuable in themselves and in some sense representative of the major periods of tragic achievement, but which contain enough common features to enable the student to make meaningful comparisons and judgments among them, and to derive meaningful generalizations from them. A number of these common features are indicated in the critical documents in Parts Three and Four and in the suggestions for written assignments.

Part Two supplements the tragedies in several different ways. The various versions of the material used in three of them—Seneca's complete play dealing with the same portion of the Oedipus legend as Sophocles' *Oedipus Rex*, the original source (also complete) from which Shakespeare derived the plot of *Othello*, and a passage from one of Ibsen's early drafts of *Ghosts*—provide for some additional kinds of comparisons and evaluations; and the notes and comments of Ibsen and O'Neill should help to give the student some insight into how these playwrights conceived of their works.

Part Three consists of critical documents dealing with the nature of tragedy selected for their striking differences in doctrine and method and for their applicability to the plays in Part One. Only complete essays are used (except for the *Poetics,* the final portions of which are abridged), so that each critic is represented, not by some isolated and apparently arbitrary opinions, but by a coherent critical position.

Part Four includes a significant sampling of the many contrasting interpretations and judgments that have been evoked by *Oedipus Rex* and *Ghosts*. While these commentaries are necessarily excerpts, each is sufficient to make a coherent point about the play. Besides providing material for comparison and contrast, these selections will serve as models for the student's own analyses of *Othello* and *The Hairy Ape,* which he is left to interpret independently.

The suggestions for written assignments at the end of the book are arranged in an approximate sequence of increasing length and complexity. Beginning with short and carefully controlled exercises on each play and major critical document, they proceed to more complex assignments involving the comparison of some aspect of two or more plays or critical pieces, then to the application of specified critical doctrines to the plays, and terminate in full-length research papers which require the student to select his own material out of all these sources (including both plays and critical documents) and to give it a coherent shape. Finally, some suggestions for papers involving library research have been added. It is hoped that the earlier and simpler assignments will not only provide useful training in composition (they include the basic rhetorical forms usually taught in composition courses: narration, description, comparison, classification, cause-and-effect analysis, etc.) but will also prepare the student to cope with some of the substantive problems he will face in the terminal essay to which the book is directed. Those suggestions which are not used for written assignments might serve as study questions and subjects for class discussion.

In documenting these papers the student can, of course, simply refer to the pages of this edition. However, the source of each selection is fully identified to make it possible for him to cite the sources themselves, if his instructor prefers this method. A reference to a nondramatic work can cite the pages numbers (and, for newspaper articles, the column numbers) of that source, which are inserted into the text immediately following the last word taken from the page. A reference to a play can be made by act or scene number, to a verse drama, by line number. In Sophocles' and Seneca's plays, where the lineation is continuous, the line numbers alone will identify a passage; in *Othello,* where the lineation begins with each scene, it is necessary to cite act, scene, and line numbers (for example, see the footnote on " Consuls " on the first page of *Othello*).

Every effort has been made to reprint each selection as it appears in the edition named as its source, although some minor mechanical details have been altered to make the usage consistent in this book, and a few obvious errors have been corrected. Hume's spelling and punctuation have been modernized. Omissions are indicated by ellipses, and editorial insertions are bracketed. The *dramatis personae* for *Oedipus Rex, Ghosts,* and *The Hairy Ape* have been added by the present editor; for *Othello,* by G. B. Harrison.

The editor is indebted generally to the earlier sourcebooks of this type, which demonstrated the possibilities of this project, and, in particular, to Professor Hans J. Gottlieb of New York University, Professor David Levin of Stanford University, and Professor Richard B. Sewall of Yale University, whose criticisms of the original manuscript provided some valuable suggestions which have been incorporated into the book.

RICHARD LEVIN

State University College on Long Island
February, 1960

Contents

1. Four Tragedies

Oedipus Rex is the commonly used Latin title for Sophocles' *Oedipus Tyrranos,* which was produced about 430 B.C. in Athens at the annual festival of Dionysos. The usual English translation is *Oedipus the King.*

The opening of the play will be clearer to the reader if he understands some of the preceding events that are known to all the characters and frequently alluded to by them. Laïos, the previous King of Thebes, had been mysteriously killed, perhaps about ten years before the play begins. Shortly after his death a monster, the Sphinx, settled in the area and killed all passers-by who could not solve the riddle she asked them. When Oedipus reached Thebes in his flight from his home in Corinth, he encountered the Sphinx and, by answering the riddle, destroyed her. In gratitude the people of Thebes made him their King, and he married Iokastê, the widow of Laïos. They had two sons and two daughters, and all went well with Thebes for years until a terrible plague struck the city.

The designations of the parts of the play (Prologue, Párodos, Éxodos, etc.) are explained in Chapter 12 of Aristotle's *Poetics,* in Part Three of this book. The present translators have used the term "scene" for what Aristotle calls an "episode," and "ode" for what he calls the "stasimon." The Chorus sang or chanted the Párodos and Odes to a musical accompaniment while they performed an interpretive dance, probably dancing in one direction during the Strophe and executing the same movement in the opposite direction during the Antistrophe. At the end of their song they probably remained in the orchestra, silently observing the action until the next Ode, although their leader (the Choragos) sometimes conversed with the characters and, at points of great emotional intensity, might join with them in a kind of responsive song or chant, which Aristotle calls a Commos (see the passages in this play beginning with Scene ii. 615 and Éxodos, 1267). Perhaps the entire Chorus joined in during the Commos.

The version by Dudley Fitts and Robert Fitzgerald printed here incorporates their latest revisions made in 1959, and is taken from *Four Greek Plays,* edited by Dudley Fitts (N.Y.: Harcourt, Brace, 1960).

The exact date of *The Tragedy of Othello, the Moor of Venice* is not known, but it was probably written and produced in 1602 or 1603, shortly after *Hamlet* and before *King Lear.* It was published in quarto form in 1622, and the following year it was included, in a somewhat different version, in the First Folio of Shakespeare's collected plays (these two editions are referred to in the footnotes as Q1 and F1, respectively).

The text of the play used here and all the footnotes are taken from *Shakespeare: The Complete Plays,* edited by G. B. Harrison (N.Y.: Harcourt, Brace, 1948). Some notes refer to other plays of Shakespeare by their common abbreviations.

When *Ghosts* (*Gengangere*) was published in 1881, it was attacked so violently that no Scandinavian theater would touch it for some time. (See the letter Ibsen wrote during this period, reprinted in Part Two.) It was apparently first produced in Chicago in 1882, in its original tongue (the Dano-Norwegian literary language), and its first European performance took place in August 1883 in Helsingborg, Sweden.

The translation by Eva LeGallienne used here is taken from *Six Plays by Henrik Ibsen* (N.Y.: Random House, n.d.).

The Hairy Ape: A Comedy of Ancient and Modern Life in Eight Scenes originated as a short story, written in 1917 and never published. O'Neill rewrote it in its present form in 1921; it was first produced in New York City on March 9, 1922. The text is taken from *The Plays of Eugene O'Neill* (N.Y.: Random House, n.d.), Vol. III.

Oedipus Rex

by Sophocles

OEDIPUS, *King of Thebes, supposed son of Polybos and Meropê, King and Queen of Corinth*

IOKASTÊ, *wife of Oedipus and widow of the late King Laïos*

KREON, *brother of Iokastê, a prince of Thebes*

TEIRESIAS, *a blind seer who serves Apollo*

PRIEST

MESSENGER, *from Corinth*

SHEPHERD, *former servant of Laïos*

SECOND MESSENGER, *from the palace*

CHORUS OF THEBAN ELDERS

CHORAGOS, *leader of the Chorus*

ANTIGONE *and* ISMENE, *young daughters of Oedipus and Iokastê (They appear in the Éxodos but do not speak.)*

SUPPLIANTS, GUARDS, SERVANTS

THE SCENE. *Before the palace of Oedipus, King of Thebes. A central door and two lateral doors open onto a platform which runs the length of the façade. On the platform, right and left, are altars; and three steps lead down into the* orchêstra, *or chorus-ground. At the beginning of the action these steps are crowded by suppliants who have brought branches and chaplets of olive leaves and who sit in various attitudes of despair.* OEDIPUS *enters.*

Prologue

OED. My children, generations of the living
In the line of Kadmos,° nursed at his ancient
    hearth:
Why have you strewn yourselves before these altars
In supplication, with your boughs and garlands?
The breath of incense rises from the city   5
With a sound of prayer and lamentation.
                            Children,
I would not have you speak through messengers,
And therefore I have come myself to hear you —
I, Oedipus, who bear the famous name.
[*To a* PRIEST] You, there, since you are eldest in
    the company,   10
Speak for them all, tell me what preys upon you,
Whether you come in dread, or crave some bless-
    ing:
Tell me, and never doubt that I will help you
In every way I can; I should be heartless
Were I not moved to find you suppliant here.   15
    PRIEST. Great Oedipus, O powerful king of
    Thebes!
You see how all the ages of our people
Cling to your altar steps: here are boys
Who can barely stand alone, and here are priests
By weight of age, as I am a priest of God,   20
And young men chosen from those yet unmarried;
As for the others, all that multitude,
They wait with olive chaplets in the squares,
At the two shrines of Pallas,° and where Apollo°
Speaks in the glowing embers.
                      Your own eyes   25
Must tell you: Thebes is tossed on a murdering sea
And can not lift her head from the death surge.
A rust consumes the buds and fruits of the earth;
The herds are sick; children die unborn,
And labor is vain. The god of plague and pyre   30
Raids like detestable lightning through the city,
And all the house of Kadmos is laid waste,
All emptied, and all darkened: Death alone
Battens upon the misery of Thebes.

You are not one of the immortal gods, we know;   35
Yet we have come to you to make our prayer
As to the man surest in mortal ways
And wisest in the ways of God. You saved us
From the Sphinx, that flinty singer, and the tribute
We paid to her so long; yet you were never   40
Better informed than we, nor could we teach you:
A god's touch, it seems, enabled you to help us.

Therefore, O mighty power, we turn to you:
Find us our safety, find us a remedy,
Whether by counsel of the gods or of men.   45
A king of wisdom tested in the past
Can act in a time of troubles, and act well.
Noblest of men, restore
Life to your city! Think how all men call you
Liberator for your boldness long ago;   50
Ah, when your years of kingship are remembered,

---

1. Kadmos: the founder of Thebes and great-grandfather of Laïos. See Scene i. 254–55. The "line of Kadmos" would be all the citizens of Thebes, just as Thebes itself is called the "house of Kadmos." See Prologue, 32.

24. Pallas: Athenê, the goddess regarded as the preserver of the state and the patroness of the fine and useful arts, particularly agriculture. **Apollo:** the god of punishment, and also the god of healing, of music, and of prophecy. He is the patron of Teiresias and of the oracle at Delphi.

Let them not say *We rose, but later fell* —
Keep the State from going down in the storm!
Once, years ago, with happy augury,
You brought us fortune; be the same again!   55
No man questions your power to rule the land:
But rule over men, not over a dead city!
Ships are only hulls, high walls are nothing,
When no life moves in the empty passageways.
    OED. Poor children! You may be sure I know   60
All that you longed for in your coming here.
I know that you are deathly sick; and yet,
Sick as you are, not one is as sick as I.
Each of you suffers in himself alone
His anguish, not another's; but my spirit   65
Groans for the city, for myself, for you.

I was not sleeping, you are not waking me.
No, I have been in tears for a long while
And in my restless thought walked many ways.
In all my search I found one remedy,   70
And I have adopted it: I have sent Kreon,
Son of Menoikeus, brother of the queen,
To Delphi, Apollo's place of revelation,
To learn there, if he can,
What act or pledge of mine may save the city.   75
I have counted the days, and now, this very day,
I am troubled, for he has overstayed his time.
What is he doing? He has been gone too long.
Yet whenever he comes back, I should do ill
Not to take any action the god orders.   80
    PRIEST. It is a timely promise. At this instant
They tell me Kreon is here.
    OED.   O Lord Apollo!
May his news be fair as his face is radiant!
    PRIEST. Good news, I gather! he is crowned with
bay,°
The chaplet is thick with berries.
    OED.   We shall soon
    know;   85
He is near enough to hear us now.
                [*Enter* KREON.]
                    O prince:
Brother: son of Menoikeus:
What answer do you bring us from the god?
    KRE. A strong one. I can tell you, great afflictions
Will turn out well, if they are taken well.   90
    OED. What was the oracle? These vague words
Leave me still hanging between hope and fear.
    KRE. Is it your pleasure to hear me with all these
Gathered around us? I am prepared to speak,
But should we not go in?
    OED.   Speak to them all,   95
It is for them I suffer, more than for myself.
    KRE. Then I will tell you what I heard at Delphi.

---

84. bay: the laurel, sacred to Apollo, worn in a chaplet or wreath
around the head as a symbol of victory.

In plain words
The god commands us to expel from the land of
    Thebes
An old defilement we are sheltering.   100
It is a deathly thing, beyond cure;
We must not let it feed upon us longer.
    OED. What defilement? How shall we rid our-
selves of it?
    KRE. By exile or death, blood for blood. It was
Murder that brought the plague-wind on the city.
    OED. Murder of whom? Surely the god has
named him?   106
    KRE. My lord: Laïos once ruled this land,
Before you came to govern us.
    OED.   I know;
I learned of him from others; I never saw him.
    KRE. He was murdered; and Apollo commands
us now   110
To take revenge upon whoever killed him.
    OED. Upon whom? Where are they? Where shall
we find a clue
To solve that crime, after so many years?
    KRE. Here in this land, he said. Search reveals
Things that escape an inattentive man.   115
    OED. Tell me: Was Laïos murdered in his house,
Or in the fields, or in some foreign country?
    KRE. He said he planned to make a pilgrimage.
He did not come home again.
    OED.   And was there no one,
No witness, no companion, to tell what happened?
    KRE. They were all killed but one, and he got
away   121
So frightened that he could remember one thing
only.
    OED. What was that one thing? One may be the
key
To everything, if we resolve to use it.
    KRE. He said that a band of highwaymen attacked
them,   125
Outnumbered them, and overwhelmed the king.
    OED. Strange, that a highwayman should be so
daring —
Unless some faction here bribed him to do it.
    KRE. We thought of that. But after Laïos' death
New troubles arose and we had no avenger.   130
    OED. What troubles could prevent your hunting
down the killers?
    KRE. The riddling Sphinx's song
Made us deaf to all mysteries but her own.
    OED. Then once more I must bring what is dark
to light.
It is most fitting that Apollo shows,   135
As you do, this compunction for the dead.
You shall see how I stand by you, as I should,
Avenging this country and the god as well,
And not as though it were for some distant friend,
But for my own sake, to be rid of evil.   140

Whoever killed King Laïos might — who knows? —
Lay violent hands even on me — and soon.
I act for the murdered king in my own interest.

Come, then, my children: leave the altar steps,
Lift up your olive boughs!
              One of you go   145
And summon the people of Kadmos to gather here.
I will do all that I can; you may tell them that.
                    [*Exit a* PAGE.]

So, with the help of God,
We shall be saved — or else indeed we are lost.

PRIEST. Let us rise, children. It was for this we
     came,   150
And now the king has promised it.
Phoibos° has sent us an oracle; may he descend
Himself to save us and drive out the plague.

     [*Exeunt* OEDIPUS *and* KREON *into the palace by
the central door. The* PRIEST *and the* SUPPLI-
ANTS *disperse R and L. After a short pause the*
CHORUS *enters the* orchêstra.]

Párodos

                         [STROPHE 1]
     CHOR. What is God° singing in his profound
Delphi of gold and shadow?   155
What oracle for Thebes, the sunwhipped city?
Fear unjoints me, the roots of my heart tremble.
Now I remember, O Healer, your power, and
     wonder:
Will you send doom like a sudden cloud, or weave
     it
Like nightfall of the past?   160
Speak to me, tell me, O
Child of golden Hope, immortal Voice.

                     [ANTISTROPHE 1]
Let me pray to Athenê, the immortal daughter of
     Zeus,
And to Artemis° her sister
Who keeps her famous throne in the market ring,
And to Apollo, archer° from distant heaven —   166
O gods, descend! Like three streams leap against
The fires of our grief, the fires of darkness;
Be swift to bring us rest!
As in the old time from the brilliant house   170
Of air you stepped to save us, come again!

Now our afflictions have no end,   [STROPHE 2]
Now all our stricken host lies down

And no man fights off death with his mind;
The noble plowland bears no grain,   175
And groaning mothers can not bear —
See, how our lives like birds take wing,
Like sparks that fly when a fire soars,
To the shore of the god of evening.

The plague burns on, it is pitiless, [ANTISTROPHE 2]
Though pallid children laden with death   181
Lie unwept in the stony ways,
And old gray women by every path
Flock to the strand about the altars
There to strike their breasts and cry   185
Worship of Phoibos in wailing prayers:
Be kind, God's golden child!

                     [STROPHE 3]
There are no swords in this attack by fire,
No shields, but we are ringed with cries.
Send the besieger plunging from our homes   190
Into the vast sea-room of the Atlantic
Or into the waves that foam eastward of Thrace —
For the day ravages what the night spares —
Destroy our enemy, lord of the thunder!
Let him be riven by lightning from heaven!   195

                   [ANTISTROPHE 3]
Phoibos Apollo, stretch the sun's bowstring,
That golden cord, until it sing for us,
Flashing arrows in heaven!
                   Artemis, Huntress,
Race with flaring lights upon our mountains!
O scarlet god, O golden-banded brow,   200
O Theban Bacchos in a storm of Maenads,°
               [*Enter* OEDIPUS, *C.*]
Whirl upon Death, that all the Undying hate!
Come with blinding torches, come in joy!

Scene 1

     OED. Is this your prayer? It may be answered.
     Come,
Listen to me, act as the crisis demands,   205
And you shall have relief from all these evils.

Until now I was a stranger to this tale,
As I had been a stranger to the crime.
Could I track down the murderer without a clue?
But now, friends,   210

---

152. Phoibos: Apollo; the name means "light" or "pure."
154. God: Apollo, whose oracle is at Delphi. Four lines below
he is named by another of his attributes: the Healer. **164. Artemis:** twin sister of Apollo, who has many of his attributes
and is regarded especially as the goddess of flocks and of hunting. **166. archer:** Apollo is also the god of archery. See
Párodos, 196–98.

201. Theban . . . Maenads: Bacchos (or Dionysos), the son of
Zeus and Semele, who was the daughter of Kadmos, was born
in Thebes and regarded as its patron. He is the god of wine
and fertility, and is called "scarlet" here because he is flushed
from drinking. The Maenads (or Bacchae) are his priestesses,
who worked themselves into a kind of frenzy (hence "storm"
and "whirl") at the Dionysiac festivals, out of which the
Greek drama is believed to have evolved (see the *Poetics*,
Chap. 4).

As one who became a citizen after the murder,
I make this proclamation to all Thebans:
If any man knows by whose hand Laïos, son of
    Labdakos,°
Met his death, I direct that man to tell me every-
    thing,
No matter what he fears for having so long with-
    held it.   215
Let it stand as promised that no further trouble
Will come to him, but he may leave the land in
    safety.

Moreover: If anyone knows the murderer to be for-
    eign,
Let him not keep silent: he shall have his reward
    from me.
However, if he does conceal it; if any man   220
Fearing for his friend or for himself disobeys this
    edict,
Hear what I propose to do:

I solemnly forbid the people of this country,
Where power and throne are mine, ever to receive
    that man
Or speak to him, no matter who he is, or let him
Join in sacrifice, lustration, or in prayer.   226
I decree that he be driven from every house,
Being, as he is, corruption itself to us: the Delphic
Voice of Apollo has pronounced this revelation.
Thus I associate myself with the oracle   230
And take the side of the murdered king.

As for the criminal, I pray to God —
Whether it be a lurking thief, or one of a num-
    ber —
I pray that that man's life be consumed in evil and
    wretchedness.
And as for me, this curse applies no less   235
If it should turn out that the culprit is my guest
    here,
Sharing my hearth.
                  You have heard the penalty.
I lay it on you now to attend to this
For my sake, for Apollo's, for the sick
Sterile city that heaven has abandoned.   240
Suppose the oracle had given you no command:
Should this defilement go uncleansed for ever?
You should have found the murderer: your king,
A noble king, had been destroyed!
                       Now I,
Having the power that he held before me,   245
Having his bed, begetting children there
Upon his wife, as he would have, had he lived —
Their son would have been my children's brother,
If Laïos had had luck in fatherhood!
(And now his bad fortune has struck him down) —
I say I take the son's part, just as though   251

I were his son, to press the fight for him
And see it won! I'll find the hand that brought
Death to Labdakos' and Polydoros' child,
Heir of Kadmos' and Agenor's line.°   255
And as for those who fail me,
May the gods deny them the fruit of the earth,
Fruit of the womb, and may they rot utterly!
Let them be wretched as we are wretched, and
    worse!

For you, for loyal Thebans, and for all   260
Who find my actions right, I pray the favor
Of justice, and of all the immortal gods.
    CHORAG. Since I am under oath, my lord, I swear
I did not do the murder, I can not name
The murderer. Phoibos ordained the search;   265
Why did he not say who the culprit was?
    OED. An honest question. But no man in the
    world
Can make the gods do more than the gods will.
    CHORAG. There is an alternative, I think —
    OED.   Tell me.
Any or all, you must not fail to tell me.   270
    CHORAG. A lord clairvoyant to the lord Apollo,
As we all know, is the skilled Teiresias.
One might learn much about this from him, Oedi-
    pus.
    OED. I am not wasting time:
Kreon spoke of this, and I have sent for him —   275
Twice, in fact; it is strange that he is not here.
    CHORAG. The other matter — that old report —
    seems useless.
    OED. What was that? I am interested in all re-
    ports.
    CHORAG. The king was said to have been killed
    by highwaymen.   279
    OED. I know. But we have no witnesses to that.
    CHORAG. If the killer can feel a particle of dread,
Your curse will bring him out of hiding!
    OED.   No.
The man who dared that act will fear no curse.
    [*Enter the blind seer* TEIRESIAS, *led by a* PAGE.]
    CHORAG. But there is one man who may detect the
    criminal.
This is Teiresias, this is the holy prophet   285
In whom, alone of all men, truth was born.
    OED. Teiresias: seer: student of mysteries,
Of all that's taught and all that no man tells,
Secrets of Heaven and secrets of the earth:
Blind though you are, you know the city lies   290
Sick with plague; and from this plague, my lord,
We find that you alone can guard or save us.

Possibly you did not hear the messengers?

---

213. **Labdakos:** See Scene i. 254–55.

254–55. **Labdakos' . . . line:** The child is Laïos, whose father
was Labdakos. Labdakos' father was Polydoros, the son of
Kadmos, and Kadmos' father was Agenor.

Apollo, when we sent to him,
Sent us back word that this great pestilence   295
Would lift, but only if we established clearly
The identity of those who murdered Laïos.
They must be killed or exiled.

                                    Can you use
Birdflight° or any art of divination
To purify yourself, and Thebes, and me   300
From this contagion? We are in your hands.
There is no fairer duty
Than that of helping others in distress.

TEIR. How dreadful knowledge of the truth can
be   304
When there's no help in truth! I knew this well,
But did not act on it: else I should not have come.

OED. What is troubling you? Why are your eyes
so cold?

TEIR. Let me go home. Bear your own fate, and
I'll
Bear mine. It is better so: trust what I say.   309

OED. What you say is ungracious and unhelpful
To your native country. Do not refuse to speak.

TEIR. When it comes to speech, your own is neither temperate
Nor opportune. I wish to be more prudent.

OED. In God's name, we all beg you —

TEIR.   You are all ignorant.
No; I will never tell you what I know.   315
Now it is my misery; then, it would be yours.

OED. What! You do know something, and will
not tell us?
You would betray us all and wreck the State?

TEIR. I do not intend to torture myself, or you.
Why persist in asking? You will not persuade me.

OED. What a wicked old man you are! You'd try
a stone's   321
Patience! Out with it! Have you no feeling at all?

TEIR. You call me unfeeling. If you could only
see
The nature of your own feelings . . .

OED.   Why,
Who would not feel as I do? Who could endure
Your arrogance toward the city?   326

TEIR.   What does it matter?
Whether I speak or not, it is bound to come.

OED. Then, if "it" is bound to come, you are
bound to tell me.

TEIR. No, I will not go on. Rage as you please.

OED. Rage? Why not!
                    And I'll tell you what I think: 330
You planned it, you had it done, you all but
Killed him with your own hands: if you had eyes,
I'd say the crime was yours, and yours alone.

TEIR. So? I charge you, then,
Abide by the proclamation you have made: 335
From this day forth
Never speak again to these men or to me;
You yourself are the pollution of this country.

OED. You dare say that! Can you possibly think
you have
Some way of going free, after such insolence?   340

TEIR. I have gone free. It is the truth sustains me.

OED. Who taught you shamelessness? It was not
your craft.

TEIR. You did. You made me speak. I did not
want to.

OED. Speak what? Let me hear it again more
clearly.

TEIR. Was it not clear before? Are you tempting
me?   345

OED. I did not understand it. Say it again.

TEIR. I say that you are the murderer whom you
seek.

OED. Now twice you have spat out infamy. You'll
pay for it!

TEIR. Would you care for more? Do you wish to
be really angry?

OED. Say what you will. Whatever you say is
worthless.   350

TEIR. I say you live in hideous shame with those
Most dear to you. You can not see the evil.

OED. Can you go on babbling like this for ever?

TEIR. I can, if there is power in truth.

OED.   There is:
But not for you, not for you,   355
You sightless, witless, senseless, mad old man!

TEIR. You are the madman. There is no one here
Who will not curse you soon, as you curse me.

OED. You child of total night! I would not touch
you;
Neither would any man who sees the sun.   360

TEIR. True: it is not from you my fate will come.
That lies within Apollo's competence,
As it is his concern.

OED.   Tell me, who made
These fine discoveries? Kreon? or someone else?

TEIR. Kreon is no threat. You weave your own
doom.   365

OED. Wealth, power, craft of statesmanship!
Kingly position, everywhere admired!
What savage envy is stored up against these,
If Kreon, whom I trusted, Kreon my friend,
For this great office which the city once   370
Put in my hands unsought — if for this power
Kreon desires in secret to destroy me!

He has bought this decrepit fortune-teller, this
Collector of dirty pennies, this prophet fraud —
Why, he is no more clairvoyant than I am!

                                    Tell us:

---

299. Birdflight: Seers such as Teiresias could prophesy from
the flight of birds.   See Scene i. 380–84; Ode I. 468; Scene iii.
919.

Has your mystic mummery ever approached the
    truth?   376
When that hellcat the Sphinx was performing here,
What help were you to these people?
Her magic was not for the first man who came
    along:
It demanded a real exorcist. Your birds —   380
What good were they? or the gods, for the matter
    of that?
But I came by,
Oedipus, the simple man, who knows nothing —
I thought it out for myself, no birds helped me!
And this is the man you think you can destroy,   385
That you may be close to Kreon when he's king!
Well, you and your friend Kreon, it seems to me,
Will suffer most. If you were not an old man,
You would have paid already for your plot.

    CHORAG. We can not see that his words or yours
Have been spoken except in anger, Oedipus,   391
And of anger we have no need. How to accomplish
The god's will best: that is what most concerns us.

    TEIR. You are a king. But where argument's con-
        cerned
I am your man, as much a king as you.   395
I am not your servant, but Apollo's.
I have no need of Kreon or Kreon's name.

Listen to me. You mock my blindness, do you?
But I say that you, with both your eyes, are blind:
You can not see the wretchedness of your life,   400
Nor in whose house you live, no, nor with whom.
Who are your father and mother? Can you tell me?
You do not even know the blind wrongs
That you have done them, on earth and in the
    world below.
But the double lash of your parents' curse will whip
    you   405
Out of this land some day, with only night
Upon your precious eyes.
Your cries then — where will they not be heard?
What fastness of Kithairon° will not echo them?
And that bridal-descant of yours — you'll know it
    then,   410
The song they sang when you came here to Thebes
And found your misguided berthing.
All this, and more, that you can not guess at now,
Will bring you to yourself among your children.

Be angry, then. Curse Kreon. Curse my words.
I tell you, no man that walks upon the earth   416
Shall be rooted out more horribly than you.

    OED. Am I to bear this from him? — Damnation
Take you! Out of this place! Out of my sight!

    TEIR. I would not have come at all if you had not
        asked me.   420

---

409. Kithairon: a mountain near Thebes which assumes greater
importance later in the play.

    OED. Could I have told that you'd talk nonsense,
    that
You'd come here to make a fool of yourself, and of
    me?

    TEIR. A fool? Your parents thought me sane
    enough.

    OED. My parents again! — Wait: who were my
    parents?

    TEIR. This day will give you a father, and break
    your heart.   425

    OED. Your infantile riddles! Your damned abraca-
    dabra!

    TEIR. You were a great man once at solving rid-
    dles.

    OED. Mock me with that if you like; you will find
    it true.

    TEIR. It was true enough. It brought about your
    ruin.   429

    OED. But if it saved this town?

    TEIR. [*To the* PAGE] Boy, give me your hand.

    OED. Yes, boy; lead him away.   430
                   — While you are here
We can do nothing. Go; leave us in peace.

    TEIR. I will go when I have said what I have to
    say.
How can you hurt me? And I tell you again:
The man you have been looking for all this time,
The damned man, the murderer of Laïos,   436
That man is in Thebes. To your mind he is foreign-
    born,
But it will soon be shown that he is a Theban,
A revelation that will fail to please.
                           A blind man,
Who has his eyes now; a penniless man, who is rich
    now;   440
And he will go tapping the strange earth with his
    staff.
To the children with whom he lives now he will be
Brother and father — the very same; to her
Who bore him, son and husband — the very same
Who came to his father's bed, wet with his father's
    blood.   445

Enough. Go think that over.
If later you find error in what I have said,
You may say that I have no skill in prophecy.

    [*Exit* TEIRESIAS, *led by his* PAGE. OEDIPUS *goes
    into the palace.*]

Ode I

                              [STROPHE 1]
    CHOR. The Delphic stone of prophecies
Remembers ancient regicide   450
And a still bloody hand.

That killer's hour of flight has come.
He must be stronger than riderless
Coursers of untiring wind,
For the son of Zeus° armed with his father's thun-
    der   455
Leaps in lightning after him;
And the Furies hold his track, the sad Furies.°

Holy Parnassos'° peak of snow   [ANTISTROPHE 1]
Flashes and blinds that secret man,
That all shall hunt him down: 460
Though he may roam the forest shade
Like a bull gone wild from pasture
To rage through glooms of stone.
Doom comes down on him; flight will not avail
    him;
For the world's heart calls him desolate,   465
And the immortal voices follow, for ever follow.

But now a wilder thing is heard   [STROPHE 2]
From the old man skilled at hearing Fate in the
    wing-beat of a bird.
Bewildered as a blown bird, my soul hovers and
    can not find
Foothold in this debate, or any reason or rest of
    mind.   470
But no man ever brought — none can bring
Proof of strife between Thebes' royal house,
Labdakos' line, and the son of Polybos;°
And never until now has any man brought word
Of Laïos' dark death staining Oedipus the King.

Divine Zeus and Apollo hold   [ANTISTROPHE 2]
Perfect intelligence alone of all tales ever told;   477
And well though this diviner works, he works in
    his own night;
No man can judge that rough unknown or trust in
    second sight,
For wisdom changes hands among the wise.   480
Shall I believe my great lord criminal
At a raging word that a blind old man let fall?
I saw him, when the carrion woman° faced him of
    old,
Prove his heroic mind. These evil words are lies.

Scene II

KRE. Men of Thebes: 485
I am told that heavy accusations
Have been brought against me by King Oedipus.

I am not the kind of man to bear this tamely.

If in these present difficulties

455. son of Zeus: Apollo.   457. Furies: deities of retribution.
458. Parnassos: mountain in Phokis, sacred to Apollo, near the
Delphic oracle.   473. son of Polybos: Oedipus.   483. carrion woman: the Sphinx.

He holds me accountable for any harm to him   490
Through anything I have said or done — why,
    then,
I do not value life in this dishonor.
It is not as though this rumor touched upon
Some private indiscretion. The matter is grave.
The fact is that I am being called disloyal   495
To the State, to my fellow citizens, to my friends.
    CHORAG. He may have spoken in anger, not from
        his mind.
    KRE. But did you not hear him say I was the
        one
Who seduced the old prophet into lying?
    CHORAG. The thing was said; I do not know how
        seriously.   500
    KRE. But you were watching him! Were his eyes
        steady?
Did he look like a man in his right mind?
    CHORAG.   I do not know.
I can not judge the behavior of great men.
But here is the king himself.
                  [Enter OEDIPUS.]
    OED.   So you dared come back.
Why? How brazen of you to come to my house,
You murderer!
              Do you think I do not know   506
That you plotted to kill me, plotted to steal my
    throne?
Tell me, in God's name: am I coward, a fool,
That you should dream you could accomplish this?
A fool who could not see your slippery game?   510
A coward, not to fight back when I saw it?
You are the fool, Kreon, are you not? hoping
Without support or friends to get a throne?
Thrones may be won or bought: you could do nei-
    ther.
    KRE. Now listen to me. You have talked; let me
        talk, too.   515
You can not judge unless you know the facts.
    OED. You speak well: there is one fact; but I find
        it hard
To learn from the deadliest enemy I have.
    KRE. That above all I must dispute with you.
    OED. That above all I will not hear you deny.   520
    KRE. If you think there is anything good in be-
        ing stubborn
Against all reason, then I say you are wrong.
    OED. If you think a man can sin against his own
        kind
And not be punished for it, I say you are mad.
    KRE. I agree. But tell me: what have I done to
        you?   525
    OED. You advised me to send for that wizard, did
        you not?
    KRE. I did. I should do it again.
    OED.   Very well. Now tell me:
How long has it been since Laïos —

KRE.   What of Laïos?
OED. Since he vanished in that onset by the road?
KRE. It was long ago, a long time.
OED.   And this prophet,   530
Was he practicing here then?
KRE.   He was; and with honor, as now.
OED. Did he speak of me at that time?
KRE.   He never did;
At least, not when I was present.
OED.   But . . . the enquiry?
I suppose you held one?
KRE.   We did, but we learned nothing.
OED. Why did the prophet not speak against me
     then?
                                             535
KRE. I do not know; and I am the kind of man
Who holds his tongue when he has no facts to go
on.
OED. There's one fact that you know, and you
     could tell it.
KRE. What fact is that? If I know it, you shall
     have it.
OED. If he were not involved with you, he could
     not say   540
That it was I who murdered Laïos.
KRE. If he says that, you are the one that knows
     it! —
But now it is my turn to question you.
OED. Put your questions. I am no murderer.
KRE. First, then: You married my sister?
OED.   I married your sister.   545
KRE. And you rule the kingdom equally with
     her?
OED. Everything that she wants she has from me.
KRE. And I am the third, equal to both of you?
OED. That is why I call you a bad friend.
KRE. No. Reason it out, as I have done.   550
Think of this first: Would any sane man prefer
Power, with all a king's anxieties,
To that same power and the grace of sleep?
Certainly not I.
I have never longed for the king's power — only his
     rights.   555
Would any wise man differ from me in this?
As matters stand, I have my way in everything
With your consent, and no responsibilities.
If I were king, I should be a slave to policy.

How could I desire a scepter more   560
Than what is now mine — untroubled influence?
No, I have not gone mad; I need no honors,
Except those with the perquisites I have now.
I am welcome everywhere; every man salutes me,
And those who want your favor seek my ear,   565
Since I know how to manage what they ask.
Should I exchange this ease for that anxiety?
Besides, no sober mind is treasonable.
I hate anarchy

And never would deal with any man who likes
     it.   570
Test what I have said. Go to the priestess
At Delphi, ask if I quoted her correctly.
And as for this other thing: if I am found
Guilty of treason with Teiresias,
Then sentence me to death. You have my word
It is a sentence I should cast my vote for — 576
But not without evidence!
                    You do wrong
When you take good men for bad, bad men for
     good.
A true friend thrown aside — why, life itself
Is not more precious!
                    In time you will know this well: 580
For time, and time alone, will show the just man,
Though scoundrels are discovered in a day.
CHORAG. This is well said, and a prudent man
     would ponder it.
Judgments too quickly formed are dangerous.
OED. But is he not quick in his duplicity?   585
And shall I not be quick to parry him?
Would you have me stand still, hold my peace, and
     let
This man win everything, through my inaction?
KRE. And you want — what is it, then? To ban-
     ish me?
OED. No, not exile. It is your death I want,   590
So that all the world may see what treason means.
KRE. You will persist, then? You will not believe
     me?
OED. How can I believe you?
KRE.   Then you are a fool.
OED. To save myself?
KRE.   In justice, think of me.
OED. You are evil incarnate.
KRE.   But suppose that you are wrong?   595
OED. Still I must rule.
KRE.   But not if you rule badly.
OED. O city, city!
KRE.   It is my city, too!
CHORAG. Now, my lords, be still. I see the queen,
Iokastê, coming from her palace chambers;   599
And it is time she came, for the sake of you both.
This dreadful quarrel can be resolved through her.
                    [Enter IOKASTÊ.]
IOK. Poor foolish men, what wicked din is this?
With Thebes sick to death, is it not shameful
That you should rake some private quarrel up?
[To OEDIPUS] Come into the house.
                    — And you, Kreon, go now: 605
Let us have no more of this tumult over nothing.
KRE. Nothing? No, sister: what your husband
     plans for me
Is one of two great evils: exile or death.
OED. He is right.

    Why, woman I have caught him squarely
Plotting against my life.

KRE.   No! Let me die   610
Accurst if ever I have wished you harm!

IOK. Ah, believe it, Oedipus!
In the name of the gods, respect this oath of his
For my sake, for the sake of these people here!

[STROPHE 1°]

CHORAG. Open your mind to her, my lord. Be
    ruled by her, I beg you!   615

OED. What would you have me do?

CHORAG. Respect Kreon's word. He has never
    spoken like a fool,
And now he has sworn an oath.

OED.   You know what you ask?

CHORAG.   I do.

OED.   Speak on, then.

CHORAG. A friend so sworn should not be baited
    so,   620
In blind malice, and without final proof.

OED. You are aware, I hope, that what you say
Means death for me, or exile at the least.

[STROPHE 2]

CHORAG. No, I swear by Helios,° first in Heaven!
May I die friendless and accurst,   625
The worst of deaths, if ever I meant that!
    It is the withering fields
      That hurt my sick heart:
      Must we bear all these ills,
        And now your bad blood as well?   630

OED. Then let him go. And let me die, if I must,
Or be driven by him in shame from the land of
    Thebes.
It is your unhappiness, and not his talk,
That touches me.
             As for him —
Wherever he goes, hatred will follow him.   635

KRE. Ugly in yielding, as you were ugly in rage!
Natures like yours chiefly torment themselves.

OED. Can you not go? Can you not leave me?

KRE.   I can.
You do not know me; but the city knows me,
And in its eyes I am just, if not in yours.   640

[*Exit* KREON.]

[ANTISTROPHE 1]

CHORAG. Lady Iokastê, did you not ask the King
    to go to his chambers?

IOK. First tell me what has happened.

CHORAG. There was suspicion without evidence;
    yet it rankled
As even false charges will.

IOK.   On both sides?

CHORAG.   On both.

IOK.   But what was said?

CHORAG. Oh let it rest, let it be done with!   646
Have we not suffered enough?

OED. You see to what your decency has brought
    you:
You have made difficulties where my heart saw
    none.

[ANTISTROPHE 2]

CHORAG. Oedipus, it is not once only I have told
    you —   650
You must know I should count myself unwise
To the point of madness, should I now forsake
    you —
    You, under whose hand,
      In the storm of another time,
    Our dear land sailed out free.   655
      But now stand fast at the helm!

IOK. In God's name, Oedipus, inform your wife
    as well:
Why are you so set in this hard anger?

OED. I will tell you, for none of these men de-
    serves
My confidence as you do. It is Kreon's work,   660
His treachery, his plotting against me.

IOK. Go on, if you can make this clear to me.

OED. He charges me with the murder of Laïos.

IOK. Has he some knowledge? Or does he speak
    from hearsay?

OED. He would not commit himself to such a
    charge,   665
But he has brought in that damnable soothsayer
To tell his story.

IOK.   Set your mind at rest.
If it is a question of soothsayers, I tell you
That you will find no man whose craft gives knowl-
    edge
Of the unknowable.

            Here is my proof: 670

An oracle was reported to Laïos once
(I will not say from Phoibos himself, but from
His appointed ministers, at any rate)
That his doom would be death at the hands of his
    own son —
His son, born of his flesh and of mine!   675

Now, you remember the story: Laïos was killed
By marauding strangers where three highways
    meet;
But his child had not been three days in this
    world
Before the king had pierced the baby's ankles
And left him to die on a lonely mountainside.   680

Thus, Apollo never caused that child

To kill his father, and it was not Laïos' fate
To die at the hands of his son, as he had feared.
This is what prophets and prophecies are worth!
Have no dread of them.

                It is God himself   685
Who can show us what he wills, in his own way.

    OED. How strange a shadowy memory crossed my
      mind,
Just now while you were speaking; it chilled my
  heart.

    IOK. What do you mean? What memory do you
      speak of?

    OED. If I understand you, Laïos was killed   690
At a place where three roads meet.

    IOK.   So it was said;
We have no later story.

    OED.   Where did it happen?

    IOK. Phokis, it is called: at a place where the
      Theban Way
Divides into the roads toward Delphi and Daulia.

    OED. When?

    IOK. We had the news not long before you came
And proved the right to your succession here.   696

    OED. Ah, what net has God been weaving for me?

    IOK. Oedipus! Why does this trouble you?

    OED.   Do not ask me yet.
First, tell me how Laïos looked, and tell me
How old he was.

    IOK.   He was tall, his hair just touched   700
With white; his form was not unlike your own.

    OED. I think that I myself may be accurst
By my own ignorant edict.

    IOK.   You speak strangely.
It makes me tremble to look at you, my king.

    OED. I am not sure that the blind man can not
      see.   705
But I should know better if you were to tell me —

    IOK. Anything — though I dread to hear you ask
      it.

    OED. Was the king lightly escorted, or did he
      ride
With a large company, as a ruler should?

    IOK. There were five men with him in all: one
      was a herald;
                   710
And a single chariot, which he was driving.

    OED. Alas, that makes it plain enough!

                     But who —
Who told you how it happened?

    IOK.   A household servant,
The only one to escape.

    OED.   And is he still
A servant of ours?

    IOK.   No; for when he came back at last   715
And found you enthroned in the place of the dead
  king,
He came to me, touched my hand with his, and
  begged

That I would send him away to the frontier dis-
  trict
Where only the shepherds go —
As far away from the city as I could send him.
I granted his prayer; for although the man was a
  slave,   721
He had earned more than this favor at my hands.

    OED. Can he be called back quickly?

    IOK.   Easily.
But why?

    OED.   I have taken too much upon myself   724
Without enquiry; therefore I wish to consult him.

    IOK. Then he shall come.

                But am I not one also
To whom you might confide these fears of yours?

    OED. That is your right; it will not be denied you,
Now least of all; for I have reached a pitch
Of wild foreboding. Is there anyone   730
To whom I should sooner speak?

Polybos of Corinth is my father.
My mother is a Dorian: Meropê.
I grew up chief among the men of Corinth
Until a strange thing happened —   735
Not worth my passion, it may be, but strange.

At a feast, a drunken man maundering in his cups
Cries out that I am not my father's son!

I contained myself that night, though I felt anger
And a sinking heart. The next day I visited   740
My father and mother, and questioned them. They
  stormed,
Calling it all the slanderous rant of a fool;
And this relieved me. Yet the suspicion
Remained always aching in my mind;
I knew there was talk; I could not rest;   745
And finally, saying nothing to my parents,
I went to the shrine at Delphi.

The god dismissed my question without reply;
He spoke of other things.

                 Some were clear,
Full of wretchedness, dreadful, unbearable: 750
As, that I should lie with my own mother, breed
Children from whom all men would turn their
  eyes;
And that I should be my father's murderer.

I heard all this, and fled. And from that day
Corinth to me was only in the stars   755
Descending in that quarter of the sky,
As I wandered farther and farther on my way
To a land where I should never see the evil
Sung by the oracle. And I came to this country
Where, so you say, King Laïos was killed.   760

I will tell you all that happened there, my lady.

There were three highways

Coming together at a place I passed;
And there a herald came towards me, and a chariot
Drawn by horses, with a man such as you describe
Seated in it. The groom leading the horses   766
Forced me off the road at his lord's command;
But as this charioteer lurched over towards me
I struck him in my rage. The old man saw me
And brought his double goad down upon my head
As I came abreast.

                He was paid back, and more!
Swinging my club in this right hand I knocked
    him   772
Out of his car, and he rolled on the ground.

                             I killed him.

I killed them all.
Now if that stranger and Laïos were — kin,   775
Where is a man more miserable than I?
More hated by the gods? Citizen and alien alike
Must never shelter me or speak to me —
I must be shunned by all.

                  And I myself
Pronounced this malediction upon myself!   780

Think of it: I have touched you with these hands,
These hands that killed your husband. What defilement!

Am I all evil, then? It must be so,
Since I must flee from Thebes, yet never again
See my own countrymen, my own country,   785
For fear of joining my mother in marriage
And killing Polybos, my father.

                      Ah,
If I was created so, born to this fate,
Who could deny the savagery of God?

O holy majesty of heavenly powers!   790
May I never see that day! Never!
Rather let me vanish from the race of men
Than know the abomination destined me!
    CHORAG. We too, my lord, have felt dismay at
    this.
But there is hope: you have yet to hear the shep-
    herd.   795
    OED. Indeed, I fear no other hope is left me.
    IOK. What do you hope from him when he
    comes?
    OED.   This much:
If his account of the murder tallies with yours,
Then I am cleared.
    IOK.   What was it that I said
Of such importance?
    OED.   Why, " marauders," you said,
Killed the king, according to this man's story.   801
If he maintains that still, if there were several,
Clearly the guilt is not mine: I was alone.
But if he says one man, singlehanded, did it,
Then the evidence all points to me.   805

    IOK. You may be sure that he said there were sev-
    eral;
And can he call back that story now? He can not
The whole city heard it as plainly as I.
But suppose he alters some detail of it:
He can not ever show that Laïos' death   810
Fulfilled the oracle: for Apollo said
My child was doomed to kill him; and my child —
Poor baby! — it was my child that died first.

No. From now on, where oracles are concerned,
I would not waste a second thought on any.   815
    OED. You may be right.
                      But come: let someone go
For the shepherd at once. This matter must be set-
tled.
    IOK. I will send for him.
I would not wish to cross you in anything,
And surely not in this. — Let us go in.   820
                    [Exeunt into the palace.]

Ode II

                                  [STROPHE 1]
    CHOR. Let me be reverent in the ways of right,
Lowly the paths I journey on;
Let all my words and actions keep
The laws of the pure universe
From highest Heaven handed down.   825
For Heaven is their bright nurse,
Those generations of the realms of light;
Ah, never of mortal kind were they begot,
Nor are they slaves of memory, lost in sleep:
Their Father is greater than Time, and ages not.

The tyrant is a child of Pride   [ANTISTROPHE 1]
Who drinks from his great sickening cup   832
Recklessness and vanity,
Until from his high crest headlong
He plummets to the dust of hope.   835
That strong man is not strong.
But let no fair ambition be denied;
May God protect the wrestler for the State
In government, in comely policy,
Who will fear God, and on His ordinance wait.

                                    [STROPHE 2]
Haughtiness and the high hand of disdain   841
Tempt and outrage God's holy law;
And any mortal who dares hold
No immortal Power in awe
Will be caught up in a net of pain: 845
The price for which his levity is sold.
Let each man take due earnings, then,
And keep his hands from holy things,
And from blasphemy stand apart —
Else the crackling blast of heaven   850

Blows on his head, and on his desperate heart.
Though fools will honor impious men,
In their cities no tragic poet sings.

[ANTISTROPHE 2]
Shall we lose faith in Delphi's obscurities,
We who have heard the world's core   855
Discredited, and the sacred wood
Of Zeus at Elis praised no more?
The deeds and the strange prophecies
Must make a pattern yet to be understood.
Zeus, if indeed you are lord of all,   860
Throned in light over night and day,
Mirror this in your endless mind:
Our masters call the oracle
Words on the wind, and the Delphic vision blind!
Their hearts no longer know Apollo,   865
And reverence for the gods has died away.

Scene III

[*Enter* IOKASTÊ.]
IOK. Princes of Thebes, it has occurred to me
To visit the altars of the gods, bearing
These branches as a suppliant, and this incense.
Our king is not himself: his noble soul   870
Is overwrought with fantasies of dread,
Else he would consider
The new prophecies in the light of the old.
He will listen to any voice that speaks disaster,
And my advice goes for nothing.
[*She approaches the altar, R.*]
         To you, then, Apollo,   875
Lycéan° lord, since you are nearest, I turn in prayer.
Receive these offerings, and grant us deliverance
From defilement. Our hearts are heavy with fear
When we see our leader distracted, as helpless
     sailors   879
Are terrified by the confusion of their helmsman.
[Enter MESSENGER.]
MESS. Friends, no doubt you can direct me:
Where shall I find the house of Oedipus,
Or, better still, where is the king himself?
CHORAG. It is this very place, stranger; he is inside.
This is his wife and mother of his children.   885
MESS. I wish her happiness in a happy house,
Blest in all the fulfillment of her marriage.
IOK. I wish as much for you: your courtesy
Deserves a like good fortune. But now, tell me:
Why have you come? What have you to say to
     us?   890
MESS. Good news, my lady, for your house and
     your husband.
IOK. What news? Who sent you here?

MESS.   I am from Corinth.
The news I bring ought to mean joy for you,
Though it may be you will find some grief in it.
IOK. What is it? How can it touch us in both
     ways?   895
MESS. The word is that the people of the Isthmus
Intend to call Oedipus to be their king.
IOK. But old King Polybos — is he not reigning
     still?
MESS. No. Death holds him in his sepulchre.
IOK. What are you saying? Polybos is dead?   900
MESS. If I am not telling the truth, may I die
     myself.
IOK. [*To a* MAIDSERVANT] Go in, go quickly; tell
     this to your master.

O riddlers of God's will, where are you now!
This was the man whom Oedipus, long ago,   904
Feared so, fled so, in dread of destroying him —
But it was another fate by which he died.
[*Enter* OEDIPUS, *C.*]
OED. Dearest Iokastê, why have you sent for me?
IOK. Listen to what this man says, and then tell
     me
What has become of the solemn prophecies.   909
OED. Who is this man? What is his news for me?
IOK. He has come from Corinth to announce your
     father's death!
OED. Is it true, stranger? Tell me in your own
     words.
MESS. I can not say it more clearly: the king is
     dead.
OED. Was it by treason? Or by an attack of ill-
     ness?   914
MESS. A little thing brings old men to their rest.
OED. It was sickness, then?
MESS.   Yes, and his many years.
OED. Ah!
Why should a man respect the Pythian hearth,° or
Give heed to the birds that jangle above his head?
They prophesied that I should kill Polybos,   920
Kill my own father; but he is dead and buried,
And I am here — I never touched him, never,
Unless he died of grief for my departure,
And thus, in a sense, through me. No. Polybos
Has packed the oracles off with him underground.
They are empty words.   926
IOK.   Had I not told you so?
OED. You had; it was my faint heart that be-
     trayed me.
IOK. From now on never think of those things
     again.
OED. And yet — must I not fear my mother's
     bed?   929

876. Lycéan: another name for Apollo, meaning "god of light."

918. Pythian hearth: the Delphic oracle, so called because
Apollo killed the serpent Python on the spot where he established the oracle

IOK. Why should anyone in this world be afraid,
Since Fate rules us and nothing can be foreseen?
A man should live only for the present day.

Have no more fear of sleeping with your mother:
How many men, in dreams, have lain with their
   mothers!
No reasonable man is troubled by such things. 935
  OED. That is true; only —
If only my mother were not still alive!
But she is alive. I can not help my dread.
    IOK. Yet this news of your father's death is won-
     derful.   939
  OED. Wonderful. But I fear the living woman.
  MESS. Tell me, who is this woman that you fear?
  OED. It is Meropê, man; the wife of King Polybos.
  MESS. Meropê? Why should you be afraid of her?
  OED. An oracle of the gods, a dreadful saying.
    MESS. Can you tell me about it or are you sworn
     to silence?   945
  OED. I can tell you, and I will.

Apollo said through his prophet that I was the man
Who should marry his own mother, shed his fa-
   ther's blood
With his own hands. And so, for all these years
I have kept clear of Corinth, and no harm has
   come —   950
Though it would have been sweet to see my parents
   again.
    MESS. And is this the fear that drove you out of
     Corinth?
  OED. Would you have me kill my father?
  MESS.   As for that
You must be reassured by the news I gave you.
    OED. If you could reassure me, I would reward
     you.   955
  MESS. I had that in mind, I will confess: I thought
I could count on you when you returned to Corinth.
  OED. No: I will never go near my parents again.
    MESS. Ah, son, you still do not know what you
     are doing —
    OED. What do you mean? In the name of God
     tell me!   960
    MESS. — If these are your reasons for not going
     home.
  OED. I tell you, I fear the oracle may come true.
    MESS. And guilt may come upon you through
     your parents?
  OED. That is the dread that is always in my heart.
    MESS. Can you not see that all your fears are
     groundless?   965
  OED. Groundless? Am I not my parents' son?
  MESS. Polybos was not your father.
  OED.   Not my father?
    MESS. No more your father than the man speak-
     ing to you.
  OED. But you are nothing to me!

  MESS.   Neither was he.
  OED. Then why did he call me son?
  MESS.   I will tell you:
Long ago he had you from my hands, as a gift.
    OED. Then how could he love me so, if I was not
     his?   972
    MESS. He had no children, and his heart turned
     to you.
    OED. What of you? Did you buy me? Did you
     find me by chance?
    MESS. I came upon you in the woody vales of
     Kithairon.°   975
  OED. And what were you doing there?
  MESS.   Tending my flocks.
  OED. A wandering shepherd?
  MESS.   But your savior, son, that day.
  OED. From what did you save me?
  MESS.   Your ankles should tell you that.
    OED. Ah, stranger, why do you speak of that
     childhood pain?
    MESS. I pulled the skewer that pinned your feet
     together.   980
    OED. I have had the mark as long as I can re-
     member.
    MESS. That was why you were given the name
     you bear.°
    OED. God! Was it my father or my mother who
     did it?
Tell me!
    MESS. I do not know. The man who gave you
     to me
Can tell you better than I.   985
  OED. It was not you that found me, but another?
  MESS. It was another shepherd gave you to me.
  OED. Who was he? Can you tell me who he was?
    MESS. I think he was said to be one of Laïos'
     people.
    OED. You mean the Laïos who was king here
     years ago?   990
    MESS. Yes; King Laïos; and the man was one of
     his herdsmen.
  OED. Is he still alive? Can I see him?
  MESS.   These men here
Know best about such things.
  OED.   Does anyone here
Know this shepherd that he is talking about?   994
Have you seen him in the fields, or in the town?
If you have, tell me. It is time things were made
   plain.
    CHORAG. I think the man he means is that same
     shepherd
You have already asked to see. Iokastê perhaps
Could tell you something.
  OED.   Do you know anything

975. Kithairon: See Scene i. 409.   **982. name you bear:** Oedipus means "swollen foot."

About him, Lady? Is he the man we have sum-
    moned?   1000
Is that the man this shepherd means?

IOK.   Why think of him?
Forget this herdsman. Forget it all.
This talk is a waste of time.

OED.   How can you say that,
When the clues to my true birth are in my hands?

IOK. For God's love, let us have no more ques-
    tioning!   1005
Is your life nothing to you?
My own is pain enough for me to bear.

OED. You need not worry. Suppose my mother
    a slave,
And born of slaves: no baseness can touch you.

IOK. Listen to me, I beg you: do not do this
    thing!   1010

OED. I will not listen; the truth must be made
    known.

IOK. Everything that I say is for your own good!

OED.   My own good
Snaps my patience, then; I want none of it.

IOK. You are fatally wrong! May you never learn
    who you are!

OED. Go, one of you, and bring the shepherd
    here.   1015
Let us leave this woman to brag of her royal name.

IOK. Ah, miserable!
That is the only word I have for you now.
That is the only word I can ever have.

                 [*Exit into the palace.*]

CHORAG. Why has she left us, Oedipus? Why has
    she gone   1020
In such a passion of sorrow? I fear this silence:
Something dreadful may come of it.

OED.   Let it come!
However base my birth, I must know about it.
The Queen, like a woman, is perhaps ashamed
To think of my low origin. But I   1025
Am a child of Luck; I can not be dishonored.
Luck is my mother; the passing months, my
    brothers,
Have seen me rich and poor.

                 If this is so,
How could I wish that I were someone else?
How could I not be glad to know my birth?   1030

Ode III

                   [STROPHE]

CHOR. If ever the coming time were known
To my heart's pondering,
Kithairon, now by Heaven I see the torches
At the festival of the next full moon,
And see the dance, and hear the choir sing   1035

A grace to your gentle shade:
Mountain where Oedipus was found,
O mountain guard of a noble race!
May the god° who heals us lend his aid,
And let that glory come to pass   1040
For our king's cradling-ground.

                 [ANTISTROPHE]

Of the nymphs that flower beyond the years,
Who bore you, royal child,
To Pan of the hills or the timberline Apollo,
Cold in delight where the upland clears,   1045
Or Hermês for whom Kyllenê's° heights are piled?
Or flushed° as evening cloud,
Great Dionysos, roamer of mountains,
He — was it he who found you there,
And caught you up in his own proud   1050
Arms from the sweet god-ravisher°
Who laughed by the Muses' fountains?°

Scene IV

OED. Sirs: though I do not know the man,
I think I see him coming, this shepherd we want:
He is old, like our friend here, and the men   1055
Bringing him seem to be servants of my house.
But you can tell, if you have ever seen him.

    [*Enter* SHEPHERD *escorted by servants.*]

CHORAG. I know him, he was Laïos' man. You
    can trust him.

OED. Tell me first, you from Corinth: is this the
    shepherd
We were discussing?

MESS.   This is the very man.   1060

OED. [*To* SHEPHERD] Come here. No, look at me.
    You must answer
Everything I ask.—You belonged to Laïos?

SHEP. Yes: born his slave, brought up in his
    house.

OED. Tell me: what kind of work did you do for
    him?   1064

SHEP. I was a shepherd of his, most of my life.

OED. Where mainly did you go for pasturage?

SHEP. Sometimes Kithairon, sometimes the hills
    near-by.

OED. Do you remember ever seeing this man out
    there?

SHEP. What would he be doing there? This man?

OED. This man standing here. Have you ever
    seen him before?   1070

1039. god: Apollo, the healer.   1046. Kyllenê: mountain sacred
to Hermês, god of eloquence and prudence, and herald of Zeus.
1047. flushed: Dionysos (Bacchos), again, is flushed with wine.
See Párodos, 200.   1051. god-ravisher: the nymph, whom the
Chorus suggests was Oedipus' mother.   1052. Muses' fountains: springs of Helicon, a mountain range sacred to Apollo
and the Muses.

SHEP. No. At least, not to my recollection.

MESS. And that is not strange, my lord. But I'll refresh
His memory: he must remember when we two
Spent three whole seasons together, March to September,   1074
On Kithairon or thereabouts. He had two flocks;
I had one. Each autumn I'd drive mine home
And he would go back with his to Laïos' sheepfold. —
Is this not true, just as I have described it?

SHEP. True, yes; but it was all so long ago.

MESS. Well, then: do you remember, back in those days,   1080
That you gave me a baby boy to bring up as my own?

SHEP. What if I did? What are you trying to say?

MESS. King Oedipus was once that little child.

SHEP. Damn you, hold your tongue!

OED.   No more of that!   1084
It is your tongue needs watching, not this man's.

SHEP. My king, my master, what is it I have done wrong?

OED. You have not answered his question about the boy.

SHEP. He does not know . . . He is only making trouble . . .

OED. Come, speak plainly, or it will go hard with you.   1089

SHEP. In God's name, do not torture an old man!

OED. Come here, one of you; bind his arms behind him.

SHEP. Unhappy king! What more do you wish to learn?

OED. Did you give this man the child he speaks of?

SHEP.   I did.
And I would to God I had died that very day.

OED. You will die now unless you speak the truth.

SHEP. Yet if I speak the truth, I am worse than dead.   1096

OED. [To ATTENDANT] He intends to draw it out, apparently —

SHEP. No! I have told you already that I gave him the boy.

OED. Where did you get him? From your house? From somewhere else?   1099

SHEP. Not from mine, no. A man gave him to me.

OED. Is that man here? Whose house did he belong to?

SHEP. For God's love, my king, do not ask me any more!

OED. You are a dead man if I have to ask you again.

SHEP. Then . . . Then the child was from the palace of Laïos.   1104

OED. A slave child? or a child of his own line?

SHEP. Ah, I am on the brink of dreadful speech!

OED. And I of dreadful hearing. Yet I must hear.

SHEP. If you must be told, then . . .
                    They said it was Laïos' child;
But it is your wife who can tell you about that.

OED. My wife! — Did she give it to you?

SHEP.   My lord, she did.   1110

OED. Do you know why?

SHEP.   I was told to get rid of it.

OED. Oh heartless mother!

SHEP.   But in dread of prophecies . . .

OED. Tell me.

SHEP.   It was said that the boy would kill his own father.

OED. Then why did you give him over to this old man?

SHEP. I pitied the baby, my king,   1115
And I thought that this man would take him far away
To his own country.
                    He saved him — but for what a fate!
For if you are what this man says you are,
No man living is more wretched than Oedipus.

OED. Ah God!   1120
It was true!
            All the prophecies!
                                — Now,
O Light, may I look on you for the last time!
I, Oedipus,
Oedipus, damned in his birth, in his marriage damned,   1124
Damned in the blood he shed with his own hand!
[He rushes into the palace.]

Ode IV

CHOR. Alas for the seed of men.   [STROPHE I]
What measure shall I give these generations
That breathe on the void and are void
And exist and do not exist?
Who bears more weight of joy   1130
Than mass of sunlight shifting in images,
Or who shall make his thought stay on
That down time drifts away?
Your splendor is all fallen.
O naked brow of wrath and tears,   1135
O change of Oedipus!
I who saw your days call no man blest —
Your great days like ghósts góne.

That mind was a strong bow.   [ANTISTROPHE I]
Deep, how deep you drew it then, hard archer,
At a dim fearful range,   1141
And brought dear glory down!
You overcame the stranger° —

1143. stranger: the Sphinx.

The virgin with her hooking lion claws —
And though death sang, stood like a tower 1145
To make pale Thebes take heart.
Fortress against our sorrow!
True king, giver of laws,
Majestic Oedipus!
No prince in Thebes had ever such renown, 1150
No prince won such grace of power.

And now of all men ever known [STROPHE 2]
Most pitiful is this man's story:
His fortunes are most changed, his state
Fallen to a low slave's 1155
Ground under bitter fate.
O Oedipus, most royal one!
The great door that expelled you to the light
Gave at night — ah, gave night to your glory:
As to the father, to the fathering son. 1160
All understood too late.
How could that queen whom Laïos won,
The garden that he harrowed at his height,
Be silent when that act was done?

But all eyes fail before time's eye, [ANTISTROPHE 2]
All actions come to justice there. 1166
Though never willed, though far down the deep
 past,
Your bed, your dread sirings,
Are brought to book at last.
Child by Laïos doomed to die, 1170
Then doomed to lose that fortunate little
 death,
Would God you never took breath in this air
That with my wailing lips I take to cry:
For I weep the world's outcast.
I was blind, and now I can tell why: 1175
Asleep, for you had given ease of breath
To Thebes, while the false years went by.

Exodos

[*Enter, from the palace,* SECOND MESSENGER.]
2. MESS. Elders of Thebes, most honored in this
 land,
What horrors are yours to see and hear, what
 weight
Of sorrow to be endured, if, true to your birth,
You venerate the line of Labdakos! 1181
I think neither Istros nor Phasis, those great rivers,
Could purify this place of all the evil
It shelters now, or soon must bring to light —
Evil not done unconsciously, but willed. 1185

The greatest griefs are those we cause ourselves.
 CHORAG. Surely, friend, we have grief enough al-
 ready;
What new sorrow do you mean?

2. MESS.   The queen is dead.
CHORAG. O miserable queen! But at whose hand?
2. MESS.   Her own.
The full horror of what happened you can not
 know, 1190
For you did not see it; but I, who did, will tell you
As clearly as I can how she met her death.

When she had left us,
In passionate silence, passing through the court,
She ran to her apartment in the house, 1195
Her hair clutched by the fingers of both hands.
She closed the doors behind her; then, by that bed
Where long ago the fatal son was conceived —
That son who should bring about his father's
 death —
We heard her call upon Laïos, dead so many
 years, 1200
And heard her wail for the double fruit of her
 marriage,
A husband by her husband, children by her child.

Exactly how she died I do not know:
For Oedipus burst in moaning and would not let us
Keep vigil to the end: it was by him 1205
As he stormed about the room that our eyes were
 caught.
From one to another of us he went, begging a
 sword,
Hunting the wife who was not his wife, the
 mother
Whose womb had carried his own children and
 himself.
I do not know: it was none of us aided him, 1210
But surely one of the gods was in control!
For with a dreadful cry
He hurled his weight, as though wrenched out of
 himself,
At the twin doors: the bolts gave, and he rushed in.
And there we saw her hanging, her body sway-
 ing 1215
From the cruel cord she had noosed about her neck.
A great sob broke from him, heartbreaking to hear,
As he loosed the rope and lowered her to the
 ground.

I would blot out from my mind what happened
 next!
For the king ripped from her gown the golden
 brooches 1220
That were her ornament, and raised them, and
 plunged them down
Straight into his own eyeballs, crying, "No more,
No more shall you look on the misery about me,
The horrors of my own doing! Too long you have
 known
The faces of those whom I should never have
 seen, 1225

Too long been blind to those for whom I was
    searching!
From this hour, go in darkness! " And as he spoke,
He struck at his eyes — not once, but many times;
And the blood spattered his beard,
Bursting from his ruined sockets like red hail.   1230

So from the unhappiness of two this evil has
    sprung,
A curse on the man and woman alike. The old
Happiness of the house of Labdakos
Was happiness enough: where is it today?
It is all wailing and ruin, disgrace, death — all
The misery of mankind that has a name —   1236
And it is wholly and for ever theirs.
    CHORAG. Is he in agony still? Is there no rest for
      him?
    2. MESS. He is calling for someone to open the
      doors wide
So that all the children of Kadmos may look upon
His father's murderer, his mother's — no,   1241
I can not say it!
                  And then he will leave Thebes,
Self-exiled, in order that the curse
Which he himself pronounced may depart from the
    house.
He is weak, and there is none to lead him,   1245
So terrible is his suffering.
                  But you will see:
Look, the doors are opening; in a moment
You will see a thing that would crush a heart of
    stone.
[*The central door is opened;* OEDIPUS, *blinded, is
    led in.*]
    CHORAG. Dreadful indeed for men to see.
Never have my own eyes   1250
Looked on a sight so full of fear.

Oedipus!
What madness came upon you, what daemon
Leaped on your life with heavier
Punishment than a mortal man can bear?   1255
No: I can not even
Look at you, poor ruined one.
And I would speak, question, ponder,
If I were able. No.
You make me shudder.   1260
    OED. God.   God.
Is there a sorrow greater?
Where shall I find harbor in this world?
My voice is hurled far on a dark wind.
What has God done to me?   1265
    CHORAG. Too terrible to think of, or to see.

    OED. O cloud of night,   [STROPHE 1°]
Never to be turned away: night coming on,
I can not tell how: night like a shroud!

1267. **Strophe** I: another Commos.   See Scene ii. 615.

My fair winds brought me here.
                      O God. Again
The pain of the spikes where I had sight,   1271
The flooding pain
Of memory, never to be gouged out.
    CHORAG. This is not strange.
You suffer it all twice over, remorse in pain,   1275
Pain in remorse.

    OED. Ah dear friend   [ANTISTROPHE 1]
Are you faithful even yet, you alone?
Are you still standing near me, will you stay here,
Patient, to care for the blind?
                    The blind man!   1280
Yet even blind I know who it is attends me,
By the voice's tone —
Though my new darkness hide the comforter.
    CHORAG. Oh fearful act!
What god was it drove you to rake black   1285
Night across your eyes?

    OED. Apollo. Apollo. Dear   [STROPHE 2]
Children, the god was Apollo.
He brought my sick, sick fate upon me.
But the blinding hand was my own!   1290
How could I bear to see
When all my sight was horror everywhere?
    CHORAG. Everywhere; that is true.
    OED. And now what is left?
Images? Love? A greeting even,   1295
Sweet to the senses? Is there anything?
Ah, no, friends: lead me away.
Lead me away from Thebes.
                  Lead the great wreck
And hell of Oedipus, whom the gods hate.
    CHORAG. Your misery, you are not blind to
      that.   1300
Would God you had never found it out!

                       [ANTISTROPHE 2]
    OED. Death take the man who unbound
My feet on that hillside
And delivered me from death to life! What life?
If only I had died,   1305
This weight of monstrous doom
Could not have dragged me and my darlings down.
    CHORAG. I would have wished the same.
    OED. Oh never to have come here
With my father's blood upon me! Never   1310
To have been the man they call his mother's hus-
    band!
Oh accurst! Oh child of evil,
To have entered that wretched bed —
                    the selfsame one!
More primal than sin itself, this fell to me.
    CHORAG. I do not know what words to offer you.
You were better dead than alive and blind.   1316

OED. Do not counsel me any more. This punishment
That I have laid upon myself is just.
If I had eyes,
I do not know how I could bear the sight   1320
Of my father, when I came to the house of Death,
Or my mother: for I have sinned against them both
So vilely that I could not make my peace
By strangling my own life.

                   Or do you think my children,
Born as they were born, would be sweet to my
    eyes?   1325
Ah never, never! Nor this town with its high walls,
Nor the holy images of the gods.

                 For I,
Thrice miserable! — Oedipus, noblest of all the line
Of Kadmos, have condemned myself to enjoy
These things no more, by my own malediction
Expelling that man whom the gods declared   1331
To be a defilement in the house of Laïos.
After exposing the rankness of my own guilt,
How could I look men frankly in the eyes?
No, I swear it,   1335
If I could have stifled my hearing at its source,
I would have done it and made all this body
A tight cell of misery, blank to light and sound:
So I should have been safe in my dark mind
Beyond external evil.

             Ah Kithairon!   1340
Why did you shelter me? When I was cast upon
    you,
Why did I not die? Then I should never
Have shown the world my execrable birth.

Ah Polybos! Corinth, city that I believed
The ancient seat of my ancestors: how fair   1345
I seemed, your child! And all the while this evil
Was cancerous within me!

             For I am sick
In my own being, sick in my origin.

O three roads, dark ravine, woodland and way
Where three roads met: you, drinking my father's
    blood,   1350
My own blood, spilled by my own hand: can you
    remember
The unspeakable things I did there, and the things
I went on from there to do?

           O marriage, marriage!
The act that engendered me, and again the act
Performed by the son in the same bed —

              Ah, the net
Of incest, mingling fathers, brothers, sons,   1356
With brides, wives, mothers: the last evil
That can be known by men: no tongue can say
How evil!

    No. For the love of God, conceal me

Somewhere far from Thebes; or kill me; or hurl
    me   1360
Into the sea, away from men's eyes for ever.

Come, lead me. You need not fear to touch me.
Of all men, I alone can bear this guilt.
          [*Enter* KREON.]
    CHORAG. Kreon is here now. As to what you ask,
He may decide the course to take. He only   1365
Is left to protect the city in your place.
    OED. Alas, how can I speak to him? What right
    have I
To beg his courtesy whom I have deeply wronged?
    KRE. I have not come to mock you, Oedipus,
Or to reproach you, either.

[*To* ATTENDANTS]   — You, standing there:
If you have lost all respect for man's dignity,   1371
At least respect the flame of Lord Helios:
Do not allow this pollution to show itself
Openly here, an affront to the earth
And Heaven's rain and the light of day. No, take
    him   1375
Into the house as quickly as you can.
For it is proper
That only the close kindred see his grief.
    OED. I pray you in God's name, since your courtesy
Ignores my dark expectation, visiting   1380
With mercy this man of all men most execrable:
Give me what I ask — for your good, not for mine.
    KRE. And what is it that you turn to me begging
    for?
    OED. Drive me out of this country as quickly as
    may be
To a place where no human voice can ever greet
    me.   1385
    KRE. I should have done that before now — only,
God's will had not been wholly revealed to me.
    OED. But his command is plain: the parricide
Must be destroyed. I am that evil man.   1389
    KRE. That is the sense of it, yes; but as things are,
We had best discover clearly what is to be done.°
    OED. You would learn more about a man like me?
    KRE. You are ready now to listen to the god.
    OED. I will listen. But it is to you
That I must turn for help. I beg you, hear me.

The woman in there —   1396
Give her whatever funeral you think proper:
She is your sister.

           — But let me go, Kreon!   1398
Let me purge my father's Thebes of the pollution
Of my living here, and go out to the wild hills,
To Kithairon, that has won such fame with me,

<hr>

1391. We ... done: Apparently Kreon will consult the Delphic
oracle once more.

The tomb my mother and father appointed for me,
And let me die there, as they willed I should.
And yet I know
Death will not ever come to me through sickness
Or in any natural way: I have been preserved   1406
For some unthinkable fate. But let that be.

As for my sons, you need not care for them.
They are men, they will find some way to live.
But my poor daughters, who have shared my table,
Who never before have been parted from their
    father —   1411
Take care of them, Kreon; do this for me.

And will you let me touch them with my hands
A last time, and let us weep together?
Be kind, my lord,   1415
Great prince, be kind!
                    Could I but touch them,
They would be mine again, as when I had my eyes.
        [Enter ANTIGONE and ISMENE, attended.]
Ah, God!
Is it my dearest children I hear weeping?
Has Kreon pitied me and sent my daughters?   1420
    KRE. Yes, Oedipus: I knew that they were dear
    to you
In the old days, and know you must love them still.
    OED. May God bless you for this — and be a
    friendlier
Guardian to you than he has been to me!

Children, where are you?   1425
Come quickly to my hands: they are your broth-
    er's —
Hands that have brought your father's once clear
    eyes
To this way of seeing —
                    Ah dearest ones,
I had neither sight nor knowledge then, your father
By the woman who was the source of his own
    life!   1430
And I weep for you — having no strength to see
    you —,
I weep for you when I think of the bitterness
That men will visit upon you all your lives.
What homes, what festivals can you attend
Without being forced to depart again in tears?
And when you come to marriageable age,   1436
Where is the man, my daughters, who would dare
Risk the bane that lies on all my children?
Is there any evil wanting? Your father killed   1439
His father; sowed the womb of her who bore him;
Engendered you at the fount of his own existence!
That is what they will say of you.

                    Then, whom
Can you ever marry? There are no bridegrooms for
    you,

And your lives must wither away in sterile dream-
    ing.

O Kreon, son of Menoikeus!   1445
You are the only father my daughters have,
Since we, their parents, are both of us gone for
    ever.
They are your own blood: you will not let them
Fall into beggary and loneliness;
You will keep them from the miseries that are
    mine!   1450
Take pity on them; see, they are only children,
Friendless except for you. Promise me this,
Great prince, and give me your hand in token
    of it.
        [KREON clasps his right hand.]

Children:
I could say much, if you could understand
    me,
But as it is, I have only this prayer for you: 1456
Live where you can, be as happy as you can —
Happier, please God, than God has made your
    father.
    KRE. Enough. You have wept enough. Now go
    within.   1459
    OED. I must; but it is hard.
    KRE.   Time eases all things.
    OED. You know my mind, then?
    KRE.   Say what you desire.
    OED. Send me from Thebes!
    KRE.   God grant that I may!
    OED. But since God hates me . . .
    KRE.   No, he will grant your wish.
    OED. You promise?
    KRE.   I can not speak beyond my knowl-
    edge.
    OED. Then lead me in.
    KRE. Come now, and leave your children.   1465
    OED. No! Do not take them from me!
    KRE.   Think no longer
That you are in command here, but rather think
How, when you were, you served your own de-
    struction.

        [Exeunt into the house all but the CHORUS; the
        CHORAGOS chants directly to the audience.]

    CHORAG. Men of Thebes: look upon Oedipus.

This is the king who solved the famous riddle
And towered up, most powerful of men.   1471
No mortal eyes but looked on him with envy,
Yet in the end ruin swept over him.

Let every man in mankind's frailty
Consider his last day; and let none   1475
Presume on his good fortune until he find
Life, at his death, a memory without pain.

Othello

by William Shakespeare

DUKE OF VENICE
BRABANTIO, *a Senator*
OTHER SENATORS
GRATIANO, *brother to Brabantio*
LODOVICO, *kinsman to Brabantio*
OTHELLO, *a noble Moor in the service of the Venetian state*
CASSIO, *his lieutenant*
IAGO, *his ancient*
MONTANO, *Othello's predecessor in the government of Cyprus*

RODERIGO, *a Venetian gentleman*
CLOWN, *servant to Othello*

DESDEMONA, *daughter to Brabantio and wife to Othello*
EMILIA, *wife to Iago*
BIANCA, *mistress to Cassio*

SAILOR, MESSENGER, HERALD, OFFICERS, GENTLEMEN, MUSICIANS, *and* ATTENDANTS

SCENE — *Venice: a seaport in Cyprus.*

Act I

SCENE I. *Venice. A street.*

[*Enter* RODERIGO *and* IAGO.]

ROD. Tush, never tell me. I take it much unkindly
That thou, Iago, who hast had° my purse
As if the strings were thine, shouldst know of this.
IAGO. 'Sblood,° but you will not hear me.
If ever I did dream of such a matter,   5
Abhor me.
ROD. Thou told'st me thou didst hold him in thy
hate.
IAGO. Despise me if I do not. Three great ones of
the city,
In personal suit° to make me his Lieutenant,
Off-capped° to him. And, by the faith of man,   10
I know my price, I am worth no worse a place.
But he, as loving his own pride and purposes,
Evades them, with a bombast circumstance°
Horribly stuffed with epithets of war.°
And, in conclusion,   15
Nonsuits° my mediators, for, " Certes,"° says he,
" I have already chose my officer."
And what was he?
Forsooth, a great arithmetician,°
One Michael Cassio, a Florentine,   20
A fellow almost damned in a fair wife,°

That never set a squadron in the field,
Nor the division of a battle° knows
More than a spinster, unless the bookish theoric,°
Wherein the toged° Consuls° can propose   25
As masterly as he — mere prattle without practice
Is all his soldiership. But he, sir, had the election.
And I, of whom his eyes had seen the proof
At Rhodes, at Cyprus, and on other grounds   29
Christian and heathen, must be beleed° and calmed
By debitor and creditor. This countercaster,°
He, in good time,° must his Lieutenant be,
And I — God bless the mark!° — his Moorship's
Ancient.°
ROD. By Heaven, I rather would have been his
hangman.
IAGO. Why, there's no remedy. 'Tis the curse of
service,   35
Preferment goes by letter and affection,
And not by old gradation,° where each second
Stood heir to the first. Now, sir, be judge yourself
Whether I in any just term am affined°
To love the Moor.
ROD.   I would not follow him, then.   40
IAGO. Oh, sir, content you,
I follow him to serve my turn upon him.
We cannot all be masters, nor all masters
Cannot be truly followed. You shall mark
Many a duteous and knee-crooking knave   45

Act I, Sc. i: 2. had: i.e., used.   **4. 'Sblood:** by God's blood.
9. In . . . suit: making this request in person.   **10. Off-capped:**
stood cap in hand.   **13. bombast circumstance:** bombastic
phrases. Bombast is cotton padding used to stuff out a gar-
ment.   **14. stuffed . . . war:** padded out with military terms.
16. Nonsuits: rejects the petition of. **Certes:** assuredly.
19. arithmetician: Contemporary books on military tactics are
full of elaborate diagrams and numerals to explain military for-
mations. Cassio is a student of such books.   **21. almost . . . wife:**
A much-disputed phrase. There is an Italian proverb, "You have
married a fair wife? You are damned." If Iago has this in mind,
he means by *almost* that Cassio is about to marry.

23. division . . . battle: organization of an army.   **24. bookish
theoric:** student of war; not a practical soldier.   **25. toged:**
wearing a toga. **Consuls:** councilors. Cf. I.ii.43.   **30. beleed:**
placed on the lee (or unfavorable) side.   **31. countercaster:**
calculator (repeating the idea of arithmetician). Counters were
used in making calculations.   **32. in . . . time:** A phrase expressing indignation.   **33. God . . . mark:** An exclamation of impatience. **Ancient:** ensign, the third officer in the company of which
Othello is Captain and Cassio Lieutenant.   **36–37. Preferment
. . . gradation:** promotion comes through private recommenda-
tion and favoritism and not by order of seniority.   **39. affined:**
tied by affection.

That doting on his own obsequious bondage
Wears out his time, much like his master's ass,
For naught but provender, and when he's old,
    cashiered.°
Whip me such honest knaves. Others there are
Who, trimmed in forms and visages of duty,°   50
Keep yet their hearts attending on themselves,
And throwing but shows of service° on their lords
Do well thrive by them, and when they have lined
    their coats
Do themselves homage.° These fellows have some
    soul,
And such a one do I profess myself. For, sir,   55
It is as sure as you are Roderigo,
Were I the Moor, I would not be Iago.
In following him, I follow but myself.
Heaven is my judge, not I for love and duty,
But seeming so, for my peculiar° end.   60
For when my outward action doth demónstrate
The native act and figure of my heart°
In compliment extern,° 'tis not long after
But I will wear my heart upon my sleeve
For daws° to peck at. I am not what I am.°   65
    ROD. What a full fortune° does the thick-lips owe°
If he can carry 't thus!°
    IAGO.   Call up her father,
Rouse him. Make after him, poison his delight,
Proclaim him in the streets. Incense her kinsmen,
And though he in a fertile climate dwell,   70
Plague him with flies. Though that his joy be joy,
Yet throw such changes of vexation on 't
As it may lose some color.°
    ROD. Here is her father's house, I'll call aloud.
    IAGO. Do, with like timorous° accent and dire yell
As when, by night and negligence, the fire   76
Is spied in populous cities.
    ROD. What ho, Brabantio! Signior Brabantio, ho!
    IAGO. Awake! What ho, Brabantio! Thieves!
    Thieves! Thieves!
Look to your house, your daughter and your bags!°
Thieves! Thieves!   81

    [BRABANTIO *appears above, at a window.*]
    BRA. What is the reason of this terrible summons?
What is the matter there?
    ROD. Signior, is all your family within?
    IAGO. Are your doors locked?
    BRA.   Why, wherefore ask you this?   85

    IAGO. 'Zounds,° sir, you're robbed. For shame,
    put on your gown,°
Your heart is burst, you have lost half your soul.
Even now, now, very now, an old black ram
Is tupping° your white ewe. Arise, arise,
Awake the snorting° citizens with the bell,   90
Or else the Devil° will make a grandsire of you.
Arise, I say.
    BRA.   What, have you lost your wits?
    ROD. Most reverend signior, do you know my
    voice?
    BRA. Not I. What are you?
    ROD. My name is Roderigo.   94
    BRA.   The worser welcome.
I have charged thee not to haunt about my doors.
In honest plainness thou hast heard me say
My daughter is not for thee, and now, in madness,
Being full of supper and distempering draughts,°
Upon malicious bravery° dost thou come   100
To start° my quiet.
    ROD. Sir, sir, sir ——
    BRA.   But thou must needs be sure
My spirit and my place have in them power
To make this bitter to thee.
    ROD.   Patience, good sir.
    BRA. What tell'st thou me of robbing? This is
    Venice,   105
My house is not a grange.°
    ROD.   Most grave Brabantio,
In simple and pure soul I come to you.
    IAGO. 'Zounds, sir, you are one of those that will
not serve God if the Devil bid you. Because we come
to do you service and you think we are ruffians,   110
you'll have your daughter covered with a Barbary°
horse, you'll have your nephews° neigh to you, you'll
have coursers for cousins,° and jennets° for germans.°
    BRA. What profane wretch art thou?   115
    IAGO. I am one, sir, that comes to tell you your
daughter and the Moor are now making the beast
with two backs.
    BRA. Thou art a villain.
    IAGO.   You are —— a Senator.
    BRA. This thou shalt answer. I know thee, Roder-
igo.   120
    ROD. Sir, I will answer anything. But I beseech you
If 't be your pleasure and most wise consent,
As partly I find it is, that your fair daughter,
At this odd-even° and dull° watch o' the night,
Transported with no worse nor better guard   125

---

48. **cashiered:** dismissed. The word at this time did not imply dishonorable discharge.   50. **trimmed ... duty:** decking themselves out with the outward forms of loyal service.   52. **throwing ... service:** serving merely in outward show.   54. **Do ... homage:** serve themselves. **homage:** an outward act signifying obedience.   60. **peculiar:** particular, personal.   62. **native ... heart:** natural actions and shape of my secret designs.   63. **extern:** outward.   65. **daws:** jackdaws; i.e., fools. **I ... am:** i.e., I am in secret a devil.   66. **full fortune:** overflowing good luck. **owe:** own.   67. **carry't thus:** i.e., bring off this marriage.   72–73. **throw ... color:** cause him some annoyance by way of variety to tarnish his joy.   75. **timorous:** terrifying.   80. **bags:** moneybags.

86. **'Zounds:** by God's wounds. **gown:** dressing gown.   89. **tupping:** covering.   90. **snorting:** snoring.   91. **Devil:** The Devil in old pictures and woodcuts was represented as black.   99. **distempering draughts:** liquor that makes senseless.   100. **bravery:** defiance.   101. **start:** startle.   106. **grange:** lonely farm.   111. **Barbary:** Moorish.   112. **nephews:** grandsons.   113. **cousins:** near relations. **jennets:** Moorish ponies.   114. **germans:** kinsmen.   124. **odd-even:** about midnight. **dull:** heavy, sleepy.

But with a knave of common hire, a gondolier,
To the gross clasps of a lascivious Moor —
If this be known to you, and your allowance,°
We then have done you bold and saucy wrongs.
But if you know not this, my manners tell me   130
We have your wrong rebuke. Do not believe
That from the sense of all civility°
I thus would play and trifle with your reverence.
Your daughter, if you have not given her leave,
I say again, hath made a gross revolt,°   135
Tying her duty, beauty, wit, and fortunes
In an extravagant° and wheeling° stranger
Of here and everywhere. Straight satisfy yourself.
If she be in her chamber or your house,
Let loose on me the justice of the state   140
For thus deluding you.
    BRA.   Strike on the tinder,° ho!
Give me a taper!° Call up all my people!
This accident is not unlike my dream.
Belief of it oppresses me already.
Light, I say! Light!   [*Exit above.*]
    IAGO.   Farewell, for I must leave you.   145
It seems not meet, nor wholesome to my place,°
To be produced — as if I stay I shall —
Against the Moor. For I do know the state,
However this may gall° him with some check,°
Cannot with safety cast° him. For he's embarked
With such loud reason to the Cyprus wars,   151
Which even now stand in act,° that, for their souls,
Another of his fathom° they have none
To lead their business. In which regard,
Though I do hate him as I do Hell pains,   155
Yet for necessity of present life
I must show out a flag° and sign of love,
Which is indeed but sign. That you shall surely find
    him,
Lead to the Sagittary° the raisèd search,   159
And there will I be with him. So farewell.   [*Exit.*]
[*Enter, below,* BRABANTIO, *in his nightgown, and*
       SERVANTS *with torches.*]
    BRA. It is too true an evil. Gone she is,
And what's to come of my despisèd time°
Is naught but bitterness. Now, Roderigo,
Where didst thou see her? Oh, unhappy girl!
With the Moor, say'st thou? Who would be a
    father!   165

How didst thou know 'twas she? Oh, she deceives
    me
Past thought! What said she to you? Get more ta-
    pers.
Raise all my kindred. Are they married, think you?
    ROD. Truly, I think they are.
    BRA. Oh Heaven! How got she out? Oh, treason
     of the blood!°   170
Fathers, from hence trust not your daughters' minds
By what you see them act. Are there not charms°
By which the property° of youth and maidhood
May be abused?° Have you not read, Roderigo,
Of some such thing?
    ROD.   Yes, sir, I have indeed.   175
    BRA. Call up my brother. Oh, would you had had
     her!
Some one way, some another. Do you know
Where we may apprehend her and the Moor?
    ROD. I think I can discover him, if you please
To get good guard and go along with me.   180
    BRA. Pray you, lead on. At every house I'll call,
I may command° at most. Get weapons, ho!
And raise some special officers of night.
On, good Roderigo, I'll deserve your pains.°
                    [*Exeunt.*]

SCENE II. *Another street.*

[*Enter* OTHELLO, IAGO, *and* ATTENDANTS
       with torches.]
    IAGO. Though in the trade of war I have slain
     men,
Yet do I hold it very stuff° o' the conscience
To do no contrivèd° murder. I lack iniquity
Sometimes to do me service. Nine or ten times
I had thought to have yerked° him here under the
    ribs.   5
    OTH. 'Tis better as it is.
    IAGO.   Nay, but he prated
And spoke such scurvy and provoking terms
Against your honor
That, with the little godliness I have,
I did full hard forbear him.° But I pray you, sir,   10
Are you fast° married? Be assured of this,
That the Magnifico° is much beloved,
And hath in his effect° a voice potential
As double as° the Duke's. He will divorce you,
Or put upon you what restraint and grievance   15

128. your allowance: by your permission. 132. from . . . civility:
disregarding all sense of decent behavior. 135. gross revolt:
indecent rebellion. 137. extravagant: vagabond. wheeling: wandering. 141. tinder: the primitive method of making fire, used
before the invention of matches. A spark, made by striking flint
on steel, fell on the tinder, some inflammable substance such
as charred linen, which was blown into flame. 142. taper: candle.
146. place: i.e., as Othello's officer. 149. gall: make sore.
check: rebuke. 150. cast: dismiss from service. 152. stand
in act: are on the point of beginning. 153. fathom: depth.
157. flag: a sign of welcome. 159. Sagittary: presumably some
building in Venice, not identified, used as a meeting place for
the Council. 162. what's . . . time: the rest of my wretched life.

170. treason . . . blood: treachery of my own child. 172. charms:
magic spells. 173. property: nature. 174. abused: deceived.
182. command: find supporters. 184. deserve . . . pains:
reward your labor.
    Sc. ii: 2. stuff: material, nature. 3. contrived: deliberately
planned. 5. yerked: jabbed. 10. full . . . him: had a hard
job to keep my hands off him. 11. fast: securely. 12. Magni-
fico: the title of the chief men of Venice. 13. in . . . effect:
what he can do. 13-14. potential . . . as: twice as powerful as.

The law, with all his might to enforce it on,
Will give him cable.°

OTH.   Let him do his spite.
My services which I have done the signiory°
Shall outtongue his complaints. 'Tis yet to know° —
Which, when I know that boasting is an honor, 20
I shall promulgate° — I fetch my life and being°
From men of royal siege,° and my demerits°
May speak unbonneted° to as proud a fortune
As this that I have reached. For know, Iago,
But that I love the gentle Desdemona,   25
I would not my unhousèd° free condition
Put into circumscription and confine°
For the sea's worth. But look! What lights come
    yond?

IAGO. Those are the raisèd father and his friends.
You were best go in.

OTH.   Not I, I must be found.   30
My parts,° my title, and my perfect° soul
Shall manifest me rightly. Is it they?

IAGO. By Janus,° I think no.

[*Enter* CASSIO, *and certain* OFFICERS *with torches*.]

OTH. The servants of the Duke, and my Lieutenant.
The goodness of the night upon you, friends!   35
What is the news?

CAS.   The Duke does greet you, General,
And he requires your haste-posthaste° appearance,
Even on the instant.

OTH.   What is the matter, think you?

CAS. Something from Cyprus, as I may divine.
It is a business of some heat. The galleys°   40
Have sent a dozen sequent° messengers
This very night at one another's heels,
And many of the consuls, raised and met,
Are at the Duke's already. You have been hotly
    called for
When, being not at your lodging to be found,   45
The Senate hath sent about three several° quests
To search you out.

OTH.   'Tis well I am found by you.
I will but spend a word here in the house
And go with you.   [*Exit*.]

CAS.   Ancient, what makes he here?

IAGO. Faith, he tonight hath boarded a land carrack.°   50
If it prove lawful prize, he's made forever.

CAS. I do not understand.

IAGO.   He's married.

CAS.   To who?

[*Re-enter* OTHELLO.]

IAGO. Marry,° to —— Come, Captain, will you
go?

OTH.   Have with you.

CAS. Here comes another troop to seek for you.

IAGO. It is Brabantio. General, be advised,°   55
He comes to bad intent.

[*Enter* BRABANTIO, RODERIGO, *and* OFFICERS *with
torches and weapons*.]

OTH.   Holloa! Stand there!

ROD. Signior, it is the Moor.

BRA.   Down with him, thief!

[*They draw on both sides*.]

IAGO. You, Roderigo! Come, sir, I am for you.

OTH. Keep up° your bright swords, for the dew
will rust them.
Good signior, you shall more command with years
Than with your weapons.   61

BRA. O thou foul thief, where hast thou stowed
my daughter!
Damned as thou art, thou hast enchanted her.
For I'll refer me to all things of sense°
If she in chains of magic were not bound,   65
Whether a maid so tender, fair, and happy,
So opposite to marriage that she shunned
The wealthy curlèd darlings of our nation,
Would ever have, to incur a general mock,
Run from her guardage° to the sooty bosom   70
Of such a thing as thou, to fear, not to delight.
Judge me the world if 'tis not gross in sense°
That thou hast practiced on her with foul charms,
Abused her delicate youth with drugs or minerals
That weaken motion.° I'll have 't disputed on,° 75
'Tis probable, and palpable° to thinking.
I therefore apprehend and do attach° thee
For an abuser of the world, a practicer
Of arts inhibited and out of warrant.°
Lay hold upon him. If he do resist,   80
Subdue him at his peril.

OTH.   Hold your hands,
Both you of my inclining and the rest.
Were it my cue to fight, I should have known it
Without a prompter. Where will you that I go

---

17. **cable**: rope.   18. **signiory**: the state of Venice.   19. **'Tis ... know**: it has still to be made known.   21. **promulgate**: proclaim. **fetch ... being**: am descended.   22. **royal siege**: throne. **demerits**: deserts.   23. **unbonneted**: A disputed phrase. Usually it means "without a cap"; i.e., in sign that the wearer is standing before a superior. But Othello means that his merits are such that he need show deference to no man.   26. **unhoused**: unmarried.   27. **confine**: confinement.   31. **parts**: abilities. **perfect**: ready.   33. **Janus**: the two-faced God of the Romans, an appropriate deity for Iago.   37. **haste-posthaste**: with the quickest possible speed. When it was necessary to urge the postboy to greater speed than usual, the letter or dispatch was inscribed "haste, posthaste." The Earl of Essex once inscribed a letter "haste, haste, haste posthaste, haste for life."   40. **galleys**: Venetian ships which were manned and rowed by slaves; the fastest of craft.   41. **sequent**: following one after another.   46. **several**: separate.

50. **carrack**: the largest type of Spanish merchant ship. 53. **Marry**: Mary, by the Virgin — with a pun.   55. **advised**: careful.   59. **Keep up**: sheathe.   64. **refer ... sense**: i.e., by every rational consideration.   70. **guardage**: guardianship. 72. **gross in sense**: i.e., plain to the perception.   75. **motion**: sense. **disputed on**: argued in the courts of law.   76. **palpable**: clear.   77. **attach**: arrest.   79. **arts ... warrant**: forbidden and illegal acts; i.e., magic and witchcraft.

To answer this your charge?

BRA.   To prison, till fit time   85
Of law and course of direct session°
Call thee to answer.

OTH.   What if I do obey?
How may the Duke be therewith satisfied,
Whose messengers are here about my side
Upon some present° business of the state   90
To bring me to him?

I. OFF.   'Tis true, most worthy signior.
The Duke's in Council, and your noble self
I am sure is sent for.

BRA.   How! The Duke in Council!
In this time of the night! Bring him away.
Mine's not an idle° cause. The Duke himself,   95
Or any of my brothers of the state,
Cannot but feel this wrong as 'twere their own.
For if such actions may have passage free,°
Bondslaves and pagans shall our statesmen be.

                         [*Exeunt.*]

SCENE III. *A council chamber.*

[*The* DUKE *and* SENATORS *sitting at a table,* OFFICERS *attending.*]

DUKE. There is no composition° in these news°
That gives them credit.

I. SEN.   Indeed they are disproportioned.
My letters say a hundred and seven galleys.

DUKE. And mine, a hundred and forty.

2. SEN.   And mine, two hundred.
But though they jump not on a just account° —   5
As in these cases, where the aim reports,°
'Tis oft with difference — yet do they all confirm
A Turkish fleet, and bearing up° to Cyprus.

DUKE. Nay, it is possible enough to judgment.
I do not so secure me in the error,°   10
But the main article° I do approve
In fearful° sense.

SAILOR. [*Within*] What ho! What ho! What ho!

I. OFF. A messenger from the galleys.

             [*Enter* SAILOR.]

DUKE.   Now, what's the business?

SAIL. The Turkish preparation makes for Rhodes.
So was I bid report here to the state   15
By Signior Angelo.

DUKE. How say you by this change?

---

86. course . . . session: trial in the ordinary courts, where witches and other criminals are tried — and not by special commission as a great man.   90. present: immediate.   95. idle: trivial. 98. have . . . free: be freely allowed.
     Sc. iii: 1. composition: agreement. news: reports.   5. jump . . . account: do not agree with an exact estimate.   6. aim reports: i.e., intelligence reports of an enemy's intention often differ in the details.   8. bearing up: making course for.   10. I . . . error: I do not consider myself free from danger, because the reports may not all be accurate.   11. main article: general purport.   12. fearful: to be feared.

I. SEN.   This cannot be,
By no assay of reason.° 'Tis a pageant°
To keep us in false gaze.° When we consider
The importancy of Cyprus to the Turk,
And let ourselves again but understand   20
That as it more concerns the Turk than Rhodes,
So may he with more facile question bear° it,
For that it stands not in such warlike brace°
But altogether lacks the abilities   25
That Rhodes is dressed° in — if we make thought
   of this,
We must not think the Turk is so unskillful
To leave that latest which concerns him first,
Neglecting an attempt of ease and gain
To wake and wage° a danger profitless.   30

DUKE. Nay, in all confidence, he's not for Rhodes.

I. OFF. Here is more news.

            [*Enter a* MESSENGER.]

MESS. The Ottomites,° Reverend and Gracious,
Steering with due course toward the isle of Rhodes,
Have there injointed° them with an after-fleet.°   35

I. SEN. Aye, so I thought. How many, as you
   guess?

MESS. Of thirty sail. And now they do restem°
Their backward course, bearing with frank appearance°
Their purposes toward Cyprus. Signior Montano,
Your trusty and most valiant servitor,
With his free duty recommends you thus,°   40
And prays you to believe him.

DUKE. 'Tis certain then for Cyprus.
Marcus Luccicos, is not he in town?

I. SEN. He's now in Florence.

DUKE. Write from us to him, post-posthaste dispatch.   45

I. SEN. Here comes Brabantio and the valiant
   Moor.

[*Enter* BRABANTIO, OTHELLO, IAGO, RODERIGO, *and* OFFICERS.]

DUKE. Valiant Othello, we must straight employ
   you
Against the general enemy Ottoman.
[*To* BRABANTIO] I did not see you. Welcome, gentle
   signior,   50
We lacked your counsel and your help tonight.

BRA. So did I yours. Good your Grace, pardon
   me,
Neither my place nor aught I heard of business
Hath raised me from my bed, nor doth the general
   care
Take hold on me. For my particular° grief   55

---

18. assay of reason: reasonable test. pageant: show.   19. false gaze: looking the wrong way.   22. with . . . bear: take it more easily.   24. brace: state of defense.   26. dressed: prepared. 30. wage: risk.   33. Ottomites: Turks.   35. injointed: joined. after-fleet: following, second fleet.   37. restem: steer again. 38. frank appearance: no attempt at concealment.   41. With . . . thus: with all due respect thus advises.   55. particular: personal.

Is of so floodgate° and o'erbearing nature
That it engluts° and swallows other sorrows,
And it is still itself.
    DUKE.   Why, what's the matter?
    BRA. My daughter! Oh, my daughter!
    ALL.   Dead?
    BRA.   Aye, to me.
She is abused, stol'n from me and corrupted   60
By spells and medicines bought of mountebanks.°
For nature so preposterously to err,
Being not deficient, blind, or lame of sense,
Sans° witchcraft could not.
    DUKE. Whoe'er he be that in this foul proceeding
Hath thus beguiled your daughter of herself°   66
And you of her, the bloody book of law
You shall yourself read in the bitter letter
After your own sense — yea, though our proper° son
Stood in your action.
    BRA.   Humbly I thank your Grace. 70
Here is the man, this Moor, whom now, it seems,
Your special mandate for the state affairs
Hath hither brought.
    ALL.   We are very sorry for 't.
    DUKE. [*To* OTHELLO] What in your own part can
    you say to this?
    BRA. Nothing but this is so.   75
    OTH. Most potent, grave, and reverend signiors,
My very noble and approved° good masters,
That I have ta'en away this old man's daughter,
It is most true — true, I have married her.
The very head and front° of my offending   80
Hath this extent, no more. Rude° am I in my speech,
And little blest with the soft phrase of peace.
For since these arms of mine had seven years' pith°
Till now some nine moons wasted, they have used
Their dearest° action in the tented field.   85
And little of this great world can I speak,
More than pertains to feats of broil and battle,
And therefore little shall I grace my cause
In speaking for myself. Yet, by your gracious pa-
    tience,
I will a round unvarnished tale° deliver   90
Of my whole course of love — what drugs, what
    charms,
What conjuration and what mighty magic —
For such proceeding I am charged withal —
I won his daughter.
    BRA.   A maiden never bold,
Of spirit so still and quiet that her motion   95

Blushed at herself,° and she — in spite of nature,
Of years, of country, credit,° everything —
To fall in love with what she feared to look on!
It is a judgment maimed and most imperfect
That will confess° perfection so could err   100
Against all rules of nature, and must be driven
To find out practices° of cunning Hell
Why this should be. I therefore vouch° again
That with some mixtures° powerful o'er the blood,°
Or with some dram conjured° to this effect,   105
He wrought upon her.
    DUKE.   To vouch this is no proof
Without more certain and more overt° test
Than these thin habits° and poor likelihoods°
Of modern seeming° do prefer° against him.
    I. SEN. But, Othello, speak.   110
Did you by indirect and forcèd° courses
Subdue and poison this young maid's affections?
Or came it by request, and such fair question
As soul to soul affordeth?
    OTH.   I do beseech you
Send for the lady to the Sagittary,   115
And let her speak of me before her father.
If you do find me foul in her report,
The trust, the office I do hold of you,
Not only take away, but let your sentence
Even fall upon my life.
    DUKE.   Fetch Desdemona hither.   120
    OTH. Ancient, conduct them, you best know the
    place.   [*Exeunt* IAGO *and* ATTENDANTS.]
And till she come, as truly as to Heaven
I do confess the vices of my blood,
So justly to your grave ears I'll present
How I did thrive in this fair lady's love   125
And she in mine.
    DUKE.   Say it, Othello.
    OTH. Her father loved me, oft invited me,
Still° questioned me the story of my life
From year to year, the battles, sieges, fortunes,   130
That I have passed.
I ran it through, even from my boyish days
To the very moment that he bade me tell it.
Wherein I spake of most disastrous chances,°
Of moving accidents° by flood and field,   135
Of hairbreadth 'scapes i' the imminent deadly
    breach,°
Of being taken by the insolent foe
And sold to slavery, of my redemption thence,

---

56. floodgate: i.e., like water rushing through an opened sluice.
57. engluts: swallows. **61. mountebanks:** quack doctors, who
dealt in poisons and love potions. Cf. *Haml.*, IV.vii.142.
64. Sans: without. **66. beguiled . . . herself:** cheated your
daughter of herself; i.e., caused her to be "beside herself."
69. proper: own. **77. approved:** tested; i.e., found good masters
by experience. **80. front:** forehead. **81. Rude:** rough, uncul-
tured. **83. pith:** marrow. **85. dearest:** most important.
90. round . . . tale: direct, unadorned account.

95–96. Of . . . herself: she was so shy that she blushed at the
slightest cause. **motion:** outward behavior. **97. credit:** reputation. **100. will confess:** would believe. **102. practices:** plots.
103. vouch: declare. **104. mixtures:** drugs. **blood:** passions.
105. conjured: mixed with spells. **107. overt:** open. **108. thin
habits:** slight evidence; lit., thin clothes. **poor likelihoods:** unconvincing charges. **109. modern seeming:** slight suspicion. **prefer:** make a charge against. **111. forced:** unnatural. **129. Still:**
always, continually. **134. chances:** accidents. **135. accidents:**
occurrences. **136. breach:** assault on a city.

And portance° in my travels' history.
Wherein of antres° vast and deserts idle,°　　140
Rough quarries, rocks, and hills whose heads touch
　　heaven,
It was my hint° to speak — such was the process.°
And of the cannibals that each other eat,
The anthropophagi,° and men whose heads
Do grow beneath their shoulders.° This to hear
Would Desdemona seriously incline.　　146
But still the house affairs would draw her thence,
Which ever as she could with haste dispatch,
She'd come again, and with a greedy ear
Devour up my discourse. Which I observing,　　150
Took once a pliant° hour and found good means
To draw from her a prayer of earnest heart
That I would all my pilgrimage dilate,°
Whereof by parcels° she had something heard,
But not intentively.° I did consent,　　155
And often did beguile her of° her tears
When I did speak of some distressful stroke
That my youth suffered. My story being done,
She gave me for my pains a world of sighs.
She swore, in faith, 'twas strange, 'twas passing
　　strange,　　160
'Twas pitiful, 'twas wondrous pitiful.
She wished she had not heard it, yet she wished
That Heaven had made her° such a man. She
　　thanked me,
And bade me, if I had a friend that loved her,
I should but teach him how to tell my story　　165
And that would woo her. Upon this hint I spake.
She loved me for the dangers I had passed,
And I loved her that she did pity them.
This only is the witchcraft I have used.
Here comes the lady, let her witness it.　　170
　　　[Enter DESDEMONA, IAGO, and ATTENDANTS.]
　DUKE. I think this tale would win my daughter
　　too.
Good Brabantio,
Take up this mangled matter at the best.°
Men do their broken weapons rather use
Than their bare hands.
　BRA.　　　　　　I pray you hear her speak.　　175
If she confess that she was half the wooer,
Destruction on my head if my bad blame
Light on the man! Come hither, gentle mistress.
Do you perceive in all this noble company
Where most you owe obedience?
　DES.　　　　　　　My noble Father,　　180
I do perceive here a divided duty.

To you I am bound for life and education,
My life and education both do learn° me
How to respect you, you are the lord of duty,°
I am hitherto your daughter. But here's my hus-
　　band,　　185
And so much duty as my mother showed
To you, preferring you before her father
So much I challenge that I may profess
Due to the Moor my lord.
　BRA.　　　　　God be with you! I have done.
Please it your Grace, on to the state affairs.　　190
I had rather to adopt a child than get° it.
Come hither, Moor.
I here do give thee that with all my heart
Which, but thou hast already, with all my heart
I would keep from thee. For your sake, jewel,　　195
I am glad at soul I have no other child,
For thy escape would teach me tyranny,
To hang clogs on them. I have done, my lord.
　DUKE. Let me speak like yourself, and lay a sen-
　　tence°
Which, as a grise° or step, may help these lovers
Into your favor.　　201
When remedies are past, the griefs are ended
By seeing the worst, which late on hopes depended.°
To mourn a mischief that is past and gone
Is the next way to draw new mischief on.　　205
What cannot be preserved when fortune takes,
Patience her injury a mockery makes.°
The robbed that smiles steals something from the
　　thief.
He robs himself that spends a bootless° grief.
　BRA. So° let the Turk of Cyprus us beguile,　　210
We lose it not so long as we can smile.
He bears the sentence well that nothing bears
But the free comfort which from thence he hears.
But he bears both the sentence and the sorrow
That, to pay grief, must of poor patience borrow.
These sentences, to sugar or to gall,　　216
Being strong on both sides, are equivocal.
But words are words. I never yet did hear
That the bruised heart was piercèd through the ear.
I humbly beseech you, proceed to the affairs of
　　state.　　220
　DUKE. The Turk with a most mighty preparation
makes for Cyprus. Othello, the fortitude of the place

139. portance: bearing.　140. antres: caves. idle: worthless.
142. hint: occasion. process: proceeding, order.　144. anthropophagi: cannibals.　144–45. men . . . shoulders: See Temp,
III.iii.46–47,n.　151. pliant: suitable.　153. dilate: relate at
length.　154. parcels: portions.　155. intentively: intently.
156. beguile . . . of: draw from her.　163. her: for her.　173. Take
. . . best: make the best settlement you can of this confused business.

183. learn: teach.　184. lord of duty: the man to whom I owe
duty.　191. get: beget.　199. sentence: proverbial saying.
200. grise: degree, step.　202–03. When . . . depended: our
anxieties end when the feared event happens.　207. Patience . . .
makes: i.e., when we are not unduly disturbed by our misfortunes, we mock Fortune.　209. bootless: vain.　210–19. So . . .
ear: Brabantio retaliates sarcastically with a few "sentences"
of his own: Let the Turk take Cyprus; it is no loss if we smile at it.
It is easy enough to produce sententious consolation, it costs
nothing; but the man who has to endure both consolation and the
sorrow itself must needs be patient. These sentences work both
ways; mere words hurt no one. Cf. Leonato's similar outburst,
M Ado, V.i.3–38.

is best known to you, and though we have there a
substitute° of most allowed° sufficiency,° yet opinion, a sovereign mistress of effects, throws a more
safer voice on you.° You must therefore be content
to slubber° the gloss of your new fortunes with this
more stubborn and boisterous expedition.   229

OTH. The tyrant custom, most grave Senators,
Hath made the flinty and steel couch of war
My thrice-driven° bed of down. I do agnize°
A natural and prompt alacrity
I find in hardness,° and do undertake
These present wars against the Ottomites.   235
Most humbly therefore bending to your state,
I crave fit disposition for my wife,
Due reference of place° and exhibition,°
With such accommodation and besort°
As levels with her breeding.°

DUKE.   If you please,   240
Be 't at her father's.

BRA.   I'll not have it so.

OTH. Nor I.

DES.   Nor I. I would not there reside,
To put my father in impatient thoughts
By being in his eye. Most gracious Duke,
To my unfolding° lend your prosperous° ear,   245
And let me find a charter° in your voice
To assist my simpleness.

DUKE. What would you, Desdemona?

DES. That I did love the Moor to live with him,
My downright violence and storm of fortunes   250
May trumpet to the world. My heart's subdued
Even to the very quality of my lord.°
I saw Othello's visage in his mind,
And to his honors and his valiant parts
Did I my soul and fortunes consecrate.   255
So that, dear lords, if I be left behind,
A moth of peace,° and he go to the war,
The rites for which I love him are bereft me,
And I a heavy interim° shall support
By his dear absence. Let me go with him.   260

OTH. Let her have your voices.
Vouch° with me, Heaven, I therefore beg it not
To please the palate of my appetite,
Nor to comply with heat — the young affects
In me defunct° — and proper satisfaction,   265

But to be free and bounteous° to her mind.°
And Heaven defend° your good souls, that you think
I will your serious and great business scant
For she is with me. No, when light-winged toys°
Of feathered Cupid seel° with wanton dullness   270
My speculative and officed instruments,°
That my disports° corrupt and taint my business,
Let housewives make a skillet° of my helm,
And all indign° and base adversities
Make head against° my estimation!°   275

DUKE. Be it as you shall privately determine,
Either for her stay or going. The affair cries haste,
And speed must answer 't. You must hence tonight.

DES. Tonight, my lord?

DUKE.   This night.

OTH.   With all my heart.

DUKE. At nìne i' the morning here we'll meet
again.   280
Othello, leave some officer behind,
And he shall our commission° bring to you,
With such things else of quality and respect
As doth import you.°

OTH.   So please your Grace, my Ancient,
A man he is of honesty and trust.   285
To his conveyance I assign my wife,
With what else needful your good grace shall think
To be sent after me.

DUKE.   Let it be so.
Good night to everyone. [*To* BRABANTIO] And, noble
signior,
If virtue no delighted beauty lack,   290
Your son-in-law is far more fair than black.°

I. SEN. Adieu, brave Moor. Use Desdemona well.

BRA. Look to her, Moor, if thou hast eyes to see.
She has deceived her father, and may thee.°

        [*Exeunt* DUKE, SENATORS, OFFICERS, *etc.*]

OTH. My life upon her faith! Honest Iago,   295
My Desdemona must I leave to thee.
I prithee, let thy wife attend on her,
And bring them after in the best advantage.°
Come, Desdemona, I have but an hour
Of love, of worldly matters and direction,   300
To spend with thee. We must obey the time.

        [*Exeunt* OTHELLO *and* DESDEMONA.]

---

224. **substitute:** deputy commander. **allowed:** admitted. **sufficiency:** efficiency.   224–27. **yet . . . you:** yet public opinion,
which controls our actions, is such that we regard you as a safer
choice.   228. **slubber:** tarnish.   232. **thrice-driven:** three times
refined. **agnize:** confess.   234. **hardness:** hardship.   238. **Due
. . . place:** i.e., that she shall be treated as becomes my wife.
exhibition: allowance.   239. **besort:** attendants.   240. **levels
. . . breeding:** as suits her birth.   245. **unfolding:** plan; lit., re-
vealing. **prosperous:** favorable.   246. **charter:** privilege.
249–52. **That . . . lord:** my love for the Moor is publicly shown by
the way in which I have violently taken my fortunes in my hands;
my heart has become a soldier like my husband. **quality:** profession.   257. **moth of peace:** a useless creature living in luxury.
259. **interim:** interval.   262. **Vouch:** certify.   264–65. **young
. . . defunct:** in me the passion of youth is dead.

266. **bounteous:** generous. **to . . . mind:** Othello repeats Desdemona's claim that this is a marriage of minds.   267. **defend:** forbid.   269. **toys:** trifles.   270. **seel:** close up; a technical term
from falconry.   271. **speculative . . . instruments:** powers of
sight and action; i.e., my efficiency as your general.   272. **dis-
ports:** amusements.   273. **skillet:** saucepan.   274. **indign:**
unworthy.   275. **Make . . . against:** overcome. **estimation:**
reputation.   282. **commission:** formal document of appoint-
ment.   283–84. **With . . . you:** with other matters that concern
your position and honor.   290–91. **If . . . black:** if worthiness is
a beautiful thing in itself, your son-in-law, though black, has
beauty.   293–94. **Look . . . thee:** Iago in the background takes
note of these words, and later reminds Othello of them with
deadly effect. See III.iii.206.   298. **in . . . advantage:** at the best
opportunity.

ROD. Iago!

IAGO. What say'st thou, noble heart?

ROD. What will I do, thinkest thou?

IAGO. Why, go to bed and sleep.　　305

ROD. I will incontinently° drown myself.

IAGO. If thou dost, I shall never love thee after. Why, thou silly gentleman!

ROD. It is silliness to live when to live is torment, and then have we a prescription to die when death is our physician.　　311

IAGO. Oh, villainous! I have looked upon the world for four times seven years, and since I could distinguish betwixt a benefit and an injury I never found man that knew how to love himself. Ere I would say I would drown myself for the love of a guinea hen, I would change my humanity with a baboon.　318

ROD. What should I do? I confess it is my shame to be so fond,° but it is not in my virtue° to amend it.

IAGO. Virtue! A fig! 'Tis in ourselves that we are thus or thus. Our bodies are gardens, to the which our wills° are gardeners. So that if we will plant nettles or sow lettuce, set hyssop and weed up　325 thyme, supply it with one gender° of herbs or distract it with many, either to have it sterile with idleness or manured with industry — why, the power and corrigible° authority of this lies in our wills. If the balance of our lives had not one scale of　330 reason to poise° another of sensuality, the blood and baseness of our natures would conduct us to most preposterous conclusions. But we have reason to cool our raging motions, our carnal stings,° our unbitted° lusts, whereof I take this that you call love to be a sect or scion.°　　337

ROD. It cannot be.

IAGO. It is merely a lust of the blood and a permission of the will. Come, be a man. Drown thyself! Drown cats and blind puppies. I have professed me thy friend, and I confess me knit to thy deserving with cables of perdurable° toughness. I could never better stead° thee than now. Put money in thy purse, follow thou the wars, defeat thy favor with an　345 usurped beard° — I say put money in thy purse. It cannot be that Desdemona should long continue her love to the Moor — put money in thy purse — nor he his to her. It was a violent commencement,　350 and thou shalt see an answerable sequestration° — put but money in thy purse. These Moors are changeable in their wills. — Fill thy purse with money. The

food that to him now is as luscious as locusts° shall be to him shortly as bitter as coloquintida.°　355 She must change for youth. When she is sated with his body, she will find the error of her choice. She must have change, she must — therefore put money in thy purse. If thou wilt needs damn thyself, do it a more delicate way than drowning. Make all　360 the money thou canst.° If sanctimony and a frail vow betwixt an erring° barbarian and a supersubtle Venetian be not too hard for my wits and all the tribe of Hell, thou shalt enjoy her — therefore make money. A pox of drowning thyself! It is clean out of the way. Seek thou rather to be hanged in　366 compassing° thy joy than to be drowned and go without her.

ROD. Wilt thou be fast to my hopes if I depend on the issue?　　370

IAGO. Thou art sure of me. Go, make money. I have told thee often, and I retell thee again and again, I hate the Moor. My cause is hearted,° thine hath no less reason. Let us be conjunctive° in our revenge against him. If thou canst cuckold° him,　375 thou dost thyself a pleasure, me a sport. There are many events in the womb of time, which will be delivered. Traverse,° go, provide thy money. We will have more of this tomorrow. Adieu.　　380

ROD. Where shall we meet i' the morning?

IAGO. At my lodging.

ROD. I'll be with thee betimes.°

IAGO. Go to, farewell. Do you hear, Roderigo?

ROD. What say you?　　386

IAGO. No more of drowning, do you hear?

ROD. I am changed. I'll go sell all my land. [Exit.]

IAGO. Thus do I ever make my fool my purse,
For I mine own gained knowledge should profane
If I would time expend with such a snipe　　391
But for my sport and profit. I hate the Moor,
And it is thought abroad that 'twixt my sheets
He has done my office. I know not if 't be true,
But I for mere suspicion in that kind　　395
Will do as if for surety. He holds me well,
The better shall my purpose work on him.
Cassio's a proper° man. Let me see now,
To get his place, and to plume up° my will
In double knavery — How, how? — Let's see. —
After some time, to abuse Othello's ear　　401
That he is too familiar with his wife.
He hath a person and a smooth dispose
To be suspected,° framed to make women false.

306. incontinently: immediately.　**320.** fond: foolishly in love. virtue: manhood.　**324.** wills: desires.　**326.** gender: kind. **329.** corrigible: correcting, directing.　**331.** poise: weigh. **335.** carnal stings: fleshly desires.　**336.** unbitted: uncontrolled. **337.** sect or scion: Both words mean a slip taken from a tree and planted to produce a new growth.　**343.** perdurable: very hard.　**344.** stead: help.　**345–46.** defeat . . . beard: disguise your face by growing a beard.　**351.** answerable sequestration: corresponding separation; i.e., reaction.

354. locusts: It is not known what fruit was called a locust. **355.** coloquintida: known as "bitter apple," a form of gherkin from which a purge was made.　**360–61.** Make . . . canst: turn all you can into ready cash.　**362.** erring: vagabond.　**367.** compassing: achieving.　**373.** hearted: heartfelt.　**374.** conjunctive: united.　**375.** cuckold: make him a cuckold.　**379.** Traverse: quickstep.　**384.** betimes: in good time, early.　**398.** proper: handsome.　**399.** plume up: glorify.　**403–04.** He . . . suspected: an easy way with him that is naturally suspected.

The Moor is of a free and open nature   405
That thinks men honest that but seem to be so,
And will as tenderly be led by the nose
As asses are.
I have 't. It is engendered.° Hell and night   409
Must bring this monstrous birth to the world's light.
                 [*Exit.*]

Act II

SCENE I. *A seaport in Cyprus. An open place near the wharf.*

[*Enter* MONTANO *and two* GENTLEMEN.]

MON. What from the cape can you discern at sea?
1. GENT. Nothing at all. It is a high-wrought flood.°
I cannot 'twixt the heaven and the main°
Descry a sail.
     MON. Methinks the wind hath spoke aloud at land,   5
A fuller blast ne'er shook our battlements.
If it hath ruffianed° so upon the sea,
What ribs of oak, when mountains melt on them,
Can hold the mortise?° What shall we hear of this?
     2. GENT. A segregation° of the Turkish fleet.   10
For do but stand upon the foaming shore,
The chidden billow seems to pelt the clouds,
The wind-shaked surge, with high and monstrous mane,
Seems to cast water on the burning Bear,°
And quench the guards of the ever-fixèd Pole.°   15
I never did like molestation° view
On the enchafèd° flood.
     MON.   If that the Turkish fleet
Be not ensheltered and embayed,° they are drowned.
It is impossible to bear it out.
          [*Enter a* THIRD GENTLEMAN.]
     3. GENT. News, lads! Our wars are done.   20
The desperate tempest hath so banged the Turks
That their designment halts.° A noble ship of Venice
Hath seen a grievous wreck and sufferance°
On most part of their fleet.

MON. How! Is this true?
3. GENT.   The ship is here put in,   25
A Veronesa. Michael Cassio,
Lieutenant to the warlike Moor Othello,
Is come on shore, the Moor himself at sea,
And is in full commission° here for Cyprus.
     MON. I am glad on 't. 'Tis a worthy governor.   30
     3. GENT. But this same Cassio, though he speak of comfort
Touching the Turkish loss, yet he looks sadly
And prays the Moor be safe, for they were parted
With foul and violent tempest.
     MON.   Pray Heavens he be,
For I have served him, and the man commands   35
Like a full° soldier. Let's to the seaside, ho!
As well to see the vessel that's come in
As to throw out our eyes for brave Othello,
Even till we make the main and the aerial blue
An indistinct regard.°
     3. GENT.   Come, let's do so.   40
For every minute is expectancy
Of more arrivance.°
          [*Enter* CASSIO.]
     CAS. Thanks, you the valiant of this warlike isle
That so approve the Moor! Oh, let the heavens
Give him defense against the elements,   45
For I have lost him on a dangerous sea.
     MON. Is he well shipped?°
     CAS. His bark is stoutly timbered, and his pilot
Of very expert and approved allowance.°
Therefore my hopes, not surfeited° to death,   50
Stand in bold cure.°   [*A cry within:*
            "A sail, a sail, a sail!"]
       [*Enter a* FOURTH GENTLEMAN.]
     CAS. What noise?
     4. GENT. The town is empty. On the brow o' the sea
Stand ranks of people, and they cry " A sail! "   54
     CAS. My hopes do shape° him for the governor.
            [*Guns heard*]
     2. GENT. They do discharge their shot of courtesy.
Our friends, at least.
     CAS.   I pray you, sir, go forth,
And give us truth who 'tis that is arrived.
     2. GENT. I shall.   [*Exit.*]
     MON. But, good Lieutenant, is your General wived?   60
     CAS. Most fortunately. He hath achieved° a maid
That paragons° description and wild fame,
One that excels the quirks of blazoning pens
And in the essential vesture of creation

---

409. engendered: conceived.

    Act II, Sc. i: 2. high-wrought flood: heavy sea.   **3. main: sea.**   **7. ruffianed:** played the ruffian.   **9. hold . . . mortise:** remain fast joined.   **10. segregation:** separation.   **14. Bear:** the Great Bear.   **15. guards . . . Pole:** stars in the "tail" of the Little Bear constellation.   **16. molestation:** disturbance.   **17. enchafed:** angry.   **18. embayed:** anchored in some bay.   **22. designment halts:** plan is made lame.   **23. sufferance:** damage.

29. in . . . commission: with full powers. See I.iii.281–82. **36. full:** perfect. **39–40. Even . . . regard:** until we can no longer distinguish between sea and sky. **41–42. For . . . arrivance:** every minute more arrivals are expected. **47. well shipped:** in a good ship. **49. approved allowance:** proved skill. **50. surfeited:** sickened. **51. Stand . . . cure:** have every hope of cure. **55. shape:** imagine. **61. achieved:** won. **62. paragons:** surpasses.

Does tire the ingener.°

[*Re-enter* SECOND GENTLEMAN.] How now! Who has
 put in? 65

2. GENT. 'Tis one Iago, Ancient to the General.

CAS. He has had most favorable and happy speed.
Tempests themselves, high seas, and howling
 winds,
The guttered° rocks, and congregated sands,
Traitors ensteeped° to clog the guiltless keel, 70
As having sense of beauty, do omit
Their mortal natures,° letting go safely by
The divine Desdemona.

MON. What is she?

CAS. She that I spake of, our great Captain's cap-
 tain,
Left in the conduct° of the bold Iago, 75
Whose footing° here anticipates our thoughts
A sennight's° speed. Great Jove, Othello guard,
And swell his sail with thine own powerful breath,
That he may bless this bay with his tall ship,
Make love's quick pants in Desdemona's arms, 80
Give renewed fire to our extincted° spirits,
And bring all Cyprus comfort.

[*Enter* DESDEMONA, EMILIA, IAGO, RODERIGO,
 and ATTENDANTS.]

 Oh, behold,
The riches of the ship is come on shore!
Ye men of Cyprus, let her have your knees.
Hail to thee, lady! And the grace of Heaven, 85
Before, behind thee, and on every hand,
Enwheel° thee round!

DES. I thank you, valiant Cassio.
What tidings can you tell me of my lord?

CAS. He is not yet arrived, nor know I aught
But that he's well and will be shortly here. 90

DES. Oh, but I fear—— How lost you company?

CAS. The great contention of the sea and skies
Parted our fellowship.° — But, hark! A sail.

[*A cry within:* "A sail, a sail!" *Guns heard.*]

2. GENT. They give their greeting to the citadel.
This likewise is a friend.

CAS. See for the news. [*Exit* GENTLEMAN.]
Good Ancient, you are welcome. [*To* EMILIA] Wel-
 come, mistress.
Let it not gall your patience, good Iago,
That I extend my manners.° 'Tis my breeding°
That gives me this bold show of courtesy.° 100

[*Kissing her.*]

IAGO. Sir, would she give you so much of her lips
As of her tongue she oft bestows on me,
You'd have enough.

DES. Alas, she has no speech.

IAGO. In faith, too much,
I find it still° when I have list° to sleep. 105
Marry, before your ladyship, I grant,
She puts her tongue a little in her heart
And chides with thinking.

EMIL. You have little cause to say so.

IAGO. Come on, come on. You are pictures° out of
 doors, 110
Bells° in your parlors, wildcats in your kitchens,
Saints in your injuries,° devils being offended,
Players in your housewifery, and housewives in your
 beds.

DES. Oh, fie upon thee, slanderer!

IAGO. Nay, it is true, or else I am a Turk.° 115
You rise to play, and go to bed to work.

EMIL. You shall not write my praise.

IAGO. No, let me not.

DES. What wouldst thou write of me if thou
 shouldst praise me?

IAGO. O gentle lady, do not put me to 't,
For I am nothing if not critical.° 120

DES. Come on, assay.° — There's one gone to the
 harbor?

IAGO. Aye, madam.

DES. I am not merry, but I do beguile
The thing I am by seeming otherwise.
Come, how wouldst thou praise me? 125

IAGO. I am about it, but indeed my invention
Comes from my pate as birdlime does from
 frieze° —
It plucks out brains and all. But my Muse labors,
And thus she is delivered.
If she be fair and wise, fairness and wit, 130
The one's for use, the other useth it.

DES. Well praised! How if she be black and witty?

IAGO. If she be black, and thereto have a wit,
She'll find a white° that shall her blackness fit.

DES. Worse and worse. 135

EMIL. How if fair and foolish?

IAGO. She never yet was foolish that was fair,
For even her folly helped her to an heir.

DES. These are old fond paradoxes° to make fools
laugh i' the alehouse. What miserable praise hast
thou for her that's foul and foolish? 141

63–65. One . . . ingener: one that is too good for the fancy
phrases (*quirks*) of painting pens (i.e., poets) and in her absolute
perfection wearies the artist (i.e., the painter). (Cassio is full of
gallant phrases and behavior, in contrast to Iago's bluntness.) ingener: inventor. 69. guttered: worn into channels. 70. en-
steeped: submerged. 71–72. omit . . . natures: forbear their
deadly nature. 75. conduct: escort. 76. footing: arrival.
77. sennight: week. 81. extincted: extinguished. 87. En-
wheel: encompass. 93. fellowship: company. 99. extend my
manners: i.e., salute your wife. breeding: bringing-up. 100. bold
. . . courtesy: i.e., of saluting your wife with a kiss — a piece of
presumptuous behavior which indicates that Cassio regards himself as Iago's social superior. 105. still: continuously. list: desire.
110. pictures: i.e., painted and dumb. 111. Bells: i.e., ever
clacking. 112. Saints . . . injuries: saints when you hurt anyone
else. 115. Turk: heathen. 120. critical: bitter. 121. assay:
try. 126–27. my . . . frieze: my literary effort (*invention*) is as
hard to pull out of my head as frieze (cloth with a nap) stuck to
birdlime. 134. white: with a pun on *wight* (l. 159), man, person.
139. fond paradoxes: foolish remarks, contrary to general
opinion.

IAGO. There's none so foul, and foolish thereunto,
But does foul pranks which fair and wise ones do.

DES. Oh, heavy ignorance! Thou praisest the worst
best. But what praise couldst thou bestow on a deserving woman indeed, one that in the authority of
her merit did justly put on the vouch of very malice
itself?°   148

IAGO. She that was ever fair and never proud,
Had tongue at will° and yet was never loud,
Never lacked gold and yet went never gay,
Fled from her wish and yet said " Now I may."
She that, being angered, her revenge being nigh,
Bade her wrong stay and her displeasure fly.
She that in wisdom never was so frail   155
To change the cod's head for the salmon's tail.°
She that could think and ne'er disclose her mind,
See suitors following and not look behind.
She was a wight, if ever such wight were ——

DES. To do what?   160

IAGO. To suckle fools and chronicle small beer.°

DES. Oh, most lame and impotent conclusion! Do
not learn of him, Emilia, though he be thy husband.
How say you, Cassio? Is he not a most profane and
liberal° counselor?   165

CAS. He speaks home,° madam. You may relish°
him more in the soldier than in the scholar.

IAGO. [*Aside*] He° takes her by the palm. Aye,
well said, whisper. With as little a web as this will I
ensnare as great a fly as Cassio. Aye, smile upon   170
her, do, I will gyve° thee in thine own courtship.
You say true, 'tis so indeed. If such tricks as these
strip you out of your Lieutenantry, it had been better
you had not kissed your three fingers° so oft, which
now again you are most apt to play the sir° in.   175
Very good, well kissed! An excellent courtesy! 'Tis
so indeed. Yet again your fingers to your lips? Would
they were clyster pipes° for your sake! [*Trumpet
within.*] The Moor! I know his trumpet.   180

CAS. 'Tis truly so.

DES. Let's meet him and receive him.

CAS. Lo where he comes!

[*Enter* OTHELLO *and* ATTENDANTS.]

OTH. O my fair warrior!°

DES.   My dear Othello!

OTH. It gives me wonder great as my content   185
To see you here before me. O my soul's joy!
If after every tempest come such calms,

May the winds blow till they have wakened death!
And let the laboring bark climb hills of seas
Olympus-high,° and duck again as low   190
As Hell's from Heaven! If it were now to die,
'Twere now to be most happy, for I fear
My soul hath her content so absolute
That not another comfort like to this
Succeeds in unknown fate.   194

DES.   The Heavens forbid
But that our loves and comforts should increase,
Even as our days do grow!

OTH.   Amen to that, sweet powers!
I cannot speak enough of this content.
It stops me here,° it is too much of joy.
And this, and this, the greatest discords be   200

[*Kissing her*]

That e'er our hearts shall make!

IAGO. [*Aside*]   Oh, you are well tuned now,
But I'll set down the pegs° that make this music,
As honest as I am.

OTH.   Come, let us to the castle.
News, friends. Our wars are done, the Turks are
    drowned.
How does my old acquaintance of this isle?   205
Honey, you shall be well desired in Cyprus,
I have found great love amongst them. O my sweet,
I prattle out of fashion,° and I dote
In mine own comforts. I prithee, good Iago,
Go to the bay and disembark my coffers.°   210
Bring thou the master° to the citadel.
He is a good one, and his worthiness
Does challenge° much respect. Come, Desdemona,
Once more well met at Cyprus.   214

[*Exeunt all but* IAGO *and* RODERIGO.]

IAGO. Do thou meet me presently° at the harbor.
Come hither. If thou beest valiant — as they say base
men being in love have then a nobility in their natures more than is native to them — list me. The
Lieutenant tonight watches on the court of guard.°
First, I must tell thee this. Desdemona is directly in
love with him.   221

ROD. With him! Why, 'tis not possible.

IAGO. Lay thy finger thus,° and let thy soul be instructed. Mark me with what violence she first loved
the Moor, but for° bragging and telling her   225
fantastical lies. And will she love him still for prat-
ing? Let not thy discreet heart think it. Her eye must
be fed, and what delight shall she have to look on the
Devil?° When the blood is made dull with the act

146–48. one . . . itself: one so deserving that even malice would
declare her good.   **150. tongue . . . will:** a ready flow of words.
156. To . . . tail: to prefer the tail end of a good thing to the
head of a poor thing.   **161. chronicle . . . beer:** write a whole
history about trifles (*small beer:* thin drink).   **165. liberal:**
gross.   **166. home:** to the point. **relish:** appreciate.   **168–79. He
. . . sake:** As so often, Shakespeare without using elaborate stage
directions exactly indicates the action in the dialogue. Cf. *W Tale*,
I.ii.111–18.   **171. gyve:** fetter.   **174. kissed . . . fingers:** a
gesture of gallantry.   **175. play . . . sir:** act the fine gentleman.   **179. clyster pipes:** an enema syringe.   **184. warrior:**
because she is a soldier's wife. See I.iii.249.

190. Olympus-high: high as Olympus, the highest mountain in
Greece.   **199. here:** i.e., in the heart.   **202. set . . . pegs:** i.e.,
make you sing in a different key. A stringed instrument was
tuned by the pegs.   **208. prattle . . . fashion:** talk idly.
210. coffers: trunks.   **211. master:** captain of the ship.   **213. challenge:** claim.   **215. presently:** immediately.   **219. watches . . .
guard:** is on duty with the guard. The court of guard meant
both the guard itself and the guardroom.   **223. finger thus:** i.e.,
on the lips.   **225. but for:** only for.   **229. Devil:** See I.i.91,n.

of sport, there should be, again to inflame it   230
and to give satiety a fresh appetite, loveliness in favor,° sympathy in years, manners, and beauties, all
which the Moor is defective in. Now, for want of
these required conveniences, her delicate tenderness
will find itself abused, begin to heave the   235
gorge,° disrelish and abhor the Moor. Very nature
will instruct her in it and compel her to some second
choice. Now, sir, this granted—as it is a most pregnant and unforced position°—who stands so eminently in the degree of this fortune as Cassio   240
does? A knave very voluble, no further conscion-
able° than in putting on the mere form of civil and
humane seeming° for the better compassing of his
salt° and most hidden loose affection? Why, none,
why, none. A slipper° and subtle knave, a finder-
out of occasions, that has an eye can stamp   246
and counterfeit advantages,° though true advantage
never present itself. A devilish knave! Besides, the
knave is handsome, young, and hath all those requisites in him that folly and green° minds look   250
after. A pestilent complete knave, and the woman
hath found him already.

ROD. I cannot believe that in her. She's full of
most blest condition.°   255

IAGO. Blest fig's-end!° The wine she drinks is
made of grapes. If she had been blest, she would
never have loved the Moor. Blest pudding! Didst
thou not see her paddle° with the palm of his hand?
Didst not mark that?   260

ROD. Yes, that I did, but that was but courtesy.

IAGO. Lechery, by this hand, an index° and obscure prologue to the history of lust and foul
thoughts. They met so near with their lips that
their breaths embraced together. Villainous   265
thoughts, Roderigo! When these mutualities° so
marshal the way, hard at hand comes the master and
main exercise, the incorporate° conclusion. Pish!
But, sir, be you ruled by me. I have brought you
from Venice. Watch you tonight. For the com-   270
mand, I'll lay 't upon you. Cassio knows you not.
I'll not be far from you. Do you find some occasion
to anger Cassio, either by speaking too loud, or taint-
ing° his discipline, or from what other course you
please which the time shall more favorably   275
minister.°

ROD. Well.

IAGO. Sir, he is rash and very sudden in choler,°
and haply° may strike at you. Provoke him, that he
may, for even out of that will I cause these of   280
Cyprus to mutiny, whose qualification° shall come
into no true taste again but by the displanting° of
Cassio. So shall you have a shorter journey to your
desires by the means I shall then have to pre-   285
fer° them, and the impediment most profitably removed without the which there were no expectation
of our prosperity.

ROD. I will do this, if I can bring it to any opportunity.   290

IAGO. I warrant thee. Meet me by and by at the
citadel. I must fetch his necessaries ashore. Farewell.

ROD. Adieu.   [*Exit.*]

IAGO. That Cassio loves her, I do well believe it.
That she loves him, 'tis apt and of great credit.°   296
The Moor, howbeit that I endure him not,
Is of a constant, loving, noble nature,
And I dare think he'll prove to Desdemona
A most dear husband. Now, I do love her too,   300
Not out of absolute lust, though peradventure
I stand accountant for as great a sin,
But partly led to diet° my revenge
For that I do suspect the lusty Moor   304
Hath leaped into my seat. The thought whereof
Doth like a poisonous mineral° gnaw my inwards.
And nothing can or shall content my soul
Till I am evened with him, wife for wife.
Or failing so, yet that I put the Moor
At least into a jealousy so strong   310
That judgment° cannot cure. Which thing to do,
If this poor trash of Venice, whom I trash°
For his quick hunting,° stand the putting-on,°
I'll have our Michael Cassio on the hip,
Abuse him to the Moor in the rank garb°—   315
For I fear Cassio with my nightcap too—
Make the Moor thank me, love me, and reward me
For making him egregiously° an ass
And practicing upon° his peace and quiet
Even to madness. 'Tis here, but yet confused.   320
Knavery's plain face is never seen till used.   [*Exit.*]

278. **choler:** anger.   279. **haply:** perhaps.   281. **qualification:** appeasement.   282. **displanting:** removal.   286. **prefer:** promote.   296. **apt . . . credit:** likely and very credible.   303. **diet:** feed.   306. **poisonous mineral:** corrosive poison. See I.ii.74.   311. **judgment:** reason.   312. **trash . . . trash:** rubbish . . . discard.   312–13. **trash . . . hunting:** F1 reads "trace" and Q1 "crush." If the emendation "trash" is correct, it means "hold back from outrunning the pack." Cf. *Temp*, I.ii.81,n.   313. **putting-on:** encouraging.   315. **rank garb:** gross manner; i.e., by accusing him of being Desdemona's lover.   318. **egregiously:** notably.   319. **practicing upon:** plotting against.

232. **favor:** face.   235–36. **heave . . . gorge:** retch. **gorge:** throat.   238–39. **pregnant . . . position:** very significant and probable argument.   241–42. **no . . . consciable:** who has no more conscience.   243. **humane seeming:** courteous appearance.   244. **salt:** lecherous.   245. **slipper:** slippery.   246–47. **stamp . . . advantages:** forge false opportunities.   250. **green:** inexperienced, foolish.   255. **condition:** disposition.   256. **Blest fig's-end:** blest nonsense, a phrase used as a substitute in contempt for a phrase just used, as is also *blest pudding* (l.258).   259. **paddle:** play.   262. **index:** table of contents.   266. **mutualities:** mutual exchanges.   268. **incorporate:** bodily.   274. **tainting:** disparaging.   276. **minister:** provide.

SCENE II. *A street.*

[*Enter a* HERALD *with a proclamation,* PEOPLE *following.*]

HER. It is Othello's pleasure, our noble and valiant General, that upon certain tidings now arrived, importing the mere perdition° of the Turkish fleet, every man put himself into triumph° — some to dance, some to make bonfires, each man to what 5 sport and revels his addiction° leads him. For, besides these beneficial news, it is the celebration of his nuptial. So much was his pleasure should be proclaimed. All offices° are open, and there is full liberty of feasting from this present hour of five till 10 the bell have told eleven. Heaven bless the isle of Cyprus and our noble General Othello! [*Exeunt.*]

SCENE III. *A hall in the castle.*

[*Enter* OTHELLO, DESDEMONA, CASSIO, *and* ATTENDANTS.]

OTH. Good Michael, look you to the guard tonight. Let's teach ourselves that honorable stop, Not to outsport discretion.°

CAS. Iago hath direction what to do, But notwithstanding with my personal eye 5 Will I look to 't.

OTH. Iago is most honest. Michael, good night. Tomorrow with your earliest° Let me have speech with you. Come, my dear love, The purchase made, the fruits are to ensue — That profit's yet to come 'tween me and you. 10 Good night.

[*Exeunt* OTHELLO, DESDEMONA, *and* ATTENDANTS.]
[*Enter* IAGO.]

CAS. Welcome, Iago. We must to the watch.

IAGO. Not this hour, Lieutenant, 'tis not yet ten o' the clock. Our General cast° us thus early for the love of his Desdemona, who let us not therefore blame. He hath not yet made wanton the night with her, and she is sport for Jove. 17

CAS. She's a most exquisite lady.

IAGO. And, I'll warrant her, full of game.

CAS. Indeed she's a most fresh and delicate creature. 21

IAGO. What an eye she has! Methinks it sounds a parley to provocation.°

CAS. An inviting eye, and yet methinks right modest.

IAGO. And when she speaks, is it not an alarum° to love? 27

CAS. She is indeed perfection.

IAGO. Well, happiness to their sheets! Come, Lieutenant, I have a stoup° of wine, and here without are a brace of Cyprus gallants that would fain° have a measure to the health of black Othello. 33

CAS. Not tonight, good Iago. I have very poor and unhappy brains for drinking. I could well wish courtesy would invent some other custom of entertainment.

IAGO. Oh, they are our friends. But one cup — I'll drink for you. 39

CAS. I have drunk but one cup tonight, and that was craftily qualified° too, and behold what innovation° it makes here. I am unfortunate in the infirmity, and dare not task° my weakness with any more. 44

IAGO. What, man! 'Tis a night of revels. The gallants desire it.

CAS. Where are they?

IAGO. Here at the door. I pray you call them in.

CAS. I'll do 't, but it dislikes° me. [*Exit.*]

IAGO. If I can fasten but one cup upon him, 50 With that which he hath drunk tonight already He'll be as full of quarrel and offense As my young mistress' dog. Now my sick fool Roderigo, Whom love hath turned almost the wrong side out, To Desdemona hath tonight caroused° 55 Potations pottle-deep,° and he's to watch. Three lads of Cyprus, noble swelling° spirits That hold their honors in a wary distance,° The very elements° of this warlike isle, Have I tonight flustered with flowing cups, 60 And they watch too. Now, 'mongst this flock of drunkards, Am I to put our Cassio in some action That may offend the isle. But here they come. If consequence do but approve my dream,° My boat sails freely, both with wind and stream. 65

[*Re-enter* CASSIO, *with him* MONTANO *and* GENTLEMEN, SERVANTS *following with wine.*]

CAS. 'Fore God, they have given me a rouse° already.

MON. Good faith, a little one — not past a pint, as I am a soldier.

IAGO. Some wine, ho! [*Sings.*] 70

26. alarum: call to arms. 31. stoup: large drinking vessel. 32. fain: gladly. 41. craftily qualified: cunningly mixed. 42. innovation: revolution, disturbance. 43. task: burden. 49. dislikes: displeases. 55. caroused: drunk healths. 56. pottle-deep: "bottoms up"; a pottle held two quarts. 57. swelling: bursting with pride. 58. hold . . . distance: "have a chip on their shoulders." 59. very elements: typical specimens. 64. If . . . dream: if what follows proves my dream true. 66. rouse: a deep drink.

Sc. ii: 3. mere perdition: absolute destruction. 4. put . . . triumph: celebrate. 6. addiction: inclination. 9. offices: the kitchen and buttery — i.e., free food and drink for all.
Sc. iii: 3. outsport discretion: let the fun go too far. 7. with . . . earliest: very early. 14. cast: dismissed. 22-23. sounds . . . provocation: invites to a love talk.

"And let me the cannikin° clink, clink,
And let me the cannikin clink.
A soldier's a man,
A life's but a span.°
Why, then let a soldier drink."   75
Some wine, boys!

CAS. 'Fore God, an excellent song.

IAGO. I learned it in England, where indeed they
are most potent in potting.° Your Dane, your German, and your swag-bellied° Hollander — Drink,
ho! — are nothing to your English.   81

CAS. Is your Englishman so expert in his drinking?

IAGO. Why, he drinks you with facility your Dane
dead drunk, he sweats not° to overthrow your Almain,° he gives your Hollander a vomit° ere the
next pottle can be filled.   87

CAS. To the health of our General!

MON. I am for it, Lieutenant, and I'll do you justice.   90

IAGO. O sweet England! [*Sings.*]
" King Stephen was a worthy peer,
His breeches cost him but a crown.
He held them sixpence all too dear,°
With that he called the tailor lown.°   95

"He was a wight of high renown,
And thou art but of low degree.
'Tis pride that pulls the country down.
Then take thine auld cloak about thee."
Some wine, ho!   100

CAS. Why, this is a more exquisite song than the
other.

IAGO. Will you hear 't again?

CAS. No, for I hold him to be unworthy of his
place that does those things. Well, God's above all,
and there be souls must be saved and there be souls
must not be saved.   107

IAGO. It's true, good Lieutenant.

CAS. For mine own part — no offense to the General, nor any man of quality° — I hope to be saved.

IAGO. And so do I too, Lieutenant.   112

CAS. Aye, but, by your leave, not before me. The
Lieutenant is to be saved before the Ancient. Let's
have no more of this, let's to our affairs. God   115
forgive us our sins! Gentlemen, let's look to our business. Do not think, gentlemen, I am drunk. This is
my Ancient, this is my right hand and this is my

left. I am not drunk **now, I** can stand well enough
and speak well enough.   120

ALL. Excellent well.

CAS. Why, very well, **then,** you must not think
then that I am drunk.   [*Exit.*]

MON. To the platform,° masters. Come, let's set
the watch.°   125

IAGO. You see this fellow that is gone before.
He is a soldier fit to stand by Caesar
And give direction. And do but see his vice.
'Tis to his virtue a just equinox,°
The one as long as the other. 'Tis pity of him.   130
I fear the trust Othello puts him in
On some odd time° of his infirmity
Will shake this island.

MON.   But is he often thus?

IAGO. 'Tis evermore the prologue to his sleep.
He'll watch the horologe a double set,°   135
If drink rock not his cradle.

MON.   It were well
The General were put in mind of it.
Perhaps he sees it not, or his good nature
Prizes the virtue that appears in Cassio
And looks not on his evils. Is not this true?   140
[*Enter* RODERIGO.]

IAGO. [*Aside to him*] How now, Roderigo! I pray
you, after the Lieutenant. Go.   [*Exit* RODERIGO.]

MON. And 'tis great pity that the noble Moor
Should hazard such a place as his own second
With one of an ingraft° infirmity.   145
It were an honest action to say
So to the Moor.

IAGO.   Not I, for this fair island.
I do love Cassio well, and would do much
To cure him of this evil — But, hark! What noise?
[*A cry within:* " Help! help! "]
[*Re-enter* CASSIO, *driving in* RODERIGO.]

CAS. 'Zounds! You rogue! You rascal!

MON.   What's the matter, Lieutenant? 150

CAS. A knave teach me my duty!
But I'll beat the knave into a wicker bottle.°

ROD. Beat me!

CAS. Dost thou prate, rogue? [*Striking* RODERIGO.]

MON.   Nay, good Lieutenant, [*Staying him.*]
I pray you, sir, hold your hand.

CAS.   Let me go, sir,
Or I'll knock you o'er the mazzard.°

MON.   Come, come, you're drunk.   155

CAS. Drunk!   [*They fight.*]

---

71. cannikin: drinking pot.   74. span: lit., the measure between
the thumb and little finger of the outstretched hand; about 9
inches.   79. potent in potting: desperate drinkers.   For the
Danes' potency in potting see *Haml.*, I.iv.8–38.   80. swag-
bellied: with loose bellies. Germans and Dutchmen were almost
as famous for drinking as the Danes.   85. sweats not: has no
need to labor excessively.   86. Almain: German.   86. gives . . .
vomit: drinks as much as will make a Dutchman throw up.
94. sixpence . . . dear: too dear by sixpence.   95. lown: lout.
111. quality: rank.

124. platform: the level place on the ramparts where the cannon
were mounted.   124–25. set . . . watch: mount guard.   129. just
equinox: exact equal.   132. some . . . time: some time or other.
135. watch . . . set: stay awake the clock twice round.   145. in-
graft: engrafted, firmly fixed.   152. But . . . bottle: One of those
bad-tempered threatening phrases which have no very exact
meaning, like "I'll knock him into a cocked hat." wicker bottle:
large bottle covered with wicker, demijohn.   154. mazzard:
head, a slang word.

IAGO. [*Aside to* RODERIGO] Away, I say. Go out
  and cry a mutiny.°   [*Exit* RODERIGO.]
Nay, good Lieutenant! God's will, gentlemen!
Help, ho! — Lieutenant — sir — Montano — sir —
Help, masters! — Here's a goodly watch indeed!
              [*A bell rings.*]
Who's that that rings the bell? — Diablo,° ho!   160
The town will rise. God's will, Lieutenant, hold —
You will be shamed forever.
     [*Re-enter* OTHELLO *and* ATTENDANTS.]
  OTH.   What is the matter here?
  MON. 'Zounds, I bleed still, I am hurt to the death.
                 [*Faints.*]
  OTH. Hold, for your lives!   165
  IAGO. Hold, ho! Lieutenant — sir — Montano —
    gentlemen —
Have you forgot all sense of place and duty?
Hold! The General speaks to you. Hold, hold, for
  shame!
  OTH. Why, how now, ho! From whence ariseth
  this?
Are we turned Turks, and to ourselves do that   170
Which Heaven hath forbid the Ottomites?
For Christian shame, put by this barbarous brawl.
He that stirs next to carve for his own rage°
Holds his soul light, he dies upon his motion.°
Silence that dreadful bell. It frights the isle   175
From her propriety.° What is the matter, masters?
Honest Iago, that look'st dead with grieving,
Speak, who began this? On thy love, I charge
  thee.
  IAGO. I do not know. Friends all but now, even
  now,
In quarter and in terms like bride and groom   180
Devesting° them for bed. And then, but now,
As if some planet had unwitted men,°
Swords out, and tilting° one at other's breast
In opposition bloody. I cannot speak
Any beginning to this peevish odds,°   185
And would in action glorious I had lost
Those legs that brought me to a part of it!
  OTH. How comes it, Michael, you are thus for-
  got?°
  CAS. I pray you, pardon me, I cannot speak.
  OTH. Worthy Montano, you were wont be civil.°
The gravity and stillness° of your youth   191
The world hath noted, and your name is great
In mouths of wisest censure.° What's the matter
That you unlace° your reputation thus,

And spend **your** rich opinion° for the name   195
Of a night brawler? Give me answer to it.
  MON. Worthy Othello, I am hurt to danger.
Your officer, Iago, can inform you —
While I spare speech, which something now offends
  me —
Of all that I do know. Nor know I aught   200
By me that's said or done amiss this night,
Unless self-charity° be sometimes a vice,
And to defend ourselves it be a sin
When violence assails us.
  OTH.   Now, by Heaven,
My blood begins my safer guides to rule,   205
And passion, having my best judgment collied,°
Assays to lead the way. If I once stir,
Or do but lift this arm, the best of you
Shall sink in my rebuke. Give me to know
How this foul rout° began, who set it on,   210
And he that is approved° in this offense,
Though he had twinned with me, both at a birth,
Shall lose me. What! In a town of war,
Yet wild, the people's hearts brimful of fear,
To manage° private and domestic quarrel,   215
In night, and on the court and guard of safety!
'Tis monstrous. Iago, who began 't?
  MON. If partially affined, or leagued in office,
Thou dost deliver° more or less than truth,
Thou art no soldier.
  IAGO.   Touch me not so near.   220
I had rather have this tongue cut from my mouth
Than it should do offense to Michael Cassio.
Yet I persuade myself to speak the truth
Shall nothing wrong him. Thus it is, General.
Montano and myself being in speech,   225
There comes a fellow crying out for help,
And Cassio following him with determined sword
To execute upon him. Sir, this gentleman
Steps in to Cassio and entreats his pause.°
Myself the crying fellow did pursue,   230
Lest by his clamor — as it so fell out —
The town might fall in fright. He, swift of foot,
Outran my purpose, and I returned the rather
For that I heard the clink and fall of swords,
And Cassio high in oath, which till tonight   235
I ne'er might say before. When I came back —
For this was brief — I found them close together,
At blow and thrust, even as again they were
When you yourself did part them.
More of this matter cannot I report.   240
But men are men, the best sometimes forget
Though Cassio did some little wrong to him,
As men in rage strike those that wish them best,

---

157. cry ... mutiny: cry that a mutiny has broken out; i.e.,
raise a riot.   160. Diablo: the Devil.   173. carve ... rage: to
satisfy his hunger for rage.   174. upon ... motion: at his first
movement.   176. propriety: natural behavior.   181. Devesting:
taking off their clothes.   182. planet ... men: as if some evil
star had made men mad.   183. tilting: thrusting.   185. peevish odds: silly disagreement.   188. are ... forgot: have so forgotten yourself.   190. civil: well behaved.   191. stillness:
staid behavior.   193. censure: judgment.   194. unlace:
undo.

195. spend ... opinion: lose your good reputation.   202. self-
charity: love for oneself.   206. collied: darkened.   210. rout:
riot, uproar.   211. approved: proved guilty.   215. manage: be
concerned with.   218-19. If ... deliver: if, because you are influenced by partiality or because he is your fellow officer, you report. affined: bound.   229. entreats ... pause: begs him to stop.

Yet surely Cassio, I believe, received
From him that fled some strange indignity,   245
Which patience could not pass.

OTH.   I know, Iago,
Thy honesty and love doth mince this matter,
Making it light to Cassio. Cassio, I love thee,
But never more be officer of mine.
[*Re-enter* DESDEMONA, *attended.*] Look, if my gentle
    love be not raised up!   250
I'll make thee an example.

DES.   What's the matter?

OTH. All's well now, sweeting.° Come away to
    bed. [*To* MONTANO, *who is led off*]
Sir, for your hurts, myself will be your surgeon.
Lead him off.
Iago, look with care about the town,   255
And silence those whom this vile brawl distracted.
Come, Desdemona. 'Tis the soldiers' life
To have their balmy slumbers waked with strife.
          [*Exeunt all but* IAGO *and* CASSIO.]

IAGO. What, are you hurt, Lieutenant?

CAS. Aye, past all surgery.   260

IAGO. Marry, Heaven forbid!

CAS. Reputation, reputation, reputation! Oh, I
have lost my reputation! I have lost the immortal
part of myself, and what remains is bestial. My reputation, Iago, my reputation!   265

IAGO. As I am an honest man, I thought you had
received some bodily wound. There is more sense
in that than in reputation. Reputation is an idle and
most false imposition,° oft got without merit and
lost without deserving. You have lost no repu-   270
tation at all unless you repute yourself such a loser.
What, man! There are ways to recover the General
again. You are but now cast in his mood,° a punishment more in policy° than in malice — even so as
one would beat his offenseless dog to affright an im-
perious lion.° Sue to him again and he's yours.   277

CAS. I will rather sue to be despised than to de-
ceive so good a commander with so slight, so
drunken, and so indiscreet an officer. Drunk? And
speak parrot?° And squabble? Swagger? Swear?
And discourse fustian° with one's own shadow? O
thou invisible spirit of wine, if thou hast no name to
be known by, let us call thee devil!   284

IAGO. What was he that you followed with your
sword? What had he done to you?

CAS. I know not.

IAGO. Is 't possible?   288

CAS. I remember a mass of things, but nothing
distinctly — a quarrel, but nothing wherefore. Oh

God, that men should put an enemy in their mouths
to steal away their brains! That we should, with joy,
pleasance,° revel, and applause, transform ourselves
into beasts!   294

IAGO. Why, but you are now well enough. How
came you thus recovered?

CAS. It hath pleased the devil drunkenness to give
place to the devil wrath. One unperfectness shows
me another, to make me frankly despise myself.   300

IAGO. Come, you are too severe a moraler.° As the
time, the place, and the condition of this country
stands, I could heartily wish this had not befall-
en. But since it is as it is, mend it for your own
good.   305

CAS. I will ask him for my place again, he shall
tell me I am a drunkard! Had I as many mouths as
Hydra,° such an answer would stop them all. To be
now a sensible man, by and by a fool, and presently a beast! Oh, strange! Every inordinate° cup is
unblest, and the ingredient is a devil.   312

IAGO. Come, come, good wine is a good familiar
creature, if it be well used. Exclaim no more against
it. And, good Lieutenant, I think you think I love
you.

CAS. I have well approved it, sir. I drunk!   317

IAGO. You or any man living may be drunk at
some time, man. I'll tell you what you shall do. Our
General's wife is now the General. I may say so in
this respect, for that he hath devoted and given up
himself to the contemplation, mark, and denote-
ment° of her parts and graces. Confess yourself
freely to her, importune her help to put you in your
place again. She is of so free, so kind, so apt,° so
blessed a disposition, she holds it a vice in her   325
goodness not to do more than she is requested. This
broken joint between you and her husband entreat
her to splinter° and, my fortunes against any lay°
worth naming, this crack of your love shall grow
stronger than it was before.   331

CAS. You advise me well.

IAGO. I protest, in the sincerity of love and honest
kindness.

CAS. I think it freely, and betimes in the morning
I will beseech the virtuous Desdemona to undertake
for me. I am desperate of my fortunes if they check
me here.°

IAGO. You are in the right. Good night, Lieutenant, I must to the watch.   340

CAS. Good night, honest Iago.   [*Exit.*]

IAGO. And what's he then that says I play the villain?

---

252. sweeting: sweetheart.   269. imposition: a quality laid on
a man by others.   273. cast . . . mood: dismissed because he is in
a bad mood.   275. in policy: i.e., because he must appear to be
angry before the Cypriots.   275–77. even . . . lion: a proverb
meaning that when the lion sees the dog beaten, he will know
what is coming to him.   281. speak parrot: babble.   282. fustian:
nonsense; lit., cheap cloth.

293. pleasance: a gay time.   301. moraler: moralizer.   307. Hydra: a hundred-headed beast slain by Hercules.   311. inordinate:
excessive.   322. denotement: careful observation.   324. apt:
ready.   329. splinter: put in splints.   329. lay: bet.   337–38. I
. . . here: I despair of my future if my career is stopped short
here.

When this advice is free I give and honest,
Probal° to thinking, and indeed the course
To win the Moor again? For 'tis most easy   345
The inclining Desdemona to subdue
In any honest suit. She's framed° as fruitful
As the free elements.° And then for her
To win the Moor, were 't to renounce his baptism,
All seals and symbols of redeemèd sin,   350
His soul is so enfettered to her love
That she may make, unmake, do what she list,
Even as her appetite shall play the god
With his weak function.° How am I then a villain
To counsel Cassio to this parallel course,   355
Directly to his good? Divinity of Hell!
When devils will the blackest sins put on,
They do suggest° at first with heavenly shows,
As I do now. For whiles this honest fool
Plies° Desdemona to repair his fortunes,   360
And she for him pleads strongly to the Moor,
I'll pour this pestilence into his ear,
That she repeals° him for her body's lust.
And by how much she strives to do him good,
She shall undo her credit with the Moor.   365
So will I turn her virtue into pitch,
And out of her own goodness make the net
That shall enmesh them all.
[*Enter* RODERIGO.] How now, Roderigo!

    ROD. I do follow here in the chase, not like a hound
that hunts but one that fills up the cry.° My   370
money is almost spent, I have been tonight exceed-
ingly well cudgeled, and I think the issue will be I
shall have so much experience for my pains and so,
with no money at all and a little more wit, return
again to Venice.   375

    IAGO. How poor are they that have not patience!
What wound did ever heal but by degrees?
Thou know'st we work by wit and not by witch-
    craft,
And wit depends on dilatory Time.°
Does 't not go well? Cassio hath beaten thee,   380
And thou by that small hurt hast cashiered Cassio.
Though other things grow fair against the sun,
Yet fruits that blossom first will first be ripe.°
Content thyself awhile. By the mass, 'tis morning.
Pleasure and action make the hours seem short.   385
Retire thee, go where thou art billeted.
Away, I say. Thou shalt know more hereafter.
Nay, get thee gone. [*Exit* RODERIGO.] Two things are
    to be done:

My wife must move for° Cassio to her mistress,
I'll set her on,   390
Myself the while to draw the Moor apart
And bring him jump° when he may Cassio find
Soliciting his wife. Aye, that's the way.
Dull not device° by coldness and delay.   [*Exit.*]

Act III

SCENE I. *Before the castle.*

[*Enter* CASSIO *and some* MUSICIANS.]
CAS. Masters, play here, I will content your
    pains° —
Something that's brief, and bid "Good morrow,
    General."°   [*Music.*]
[*Enter* CLOWN.]
CLO. Why, masters, have your instruments been
in Naples,° that they speak i' the nose thus?
1. MUS. How, sir, how?   5
CLO. Are these, I pray you, wind instruments?
1. MUS. Aye, marry are they, sir.
CLO. Oh, thereby hangs a tail.
1. MUS. Whereby hangs a tale, sir?   9
CLO. Marry, sir, by many a wind instrument that
I know. But, masters, here's money for you. And the
General so likes your music that he desires you, for
love's sake, to make no more noise with it.
1. MUS. Well, sir, we will not.   15
CLO. If you have any music that may not be heard,
to 't again. But, as they say, to hear music the General does not greatly care.
1. MUS. We have none such, sir.
CLO. Then put up your pipes in your bag, for I'll
away. Go, vanish into air, away!   21
    [*Exeunt* MUSICIANS.]
CAS. Dost thou hear, my honest friend?
CLO. No, I hear not your honest friend, I hear you.
CAS. Prithee keep up thy quillets.° There's a poor
piece of gold for thee. If the gentlewoman that attends the General's wife be stirring, tell her there's
one Cassio entreats her a little favor of speech. Wilt
thou do this?   28
CLO. She is stirring, sir. If she will stir hither, I
shall seem to notify unto her.
CAS. Do, good my friend.   [*Exit* CLOWN.]

---

344. **Probal:** probable.   **347. framed:** made.   **348. free ele-**
ments: i.e., the air.   **354. function:** intelligence.   **358. suggest:**
seduce.   **360. Plies:** vigorously urges.   **363. repeals:** calls
back.   **370. one . . . cry:** See *MND*, IV.i.127–28,n.   **379. And**
. . . Time: and cleverness must wait for Time, who is in no hurry.
382–83. Though . . . ripe: though the fruit ripens in the sun, yet
the first fruit to ripen will come from the earliest blossoms;
i.e., our first plan — to get Cassio cashiered — has succeeded,
the rest will soon follow.

389. move for: petition for.   **392. jump:** at the moment, just.
394. Dull . . . device: do not spoil the plan.
    Act III, Sc. i: 1. content . . . pains: reward your labor. **2. bid**
. . . General: It was a common custom to play or sing a song beneath the bedroom window of a distinguished guest or of a newly
wedded couple on the morning after their wedding night. **4. in**
Naples: a reference to the Neapolitan (i.e., venereal) **disease.**
24. keep . . . quillets: put away your wisecracks.

[*Enter* IAGO.] In happy time,° Iago.
  IAGO. You have not been abed, then?
  CAS. Why, no, the day had broke
Before we parted. I have made bold, Iago,   35
To send in to your wife. My suit to her
Is that she will to virtuous Desdemona
Procure me some access.
  IAGO.   I'll send her to you presently,
And I'll devise a mean to draw the Moor
Out of the way, that your convérse and business   40
May be more free.
  CAS. I humbly thank you for 't. [*Exit* IAGO.] I
     never knew
A Florentine more kind° and honest.
        [*Enter* EMILIA.]
  EMIL. Good morrow, good Lieutenant. I am sorry
For your displeasure,° but all will sure be well.   45
The General and his wife are talking of it,
And she speaks for you stoutly. The Moor replies
That he you hurt is of great fame in Cyprus
And great affinity,° and that in wholesome wisdom
He might not but° refuse you. But he protests he
     loves you,   50
And needs no other suitor but his likings°
To take the safest occasion by the front
To bring you in° again.
  CAS.   Yet I beseech you,
If you think fit, or that it may be done,
Give me advantage of some brief discourse   55
With Desdemona alone.
  EMIL.   Pray you, come in.
I will bestow you where you shall have time.
To speak your bosom freely.°
  CAS.   I am much bound to you.   [*Exeunt.*]

SCENE II. *A room in the castle.*

[*Enter* OTHELLO, IAGO, *and* GENTLEMEN.]
  OTH. These letters give, Iago, to the pilot,
And by him do my duties° to the Senate.
That done, I will be walking on the works.°
Repair there to me.
  IAGO.   Well, my good lord, I'll do 't.
  OTH. This fortification, gentlemen, shall we
     see 't?   5
  GENT. We'll wait upon your lordship.   [*Exeunt.*]

SCENE III. *The garden of the castle.*

[*Enter* DESDEMONA, CASSIO, *and* EMILIA.]
  DES. Be thou assured, good Cassio, I will do
All my abilities in thy behalf.
  EMIL. Good madam, do. I warrant it grieves my
     husband
As if the case were his.
  DES. Oh, that's an honest fellow. Do not doubt,
     Cassio,   5
But I will have my lord and you again
As friendly as you were.
  CAS.   Bounteous madam,
Whatever shall become of Michael Cassio,
He's never anything but your true servant.   9
  DES. I know 't. I thank you. You do love my lord.
You have known him long, and be you well as-
     sured
He shall in strangeness stand no farther off
Than in a politic distance.°
  CAS.   Aye, but, lady,
That policy may either last so long,
Or feed upon such nice and waterish diet,°   15
Or breed itself so out of circumstance,°
That, I being absent and my place supplied,°
My General will forget my love and service.
  DES. Do not doubt° that. Before Emilia here
I give thee warrant of thy place.° Assure thee,   20
If I do vow a friendship, I'll perform it
To the last article. My lord shall never rest.
I'll watch him tame° and talk him out of patience,
His bed shall seem a school, his board a shrift.°
I'll intermingle every thing he does   25
With Cassio's suit. Therefore be merry, Cassio,
For thy solicitor shall rather die
Than give thy cause away.
       [*Enter* OTHELLO *and* IAGO, *at a distance.*]
  EMIL. Madam, here comes my lord.
  CAS. Madam, I'll take my leave.   30
  DES. Nay, stay and hear me speak.
  CAS. Madam, not now. I am very ill at ease,
Unfit for mine own purposes.°
  DES. Well, do your discretion.   [*Exit* CASSIO.]
  IAGO. Ha! I like not that.
  OTH. What dost thou say?   35
  IAGO. Nothing, my lord. Or if — I know not
     what.
  OTH. Was not that Cassio parted from my wife?

---

32. In . . . time: i.e., I am glad to see you.   **43. Florentine . . . kind:** Iago is a Venetian. Cassio means: even one of my own people could not have been kinder.   **45. your displeasure:** i.e., that Othello is displeased with you.   **49. affinity:** kindred. **50. might . . . but:** i.e., he must.   **51. likings:** affections. **52-53. safest . . . in:** to take the first opportunity to restore you to your position. **front:** forehead; i.e., to take Time by the forelock.   **58. speak . . . freely:** declare what is on your mind.
    Sc. ii: 2. do . . . duties: express my loyalty.   **3. works:** fortifications.

Sc. iii: 12-13. He . . . distance: i.e., his apparent coldness to you shall only be so much as his official position demands for reasons of policy.   **15. nice . . . diet:** have such weak encouragement.   **16. breed . . . circumstance:** become so used to the situation.   **17. supplied:** filled by another.   **19. doubt:** fear. **20. give . . . place:** guarantee that you will be restored to your position.   **23. watch . . . tame:** as wild hawks are made tame by keeping them from sleep.   **24. shrift:** place of confession and absolution.   **33. Unfit . . . purposes:** in no condition to plead my own cause.

IAGO. Cassio, my lord! No, sure, I cannot think it,
That he would steal away so guilty-like,
Seeing you coming.
　　　OTH.　　　　　I do believe 'twas he.　　　40
DES. How now, my lord!
I have been talking with a suitor here,
A man that languishes in your displeasure.
　　　OTH. Who is 't you mean?
　　　DES. Why, your Lieutenant, Cassio. Good my
　　　　lord,　　　　　　　　　　　　　　　45
If I have any grace or power to move you,
His present reconciliation take.°
For if he be not one that truly loves you,
That errs in ignorance and not in cunning,°
I have no judgment in an honest face.　　　50
I prithee call him back.
　　　OTH.　　　　　　　Went he hence now?
　　　DES. Aye, sooth, so humbled
That he hath left part of his grief with me,
To suffer with him. Good love, call him back.
　　　OTH. Not now, sweet Desdemona, some other
　　　　time.　　　　　　　　　　　　　　55
　　　DES. But shall 't be shortly?
　　　OTH.　　　　　　The sooner, sweet, for you.
　　　DES. Shall 't be tonight at supper?
　　　OTH.　　　　　　　No, not tonight.
　　　DES. Tomorrow dinner then?
　　　OTH.　　　　　　I shall not dine at home.
I meet the captains at the citadel.
　　　DES. Why, then tomorrow night or Tuesday
　　　　morn,　　　　　　　　　　　　　　60
On Tuesday noon, or night, on Wednesday morn.
I prithee name the time, but let it not
Exceed three days. In faith, he's penitent,
And yet his trespass, in our common reason° —　64
Save that, they say, the wars must make examples
Out of their best — is not almost° a fault
To incur a private check.° When shall he come?
Tell me, Othello. I wonder in my soul
What you would ask me that I should deny,　　69
Or stand so mammering° on. What! Michael Cassio,
That came a-wooing with you, and so many a
　　time
When I have spoke of you dispraisingly
Hath ta'en your part — to have so much to do
To bring him in! Trust me, I could do much ——
　　　OTH. Prithee, no more. Let him come when he
　　　　will.　　　　　　　　　　　　　　75
I will deny thee nothing.
　　　DES.　　　　　　Why, this is not a boon.°
'Tis as I should entreat you wear your gloves,
Or feed on nourishing dishes, or keep you warm,
Or sue to you to do a peculiar° profit

To your own person. Nay, when I have a suit　80
Wherein I mean to touch your love indeed,
It shall be full of poise° and difficult weight,°
And fearful to be granted.°
　　　OTH.　　　　　I will deny thee nothing.
Whereon I do beseech thee grant me this,
To leave me but a little to myself.　　　　85
　　　DES. Shall I deny you? No. Farewell, my lord.
　　　OTH. Farewell, my Desdemona. I'll come to thee
　　　　straight.
　　　DES. Emilia, come. Be as your fancies teach you.°
Whate'er you be, I am obedient.
　　　　　　　[*Exeunt* DESDEMONA *and* EMILIA.]
　　　OTH. Excellent wretch! Perdition catch my soul
But I do love thee! And when I love thee not,　91
Chaos° is come again.
　　　IAGO. My noble lord ——
　　　OTH.　　　　　　　What dost thou say, Iago?
　　　IAGO. Did Michael Cassio, when you wooed my
　　　　lady,
Know of your love?　　　　　　　　　95
　　　OTH. He did, from first to last. Why dost thou
ask?
　　　IAGO. But for a satisfaction of my thought,
No further harm.
　　　OTH.　　　　Why of thy thought, Iago?
　　　IAGO. I did not think he had been acquainted with
　　　　her.
　　　OTH. Oh yes, and went between us very oft.　100
　　　IAGO. Indeed!
　　　OTH. Indeed! Aye, indeed. Discern'st thou aught
　　　　in that?
Is he not honest?
　　　IAGO. Honest, my lord!
　　　OTH. Honest! Aye, honest.
　　　IAGO. My lord, for aught I know.
　　　OTH. What dost thou think?
　　　IAGO. Think, my lord!　　　　　　　105
　　　OTH. Think, my lord! By Heaven, he echoes me
As if there were some monster in his thought
Too hideous to be shown. Thou dost mean some-
　　thing.
I heard thee say even now thou likedst not that
When Cassio left my wife. What didst not like?
And when I told thee he was of my counsel　111
In my whole course of wooing, thou criedst "In-
　　deed!"
And didst contract and purse thy brow together
As if thou then hadst shut up in thy brain
Some horrible conceit.° If thou dost love me,　115
Show me thy thought.

---

47. His . . . take: accept his immediate apology and forgive him.
49. in cunning: knowingly.　64. common reason: common sense.
66. not almost: hardly.　67. check: rebuke.　70. mammering:
hesitating.　76. boon: great favor.　79. peculiar: particular.

82. poise: weight in the scales. difficult weight: hard to es-
timate.　83. fearful . . . granted: only granted with a sense of
fear.　88. Be . . . you: please yourself.　92. Chaos: the utter
confusion that existed before order was established in the
universe. The idea of order and chaos is worked out elabo-
rately in *Tr & Cr*, I.iii.83–124.　115. conceit: conception,
notion.

IAGO. My lord, you know I love you.

OTH.   I think thou dost,
And for° I know thou'rt full of love and honesty
And weigh'st thy words before thou givest them
    breath,
Therefore these stops of thine fright me the more.
For such things in a false disloyal knave   121
Are tricks of custom, but in a man that's just
They're close delations,° working from the heart,
That passion cannot rule.

IAGO.   For Michael Cassio,
I dare be sworn I think that he is honest.   125

OTH. I think so too.

IAGO.   Men should be what they seem,
Or those that be not, would they might seem none!°

OTH. Certain, men should be what they seem.

IAGO. Why, then I think Cassio's an honest man.

OTH. Nay, yet there's more in this.   130
I prithee speak to me as to thy thinkings,
As thou dost ruminate, and give thy worst of
    thoughts
The worst of words.

IAGO.   Good my lord, pardon me.
Though I am bound to every act of duty,
I am not bound to that all slaves are free to.   135
Utter my thoughts? Why, say they are vile and false,
As where's that palace whereinto foul things
Sometimes intrude not? Who has a breast so pure
But some uncleanly apprehensions
Keep leets and law days, and in session sit   140
With meditations lawful?°

OTH. Thou dost conspire against thy friend, Iago,
If thou but think'st him wronged and makest his
    ear
A stranger to thy thoughts.

IAGO.   I do beseech you —
Though I perchance am vicious in my guess,   145
As, I confess, it is my nature's plague
To spy into abuses, and oft my jealousy°
Shapes faults that are not — that your wisdom yet,
From one that so imperfectly conceits,°
Would take no notice, nor build yourself a trouble
Out of his scattering° and unsure observance.°   151
It were not for your quiet nor your good,
Nor for my manhood, honesty, or wisdom,
To let you know my thoughts.

OTH.   What dost thou mean?

IAGO. Good name in man and woman, dear my
    lord,   155

Is the immediate° jewel of their souls.
Who steals my purse steals trash — 'tis something,
    nothing,
'Twas mine, 'tis his, and has been slave to thou-
    sands —
But he that filches from me my good name
Robs me of that which not enriches him   160
And makes me poor indeed.

OTH. By Heaven, I'll know thy thoughts.

IAGO. You cannot if my heart were in your hand,
Nor shall not whilst 'tis in my custody.

OTH. Ha!

IAGO.   Oh, beware, my lord, of jealousy.   165
It is the green-eyed monster which doth mock°
The meat° it feeds on. That cuckold lives in bliss
Who, certain of his fate, loves not his wronger.°
But, oh, what damnèd minutes tells he o'er   169
Who dotes, yet doubts, suspects, yet strongly loves!

OTH. Oh, misery!

IAGO. Poor and content is rich, and rich enough.
But riches fineless° is as poor as winter
To him that ever fears he shall be poor.
Good Heaven, the souls of all my tribe defend   175
From jealousy!

OTH.   Why, why is this?
Think'st thou I'd make a life of jealousy,
To follow still the changes of the moon
With fresh suspicions? No, to be once in doubt
Is once to be resolved.° Exchange me for a goat   180
When I shall turn the business of my soul
To such exsufflicate and blown surmises,
Matching thy inference.° 'Tis not to make me jeal-
    ous
To say my wife is fair, feeds well, loves company,
Is free of speech, sings, plays, and dances well.   185
Where virtue is, these are more virtuous.
Nor from mine own weak merits will I draw
The smallest fear or doubt of her revolt,°
For she had eyes, and chose me. No, Iago,
I'll see before I doubt, when I doubt, prove,   190
And on the proof, there is no more but this —
Away at once with love or jealousy!

IAGO. I am glad of it, for now I shall have reason
To show the love and duty that I bear you
With franker spirit. Therefore, as I am bound,   195
Receive it from me. I speak not yet of proof.
Look to your wife. Observe her well with Cassio.
Wear your eye thus, not jealous nor secure.°

---

118. for: since.   123. close delations: concealed accusations.
127. seem none: i.e., not seem to be honest men.   138–41. Who
. . . lawful: whose heart is so pure but that some foul suggestion
will sit on the bench alongside lawful thoughts; i.e., foul thoughts
will rise even on the most respectable occasions. leet: court
held by the lord of the manor. law days: days when courts sit.
session: sitting of the court. 147. jealousy: suspicion. 149. conceits: conceives, imagines.   151. scattering: scattered, casual.
observance: observation.

156. immediate: most valuable.   166. doth mock: makes a
mockery of.   167. meat: i.e., victim.   167–68. That . . .
wronger: i.e., the cuckold who hates his wife and knows her falseness is not tormented by suspicious jealousy.   173. fine-
less: limitless.   179–80. to . . . resolved: whenever I find myself in doubt I at once seek out the truth.   181–83. When . . .
inference: when I shall allow that which concerns me most
dearly to be influenced by such trifling suggestions as yours.
exsufflicate: blown up, like a bubble.   188. revolt: faithlessness.
198. secure: overconfident.

I would not have your free and noble nature
Out of self-bounty° be abused, look to 't.   200
I know our country disposition well.
In Venice° they do let Heaven see the pranks
They dare not show their husbands. Their best con-
    science
Is not to leave 't undone, but keep 't unknown.
    OTH. Dost thou say so?   205
    IAGO. She did deceive her father,° marrying you,
And when she seemed to shake and fear your looks,
She loved them most.
    OTH.   And so she did.
    IAGO.   Why, go to, then.
She that so young could give out such a seeming
To seel° her father's eyes up close as oak ——   210
He thought 'twas witchcraft — but I am much to
    blame.
I humbly do beseech you of your pardon
For too much loving you.
    OTH.   I am bound to thee forever.
    IAGO. I see this hath a little dashed your spirits.
    OTH. Not a jot, not a jot.
    IAGO.   I' faith, I fear it has.   215
I hope you will consider what is spoke
Comes from my love, but I do see you're moved.
I am to pray you not to strain my speech
To grosser issues° nor to larger reach°
Than to suspicion.   220
    OTH. I will not.
    IAGO.   Should you do so, my lord,
My speech should fall into such vile success°
As my thoughts aim not at. Cassio's my worthy
    friend. —
My lord, I see you're moved.
    OTH.   No, not much moved.
I do not think but Desdemona's honest.°   225
    IAGO. Long live she so! And long live you to think
    so!
    OTH. And yet, how nature erring from itself ——
    IAGO. Aye, there's the point. As — to be bold with
    you —
Not to affect° many proposed matches°
Of her own clime, complexion, and degree,   230
Whereto we see in all things nature tends° ——
Foh! One may smell in such a will most rank,°
Foul disproportion, thoughts unnatural.

But pardon me. I do not in position
Distinctly speak of her, though I may fear   235
Her will, recoiling to her better judgment,
May fall to match° you with her country forms,°
And happily° repent.
    OTH.   Farewell, farewell.
If more thou dost perceive, let me know more.
Set on thy wife to observe. Leave me, Iago.   240
    IAGO. [Going] My lord, I take my leave.
    OTH. Why did I marry? This honest creature
    doubtless
Sees and knows more, much more, than he unfolds.
    IAGO. [Returning] My lord, I would I might en-
    treat your honor
To scan this thing no further. Leave it to time.   245
Though it be fit that Cassio have his place,
For sure he fills it up with great ability,
Yet if you please to hold him off awhile,
You shall by that perceive him and his means.
Note if your lady strain his entertainment°   250
With any strong or vehement importunity —
Much will be seen in that. In the meantime,
Let me be thought too busy in my fears —
As worthy cause I have to fear I am —
And hold her free, I do beseech your Honor.   255
    OTH. Fear not my government.°
    IAGO. I once more take my leave.   [Exit.]
    OTH. This fellow's of exceeding honesty,
And knows all qualities,° with a learned spirit,   259
Of human dealings.° If I do prove her haggard,
Though that her jesses were my dear heartstrings,
I'd whistle her off and let her down the wind
To prey at fortune.° Haply, for I am black
And have not those soft parts of conversation
That chamberers° have, or for I am declined   265
Into the vale of years — yet that's not much —
She's gone, I am abused, and my relief
Must be to loathe her. Oh, curse of marriage,
That we can call these delicate creatures ours,
And not their appetites! I had rather be a toad   270
And live upon the vapor of a dungeon
Than keep a corner in the thing I love
For others' uses. Yet, 'tis the plague of great ones,
Prerogatived° are they less than the base.
'Tis destiny unshunnable, like death.   275
Even then this forkèd plague° is fated to us
When we do quicken.° Desdemona comes.

---

200. self-bounty: natural goodness. 202. In Venice: Venice was
notorious for its loose women; the Venetian courtesans were
among the sights of Europe and were much commented upon by
travelers. 206. She . . . father: Iago deliberately echoes Brabantio's parting words. See I.iii.293–94. 210. seel: blind. See
I.iii.270,n. 219. grosser issues: worse conclusions. larger reach:
i.e., more widely. 222. success: result. 225. honest: When
applied to Desdemona, "honest" means "chaste," but applied to
Iago it has the modern meaning of "open and sincere." 229. af-
fect: be inclined to. proposed matches: offers of marriage. 231. in
. . . tends: i.e., a woman naturally marries a man of her own
country, color, and rank. 232. will . . . rank: desire most
lustful.

237. match: compare. country forms: the appearance of her countrymen; i.e., white men. 238. happily: haply, by chance.
250. strain . . . entertainment: urge you to receive him.
256. government: self-control. 259. qualities: different kinds.
259–60. with . . . dealings: with wide experience of human nature. 260–63. If . . . fortune: Othello keeps up the imagery of
falconry throughout. He means: If I find that she is wild, I'll
whistle her off the game and let her go where she will, for she's not
worth keeping. haggard: a wild hawk. jesses: the straps attached
to a hawk's legs. 265. chamberers: playboys. 274. Preroga-
tived: privileged. 276. forked plague: i.e., to be a cuckold.
277. quicken: stir in our mother's womb.

[*Re-enter* DESDEMONA *and* EMILIA.] If she be false, oh,
 then Heaven mocks itself!
I'll not believe 't.
  DES.   How now, my dear Othello!
Your dinner, and the generous° islanders 280
By you invited, do attend your presence.
  OTH. I am to blame.
  DES.   Why do you speak so faintly?
Are you not well?
  OTH. I have a pain upon my forehead here.
  DES. Faith, that's with watching,° 'twill away
 again. 285
Let me but bind it hard, within this hour
It will be well.
  OTH.   Your napkin° is too little,
    [*He puts the handkerchief from him,*
        and she drops it.]
Let it alone. Come, I'll go in with you.
  DES. I am very sorry that you are not well.
    [*Exeunt* OTHELLO *and* DESDEMONA.]
  EMIL. I am glad I have found this napkin. 290
This was her first remembrance from the Moor.
My wayward° husband hath a hundred times
Wooed me to steal it, but she so loves the token,
For he conjured° her she should ever keep it,
That she reserves it evermore about her 295
To kiss and talk to. I'll have the work ta'en out,°
And give 't Iago. What he will do with it
Heaven knows, not I.
I nothing but to please his fantasy.°
    [*Re-enter* IAGO.]
  IAGO. How now! What do you here alone? 300
  EMIL. Do not you chide, I have a thing for you.
  IAGO. A thing for me? It is a common thing——
  EMIL. Ha!
  IAGO. To have a foolish wife. 304
  EMIL. Oh, is that all? What will you give me now
For that same handkerchief?
  IAGO.   What handkerchief?
  EMIL. What handkerchief!
Why, that the Moor first gave to Desdemona,
That which so often you did bid me steal.
  IAGO. Hast stol'n it from her? 310
  EMIL. No, faith, she let it drop by negligence,
And, to the advantage,° I being here took 't up.
Look, here it is.
  IAGO.   A good wench. Give it me.
  EMIL. What will you do with 't, that you have
   been so earnest
To have me filch it? 314
  IAGO. [*Snatching it*] Why, what's that to you?
  EMIL. If 't be not for some purpose of import,

Give 't me again. Poor lady, she'll run mad
When she shall lack it.
  IAGO. Be not acknown on 't,° I have use for it.
Go, leave me.   [*Exit* EMILIA.]
I will in Cassio's lodging lose this napkin, 321
And let him find it. Trifles light as air
Are to the jealous confirmations strong
As proofs of Holy Writ. This may do something.
The Moor already changes with my poison. 325
Dangerous conceits are in their natures poisons,
Which at the first are scarce found to distaste,°
But with a little° act upon the blood
Burn like the mines of sulphur. I did say so.°
Look where he comes!
  [*Re-enter* OTHELLO.] Not poppy,° nor mandragora,°
Nor all the drowsy syrups of the world, 331
Shall ever medicine thee to that sweet sleep
Which thou owedst° yesterday.
  OTH.   Ha! Ha! False to me?
  IAGO. Why, how now, General! No more of that.
  OTH. Avaunt!° Be gone! Thou hast set me on the
  rack.° 335
I swear 'tis better to be much abused
Than but to know 't a little.
  IAGO.   How now, my lord!
  OTH. What sense had I of her stol'n hours of lust?
I saw 't not, thought it not, it harmed not me.
I slept the next night well, was free and merry. 340
I found not Cassio's kisses on her lips.
He that is robbed, not wanting° what is stol'n,
Let him not know 't and he's not robbed at all.
  IAGO. I am sorry to hear this.
  OTH. I had been happy if the general camp, 345
Pioners° and all, had tasted her sweet body,
So I had nothing known. Oh, now forever
Farewell the tranquil mind! Farewell content!
Farewell the plumèd° troop and the big wars
That make ambition virtue! Oh, farewell, 350
Farewell the neighing steed and the shrill trump,
The spirit-stirring drum, the ear-piercing fife,
The royal banner and all quality,°
Pride, pomp, and circumstance of glorious war!
And, O you mortal engines,° whose rude throats
The immortal Jove's dread clamors counterfeit,°
Farewell! Othello's occupation's gone! 357
  IAGO. Is 't possible, my lord?
  OTH. Villain, be sure thou prove my love a whore,
Be sure of it, give me the ocular proof. 360

319. Be ... on't: know nothing about it. 327. distaste: taste
unpleasantly. 328. with a little: in a little while. 329. I ...
so: As Iago says this, Othello is seen approaching, with all the
signs of his agitation outwardly visible. 330. poppy: opium.
mandragora: called also mandrake, a root used as a drug
to bring sleep. 333. owedst: owned, possessed. 335. Avaunt:
be off! on ... rack: i.e., in torment. 342. wanting: missing.
346. Pioners: pioneers, the lowest type of soldier. 349. plumed:
wearing plumes in the helmet. 353. quality: military rank.
355. mortal engines: deadly cannon. 356. counterfeit: imitate.

280. generous: noble, of gentle blood. 285. watching: lack of
sleep. 287. napkin: handkerchief. 292. wayward: unaccountable. 294. conjured: begged with an oath. 296. work ... out:
pattern copied. 299. fantasy: whim. 312. to ... advantage:
thereby giving me the opportunity.

Or by the worth of man's eternal soul,
Thou hadst been better have been born a dog
Than answer my waked wrath!

IAGO.   Is 't come to this?

OTH. Make me to see 't, or at the least so prove it
That the probation° bear no hinge nor loop   365
To hang a doubt on, or woe upon thy life!

IAGO. My noble lord——

OTH. If thou dost slander her and torture me,
Never pray more, abandon all remorse.°
On horror's head horrors accumulate,   370
Do deeds to make Heaven weep, all earth amazed,
For nothing canst thou to damnation add
Greater than that.

IAGO.   Oh, grace! Oh, Heaven defend me!
Are you a man? Have you a soul or sense?   374
God be wi' you, take mine office. O wretched fool,
That livest to make thine honesty a vice!
O monstrous world! Take note, take note, O world,
To be direct and honest is not safe.
I thank you for this profit,° and from hence   379
I'll love no friend, sith° love breeds such offense.

OTH. Nay, stay. Thou shouldst be honest.

IAGO. I should be wise, for honesty's a fool,
And loses that it works for.

OTH.   By the world,
I think my wife be honest, and think she is not.
I think that thou art just, and think thou art not.
I'll have some proof. Her name, that was as fresh
As Dian's° visage, is now begrimed and black   387
As mine own face. If there be cords, or knives,
Poison, or fire, or suffocating streams,
I'll not endure it. Would I were satisfied!   390

IAGO. I see, sir, you are eaten up with passion.
I do repent me that I put it to you.
You would be satisfied?

OTH.   Would! Nay, I will.

IAGO. And may, but, how? How satisfied, my
   lord?
Would you, the supervisor,° grossly gape on?   395
Behold her topped?

OTH.   Death and damnation! Oh!

IAGO. It were a tedious difficulty, I think,
To bring them to that prospect.° Damn them then,
If ever mortal eyes do see them bolster°
More than their own! What then? How then?   400
What shall I say? Where's satisfaction?
It is impossible you should see this,
Were they as prime° as goats, as hot as monkeys,
As salt° as wolves in pride,° and fools as gross
As ignorance made drunk. But yet I say   405
If imputation° and strong circumstances,

Which lead directly to the door of truth,
Will give you satisfaction, you may have 't.

OTH. Give me a living° reason she's disloyal.

IAGO. I do not like the office.   410
But sith I am entered in this cause so far,
Pricked° to 't by foolish honesty and love,
I will go on. I lay with Cassio lately,
And being troubled with a raging tooth,
I could not sleep.   415
There are a kind of men so loose of soul
That in their sleeps will mutter their affairs.
One of this kind is Cassio.
In sleep I heard him say " Sweet Desdemona,
Let us be wary, let us hide our loves."   420
And then, sir, would he gripe° and wring my
   hand,
Cry " O sweet creature! " and then kiss me hard,
As if he plucked up kisses by the roots
That grew upon my lips. Then laid his leg   424
Over my thigh, and sighed and kissed, and then
Cried " Cursed fate that gave thee to the Moor! "

OTH. Oh, monstrous! Monstrous!

IAGO.   Nay, this was but his dream.

OTH. But this denoted a foregone conclusion.
'Tis a shrewd doubt,° though it be but a dream.

IAGO. And this may help to thicken other proofs
That do demónstrate thinly.

OTH.   I'll tear her all to pieces.   431

IAGO. Nay, but be wise. Yet we see nothing done,
She may be honest yet. Tell me but this:
Have you not sometimes seen a handkerchief   434
Spotted with strawberries° in your wife's hand?

OTH. I gave her such a one, 'twas my first gift.

IAGO. I know not that. But such a handkerchief —
I am sure it was your wife's — did I today
See Cassio wipe his beard with.

OTH.   If it be that——

IAGO. If it be that, or any that was hers,   440
It speaks against her with the other proofs.

OTH. Oh, that the slave had forty thousand lives!
One is too poor, too weak, for my revenge.
Now do I see 'tis true. Look here, Iago,
All my fond love thus do I blow to Heaven —   445
'Tis gone.
Arise, black Vengeance, from thy hollow cell!
Yield up, O Love, thy crown and hearted° throne
To tyrannous hate! Swell, bosom, with thy fraught,°
For 'tis of aspics'° tongues!

IAGO.   Yet be content.   450

OTH. Oh, blood, blood, blood!

IAGO. Patience, I say. Your mind perhaps may
   change.

---

365. probation: proof.   369. remorse: pity.   379. profit: profitable lesson.   380. sith: since.   387. Dian: Diana, goddess of chastity.   395. supervisor: looker-on.   398. prospect: sight. 399. bolster: sleep together.   403. prime: lustful.   404. salt: eager. in pride: in heat.   406. imputation: probability.

409. living: tangible.   412. Pricked: spurred on.   421. gripe: grip.   429. shrewd doubt: bitter suspicion.   435. with strawberries: with a pattern of strawberries.   448. hearted: in my heart.   449. fraught: freight, load.   450. aspic: asp, a small poisonous snake. See *Ant & Cleo*, V.ii.351-56.

OTH. Never, Iago. Like to the Pontic Sea,
Whose icy current and compulsive course
Ne'er feels retiring ebb but keeps due on   455
To the Propontic and the Hellespont;°
Even so my bloody thoughts, with violent pace,
Shall ne'er look back, ne'er ebb to humble love,
Till that capable° and wide revenge   459
Swallow them up. Now, by yond marble Heaven,
In the due reverence of a sacred vow   [*Kneels.*]
I here engage° my words.
   IAGO.   Do not rise yet.   [*Kneels.*]
Witness, you ever burning lights above,
You elements that clip° us round about,
Witness that here Iago doth give up   465
The execution of his wit, hands, heart,
To wronged Othello's service! Let him command,
And to obey shall be in me remorse,°
What bloody business ever.   [*They rise.*]
   OTH.   I greet thy love,
Not with vain thanks, but with acceptance bounte-
   ous,   470
And will upon the instant put thee to 't.°
Within these three days let me hear thee say
That Cassio's not alive.
   IAGO. My friend is dead. 'Tis done at your request.
But let her live.
   OTH. Damn her, lewd minx! Oh, damn her! 475
Come, go with me apart. I will withdraw,
To furnish me with some swift means of death
For the fair devil. Now art thou my Lieutenant.
   IAGO. I am your own forever.   [*Exeunt.*]

SCENE IV. *Before the castle.*

[*Enter* DESDEMONA, EMILIA, *and* CLOWN.]
   DES. Do you know, sirrah, where Lieutenant Cas-
sio lies?
   CLO. I dare not say he lies anywhere.
   DES. Why, man?
   CLO. He's a soldier, and for one to say a soldier
lies is stabbing.   6
   DES. Go to. Where lodges he?
   CLO. To tell you where he lodges is to tell you
where I lie.
   DES. Can anything be made of this?   10
   CLO. I know not where he lodges, and for me to
devise a lodging, and say he lies here or he lies there,
were to lie in mine own throat.

DES. Can you inquire him out and be edified by
report?°   15
   CLO. I will catechize the world for him; that is,
make questions and by them answer.
   DES. Seek him, bid him come hither. Tell him I
have moved my lord on his behalf and hope all will
be well.   20
   CLO. To do this is within the compass of man's
wit, and therefore I will attempt the doing it.
                                          [*Exit.*]
   DES. Where should I lose that handkerchief,
   Emilia?
   EMIL. I know not, madam.
   DES. Believe me, I had rather have lost my purse
Full of crusados.° And, but my noble Moor   26
Is true of mind and made of no such baseness
As jealous creatures are, it were enough
To put him to ill thinking.
   EMIL.   Is he not jealous?   29
   DES. Who, he? I think the sun where he was born
Drew all such humors° from him.
   EMIL.   Look where he comes.
   DES. I will not leave him now till Cassio
Be called to him.
[*Enter* OTHELLO.] How is 't with you, my lord?
   OTH. Well, my good lady. [*Aside*] Oh, hardness to
   dissemble!
How do you, Desdemona?
   DES.   Well, my good lord.   35
   OTH. Give me your hand. This hand is moist,°
   my lady.
   DES. It yet has felt no age nor known no sorrow.
   OTH. This argues fruitfulness and liberal heart.
Hot, hot, and moist — this hand of yours requires
A sequester° from liberty, fasting and prayer,   40
Much castigation, exercise devout.
For here's a young and sweating devil here,
That commonly rebels. 'Tis a good hand,
A frank one.
   DES.   You may indeed say so,
For 'twas that hand that gave away my heart.   45
   OTH. A liberal° hand. The hearts of old gave
   hands,
But our new heraldry is hands, not hearts.°
   DES. I cannot speak of this. Come now, your prom-
   ise.

Sc. iv: **14–15. edified by report:** enlightened by the information. Desdemona speaks with mock pomposity.   **26. crusados:**
small gold Portuguese coins.   **31. humors:** moods; lit., damp-
nesses.   **36. moist:** a hot moist palm was believed to show desire.
40. sequester: separation.   **46. liberal:** overgenerous.   **46–47. The
. . . hearts:** once love and deeds went together, but now it is all
deeds (i.e., faithlessness) and no love. This phrase has been taken
as a reference to the order of baronets created by James I in 1611,
who bore on their heraldic coats of arms the device of the "bloody
hand of Ulster." If so, the lines are a later addition; but the
reference is very doubtful. The contrast between hearts (true
love and faith) and hands (actions) is natural (see *Lear* I.ii. 72–
73). As Othello's passions rise, he ceases to be entirely coherent.

453–56. Like . . . Hellespont: In Pliny's *Natural History*, translated by Philemon Holland in 1601, it was noted that "the sea
Pontus (Black Sea) evermore floweth and runneth out into Pro-
pontis (Sea of Marmora) but the sea never returneth back again
within Pontus." **Hellespont:** the Dardanelles.   **459. capable:**
comprehensive, complete.   **462. engage:** pledge.   **464. elements . . . clip:** skies that embrace, surround.   **468. remorse:**
solemn obligation.   **471. put . . . to't:** put you to the proof.

OTH. What promise, chuck?°
DES. I have sent to bid Cassio come speak with
  you.   50
OTH. I have a salt and sorry rheum° offends me.
Lend me thy handkerchief.
DES. Here, my lord.
OTH. That which I gave you.
DES. I have it not about me.
OTH. Not?
DES. No indeed, my lord.
OTH. That's a fault. That handkerchief   55
Did an Egyptian° to my mother give.
She was a charmer, and could almost read
The thoughts of people. She told her while she kept
  it
'Twould make her amiable and subdue my father
Entirely to her love, but if she lost it   60
Or made a gift of it, my father's eye
Should hold her loathed and his spirits should hunt
After new fancies. She dying gave it me,
And bid me, when my fate would have me wive,
To give it her. I did so. And take heed on 't,   65
Make it a darling like your precious eye.
To lose 't or give 't away were such perdition
As nothing else could match.
DES.   Is 't possible?
OTH. 'Tis true. There's magic in the web of it.
A sibyl° that had numbered in the world   70
The sun to course two hundred compasses
In her prophetic fury° sewed the work.
The worms were hallowed that did breed the silk,
And it was dyed in mummy° which the skillful
Conserved° of maidens' hearts.
DES.   Indeed! Is 't true?   75
OTH. Most veritable, therefore look to 't well.
DES. Then would to God that I had never seen 't.
OTH. Ha! Wherefore?
DES. Why do you speak so startlingly and rash?
OTH. Is 't lost? Is 't gone? Speak, is it out o' the
  way?   80
DES. Heaven bless us!
OTH. Say you?
DES. It is not lost, but what an if it were?
OTH. How!
DES. I say it is not lost.
OTH. Fetch 't, let me see it.   85
DES. Why, so I can, sir, but I will not now.
This is a trick to put me from my suit.
Pray you let Cassio be received again.
OTH. Fetch me the handkerchief. My mind mis-
  gives.

DES. Come, come,   90
You'll never meet a more sufficient man.
OTH. The handkerchief!
DES.   I pray talk me of Cassio.
OTH. The handkerchief!
DES.   A man that all his time
Hath founded his good fortunes on your love,
Shared dangers with you ——   95
OTH. The handkerchief!
DES. In sooth, you are to blame.
OTH. Away!   [*Exit.*]
EMIL. Is not this man jealous?
DES. I ne'er saw this before.   100
Sure there's some wonder in this handkerchief.
I am most unhappy in the loss of it.
EMIL. 'Tis not a year or two shows us a man.°
They are all but stomachs and we all but food.
They eat us hungerly, and when they are full   105
They belch us. Look you, Cassio and my husband.

    [*Enter* CASSIO *and* IAGO.]

IAGO. There is no other way, 'tis she must do 't.
And, lo, the happiness!° Go and impórtune her.
DES. How now, good Cassio! What's the news
  with you?
CAS. Madam, my former suit. I do beseech you
That by your virtuous means I may again   111
Exist, and be a member of his love
Whom I with all the office of my heart
Entirely honor. I would not be delayed.
If my offense be of such mortal kind   115
That nor my service past nor present sorrows
Nor purposed merit in futurity°
Can ransom me into his love again,
But to know so must be my benefit.
So shall I clothe me in a forced content   120
And shut myself up in some other course
To Fortune's alms.°
DES.   Alas, thrice-gentle Cassio!
My advocation° is not now in tune.
My lord is not my lord, nor should I know him
Were he in favor as in humor altered.°   125
So help me every spirit sanctified,
As I have spoken for you all my best
And stood within the blank° of his displeasure
For my free speech! You must awhile be patient.
What I can do I will, and more I will   130
Than for myself I dare. Let that suffice you.
IAGO. Is my lord angry?

EMIL.   He went hence but now,
And certainly in strange unquietness.

IAGO. Can he be angry? I have seen the cannon
When it hath blown his ranks into the air,   135
And, like the Devil, from his very arm
Puffed his own brother, and can he be angry?
Something of moment then. I will go meet him.
There's matter in 't indeed if he be angry.

DES. I prithee do so. [*Exit* IAGO.] Something sure
     of state,   140
Either from Venice, or some unhatched practice
Made demonstrable° here in Cyprus to him,
Hath puddled° his clear spirit. And in such cases
Men's natures wrangle with inferior things,
Though great ones are their object.° 'Tis even so,
For let our finger ache and it indues°   146
Our other healthful members even to that sense
Of pain. Nay, we must think men are not gods,
Nor of them look for such observancy
As fits the bridal.° Beshrew me° much, Emilia,   150
I was, unhandsome warrior° as I am,
Arraigning his unkindness with my soul,
But now I find I had suborned the witness,°
And he's indicted falsely.

EMIL. Pray Heaven it be state matters, as you
     think,   155
And no conception nor no jealous toy°
Concerning you.

DES. Alas the day, I never gave him cause!

EMIL. But jealous souls will not be answered so.
They are not ever jealous for the cause,   160
But jealous for they are jealous. 'Tis a monster
Begot upon itself, born on itself.

DES. Heaven keep that monster from Othello's
     mind!

EMIL. Lady, amen.

DES. I will go seek him. Cassio, walk hereabout.
If I do find him fit, I'll move your suit,   166
And seek to effect it to my uttermost.

CAS. I humbly thank your ladyship.

             [*Exeunt* DESDEMONA *and* EMILIA.]
             [*Enter* BIANCA.]

BIAN. Save you, friend Cassio!

CAS.   What make you from° home?
How is it with you, my most fair Bianca?   170
I' faith, sweet love, I was coming to your house.

BIAN. And I was going to your lodging, Cassio.
What, keep a week away? Seven days and nights?

Eightscore eight hours? And lovers' absent hours,
More tedious than the dial eightscore times?°   175
Oh, weary reckoning!

CAS.   Pardon me, Bianca.
I have this while with leaden thoughts been pressed,
But I shall in a more continuate time°
Strike off this score of absence. Sweet Bianca,
     [*Giving her* DESDEMONA's *handkerchief*]
Take me this work out.°

BIAN.   O Cassio, whence came this?   180
This is some token from a newer friend.
To the felt absence now I feel a cause.
Is 't come to this? Well, well.

CAS.   Go to, woman!
Throw your vile guesses in the Devil's teeth,   184
From whence you have them. You are jealous now
That this is from some mistress, some remembrance.
No, by my faith, Bianca.

BIAN.   Why, whose is it?

CAS. I know not, sweet. I found it in my chamber.
I like the work well. Ere it be demanded —
As like enough it will — I'd have it copied.   190
Take it, and do 't, and leave me for this time.

BIAN. Leave you! Wherefore?

CAS. I do attend here on the General,
And think it no addition,° nor my wish,
To have him see me womaned.°

BIAN.   Why, I pray you?   195

CAS. Not that I love you not.

BIAN.   But that you do not love me.
I pray you bring me on the way a little,
And say if I shall see you soon at night.

CAS. 'Tis but a little way that I can bring you,
For I attend here. But I'll see you soon.   200

BIAN. 'Tis very good, I must be circumstanced.°

                            [*Exeunt.*]

Act IV

SCENE I. *Cyprus. Before the castle.*

     [*Enter* OTHELLO *and* IAGO.]

IAGO. Will you think so?

OTH.   Think so, Iago!

IAGO.   What,
To kiss in private?

OTH.   An unauthorized kiss.

IAGO. Or to be naked with her friend in bed

141–42. unhatched ... demonstrable: some plot, not yet matured, which has been revealed.   143. puddled: muddied, stirred up.   143–45. in ... object: when men are disturbed by great matters, they show their temper in small things.   146. indues: endows, pervades.   150. bridal: honeymoon. Beshrew me: plague on me.   151. unhandsome warrior: clumsy soldier. Desdemona continually thinks of herself as Othello's companion in arms. Cf. I.iii.249ff.   153. suborned ... witness: corrupted the evidence; i.e., it is my fault, not his.   156. jealous toy: silly suspicion.   169. make ... from: are you doing away from.

174–75. And ... times: when one's lover is absent for a week does it not seem far longer than a hundred and sixty clock hours? 178. continuate time: i.e., when my time is not continually being interrupted.   180. Take ... out: copy this pattern.   194. addition: honor.   195. womaned: with a girl.   201. circumstanced: put off.

An hour or more, not meaning any harm?
   OTH. Naked in bed, Iago, and not mean harm!   5
It is hypocrisy against the Devil.°
They that mean virtuously and yet do so,
The Devil their virtue tempts and they tempt
    Heaven.°
   IAGO. So° they do nothing, 'tis a venial° slip.
But if I give my wife a handkerchief——   10
   OTH. What then?
   IAGO. Why, then, 'tis hers, my lord, and being
   hers,
She may, I think, bestow 't on any man.
   OTH. She is protectress of her honor too.
May she give that?   15
   IAGO. Her honor is an essence that's not seen.
They have it very oft that have it not.°
But for the handkerchief——
   OTH. By Heaven, I would most gladly have forgot
   it.
Thou said'st—oh, it comes o'er my memory,   20
As doth the raven o'er the infected house,°
Boding° to all—he had my handkerchief.
   IAGO. Aye, what of that?
   OTH.   That's not so good now.
   IAGO.   What,
If I had said I had seen him do you wrong?
Or heard him say—as knaves be such abroad,   25
Who having, by their own importunate suit,
Or voluntary dotage° of some mistress,
Convincèd or supplied° them, cannot choose
But they must blab——
   OTH.   Hath he said anything?
   IAGO. He hath, my lord, but be you well assured,
No more than he'll unswear.
   OTH.   What hath he said?   31
   IAGO. Faith, that he did——I know not what he
   did.
   OTH. What? What?
   IAGO. Lie——
   OTH.   With her?
   IAGO.   With her, on her, what you will.   34
   OTH. Lie° with her! Lie on her!—We say lie
on her when they belie her.—Lie with her!
'Zounds, that's fulsome!° Handkerchief—confes-
sions—handkerchief!—To confess, and be hanged
for his labor. First to be hanged, and then to confess.
I tremble at it. Nature would not invest herself in
such shadowing passion without some instruc-   41

tion.° It is not words that shake me thus. Pish!
Noses, ears, and lips. Is 't possible?—Confess?—
Handkerchief?—Oh, devil!   [Falls in a trance.]
   IAGO. Work on,   45
My medicine, work! Thus credulous fools are
   caught,
And many worthy and chaste dames even thus,
All guiltless, meet reproach. What ho! My lord!
My lord, I say! Othello! [Enter CASSIO.] How now,
   Cassio!
   CAS. What's the matter?   50
   IAGO. My lord is fall'n into an epilepsy.
This is his second fit, he had one yesterday.
   CAS. Rub him about the temples.
   IAGO.   No, forbear,
The lethargy° must have his quiet course.
If not, he foams at mouth and by and by   55
Breaks out to savage madness. Look, he stirs.
Do you withdraw yourself a little while,
He will recover straight. When he is gone,
I would on great occasion speak with you.
                          [Exit CASSIO.]
How is it, General? Have you not hurt your head?°
   OTH. Dost thou mock me?   61
   IAGO.   I mock you! No, by Heaven.
Would you would bear your fortune like a man!
   OTH. A hornèd man's a monster and a beast.
   IAGO. There's many a beast, then, in a populous
   city,
And many a civil° monster.   65
   OTH. Did he confess it?
   IAGO.   Good sir, be a man.
Think every bearded fellow that's but yoked°
May draw with you.° There's millions now alive
That nightly lie in those unproper beds
Which they dare swear peculiar.° Your case is bet-
   ter.   70
Oh, 'tis the spite of Hell, the Fiend's archmock,
To lip° a wanton in a secure couch°
And to suppose her chaste! No, let me know,
And knowing what I am, I know what she shall be.
   OTH. Oh, thou art wise, 'tis certain.
   IAGO.   Stand you awhile apart,   75
Confine yourself but in a patient list.°
Whilst you were here o'erwhelmèd with your
   grief—
A passion most unsuiting such a man—
Cassio came hither. I shifted him away,

Act IV, Sc. i: 6. hypocrisy . . . Devil: "double-crossing the Devil"; i.e., they are behaving in a most suspicious way. 7–8. They . . . Heaven: i.e., those who go to bed together and mean no harm are asking the Devil to tempt them, and they make God suspect their innocence. 9. So: so long as. venial: pardonable. 17. They . . . not: i.e., many are honored who have no honor. 21. As . . . house: i.e., as a bird of prey waits for its victim to die. 22. Boding: foretelling evil. 27. dotage: infatuation. 28. Convinced or supplied: overcome or satisfied their desires. 35–44. Lie . . . devil: Othello breaks into incoherent muttering before he falls down in a fit. 37. fulsome: disgusting.

40–42. Nature . . . instruction: nature would not fill me with such overwhelming emotion unless there was some cause. 54. lethargy: epileptic fit. Cf. II Hen IV, I.ii.127–29. 60. Have . . . head: With brutal cynicism Iago asks whether Othello is suffering from cuckold's headache. 65. civil: sober, well-behaved citizen. 67. yoked: married. 68. draw . . . you: lit., be your yoke fellow, share your fate. 69–70. That . . . peculiar: that lie nightly in beds which they believe are their own but which others have shared. 72. lip: kiss. secure couch: lit., a carefree bed; i.e., a bed which has been used by the wife's lover, but secretly. 76. patient list: confines of patience.

And laid good 'scuse upon your ecstasy,°   80
Bade him anon return and here speak with me,
The which he promisèd. Do but encave° yourself,
And mark the fleers,° the gibes, and notable scorns,
That dwell in every region of his face.
For I will make him tell the tale anew,   85
Where, how, how oft, how long ago, and when
He hath and is again to cope° your wife.
I say but mark his gesture. Marry, patience,
Or I shall say you are all in all in spleen,°
And nothing of a man.

OTH.   Dost thou hear, Iago?   90
I will be found most cunning in my patience,
But — dost thou hear? — most bloody.

IAGO.   That's not amiss,
But yet keep time in all. Will you withdraw?
                            [OTHELLO *retires.*]
Now will I question Cassio of Bianca,
A housewife° that by selling her desires   95
Buys herself bread and clothes. It is a creature
That dotes on Cassio, as 'tis the strumpet's plague
To beguile many and be beguiled by one.
He, when he hears of her, cannot refrain
From the excess of laughter. Here he comes.   100
[*Re-enter* CASSIO.] As he shall smile, Othello shall go
    mad,
And his unbookish° jealousy must construe°
Poor Cassio's smiles, gestures, and light behavior
Quite in the wrong. How do you now, Lieutenant?

CAS. The worser that you give me the addition°
Whose want even kills me.   106

IAGO. Ply° Desdemona well, and you are sure
    on 't.
Now, if this suit lay in Bianca's power,
How quickly should you speed!

CAS.   Alas, poor caitiff!°

OTH. Look how he laughs already!   110

IAGO. I never knew a woman love man so.

CAS. Alas, poor rogue! I think, i' faith, she loves
    me.

OTH. Now he denies it faintly and laughs it out.

IAGO. Do you hear, Cassio?

OTH.   Now he impórtunes him   115
To tell it o'er. Go to. Well said, well said.

IAGO. She gives it out that you shall marry her.
Do you intend it?

CAS. Ha, ha, ha!   120

OTH. Do you triumph, Roman?° Do you triumph?

CAS. I marry her! What, a customer!° I prithee

bear some charity to my wit. Do not think it so unwholesome. Ha, ha, ha!   125

OTH. So, so, so, so. They laugh that win.°

IAGO. Faith, the cry goes that you shall marry her.

CAS. Prithee say true.

IAGO. I am a very villain else.

OTH. Have you scored° me? Well.   130

CAS. This is the monkey's own giving out. She is
persuaded I will marry her out of her own love and
flattery, not out of my promise.

OTH. Iago beckons me, now he begins the story.

CAS. She was here even now. She haunts me in
every place. I was the other day talking on the sea
bank with certain Venetians, and thither comes the
bauble,° and, by this hand, she falls me thus about
my neck ——   140

OTH. Crying " O dear Cassio! " as it were. His gesture imports it.

CAS. So hangs and lolls and weeps upon me, so
hales° and pulls me. Ha, ha, ha!   144

OTH. Now he tells how she plucked him to my
chamber. Oh, I see that nose of yours, but not that
dog I shall throw it to.

CAS. Well, I must leave her company.

IAGO. Before me!° Look where she comes.   149

CAS. 'Tis such another fitchew!° Marry, a per-
fumed one. [*Enter* BIANCA.] What do you mean by
this haunting of me?

BIAN. Let the Devil and his dam° haunt you!
What did you mean by that same handkerchief you
gave me even now? I was a fine fool to take it.   155
I must take out the work? A likely piece of work,
that you should find it in your chamber and not
know who left it there! This is some minx's token,
and I must take out the work? There, give it your
hobbyhorse.° Wheresoever you had it, I'll take out
no work on 't.   161

CAS. How now, my sweet Bianca! How now! How
now!

OTH. By Heaven, that should be my handkerchief!   165

BIAN. An° you'll come to supper tonight, you
may. An you will not, come when you are next prepared for.   [*Exit.*]

IAGO. After her, after her.

CAS. Faith, I must, she'll rail i' the street else. 171

IAGO. Will you sup there?

CAS. Faith, I intend so.

IAGO. Well, I may chance to see you, for I would
very fain° speak with you.   175

CAS. Prithee, come, will you?

IAGO. Go to. Say no more.   [*Exit* CASSIO.]

80. ecstasy: fit.   82. encave: hide.   83. fleers: scornful grins.
87. cope: encounter.   89. spleen: hot temper. Cf. *I Hen IV*,
V.ii.19.   95. housewife: hussy.   102. unbookish: unlearned,
simple. construe: interpret.   105. addition: title (Lieutenant)
which he has lost.   107. Ply: urge.   109. caitiff: wretch.
121. triumph, Roman: The word "triumph" suggests "Roman"
because the Romans celebrated their victories with triumphs,
elaborate shows, and processions. Cf. *Caesar*, I.i.56.   123. customer: harlot.

126. They . . . win: a proverbial saying. See *Temp*, II.i.33.
130. scored: marked, as with a blow from a whip.   139. bauble:
toy, plaything.   144. hales: hauls, drags.   149. Before me:
by my soul, a mild oath.   150. fitchew: polecat, a creature most
demonstrative in the mating season.   153. dam: mother.
160. hobbyhorse: harlot.   166. An: if.   175. fain: gladly.

OTH. [*Advancing*] How shall I murder him, Iago?

IAGO. Did you perceive how he laughed at his vice?   181

OTH. Oh, Iago!

IAGO. And did you see the handkerchief?

OTH. Was that mine?

IAGO. Yours, by this hand. And to see how he prizes the foolish woman your wife! She gave it him, and he hath given it his whore.   187

OTH. I would have him nine years a-killing. A fine woman! A fair woman! A sweet woman!

IAGO. Nay, you must forget that.

OTH. Aye, let her rot, and perish, and be damned tonight, for she shall not live. No, my heart is turned to stone, I strike it and it hurts my hand. Oh, the world hath not a sweeter creature. She might lie by an emperor's side, and command him tasks.   196

IAGO. Nay, that's not your way.°

OTH. Hang her! I do but say what she is, so delicate with her needle, an admirable musician — oh, she will sing the savageness out of a bear — of so high and plenteous wit and invention ——   201

IAGO. She's the worse for all this.

OTH. Oh, a thousand thousand times. And then, of so gentle a condition!°

IAGO. Aye, too gentle.   205

OTH. Nay, that's certain. But yet the pity of it, Iago! O Iago, the pity of it, Iago!

IAGO. If you are so fond° over her iniquity, give her patent° to offend, for if it touch not you, it comes near nobody.   210

OTH. I will chop her into messes.° Cuckold me!

IAGO. Oh, 'tis foul in her.

OTH. With mine officer!

IAGO. That's fouler.   215

OTH. Get me some poison, Iago, this night. I'll not expostulate° with her, lest her body and beauty unprovide° my mind again. This night, Iago.   218

IAGO. Do it not with poison, strangle her in her bed, even the bed she hath contaminated.

OTH. Good, good. The justice of it pleases. Very good.

IAGO. And for Cassio, let me be his undertaker.° You shall hear more by midnight.   225

OTH. Excellent good. [*A trumpet within.*] What trumpet is that same?

IAGO. Something from Venice, sure. 'Tis Lodovico
Come from the Duke. And see, your wife is with him.

[*Enter* LODOVICO, DESDEMONA, *and* ATTENDANTS.]

LOD. God save the worthy General!

OTH.   With all my heart, sir.   229

LOD. The Duke and Senators of Venice greet you.
        [*Gives him a letter.*]

OTH. I kiss the instrument° of their pleasures.
        [*Opens the letter, and reads.*]

DES. And what's the news, good Cousin Lodovico?

IAGO. I am very glad to see you, signior.
Welcome to Cyprus.

LOD. I thank you. How does Lieutenant Cassio?

IAGO. Lives, sir.   236

DES. Cousin, there's fall'n between him and my lord
An unkind breach, but you shall make all well.

OTH. Are you sure of that?

DES. My lord?

OTH. [*Reads.*] "This fail you not to do, as you will ——"   240

LOD. He did not call, he's busy in the paper.
Is there division 'twixt my lord and Cassio?

DES. A most unhappy one. I would do much
To atone° them, for the love I bear to Cassio.

OTH. Fire and brimstone!

DES.   My lord?

OTH.   Are you wise?°   245

DES. What, is he angry?

LOD.   Maybe the letter moved him,
For, as I think, they do command him home,
Deputing Cassio in his government.°

DES. By my troth,° I am glad on 't.

OTH.   Indeed!

DES.   My lord?

OTH. I am glad to see you mad.

DES.   Why, sweet Othello?   250

OTH. Devil!   [*Striking her.*]

DES. I have not deserved this.

LOD. My lord, this would not be believed in Venice
Though I should swear I saw 't. 'Tis very much.°
Make her amends, she weeps.

OTH.   O devil, devil!   255
If that the earth could teem with a woman's tears,
Each drop she falls would prove a crocodile.°
Out of my sight!

DES.   I will not stay to offend you. [*Going.*]

LOD. Truly, an obedient lady.
I do beseech your lordship, call her back.   260

OTH. Mistress!

DES. My lord?

---

197. Nay ... way: i.e., don't get soft thoughts about her. 204. condition: nature. 208. fond: foolish. 209. patent: a grant by the King of some special privilege. 211. messes: little pieces. 217. expostulate: argue. 218. unprovide: weaken. 224. be ... undertaker: undertake to manage his business. In Shakespeare's plays the word does *not* mean "mortician."

231. instrument: i.e., the official letter which he has just received. 244. atone: reconcile. 245. Are ... wise: i.e., in saying you bear love to Cassio. 248. in ... government: in his place as governor. 249. troth: truth. 254. 'Tis ... much: this is too much. 256–57. If ... crocodile: if the earth could breed from woman's tears, each tear that she lets fall would become a crocodile. It was believed that the crocodile would cry and sob to attract the sympathetic passer-by, who was then snapped up.

OTH. What would you with her, sir?

LOD.   Who, I, my lord?

OTH. Aye, you did wish that I would make her
    turn.
Sir, she can turn and turn, and yet go on
And turn again. And she can weep, sir, weep.   265
And she's obedient, as you say, obedient,
Very obedient. Proceed you in your tears.
Concerning this, sir — oh, well-painted passion!° —
I am commanded home. Get you away.
I'll send for you anon. Sir, I obey the mandate,   270
And will return to Venice. Hence, avaunt!
                              [*Exit* DESDEMONA.]
Cassio shall have my place. And, sir, tonight,
I do entreat that we may sup together.
You are welcome, sir, to Cyprus. Goats and mon-
    keys!   [*Exit.*]

LOD. Is this the noble Moor whom our full Senate
Call all-in-all sufficient? This the nature   276
Whom passion could not shake? Whose solid vir-
    tue
The shot of accident nor dart of chance
Could neither graze nor pierce?

IAGO.   He is much changed.

LOD. Are his wits safe? Is he not light of brain?

IAGO. He's that he is. I may not breathe my cen-
    sure°   281
What he might be. If what he might he is not,
I would to Heaven he were!°

LOD.   What, strike his wife!

IAGO. Faith, that was not so well, yet would I knew
That stroke would prove the worst!

LOD.   Is it his use?°   285
Or did the letters work upon his blood,
And new-create this fault?

IAGO.   Alas, alas!
It is not honesty in me to speak
What I have seen and known. You shall observe
him,
And his own courses° will denote him so   290
That I may save my speech. Do but go after,
And mark how he continues.

LOD. I am sorry that I am deceived in him.
                              [*Exeunt.*]

SCENE II. *A room in the castle.*

[*Enter* OTHELLO *and* EMILIA.]

OTH. You have seen nothing, then?

EMIL. Nor ever heard, nor ever did suspect.

OTH. Yes, you have seen Cassio and she together.

EMIL. But then I saw no harm, and then I heard
Each syllable that breath made up between them.   5

OTH. What, did they never whisper?

EMIL.   Never, my lord.

OTH. Nor send you out o' the way?

EMIL. Never.

OTH. To fetch her fan, her gloves, her mask, nor
    nothing?

EMIL. Never, my lord.   10

OTH. That's strange.

EMIL. I durst, my lord, to wager she is honest,
Lay down my soul at stake.° If you think other,
Remove your thought, it doth abuse your bosom.
If any wretch have put this in your head,   15
Let Heaven requite it with the serpent's curse!°
For if she be not honest, chaste, and true,
There's no man happy, the purest of their wives
Is foul as slander.

OTH. Bid her come hither. Go.   [*Exit* EMILIA.]
She says enough. Yet she's a simple bawd°   20
That cannot say as much. This is a subtle whore,
A closet° lock and key of villainous secrets.
And yet she'll kneel and pray, I have seen her do 't.
                    [*Enter* DESDEMONA *with* EMILIA.]

DES. My lord, what is your will?

OTH.   Pray, chuck,° come hither.

DES. What is your pleasure?

OTH.   Let me see your eyes.   25
Look in my face.

DES.   What horrible fancy's this?

OTH. [*To* EMILIA] Some of your function,° mis-
    tress.
Leave procreants alone and shut the door,
Cough, or cry hem, if anybody come.
Your mystery,° your mystery. Nay, dispatch.°   30
                              [*Exit* EMILIA.]

DES. Upon my knees, what doth your speech im-
    port?
I understand a fury in your words,
But not the words.

OTH. Why, what art thou?

DES. Your wife, my lord, your true and loyal wife.

OTH. Come, swear it, damn thyself,   35
Lest, being like one of Heaven,° the devils them-
    selves
Should fear to seize thee. Therefore be double-
    damned.
Swear thou art honest.

DES.   Heaven doth truly know it.

268. well-painted passion: cleverly imitated emotion; *passion* is
any violent emotion.   281. censure: opinion, judgment.   283. I
... were: I wish he were the man he ought to be. Once more
Iago hints that he is holding back some unpleasant fact.   285. Is
... use: does he always behave like this?   290. courses: ways,
behavior.

Sc. ii: 13. at stake: as the stake, the bet.   16. serpent's
curse: i.e., the curse laid on the serpent in the Garden of Eden.
20. bawd: keeper of a brothel.   22. closet: box in which secret
papers are kept.   24. chuck: See III.iv.49,n.   27. Some ...
function: get about your business; i.e., prostitution. Othello pre-
tends that Emilia is keeper of a brothel and Desdemona one of
the women.   30. mystery: profession. dispatch: be quick.
36. being   Heaven: because you look like an angel.

OTH. Heaven truly knows that thou art false as
    Hell.

DES. To whom, my lord? With whom? How am
    I false?   40

OTH. O Desdemona! Away! Away! Away!

DES. Alas the heavy day! Why do you weep?
Am I the motive of these tears, my lord?
If haply you my father do suspect
An instrument of this your calling-back,   45
Lay not your blame on me. If you have lost him,
Why, I have lost him too.

OTH.   Had it pleased Heaven
To try me with affliction, had they rained
All kinds of sores and shames on my bare head,
Steeped me in poverty to the very lips,   50
Given to captivity me and my utmost hopes,
I should have found in some place of my soul
A drop of patience. But, alas, to make me
A fixèd figure for the time of scorn
To point his slow unmoving finger at!°   55
Yet could I bear that too, well, very well.
But there where I have garnered up my heart,°
Where either I must live or bear no life,
The fountain from the which my current runs
Or else dries up — to be discarded thence!   60
Or keep it as a cistern for foul toads
To knot and gender° in! Turn thy complexion there,
Patience, thou young and rose-lipped cherubin —
Aye, there, look grim as Hell!

DES. I hope my noble lord esteems me honest.   65

OTH. Oh, aye, as summer flies are in the sham-
    bles,°
That quicken even with blowing.° O thou weed,
Who art so lovely fair and smell'st so sweet
That the sense aches at thee, would thou hadst ne'er
    been born!   69

DES. Alas, what ignorant sin have I committed?

OTH. Was this fair paper,° this most goodly book,
Made to write " whore " upon? What committed!
Committed! O thou public commoner!°
I should make very forges of my cheeks°
That would to cinders burn up modesty   75
Did I but speak thy deeds. What committed!
Heaven stops the nose at it, and the moon winks.
The bawdy wind, that kisses all it meets,
Is hushed within the hollow mine° of earth
And will not hear it. What committed!   80
Impudent strumpet!

DES.   By Heaven, you do me wrong.

OTH. Are not you a strumpet?

DES.   No, as I am a Christian.
If to preserve this vessel for my lord
From any other foul unlawful touch
Be not to be a strumpet, I am none.   85

OTH. What, not a whore?

DES.   No, as I shall be saved.

OTH. Is 't possible?

DES. Oh, Heaven forgive us!

OTH.   I cry you mercy, then.
I took you for that cunning whore of Venice
That married with Othello. [*Raising his voice.*]
    You, mistress,   90
That have the office opposite to Saint Peter,°
And keep the gate of Hell!
[*Re-enter* EMILIA.] You, you, aye, you!
We have done our course, there's money for your
    pains.   93
I pray you turn the key, and keep our counsel.°
                                  [*Exit.*]

EMIL. Alas, what does this gentleman conceive?°
How do you, madam? How do you, my good lady?

DES. Faith, half-asleep.

EMIL. Good madam, what's the matter with my
    lord?

DES. With who?

EMIL. Why, with my lord, madam.   100

DES. Who is thy lord?

EMIL.   He that is yours, sweet lady.

DES. I have none. Do not talk to me, Emilia.
I cannot weep, nor answer have I none
But what should go by water.° Prithee tonight
Lay on my bed my wedding sheets. Remember,   105
And call thy husband hither.

EMIL.   Here's a change indeed!   [*Exit.*]

DES. 'Tis meet I should be used so, very meet.
How have I been behaved that he might stick
The small'st opinion on my least misuse?°
         [*Re-enter* EMILIA *with* IAGO.]

IAGO. What is your pleasure, madam? How is 't
    with you?   110

DES. I cannot tell. Those that do teach young babes
Do it with gentle means and easy tasks.
He might have chid me so, for, in good faith,
I am a child to chiding.

IAGO.   What's the matter, lady?   114

EMIL. Alas, Iago, my lord hath so bewhored her,
Thrown such despite and heavy terms upon her,
As true hearts cannot bear.

DES. Am I that name, Iago?

IAGO.   What name, fair lady?

54–55. A . . . at: A difficult image, much discussed. F1 reads
"slow and moving finger"; Q1 reads "slow unmoving." Probably
it means "a perpetual mark for scorn to point at with motionless finger." **time of scorn:** (perhaps) scorn for all time. **57. garnered . . . heart:** stored the harvest of my love. **62. gender:**
mate. **66. shambles:** slaughterhouse. **67. quicken . . . blowing:** come to life as soon as the eggs are laid. **71. fair paper:** i.e.,
her white body. **73. public commoner:** one who offers herself to
all comers. **74. I . . . cheeks:** i.e., my cheeks would be as hot as
a forge if I told the truth. **79. hollow mine:** i.e., the cave where
the winds were supposed to be kept.

91. office . . . Peter: St. Peter kept the keys to Heaven.
94. counsel: i.e., secret. **95. conceive:** imagine. **104. should
. . . water:** be expressed in tears. **108–09. How . . . misuse:**
what have I done that he could find the smallest reason to find
fault with my least mistake?

DES. Such as she says my lord did say I was.   119
EMIL. He called her whore. A beggar in his drink
Could not have laid such terms upon his callet.°
IAGO. Why did he so?
DES. I do not know. I am sure I am none such.
IAGO. Do not weep, do not weep. Alas the day!
EMIL. Hath she forsook so many noble matches,
Her father and her country and her friends,   126
To be called whore? Would it not make one weep?
DES. It is my wretched fortune.
IAGO.   Beshrew him for 't!
How comes this trick upon him?
DES.   Nay, Heaven doth know.
EMIL. I will be hanged if some eternal villain,
Some busy and insinuating rogue,   131
Some cogging, cozening° slave, to get some office,
Have not devised this slander. I'll be hanged else.
IAGO. Fie, there is no such man, it is impossible.
DES. If any such there be, Heaven pardon him!
EMIL. A halter pardon him! And Hell gnaw his
    bones!   136
Why should he call her whore? Who keeps her com-
    pany?
What place? What time? What form? What likeli-
    hood?
The Moor's abused by some most villainous knave,
Some base notorious knave, some scurvy fellow.
O Heaven, that such companions° Thou'dst unfold,°
And put in every honest hand a whip   142
To lash the rascals naked through the world
Even from the east to the west!
IAGO.   Speak withindoor.°
EMIL. Oh, fie upon them! Some such squire° he
    was   145
That turned your wit the seamy side without,
And made you to suspect me with the Moor.
IAGO. You are a fool. Go to.°
DES.   O good Iago,
What shall I do to win my lord again?   149
Good friend, go to him, for, by this light of Heaven,
I know not how I lost him. Here I kneel.
If e'er my will did trespass 'gainst his love
Either in discourse of thought or actual deed,
Or that mine eyes, mine ears, or any sense
Delighted them in any other form,   155
Or that I do not yet, and ever did,
And ever will, though he do shake me off
To beggarly divorcement, love him dearly,
Comfort forswear° me! Unkindness may do much,
And his unkindness may defeat° my life,   160
But never taint my love. I cannot say " whore,"
It doth abhor me now I speak the word.

To do the act that might the addition° earn
Not the world's mass of vanity° could make me.
IAGO. I pray you be content, 'tis but his humor.
The business of the state does him offense,   166
And he does chide with you.
DES. If 'twere no other——
IAGO. 'Tis but so, I warrant. [Trumpets within.]
Hark how these instruments summon to supper!
The messengers of Venice stay the meat.°   170
Go in, and weep not, all things shall be well.
                    [Exeunt DESDEMONA and EMILIA.]
[Enter RODERIGO.] How now, Roderigo!
ROD. I do not find that thou dealest justly with me.
IAGO. What in the contrary?   175
ROD. Every day thou daffest° me with some de-
vice, Iago, and rather, as it seems to me now, keep-
est from me all conveniency° than suppliest me with
the least advantage of hope. I will indeed no longer
endure it, nor am I yet persuaded to put up in peace
what already I have foolishly suffered.   182
IAGO. Will you hear me, Roderigo?
ROD. Faith, I have heard too much, for your words
and performances are no kin together.
IAGO. You charge me most unjustly.   186
ROD. With naught but truth. I have wasted myself
out of my means. The jewels you have had from me
to deliver to Desdemona would half have corrupted
a votarist.° You have told me she hath received
them, and returned me expectations and comforts of
sudden respect and acquaintance, but I find none.
IAGO. Well, go to, very well.   194
ROD. Very well! Go to! I cannot go to, man, nor
'tis not very well. By this hand, I say 'tis very scurvy,
and begin to find myself fopped° in it.
IAGO. Very well.   198
ROD. I tell you 'tis not very well. I will make myself known to Desdemona. If she will return me my
jewels, I will give over my suit and repent my unlawful solicitation. If not, assure yourself I will seek
satisfaction of you.
IAGO. You have said now.°
ROD. Aye, and said nothing but what I protest in-
tendment of doing.   206
IAGO. Why, now I see there's mettle° in thee, and
even from this instant do build on thee a better opinion than ever before. Give me thy hand, Roderigo.
Thou hast taken against me a most just exception,°
but yet I protest I have dealt most directly in thy
affair.   211
ROD. It hath not appeared.
IAGO. I grant indeed it hath not appeared, and

---

121. laid . . . callet: used such words about his moll.   132. cogging, cozening: deceiving, cheating.   141. companions: low creatures. unfold: bring to light.   144. Speak withindoor: don't
shout so loud that all the street will hear you.   145. squire:
fine fellow.   148. Go to: An expression of derision.   159. for-
swear: repudiate.   160. defeat: destroy.

163. addition: title. Cf. IV.i.105.   164. vanity: i.e., riches.
170. meat: serving of supper.   176. thou daffest: you put me
aside. Cf. I Hen IV, IV.i.96.   178. conveniency: opportunity.
190. votarist: one who has taken a vow, here a nun.   197. fopped:
fooled.   204. You . . . now: or in modern slang, "Oh yeah."
207. mettle: metal, good stuff.   209. just exception: reasonable grievance.

your suspicion is not without wit° and judgment.
But, Roderigo, if thou hast that in thee indeed 216
which I have greater reason to believe now than ever
—I mean purpose, courage, and valor—this night
show it. If thou the next night following enjoy not
Desdemona, take me from this world with treachery
and devise engines° for my life.   222

ROD. Well, what is it? Is it within reason and compass?

IAGO. Sir, there is especial commission come from
Venice to depute Cassio in Othello's place.

ROD. Is that true? Why, then Othello and Desdemona return again to Venice.   228

IAGO. Oh, no. He goes into Mauritania, and takes
away with him the fair Desdemona, unless his abode
be lingered here by some accident. Wherein none can
be so determinate° as the removing of Cassio. 233

ROD. How do you mean, "removing of" him?

IAGO. Why, by making him uncapable° of Othello's place, knocking out his brains.

ROD. And that you would have me to do?   237

IAGO. Aye, if you dare do yourself a profit and a
right. He sups tonight with a harlotry,° and thither
will I go to him. He knows not yet of his honorable
fortune. If you will watch his going thence, which I
will fashion to fall out between twelve and one, you
may take him at your pleasure. I will be near to
second your attempt, and he shall fall between us.
Come, stand not amazed at it, but go along 245
with me. I will show you such a necessity in his
death that you shall think yourself bound to put it
on him. It is now high suppertime, and the night
grows to waste. About it.   250

ROD. I will hear further reason for this.

IAGO. And you shall be satisfied.   [*Exeunt.*]

SCENE III. *Another room in the castle.*

[*Enter* OTHELLO, LODOVICO, DESDEMONA, EMILIA, *and*
ATTENDANTS.]

LOD. I do beseech you, sir, trouble yourself no
further.

OTH. Oh, pardon me, 'twill do me good to walk.

LOD. Madam, good night. I humbly thank your
ladyship.

DES. Your Honor is most welcome.

OTH.   Will you walk, sir?
Oh—Desdemona——   5

DES. My lord?

OTH. Get you to bed on the instant, I will be returned forthwith. Dismiss your attendant there.
Look it be done.

DES. I will, my lord.   10
[*Exeunt* OTHELLO, LODOVICO, *and* ATTENDANTS.]

EMIL. How goes it now? He looks gentler than
he did.

DES. He says he will return incontinent.°
He hath commanded me to go to bed,
And bade me to dismiss you.

EMIL.   Dismiss me!   14

DES. It was his bidding, therefore, good Emilia,
Give me my nightly wearing,° and adieu.
We must not now displease him.

EMIL. I would you had never seen him!

DES. So would not I. My love doth so approve°
him   19
That even his stubbornness, his checks, his frowns—
Prithee, unpin me—have grace and favor in them.

EMIL. I have laid those sheets you bade me on the
bed.

DES. All's one. Good faith, how foolish are our
minds!
If I do die before thee, prithee shroud me
In one of those same sheets.

EMIL.   Come, come, you talk. 25

DES. My mother had a maid called Barbara.
She was in love, and he she loved proved mad
And did forsake her. She had a song of "willow"°—
An old thing 'twas, but it expressed her fortune,
And she died singing it. That song tonight 30
Will not go from my mind. I have much to do
But to go hang my head all at one side
And sing it like poor Barbara. Prithee, dispatch.

EMIL. Shall I go fetch your nightgown?

DES.   No, unpin me here.
This Lodovico is a proper man.   35

EMIL. A very handsome man.

DES. He speaks well.

EMIL. I know a lady in Venice would have walked
barefoot to Palestine for a touch of his nether°
lip.   40

DES. [*Singing*]
"The poor soul sat sighing by a sycamore tree,
    Sing all a green willow.
Her hand on her bosom, her head on her knee,
    Sing willow, willow, willow.
The fresh streams ran by her, and murmured her
      moans,   45
    Sing willow, willow, willow.
Her salt tears fell from her, and softened the
      stones—"
Lay by these—[*Singing*]
    "Sing willow, willow, willow."
Prithee, hie thee, he'll come anon.°—[*Singing*] 50
"Sing all a green willow must be my garland.

215. **wit:** wisdom.   222. **engines:** instruments of torture.
233. **determinate:** decisive.   235. **uncapable:** unable to take.
239. **harlotry:** harlot.

Sc. iii: 12. **incontinent:** immediately. 16. **nightly wearing:**
nightgown. 19. **approve:** commend. 28. **willow:** the emblem
of the forlorn lover. 39. **nether:** lower. 50. **anon:** soon.

Let nobody blame him, his scorn I approve —— "
Nay, that's not next. Hark! Who is 't that knocks?
  EMIL. It's the wind.
  DES. [*Singing*]
" I called my love false love, but what said he then?
    Sing willow, willow, willow.   56
  If I court moe° women, you'll couch with moe
    men."
So get thee gone, good night. Mine eyes do itch.
Doth that bode weeping?
  EMIL.   'Tis neither here nor there.
  DES. I have heard it said so. Oh, these men, these
    men!   60
Dost thou in conscience think — tell me, Emilia —
That there be women do abuse their husbands
In such gross kind?
  EMIL.   There be some such, no question.
  DES. Wouldst thou do such a deed for all the
    world?
  EMIL. Why, would not you?
  DES.   No, by this heavenly light! 65
  EMIL. Nor I neither by this heavenly light. I might
do 't as well i' the dark.
  DES. Wouldst thou do such a deed for all the
    world?
  EMIL. The world's a huge thing. It is a great price
For a small vice.
  DES.   In troth, I think thou wouldst not. 70
  EMIL. In troth, I think I should, and undo 't when
I had done. Marry, I would not do such a thing for
a joint ring,° nor for measures of lawn,° nor for
gowns, petticoats, nor caps, nor any petty exhibi-
tion;° but for the whole world — why, who would
not make her husband a cuckold to make him a
monarch? I should venture Purgatory for 't. 77
  DES. Beshrew me if I would do such a wrong
For the whole world.
  EMIL. Why, the wrong is but a wrong i' the
world, and having the world for your labor, 'tis a
wrong in your own world and you might quickly
make it right.
  DES. I do not think there is any such woman. 84
  EMIL. Yes, a dozen, and as many to the vantage°
as would store° the world they played in.
But I do think it is their husbands' faults
If wives do fall. Say that they slack their duties
And pour our treasures into foreign laps,
Or else break out in peevish jealousies, 90
Throwing restraint° upon us, or say they strike us,
Or scant our former having in despite,°

Why, we have galls,° and though we have some
  grace,
Yet have we some revenge. Let husbands know
Their wives have sense like them. They see and smell
And have their palates both for sweet and sour, 96
As husbands have. What is it that they do
When they change us for others? Is it sport?
I think it is. And doth affection breed it?
I think it doth. Is 't frailty that thus errs? 100
It is so too. And have not we affections,
Desires for sport, and frailty, as men have?
Then let them use us well. Else let them know
The ills we do, their ills instruct us so.
  DES. Good night, good night. Heaven me such
    uses° send, 105
Not to pick bad from bad, but by bad mend!
                            [*Exeunt.*]

Act V

SCENE I. *Cyprus. A street.*

[*Enter* IAGO *and* RODERIGO.]
  IAGO. Here, stand behind this bulk,° straight° will
    he come.
Wear thy good rapier bare, and put it home.
Quick, quick, fear nothing, I'll be at thy elbow.
It makes us, or it mars us. Think on that,
And fix most firm thy resolution. 5
  ROD. Be near at hand, I may miscarry in 't.
  IAGO. Here, at thy hand. Be bold, and take thy
    stand.   [*Retires.*]
  ROD. I have no great devotion to the deed,
And yet he hath given me satisfying reasons.
'Tis but a man gone. Forth, my sword. He dies. 10
  IAGO. I have rubbed this young quat° almost to the
    sense,°
And he grows angry. Now, whether he kill Cassio,
Or Cassio him, or each do kill the other,
Every way makes my gain. Live Roderigo,
He calls me to a restitution large° 15
Of gold and jewels that I bobbed° from him
As gifts to Desdemona.
It must not be. If Cassio do remain,
He hath a daily beauty in his life
That makes me ugly,° and besides, the Moor 20
May unfold° me to him. There stand I in much
  peril.

---

57. moe: more. 73. joint ring: ring made in two pieces, a lover's
gift. measures of lawn: lengths of finest lawn, or as a modern
woman would say, "sheer nylon." 74–75. petty exhibition:
small allowance of money. 85. as . . . vantage: and more too;
vantage is that added to the exact weight to give generous measure. 86. store: stock, fill up. 91. Throwing restraint: putting
restraints. 92. scant . . . despite: for spite cut down our allowance.

93. galls: bile, the cause of bitterness. 105. uses: practices.
  Act V, Sc. i: 1. bulk: stall outside a shop. straight: straightway. 11. quat: pimple. to . . . sense: to the quick, to the raw.
15. large: full. 16. bobbed: cheated. 19–20. He . . . ugly:
by comparison with him I am a poor thing. Iago is conscious of
his lack of social graces. 21. unfold: expose.

No, he must die. Be 't so. I hear him coming.

[*Enter* CASSIO.]

ROD. I know his gait, 'tis he. Villain, thou diest!

[*Makes a pass at* CASSIO.]

CAS. That thrust had been mine enemy indeed
But that my coat is better than thou know'st.°   25
I will make proof of thine.

[*Draws, and wounds* RODERIGO.]

ROD.   Oh, I am slain!

[IAGO *from behind wounds* CASSIO
in the leg, and exit.]

CAS. I am maimed for ever. Help, ho! Murder!
Murder!   [*Falls.*]

[*Enter* OTHELLO.]

OTH. The voice of Cassio. Iago keeps his word.

ROD. Oh, villain that I am!

OTH.   It is even so.

CAS. Oh, help, ho! Light! A surgeon!   30

OTH. 'Tis he. O brave Iago, honest and just,
That hast such noble sense of thy friend's wrong!
Thou teachest me. Minion,° your dear lies dead,
And your unblest fate hies.° Strumpet, I come!
Forth of my heart those charms, thine eyes, are
blotted.   35
Thy bed lust-stained shall with lust's blood be
spotted.   [*Exit.*]

[*Enter* LODOVICO *and* GRATIANO.]

CAS. What ho! No watch?° No passage?° Murder! Murder!

GRA. 'Tis some mischance, the cry is very dire-
ful.

CAS. Oh, help!

LOD. Hark!   40

ROD. Oh, wretched villain!

LOD. Two or three groan. It is a heavy° night.
These may be counterfeits.° Let's think 't unsafe
To come in to the cry without more help.

ROD. Nobody come? Then shall I bleed to death.

LOD. Hark!

[*Re-enter* IAGO, *with a light.*]

GRA. Here's one comes in his shirt, with light and
weapons.   46

IAGO. Who's there? Whose noise is this that cries
on° murder?

LOD. We do not know.

IAGO.   Did not you hear a cry?

CAS. Here, here! For Heaven's sake, help me!

IAGO.   What's the matter?   50

GRA. This is Othello's Ancient, as I take it.

LOD. The same indeed, a very valiant fellow.

IAGO. What are you here that cry so grievously?

CAS. Iago? Oh, I am spoiled, undone by villains!
Give me some help.   55

IAGO. Oh me, Lieutenant! What villains have done
this?

CAS. I think that one of them is hereabout,
And cannot make away.

IAGO.   Oh, treacherous villains!

[*To* LODOVICO *and* GRATIANO.] What are you there?
Come in and give some help.

ROD. Oh, help me here!   60

CAS. That's one of them.

IAGO. Oh, murderous slave! Oh, villain!

[*Stabs* RODERIGO.]

ROD. Oh, damned Iago! Oh, inhuman dog!

IAGO. Kill men i' the dark! Where be these bloody
thieves?
How silent is this town! Ho! Murder! Murder!
What may you be? Are you of good or evil?   65

LOD. As you shall prove us, praise us.

IAGO. Signior Lodovico?

LOD. He, sir.

IAGO. I cry you mercy. Here's Cassio hurt by villains.

GRA. Cassio!   70

IAGO. How is 't, brother?

CAS. My leg is cut in two.

IAGO.   Marry, Heaven forbid!
Light, gentlemen. I'll bind it with my shirt.

[*Enter* BIANCA.]

BIAN. What is the matter, ho? Who is 't that
cried?

IAGO. Who is 't that cried!   75

BIAN. Oh, my dear Cassio! My sweet Cassio! Oh,
Cassio, Cassio, Cassio!

IAGO. Oh, notable strumpet! Cassio, may you suspect
Who they should be that have thus mangled you?

CAS. No.   80

GRA. I am sorry to find you thus. I have been to
seek you.

IAGO. Lend me a garter. So. Oh, for a chair,
To bear him easily hence!

BIAN. Alas, he faints! Oh, Cassio, Cassio, Cassio!

IAGO. Gentlemen all, I do suspect this trash   85
To be a party in this injury.
Patience awhile, good Cassio. Come, come,
Lend me a light. Know we this face or no?
Alas, my friend and my dear countryman
Roderigo? No — yes, sure. Oh Heaven! Roderigo.

GRA. What, of Venice?   91

IAGO. Even he, sir. Did you know him?

GRA.   Know him! Aye.

IAGO. Signior Gratiano? I cry you gentle pardon.°
These bloody accidents must excuse my manners,
That so neglected you.

GRA.   I am glad to see you.   95

IAGO. How do you, Cassio? Oh, a chair, a chair!

GRA. Roderigo!

---

25. coat ... know'st: i.e., I wear mail under my coat.   33. Minion: darling, in a bad sense.   34. hies: comes on quickly.
37. watch: police. No passage: nobody passing.   42. heavy:
thick.   43. counterfeits: fakes.   47. cries on: cries out.

93. I ... pardon: I beg you kindly pardon me.

IAGO. He, he, 'tis he. [*A chair brought in*] Oh,
that's well said, the chair.
Some good man bear him carefully from hence.
I'll fetch the General's surgeon. [*To* BIANCA] For
you, mistress,   100
Save you your labor. He that lies slain here, Cassio,
Was my dear friend. What malice was between you?
CAS. None in the world, nor do I know the man.
IAGO. [*To* BIANCA] What, look you pale? Oh, bear
him out o' the air.
[CASSIO *and* RODERIGO *are borne off.*]
Stay you, good gentlemen. Look you pale, mistress?
Do you perceive the gastness° of her eye?   106
Nay, if you stare, we shall hear more anon.
Behold her well, I pray you look upon her.
Do you see, gentlemen? Nay, guiltiness will speak,
Though tongues were out of use.   110
[*Enter* EMILIA.]
EMIL. 'Las, what's the matter? What's the matter,
husband?
IAGO. Cassio hath here been set on in the dark
By Roderigo, and fellows that are 'scaped.
He's almost slain, and Roderigo dead.   114
EMIL. Alas, good gentlemen! Alas, good Cassio!
IAGO. This is the fruit of whoring. Prithee, Emilia,
Go know of Cassio where he supped tonight.
What, do you shake at that?
BIAN. He supped at my house, but I therefore
shake not.
IAGO. Oh, did he so? I charge you, go with me.
EMIL. Fie, fie upon thee, strumpet!   121
BIAN. I am no strumpet, but of life as honest
As you that thus abuse me.
EMIL.   As I! Foh! Fie upon thee!
IAGO. Kind gentlemen, let's go see poor Cassio
dressed.°
Come, mistress, you must tell 's another tale.   125
Emilia, run you to the citadel,
And tell my lord and lady what hath happed!
Will you go on? I pray. [*Aside*] This is the night
That either makes me or fordoes° me quite.
[*Exeunt.*]

SCENE II. *A bedchamber in the castle.* DESDE-
MONA *in bed asleep, a light burning.*

[*Enter* OTHELLO.]
OTH. It is the cause,° it is the cause, my soul.
Let me not name it to you, you chaste stars!
It is the cause. Yet I'll not shed her blood,

Nor scar that whiter skin of hers than snow
And smooth as monumental alabaster.°   5
Yet she must die, else she'll betray more men.
Put out the light, and then put out the light.
If I quench thee, thou flaming minister,°
I can again thy former light restore,
Should I repent me. But once put out thy light,   10
Thou cunning'st° pattern of excelling nature,
I know not where is that Promethean heat°
That can thy light relume.° When I have plucked
the rose,
I cannot give it vital growth again,
It needs must wither. I'll smell it on the tree.   15
[*Kissing her*]
Ah, balmy breath, that dost almost persuade
Justice to break her sword! One more, one more.
Be thus when thou art dead, and I will kill thee,
And love thee after. One more, and this the last.
So sweet was ne'er so fatal. I must weep,   20
But they are cruel tears. This sorrow's heavenly,
It strikes where it doth love. She wakes.
DES. Who's there? Othello?
OTH.   Aye, Desdemona.
DES. Will you come to bed, my lord?
OTH. Have you prayed tonight, Desdemona?   25
DES. Aye, my lord.
OTH. If you bethink yourself of any crime
Unreconciled as yet to Heaven and grace,
Solicit for it straight.
DES. Alas, my lord, what may you mean by that?
OTH. Well, do it, and be brief. I will walk by.   30
I would not kill thy unpreparèd spirit.
No, Heaven forfend! I would not kill thy soul.°
DES. Talk you of killing?
OTH. Aye, I do.
DES. Then Heaven have mercy on me!
OTH. Amen, with all my heart!
DES. If you say so, I hope you will not kill me.   35
OTH. Hum!
DES. And yet I fear you, for you are fatal° then
When your eyes roll so. Why I should fear I know
not,
Since guiltiness I know not, but yet I feel I fear.
OTH. Think on thy sins.
DES.   They are loves I bear to you. 40
OTH. Aye, and for that thou diest.
DES. That death's unnatural that kills for loving.
Alas, why gnaw you so your nether lip?
Some bloody passion shakes your very frame.
These are portents,° but yet I hope, I hope,   45

106. gastness: ghastly look.   124. dressed: i.e., his wound
dressed.   129. fordoes: ruins.
    Sc. ii: 1. It . . . cause: The meaning of the opening lines of
this speech has been much discussed. The *cause* is Desdemona's
supposed faithlessness; Othello, at this moment, sees himself as
embodied vengeance, the venger of man betrayed by woman.

5. monumental alabaster: Alabaster is white translucent stone,
much used for memorial effigies on Elizabethan tombs.   8. minister: servant.   11. cunning'st: most skillfully made.   12. Promethean heat: fire from Heaven. Prometheus stole fire from
Heaven and first gave it to man.   13. relume: relight.   27-32. If
. . . soul: Othello will be a merciful murderer. Cf. *Haml*. I.v.76–
80. forfend: forbid.   37. fatal: deadly.   45. portents: signs
foretelling disaster.

They do not point on me.

OTH.   Peace, and be still!

DES. I will so. What's the matter?

OTH. That handkerchief which I so loved and gave
thee
Thou gavest to Cassio.

DES.   No, by my life and soul!
Send for the man, and ask him.

OTH.   Sweet soul, take heed,   50
Take heed of perjury, thou art on thy deathbed.

DES. Aye, but not yet to die.

OTH.   Yes, presently.°
Therefore confess thee freely of thy sin,
For to deny each article with oath
Cannot remove nor choke the strong conception°
That I do groan withal. Thou art to die.   56

DES. Then Lord have mercy on me!

OTH.   I say amen.

DES. And have you mercy too! I never did
Offend you in my life, never loved Cassio
But with such general warranty° of Heaven   60
As I might love. I never gave him token.

OTH. By Heaven, I saw my handkerchief in 's
hand.
O perjured woman! Thou dost stone° my heart,
And makest me call what I intend to do
A murder, which I thought a sacrifice.   65
I saw the handkerchief.

DES.   He found it, then,
I never gave it him. Send for him hither.
Let him confess a truth.

OTH.   He hath confessed.

DES. What, my lord?

OTH. That he hath used thee.

DES.   How? Unlawfully?   70

OTH. Aye.

DES. He will not say so.

OTH.   No, his mouth is stopped.
Honest Iago hath ta'en order for 't.

DES. Oh, my fear interprets! What, is he dead?

OTH. Had all his hairs been lives, my great revenge
Had stomach for them all.   75

DES. Alas, he is betrayed, and I undone!

OTH. Out, strumpet! Weep'st thou for him to my
face?

DES. Oh, banish me, my lord, but kill me not!

OTH. Down, strumpet!

DES. Kill me tomorrow, let me live tonight!   80

OTH. Nay, if you strive ——

DES. But half an hour!

OTH.   Being done, there is no pause.

DES. But while I say one prayer!

OTH.   It is too late.
[He stifles her.]

EMIL. [Within] My lord, my lord! What ho! My
lord, my lord!

OTH. What noise is this? Not dead? Not yet quite
dead?   85
I that am cruel am yet merciful,
I would not have thee linger in thy pain.
So, so.

EMIL. [Within] What ho! My lord, my lord!

OTH.   Who's there?

EMIL. [Within] Oh, good my lord, I would speak
a word with you!   90

OTH. Yes, 'tis Emilia. By and by. She's dead.
'Tis like she comes to speak of Cassio's death.
The noise was here. Ha! No more moving?
Still as the grave. Shall she come in? Were 't
good?
I think she stirs again. No. What's best to do?   95
If she come in, she'll sure speak to my wife.
My wife! My wife! What wife? I have no wife.
Oh, insupportable! Oh, heavy hour!
Methinks it should be now a huge eclipse
Of sun and moon, and that the affrighted globe   100
Should yawn at alteration.°

EMIL.   [Within] I do beseech you
That I may speak with you, O good my lord!

OTH. I had forgot thee. Oh, come in, Emilia.
Soft, by and by. Let me the curtains° draw.   104
Where art thou?   [Unlocks the door.]
[Enter EMILIA.] What's the matter with thee now?

EMIL. Oh, my good lord, yonder 's foul murders
done!

OTH. What, now?

EMIL. But now, my lord.

OTH. It is the very error° of the moon.
She comes more nearer earth than she was wont
And makes men mad.   111

EMIL. Cassio, my lord, hath killed a young Venetian
Called Roderigo.

OTH.   Roderigo killed!
And Cassio killed!

EMIL.   No, Cassio is not killed.

OTH. Not Cassio killed! Then murder's out of
tune,   115
And sweet revenge grows harsh.

DES. Oh, falsely, falsely murdered!

EMIL.   Alas, what cry is that?

OTH. That! What?

EMIL. Out and alas! That was my lady's voice.
Help! Help, ho! Help! O lady, speak again!   120
Sweet Desdemona! O sweet mistress, speak!

DES. A guiltless death I die.

EMIL. Oh, who hath done this deed?

DES. Nobody, I myself. Farewell.

---

101. yawn at alteration: gape with wonder at some monstrous
change.   104. curtains: i.e., of the bed.   109. error: wandering
out of her proper course.

52. presently: at once.   55. conception: thought.   60. warranty:
permission.   63. stone: turn to stone.

Commend me to my kind lord. Oh, farewell!   125
                                  [Dies.]
OTH. Why, how should she be murdered?
EMIL. Alas, who knows?
OTH. You heard her say herself it was not I.
EMIL. She said so. I must needs report the truth.
OTH. She's like a liar gone to burning Hell.
'Twas I that killed her.
    EMIL.   Oh, the more angel she,   130
And you the blacker devil!
    OTH. She turned to folly,° and she was a whore.
    EMIL. Thou dost belie her, and thou art a devil.
    OTH. She was false as water.
    EMIL.   Thou art rash as fire to say
That she was false. Oh, she was heavenly true!   135
    OTH. Cassio did top her, ask thy husband else.
Oh, I were damned beneath all depth in Hell
But that I did proceed upon just grounds
To this extremity. Thy husband knew it all.
    EMIL. My husband!   140
    OTH. Thy husband.
    EMIL. That she was false to wedlock?
    OTH. Aye, with Cassio. Nay, had she been true,
If Heaven would make me such another world
Of one entire and perfect chrysolite,°   145
I'd not have sold her for it.
    EMIL. My husband!
    OTH.   Aye, 'twas he that told me first.
An honest man he is, and hates the slime
That sticks on filthy deeds.
    EMIL.   My husband!
    OTH. What needs this iteration,° woman? I say
    thy husband.   150
    EMIL. Oh, mistress, villainy hath made mocks with
    love!
My husband say that she was false!
    OTH.   He, woman.
I say thy husband. Dost understand the word?
My friend, thy husband, honest, honest Iago.
    EMIL. If he say so, may his pernicious soul   155
Rot half a grain a day! He lies to the heart.
She was too fond of her most filthy bargain.
    OTH. Ha!
    EMIL. Do thy worst.
This deed of thine is no more worthy Heaven   160
Than thou wast worthy her.
    OTH.   Peace, you were best.
    EMIL. Thou hast not half that power to do me
    harm
As I have to be hurt. O gull!° O dolt!°
As ignorant as dirt! Thou hast done a deed——
I care not for thy sword, I'll make thee known,   165
Though I lost twenty lives. Help! Help, ho! Help!
The Moor hath killed my mistress! Murder! Murder!

[*Enter* MONTANO, GRATIANO, IAGO, *and others.*]
    MON. What is the matter? How now, General!
    EMIL. Oh, are you come, Iago? You have done
    well,
That men must lay their murders on your neck.   170
    GRA. What is the matter?
    EMIL. Disprove this villain, if thou be'st a man.
He says thou told'st him that his wife was false.
I know thou didst not, thou'rt not such a villain.
Speak, for my heart is full.   175
    IAGO. I told him what I thought, and told no more
Than what he found himself was apt° and true.
    EMIL. But did you ever tell him she was false?
    IAGO. I did.
    EMIL. You told a lie, an odious, damnèd lie,   180
Upon my soul, a lie, a wicked lie!
She false with Cassio! Did you say with Cassio?
    IAGO. With Cassio, mistress. Go to, charm your
    tongue.°
    EMIL. I will not charm my tongue, I am bound to
    speak.
My mistress here lies murdered in her bed.   185
    ALL. Oh, Heavens forfend!
    EMIL. And your reports have set the murder on.
    OTH. Nay, stare not, masters. It is true indeed.
    GRA. 'Tis a strange truth.
    MON. Oh, monstrous act!
    EMIL.   Villainy, villainy, villainy!   190
I think upon 't. I think I smell 't. Oh, villainy!
I thought so then.° I'll kill myself for grief.
Oh, villainy, villainy!
    IAGO. What, are you mad? I charge you, get you
    home.
    EMIL. Good gentlemen, let me have leave to
    speak.   195
'Tis proper I obey him, but not now.
Perchance, Iago, I will ne'er go home.
    OTH. Oh! Oh! Oh!   *[Falling on the bed.]*
    EMIL.   Nay, lay thee down and roar,
For thou hast killed the sweetest innocent
That e'er did lift up eye.
    OTH.   *[Rising]* Oh, she was foul!   200
I scarce did know you, Uncle. There lies your niece,
Whose breath indeed these hands have newly
    stopped.
I know this act shows horrible and grim.
    GRA. Poor Desdemona! I am glad thy father's
    dead.
Thy match was mortal° to him, and pure grief   205
Shore his old thread in twain.° Did he live now,
This sight would make him do a desperate turn—
Yea, curse his better angel from his side,

---

132. **folly:** lewdness.   145. **chrysolite:** a semiprecious stone, usually green in color.   150. **iteration:** repetition.   163. **gull:** dupe. **dolt:** dull-witted ass.

177. **apt:** likely.   183. **charm . . . tongue:** be silent.   192. **I . . . then:** i.e., I suspected this earlier—as for example when Iago took the handkerchief. See III.iii.313.   205. **match . . . mortal:** i.e., grief at this marriage killed him.   206. **Shore . . . twain:** cut his thread of life in two.

And fall to reprobation.°

OTH. 'Tis pitiful, but yet Iago knows   210
That she with Cassio hath the act of shame
A thousand times committed. Cassio confessed it.
And she did gratify his amorous works
With that recognizance° and pledge of love
Which I first gave her, I saw it in his hand.   215
It was a handkerchief, an antique token
My father gave my mother.

EMIL. Oh, Heaven! Oh, heavenly powers!

IAGO. 'Zounds! Hold your peace.

EMIL.   'Twill out, 'twill out. I peace!
No, I will speak as liberal as the north.°   220
Let Heaven and men and devils, let them all,
All, all, cry shame against me, yet I'll speak.

IAGO. Be wise, and get you home.

EMIL.   I will not. [IAGO *offers to stab* EMILIA.]

GRA.   Fie!
Your sword upon a woman!

EMIL. O thou dull Moor! That handkerchief thou
     speak'st of   225
I found by fortune and did give my husband,
For often with a solemn earnestness,
More than indeed belonged to such a trifle,
He begged of me to steal it.

IAGO.   Villainous whore!

EMIL. She give it Cassio! No, alas, I found it,   230
And I did give 't my husband.

IAGO.   Filth, thou liest!

EMIL. By Heaven, I do not, I do not, gentlemen.
Oh, murderous coxcomb!° What should such a fool
Do with so good a wife?

OTH.   Are there no stones° in Heaven
But what serve for the thunder? Precious villain!
     [*He runs at* IAGO. IAGO, *from behind,*
         stabs EMILIA, *and exit.*]

GRA. The woman falls. Sure, he hath killed his
     wife.   236

EMIL. Aye, aye. Oh, lay me by my mistress' side.

GRA. He's gone, but his wife's killed.

MON. 'Tis a notorious villain. Take you this
     weapon,
Which I have here recovered from the Moor.   240
Come, guard the door without, let him not pass,
But kill him rather. I'll after that same villain,
For 'tis a damnèd slave.
     [*Exeunt all but* OTHELLO *and* EMILIA.]

OTH.   I am not valiant neither.
But every puny whipster° gets my sword.
But why should honor outlive honesty?   245
Let it go all.

EMIL.   What did thy song bode, lady?
Hark, canst thou hear me? I will play the swan,

And die in music.° [*Singing*]
     "Willow, willow, willow."
Moor, she was chaste. She loved thee, cruel Moor,
So come my soul to bliss as I speak true.   250
So speaking as I think, I die, I die.   [*Dies.*]

OTH. I have another weapon in this chamber.
It is a sword of Spain,° the ice brook's temper.° —
Oh, here it is. Uncle, I must come forth.

GRA. [*Within*] If thou attempt it, it will cost thee
     dear.   255
Thou hast no weapon, and perforce must suffer.

OTH. Look in upon me then, and speak with me,
Or, naked° as I am, I will assault thee.
     [*Re-enter* GRATIANO.]

GRA. What is the matter?

OTH.   Behold, I have a weapon,
A better never did itself sustain   260
Upon a soldier's thigh. I have seen the day
That with this little arm and this good sword
I have made my way through more impediments
Than twenty times your stop. But, oh, vain boast!
Who can control his fate? 'Tis not so now.   265
Be not afraid, though you do see me weaponed.
Here is my journey's end, here is my butt°
And very sea mark of my utmost sail.°
Do you go back dismayed? 'Tis a lost fear.
Man but a rush° against Othello's breast,   270
And he retires. Where should Othello go?
Now, how dost thou look now? O ill-starred wench!
Pale as thy smock! When we shall meet at compt,°
This look of thine will hurl my soul from Heaven
And fiends will snatch at it. Cold, cold, my girl!
Even like thy chastity. Oh, cursèd slave!   276
Whip me, ye devils,
From the possession of this heavenly sight!
Blow me about in winds! Roast me in sulphur!
Wash me in steep-down gulfs° of liquid fire!   280
O Desdemona! Desdemona! Dead!
Oh! Oh! Oh!
     [*Enter* LODOVICO, MONTANO, CASSIO *carried in a chair,*
         and OFFICERS *with* IAGO, *prisoner.*]

LOD. Where is this rash and most unfortunate
     man?

OTH. That's he that was Othello. Here I am.

LOD. Where is that viper? Bring the villain forth.

OTH. I look down toward his feet,° but that's a
     fable.   286

---

209. reprobation: damnation; i.e., by self-murder.   214. recognizance: badge, token.   220. liberal ... north: as freely as the north wind, which is loud and bitter.   233. coxcomb: conceited fool.   **234. stones:** thunderbolts.   **244. whipster:** whippersnapper.

247–48. play ... music: i.e., I will sing at my death. It was believed that swans sang once only, just before they died. **253. sword of Spain:** Spanish swords and rapiers, from Toledo or Bilbao, were famous. ice ... temper: hardened in ice-cold water.   258. naked: unarmed.   267. butt: aim.   268. And ... sail: the mark that I have reached the end of my voyage. sea mark: a conspicuous object by which the mariner checks his course.   270. Man ... rush: attack with only a reed. **273. compt:** account; i.e., the Day of Judgment. **280. steep-down gulfs:** sheer whirlpools. **286. toward ... feet:** i.e., to see if he has the cloven hoof of a devil.

If that thou be'st a devil,° I cannot kill thee.
                                            [*Wounds* IAGO.]
  LOD. Wrench his sword from him.
  IAGO.   I bleed, sir, but not killed.
  OTH. I am not sorry neither. I'd have thee live,
For, in my sense, 'tis happiness to die.   290
  LOD. O thou Othello, that wert once so good,
Fall'n in the practice° of a damnèd slave,
What shall be said to thee?
  OTH.   Why, anything.
An honorable murderer, if you will,
For naught did I in hate, but all in honor.   295
  LOD. This wretch hath part confessed his villainy.
Did you and he consent in Cassio's death?
  OTH. Aye.
  CAS. Dear General, I never gave you cause.
  OTH. I do believe it, and I ask your pardon.   300
Will you, I pray, demand that demidevil
Why he hath thus ensnared my soul and body?
  IAGO. Demand me nothing. What you know, you
        know.
From this time forth I never will speak word.
  LOD. What, not to pray?
  GRA.   Torments will ope your lips.   305
  OTH. Well, thou dost best.
  LOD. Sir, you shall understand what hath befall'n,
Which, as I think, you know not. Here is a letter
Found in the pocket of the slain Roderigo,
And here another. The one of them imports   310
The death of Cassio to be undertook
By Roderigo.
  OTH. Oh, villain!
  CAS.   Most heathenish and most gross!
  LOD. Now here's another discontented paper,
Found in his pocket too. And this, it seems,   315
Roderigo meant to have sent this damnèd villain
But that, belike, Iago in the interim
Came in and satisfied him.
  OTH.   Oh, the pernicious caitiff!
How came you, Cassio, by that handkerchief
That was my wife's?
  CAS.   I found it in my chamber.   320
And he himself confessed but even now
That there he dropped it for a special purpose
Which wrought to his desire.
  OTH.   O fool! Fool! Fool!
  CAS. There is besides in Roderigo's letter
How he upbraids Iago, that he made him   325
Brave° me upon the watch, whereon it came
That I was cast.° And even but now he spake
After long seeming dead, Iago hurt him,
Iago set him on.
  LOD. You must forsake this room, and go with us.
Your power and your command is taken off,   331

And Cassio rules in Cyprus. For this slave,
If there be any cunning cruelty
That can torment him much and hold him long,°
It shall be his. You shall close prisoner rest   335
Till that the nature of your fault be known
To the Venetian state. Come, bring away.
  OTH. Soft you,° a word or two before you go.
I have done the state some service, and they know 't.
No more of that. I pray you, in your letters,   340
When you shall these unlucky deeds relate,
Speak of me as I am, nothing extenuate,
Nor set down aught in malice. Then must you speak
Of one that loved not wisely but too well,
Of one not easily jealous, but, being wrought,   345
Perplexed in the extreme, of one whose hand,
Like the base Indian, threw a pearl away
Richer than all his tribe° — of one whose subdued
        eyes,
Albeit unusèd to the melting mood,
Drop tears as fast as the Arabian trees   350
Their medicinal gum. Set you down this,
And say besides that in Aleppo once,
Where a malignant and a turbaned Turk
Beat a Venetian and traduced° the state,
I took by the throat the circumcisèd dog   355
And smote him, thus.   [*Stabs himself.*]
  LOD. Oh, bloody period!
  GRA.   All that's spoke is marred.°
  OTH. I kissed thee ere I killed thee. No way but
        this,
Killing myself, to die upon a kiss.
                [*Falls on the bed, and dies.*]
  CAS. This did I fear, but thought he had no
        weapon.   360
For he was great of heart.
  LOD.   [*To* IAGO] O Spartan° dog,
More fell° than anguish, hunger, or the sea!
Look on the tragic loading° of this bed,
This is thy work. The object poisons sight,
Let it be hid.° Gratiano, keep the house,   365
And seize upon the fortunes of the Moor,
For they succeed on you. To you, Lord Governor,
Remains the censure of this hellish villain,
The time, the place, the torture.
Oh, enforce it!
Myself will straight aboard, and to the state   370
This heavy act with heavy heart relate.   [*Exeunt.*]

Ghosts

by Henrik Ibsen

MRS. HELENE ALVING, *widow of Captain Alving (who died ten years ago)*

OSVALD ALVING, *their son, a painter*

PASTOR MANDERS

JAKOB ENGSTRAND, *widower (his wife was Johanna, former servant of the Alvings), a carpenter*

REGINE ENGSTRAND, *daughter of Engstrand, in Mrs. Alving's service*

SCENE — *The Alving country estate on one of the large fjords in the west of Norway.*

Act I

SCENE. *A spacious garden-room; in the left wall a door, and in the right wall two doors. In the center of the room a round table, with chairs about it. On the table lie books, periodicals and newspapers. In the foreground to the left a window, and by it a small sofa, with a work-table in front of it. In the background, the room is continued into a somewhat narrower conservatory, the walls of which are formed by large panes of glass. In the right-hand wall of the conservatory is a door leading down into the garden. Through the glass wall a gloomy fjord landscape is faintly visible, veiled by steady rain.*

ENGSTRAND, *the carpenter, stands by the garden door. His left leg is somewhat bent; he has a clump of wood under the sole of his boot.* REGINE, *with an empty garden syringe in her hand, hinders him from advancing.*

REG. [*In a low voice*] Well — what is it you want? No! — stay where you are — you're dripping wet!

ENG. It's only God's rain, my child.

REG. It's the devil's rain, that's what it is!

ENG. Lord, how you talk, Regine! [*Limping a few steps into the room*] But, here's what I want to tell you —

REG. Don't go clumping about with that foot of yours! The young master's upstairs asleep.

ENG. Asleep at this hour — in broad daylight?

REG. It's none of your business.

ENG. Now — look at *me* — I was on a bit of a spree last night —

REG. That's nothing new!

ENG. Well — we're all frail creatures, my child —

REG. We are that!

ENG. And temptations are manifold in this world, you see — but that didn't prevent me from going to work at half past five as usual!

REG. That's as it may me — and now, get out! I can't stand here having a rendezvous with you.

ENG. What's that?

REG. I don't want anyone to see you here — so get out!

ENG. [*Comes a few steps nearer*] Damned if I go till I've had a talk with you. Listen — I'll be through with my work at the school-house this afternoon — then I'm going right back to town by the night boat —

REG. [*Mutters*] A pleasant journey to you!

ENG. Thank you, my child! Tomorrow's the opening of the Orphanage, they'll all be celebrating — sure to be a lot of drinking too — I'll prove to them that Jakob Engstrand can keep out of the way of temptation —

REG. Ha! . . .

ENG. Lots of grand people'll be here — Pastor Manders is expected from town —

REG. He gets here today.

ENG. There — you see! Damned if I give *him* a chance to say anything against me!

REG. So that's it, is it?

ENG. That's what?

REG. [*Gives him a searching look*] What are you going to try and put over on him this time?

ENG. Are you crazy? As if I'd try and put anything over on *him!* No — Pastor Manders has been too good a friend to me — and that's just what I want to talk to you about. As I was saying, I'm going back home tonight —

REG. You can't go soon enough to please me!

ENG. But I want you to come with me, Regine.

REG. [*Open-mouthed*] I, go with *you?*

62

ENG. Yes — I want you to come home with me.

REG. [*Scornfully*] You'll never get me to do that!

ENG. Well — we'll see.

REG. Yes! You'll see all right! After being brought up here by Mrs. Alving — treated almost like one of the family — do you suppose I'd go home with you — back to that kind of a house? You're crazy!

ENG. What kind of talk's that! You'd defy your own father, would you?

REG. [*Mutters, without looking at him*] You've said often enough I'm no concern of yours —

ENG. Never mind about that —

REG. Many's the time you've cursed at me and called me a — Fi donc! [1]

ENG. When did I ever use a foul word like that?

REG. I know well enough what word you used!

ENG. Well — maybe — when I wasn't feeling quite myself — hm. Temptations are manifold in this world, Regine!

REG. Pah! . . .

ENG. And then your mother used to drive me crazy — I had to find some way to get back at her. She put on so many airs: [*Mimicking her*] "Let me go, Engstrand! Leave me alone! Don't forget I spent three years in Chamberlain Alving's house at Rosenvold!" [*Laughs*] God Almighty! She never got over the Captain being made Chamberlain [2] while she was working here!

REG. Poor mother! You certainly hounded her into her grave!

ENG. [*Shrugging his shoulders*] Oh, of course! I'm to blame for everything!

REG. [*Under her breath as she turns away*] Ugh! And then that leg of yours!

ENG. What did you say, my child?

REG. Pied de mouton! [3]

ENG. What's that? English?

REG. Yes.

ENG. Yes — well; you've certainly got educated here — and that may come in handy too.

REG. [*After a short silence*] Why do you want me to go back with you?

ENG. Why wouldn't a father want his only child with him? Aren't I a lonely, deserted widower?

REG. Oh, don't talk rubbish to me! Why do you want me with you?

ENG. Well — I'll tell you — I'm thinking of setting up in a new line of business —

REG. [*Whistles*] What, again! What is it this time?

ENG. You'll see — this time it'll be different. Christ Almighty — !

REG. Stop your swearing! [*She stamps her foot.*]

ENG. Sh! You're right, my child. Well — what I wanted to say was — I've managed to save quite a bit of money — from this work on the Orphanage —

REG. You have, have you? So much the better for you.

ENG. There's nothing to spend your money on in this God-forsaken hole —

REG. Well?

ENG. So I thought I'd invest it in a paying concern. I thought of starting a sort of tavern — for seamen —

REG. Ugh!

ENG. A really high-class tavern, you know — none of your cheap dives. No — by God! I'd cater to Captains and First-mates — really high-class people.

REG. And I suppose I'd be expected to —

ENG. Oh, you could be a great help, Regine. You wouldn't have to do anything — it wouldn't be hard on you, my child — you'd have everything your own way!

REG. Oh yes, of course!

ENG. After all there must be some women in the house — that goes without saying. We'd have to have a bit of fun in the evenings, singing and dancing — and that sort of thing. You've got to remember — these poor fellows are sailors — wanderers on the seas of the world. [*Comes nearer to her*] Don't be a fool and stand in your own way. What future is there for you out here? What good's all this education the Mrs. has paid for? You're to look after the kids in the new Orphanage I hear — is that a job for you? Do you want to wear yourself to the bone looking after a lot of dirty brats?

REG. If things turn out as I hope — well — it could be — it could be —

ENG. What "could be"?

REG. You keep your nose out of that! How much money did you save?

ENG. I'd say — in all — close to two hundred dollars.

REG. Not so bad!

ENG. Enough to get me started, my child.

REG. Do I get any of it?

ENG. You do not!

REG. Not even enough to buy myself a new dress?

ENG. You come with me — you'll get plenty of new dresses then!

REG. I can get them myself, if I set my mind to it.

ENG. But a father's guiding hand is a good thing, Regine. There's a nice little house right on Harbor Street — not much money down either — it'd be like a kind of Seamen's Home, you know.

REG. But I don't want to live with you! I don't want to have anything to do with you! So now — get out!

---

1. (*French*) Fie! For shame!   2. a nonhereditary title conferred by the King of Norway on men of wealth and position. Alving had held the army rank of Captain.   3. (*French*) sheep's foot, leg of lamb, applied derogatorily, of course, to a human.

ENG. You wouldn't be with me for long, my child — I know that well enough. All you've got to do is use your wits — you've turned into a handsome wench — do you know that?

REG. Well — what of it?

ENG. Before you know it, some First-mate'll come along — maybe even a Captain.

REG. I don't intend to marry any such trash. Sailors have no "savoir vivre." [4]

ENG. Well — I couldn't say about that —

REG. I tell you I know all about sailors. I wouldn't think of marrying one of them!

ENG. Who says you'd have to marry? You can make it pay just the same. [*More confidentially*] That Englishman — the one with the yacht — he gave three hundred dollars, he did — and she wasn't any better looking than you are.

REG. [*Goes towards him*] Get out of here!

ENG. [*Retreating*] Now, now! You wouldn't hit me, would you?

REG. You just say anything against Mother, and you'll see whether I'd hit you or not! Get out, I say! [*She pushes him towards the garden door.*] And don't bang the door; young Mister Alving —

ENG. Is asleep — I know! Why should you be so worried about him? [*In a lower tone*] God — Almighty! You don't mean to tell me that *he* — ?

REG. You must be out of your head — you fool! Go on now — get out this minute. No — not that way — here comes Pastor Manders; the back stairs for you!

ENG. [*Goes toward door right*] All right — I'll go. But listen — you have a talk with him — he'll tell you what you owe your father — for I am your father after all, you know; I can prove that by the Church Register.

[*He goes out through the other door that REGINE has opened for him and closes after him. She glances at herself quickly in the mirror, fans herself with her handkerchief and straightens her collar; then she sets about tending the flowers. PASTOR MANDERS enters the conservatory by the garden door. He wears an overcoat, carries an umbrella and has a small traveling-bag slung over his shoulder.*]

MAN. Good-day, Miss Engstrand.

REG. [*Turning in glad surprise*] Well! Good-day, Pastor Manders! Fancy! So the steamer's in, is it?

MAN. [*He comes into the room.*] Yes — just docked. Dreadful weather we've had these last few days.

REG. [*Following him*] It's a blessing for the farmers, Pastor Manders.

MAN. Quite right, Miss Engstrand! We city-folk never think of that. [*He begins taking off his overcoat.*]

REG. Do let me help you! My goodness! It's soak-

4. (*French*) good breeding, sophistication.

ing wet! I'll just hang it in the hall — and, let me take your umbrella — I'll open it up — so it'll dry quicker.

[*She goes out with the things by the second door on the right. MANDERS puts his traveling-bag on a chair with his hat. Meanwhile, REGINE comes in again.*]

MAN. It's very pleasant to be indoors. And how are things going here? All well, I trust?

REG. Yes — many thanks.

MAN. I expect you've been very busy with tomorrow's preparations.

REG. Yes — there's been so much to do!

MAN. And Mrs. Alving is at home, I hope?

REG. Oh yes, indeed. She just went upstairs to give the young master his hot chocolate.

MAN. Tell me — I heard down at the pier that Osvald had come home —

REG. He arrived the day before yesterday — we didn't expect him until today.

MAN. In good health and spirits, I trust?

REG. Yes, thank you, he seems to be — but dreadfully tired after his journey. He came straight through from Paris — without a stop; I mean, he came the whole way without a break. I think he's taking a little nap — so we must talk very quietly.

MAN. Sh! We'll be still as mice!

REG. [*She moves an armchair up to the table.*] Do sit down, Pastor Manders, and make yourself comfortable. [*He sits; she places a footstool under his feet.*] There! How does that feel?

MAN. Most comfortable, thank you! [*He looks at her.*] Do you know, Miss Engstrand, I really believe you've grown since I saw you last.

REG. Do you think so, Pastor Manders? Mrs. Alving says I've filled out too.

MAN. Filled out, eh? Yes, yes — perhaps a little — just suitably.

[*Short pause.*]

REG. Shall I tell Mrs. Alving you're here?

MAN. Thank you — there's no hurry, my dear child — Well — tell me, my dear Regine, how is your father getting on out here?

REG. Pretty well, thank you, Mr. Manders.

MAN. He came in to see me last time he was in town.

REG. Did he really? He's always so grateful for a talk with you, Mr. Manders.

MAN. I suppose you see him regularly, every day?

REG. I? — Oh, yes — of course — Whenever I have time — that is —

MAN. I'm afraid your father is not a very strong character, Miss Engstrand. He badly needs a guiding hand.

REG. Yes, I dare say he does, Mr. Manders.

MAN. He needs someone near him — someone he can lean on—whose judgment he respects. He admitted as much, quite candidly, last time he came to see me.

REG. Yes — he said something of the sort to me. But I don't know if Mrs. Alving would want to let me go — especially now that we'll have the Orphanage to manage. And I really couldn't bear to leave Mrs. Alving — she's always been so good to me.

MAN. But a daughter's duty, my dear child — of course, we would first have to gain Mrs. Alving's consent.

REG. But would it be quite the thing, at my age, to keep house for a single man?

MAN. What do you mean? My dear Miss Engstrand, it's a question of your own father!

REG. Yes, I know — but all the same — of course if it were a *proper* kind of house — belonging to a real gentleman —

MAN. Why — my dear Regine — !

REG. Oh, I mean a man I could look up to — respect — become attached to — as though I were really his daughter —

MAN. But, my dear child —

REG. Then I'd gladly live in town again — for I'm often very lonely here — and you know yourself, Mr. Manders, what it is to be all alone in the world. And I'm capable and willing — though I say it myself as shouldn't. Mr. Manders — I suppose you couldn't find me a position of that sort?

MAN. I? No — I'm really afraid I can't.

REG. But, you will think of me, dear, dear Mr. Manders — you'll keep me in mind in case —

MAN. [*Gets up*] Yes, yes — of course, Miss Engstrand —

REG. Because, you see — if I could only —

MAN. Would you be so kind as to tell Mrs. Alving I am here?

REG. I'll go and call her at once, Mr. Manders.

[*She goes out left.* MANDERS *paces up and down the room a couple of times, then stands for a moment upstage with his hands behind his back looking out into the garden. Then he comes back to the table, picks up a book and glances at the title page. He gives a start and examines some of the others.*]

MAN. Hm! — Well — well! Really!

[MRS. ALVING *comes in by the door left followed by* REGINE *who immediately goes out by the first door on the right.*]

MRS. ALV. [*With outstretched hand*] Welcome, dear Mr. Manders!

MAN. Good-day, Mrs. Alving. Well — here I am — as I promised.

MRS. ALV. And punctual as usual!

MAN. I had great trouble getting away. As you know — I'm chairman of so many organizations — and what with my committee meetings —

MRS. ALV. I'm all the more grateful to you for coming so promptly. Now we shall be able to get all our business settled before dinner. But, where is your luggage?

MAN. [*Hastily*] I left my things down at the Inn — I'll put up there for the night.

MRS. ALV. [*Repressing a smile*] Can't I really persuade you to spend the night here this time?

MAN. No, no, Mrs. Alving — thank you all the same — but I prefer to stay there as usual. It's so convenient — right by the pier, you know.

MRS. ALV. Well — just as you wish! I should have thought, that perhaps, at our age — !

MAN. Ah — yes, of course — you will have your little joke! Well — I suppose you're radiantly happy today — what with tomorrow's ceremony — and having Osvald home again —

MRS. ALV. Yes — isn't it wonderful! He hasn't been home for over two years, you know. And he's promised to spend the whole winter with me!

MAN. Has he really? That's a nice filial gesture — for I'm sure his life in Rome and Paris must offer many attractions.

MRS. ALV. Yes, no doubt — but after all, he has his mother here. God bless him — he still has a place in his heart for me.

MAN. It would be regrettable indeed if separation and his interest in such a thing as Art, were to interfere with his natural affections.

MRS. ALV. That's true. But fortunately, there's no danger of that with him. I'll be curious to see if you recognize him after all these years — he'll be down presently — he's just having a little rest upstairs. But — do sit down, dear Mr. Manders.

MAN. Thank you. You're sure I'm not disturbing you?

MRS. ALV. [*Sits by table*] Of course not!

MAN. Splendid — then suppose we get down to business. [*He goes to the chair and takes a bundle of papers out of his traveling-bag. Then sits down at the table opposite* MRS. ALVING. *He tries to arrange a space on which to lay out the papers.*] Now first of all there's the question of — [*Breaks off*] Tell me, Mrs. Alving — what are those books doing here?

MRS. ALV. These? I happen to be reading them.

MAN. You really read this sort of thing?

MRS. ALV. Of course I do.

MAN. Do you feel that this type of reading makes you any better — any happier?

MRS. ALV. It gives me a certain confidence.

MAN. Extraordinary! How do you mean?

MRS. ALV. It seems to clarify and confirm many things I've thought about myself. The strange thing is, Mr. Manders, there's really nothing new in any of these books; they deal with subjects that most of us think about and believe in; though I dare say most people don't take the trouble to look into them very deeply — or face them very honestly.

MAN. But, good Heavens — you don't seriously believe that most people — ?

MRS. ALV. I most emphatically do.

MAN. But surely not here — surely not *our* kind of people —

MRS. ALV. Yes! "Our kind of people " too.

MAN. Well — I really must say — !

MRS. ALV. But, what precisely do you object to in these books?

MAN. Object to? You don't imagine I waste my time delving into such subjects!

MRS. ALV. Then you're condemning them without knowing them?

MAN. I've read quite enough about these books to disapprove of them.

MRS. ALV. But, how can you form an opinion if you haven't — ?

MAN. My dear Mrs. Alving — in some things it is wiser to depend on the opinion of others. That is the way our world functions — and it is best that it should be so. Otherwise, what would become of Society?

MRS. ALV. Well — you may be right.

MAN. I don't deny that such books may have a certain fascination. And I don't blame you for wishing to familiarize yourself with certain intellectual trends which, I understand, are current in the sophisticated world where your son has been allowed to roam so freely. But —

MRS. ALV. But — ?

MAN. [*Lowering his voice*] But one doesn't discuss such things openly, Mrs. Alving. There is no reason to give an account to all and sundry of what one reads, or thinks, in the privacy of one's own room.

MRS. ALV. Certainly not — I agree with you —

MAN. Think of your new responsibilities towards the Orphanage. When you decided to found it, your feelings on certain subjects were decidedly at variance with those you now entertain — unless I am greatly mistaken.

MRS. ALV. I grant you that. But, let's get back to the Orphanage, Mr. Manders.

MAN. By all means — only, remember: caution, my dear Mrs. Alving! And now — to work! [*Opens an envelope and takes out some papers*] You see these papers — ?

MRS. ALV. The deeds?

MAN. Yes — all in order at last! I had great trouble in getting them in time. I had to bring strong pressure to bear on the authorities; they are painfully conscientious when it comes to property settlements of any kind, but here they are at last. [*Turns over the papers*] This is the deed of conveyance for that part of the Rosenvold estate known as the Sol-

vik property, together with all the newly erected buildings, the school, the teacher's house and the chapel. And here is the Charter of the Institution: " Charter of the Orphanage in memory of Captain Alving."

MRS. ALV. [*After examining the papers at some length*] That all seems clear —

MAN. I used the title "Captain" instead of "Court Chamberlain" — it seemed less ostentatious.

MRS. ALV. Whatever you think best.

MAN. Here is the bank-book controlling the invested capital — the interest on which will be used to defray the running expenses of the institution.

MRS. ALV. Thank you — you'll take charge of that, won't you?

MAN. Certainly, if you wish. For the time being, I think it would be wise to leave the entire sum in the bank — the interest is not very attractive it's true — but we could then take our time and later on find a good mortgage — it would of course have to be a first mortgage and on unexceptionable security — we can afford to take no risks — but we can discuss that matter at a later date.

MRS. ALV. Yes, dear Mr. Manders — I leave all that to you.

MAN. I'll keep a sharp look-out. Now, there's something else — I have meant to take it up with you several times.

MRS. ALV. And what is that?

MAN. The question of insurance. Do you wish me to take out insurance on the Orphanage or not?

MRS. ALV. Well of course it must be insured!

MAN. Just a moment, Mrs. Alving — let us examine the matter more carefully.

MRS. ALV. But, everything I own is insured — my house and its contents — the livestock — everything.

MAN. Your personal property, of course. All my things are insured too. But this is quite a different matter. The Orphanage is dedicated to a high spiritual purpose —

MRS. ALV. Yes, but —

MAN. As far as I am personally concerned, I can't see the slightest objection to safeguarding ourselves against all possible risks —

MRS. ALV. I quite agree.

MAN. But what about public opinion?

MRS. ALV. Public opinion — ?

MAN. Are there any groups of people here — people who matter, I mean — who might take exception to it?

MRS. ALV. What do you mean by "people who matter"?

MAN. I mean men of wealth and influence whose opinion it might be unwise to overlook.

MRS. ALV. I see what you mean — yes, there may
be a few people here who might object —

MAN. There, you see! In town I think there
might be a strong feeling against it — among my
colleagues for instance, and some of the more influential members of their congregations; it could
be implied that we hadn't sufficient faith in Divine
Providence.

MRS. ALV. But, surely, Mr. Manders, you have no
such feeling —

MAN. Oh, as far as I am personally concerned, I
have no qualms in the matter; but we might not be
able to prevent our action from being interpreted in
an erroneous and unfortunate light — and this in
turn might reflect on the work of the Orphanage.

MRS. ALV. Of course, if that were to be the case —

MAN. And I admit, I can't quite overlook the embarrassing — I might even say difficult position — I
should find myself in. In town this Orphanage has
been much discussed by the leading citizens. They
are well aware of the benefits that would accrue to
the town from such an institution — its existence
would undoubtedly reduce to an important degree
the yearly sums they are expected to donate to charitable works. And, since I have been your adviser in
this matter — your business representative from the
beginning — most of the blame and criticism would
inevitably fall on me —

MRS. ALV. I wouldn't want you to be exposed to
that.

MAN. Not to speak of the attacks that would unquestionably be made against me by certain newspapers —

MRS. ALV. That settles it, Mr. Manders — we'll
say no more about it!

MAN. Then, we decide against insurance?

MRS. ALV. Yes — we'll let that go.

MAN. [*Leaning back in his chair*] But, on the
other hand, Mrs. Alving, suppose there *should* be
an accident — one never knows — would you be
prepared to make good the damage?

MRS. ALV. No, I must tell you quite frankly, that
would be out of the question.

MAN. In that case we are assuming a very grave
responsibility.

MRS. ALV. Well — do you see anything else to do?

MAN. I'm afraid not — I don't really see that
there's anything else we *can* do; we don't want to
be placed in a false position — and we have no
right to arouse the antagonism of the Community.

MRS. ALV. Especially you — as a clergyman.

MAN. We must simply have faith that our institution will be under the special protection of Providence.

MRS. ALV. Let us hope so, Mr. Manders.

MAN. Then — we'll let it go?

MRS. ALV. By all means.

MAN. As you wish. [*Makes a note*] No insurance.

MRS. ALV. It's strange you should happen to bring
this up today —

MAN. I've often meant to discuss it with you —

MRS. ALV. Because only yesterday we nearly had a
fire down there.

MAN. What!

MRS. ALV. Nothing came of it, fortunately — some
wood-shavings caught fire — in the carpenter's
shop —

MAN. Where Engstrand works?

MRS. ALV. Yes. They say he's often very careless
with matches —

MAN. Poor man — he has so much on his mind
— so many worries. I'm happy to say he's decided
to turn over a new leaf.

MRS. ALV. Indeed? Who told you that?

MAN. He assured me so himself. I'm very glad —
he's such an excellent worker.

MRS. ALV. Yes — when he's sober.

MAN. That unfortunate weakness! He tells me it
relieves the pain in that poor leg of his. Last time
he came to see me in town, he was really very
touching. He was so grateful to me for getting him
this work here — where he could be near Regine.

MRS. ALV. I don't think he sees much of her.

MAN. Oh yes, he sees her every day — he told
me so himself.

MRS. ALV. Well — it's possible.

MAN. He realizes the need of someone near him,
to help him when temptation gets too strong for
him. That's what is so endearing about Jakob
Engstrand — he admits how weak he is — and is
so anxious to reform. Mrs. Alving — suppose it
should become a real necessity for him to have
Regine home with him again — ?

MRS. ALV. [*Rises quickly*] Regine — ?

MAN. I urge you not to oppose it.

MRS. ALV. I most certainly would oppose it! And
besides — Regine is to work at the Orphanage.

MAN. But — he *is* her father after all —

MRS. ALV. I know only too well the kind of father he is! No! She shall never go back to him while
I have anything to say in the matter!

MAN. [*Gets up*] But, my dear Mrs. Alving, why
be so violent about it! It's a great pity that you mis-
judge Engstrand so. One would think you were actually afraid —

MRS. ALV. [*More calmly*] That's not the point. I
am looking after Regine now and she will stay here
with me. [*Listens*] Sh! Dear Mr. Manders, let's not
discuss this any further. [*Her face lights up with
joy.*] Here comes Osvald. We'll think about *him*
now.

[*OSVALD ALVING enters left. He has on a light
overcoat and is carrying his hat. He is smoking a
large Meerschaum pipe.*]

osv. [*Standing in the doorway*] Oh, I'm sorry — I thought you were in the library — I didn't mean to disturb you. [*Comes in*] How do you do, Mr. Manders!

MAN. [*Stares at him*] Well, what an amazing —

MRS. ALV. What do you think of him, Mr. Manders?

MAN. Can it really be — ?

osv. Yes — it's the Prodigal Son, Mr. Manders!

MAN. My dear boy — !

osv. Or the wandering son returned to the fold — if you prefer.

MRS. ALV. He's only joking, Mr. Manders — He's referring to your disapproval of an artist's career.

MAN. We are not infallible in our judgments; certain steps may seem to us dangerous that turn out in the end to be — [*Shakes hands with him*] So, welcome! Welcome home, my dear Osvald! — I may still call you Osvald, I trust?

osv. What else should you call me, Mr. Manders?

MAN. Splendid! — I was just going to say — you must not imagine, my dear Osvald, that I unconditionally condemn the artist's life. I dare say there are many who succeed, in spite of everything, in preserving their integrity of character.

osv. Let us hope so!

MRS. ALV. [*Beaming with pleasure*] Well — this one's managed to do so, Mr. Manders — you've only to look at him to see that.

osv. [*Pacing the room*] There, there — Mother, dear — never mind — !

MAN. Yes, fortunately, that's undeniable! And you've begun to make quite a name for yourself. I've often seen you mentioned in the papers, and always most favorably. Though recently I haven't seen so much about your work.

osv. [*Going up to the conservatory*] No — I haven't done much painting lately.

MRS. ALV. Even an artist needs to rest now and then.

MAN. Most understandable — At such times you gather new strength, for even finer work.

osv. Quite so — Will dinner be ready soon, Mother?

MRS. ALV. In half an hour, dear. There's nothing wrong with his appetite, thank God!

MAN. And I see he's partial to tobacco too.

osv. I found this old pipe of Father's up in his study —

MAN. Oh — so that accounts for it!

MRS. ALV. How do you mean?

MAN. When Osvald came in just now — with that pipe in his mouth — I thought for a moment it was his father come to life again.

osv. Really?

MRS. ALV. How can you say that! Osvald takes after me.

MAN. Yes — perhaps; but, still, there's something about his mouth — something in the expression — that reminds me very strongly of Alving — especially when he smokes.

MRS. ALV. I don't see it at all — Osvald's mouth is much more sensitive. There's something almost ascetic about it.

MAN. It's true — some of my colleagues have a similar expression.

MRS. ALV. But put down your pipe now, Osvald, dear. I don't allow smoking in this room.

osv. [*Puts down the pipe*] Very well, Mother. I only wanted to try it; I smoked it once before you see — when I was a child.

MRS. ALV. *You* did?

osv. Yes — I was very little at the time — I remember I went up to Father's study one evening; he was in a very gay, jolly mood.

MRS. ALV. How could you possibly remember? It's so long ago!

osv. Oh, but I do! I remember it very distinctly; he sat me on his knee and told me to smoke his pipe: Smoke, Son, he said — go on, Son — have a good smoke; so I smoked away with all my might, until I felt deathly ill and great beads of perspiration stood out on my forehead. He thought it was very funny. I remember he roared with laughter at me.

MAN. What a very odd thing to do!

MRS. ALV. It's a lot of nonsense. Osvald must have dreamed it.

osv. No, Mother, I assure you I didn't! Don't you remember, you came in and rushed me off to the nursery. And then I was sick — and I noticed you'd been crying — I suppose it *was* rather odd — did Father often play tricks like that?

MAN. He was a great joker in his young days.

osv. Yet think of all the good he did. The fine and useful things he was able to accomplish — though he died comparatively young.

MAN. Yes — you have a fine heritage, Osvald Alving. It should be a great incentive to you!

osv. Yes, you're right! Indeed it should.

MAN. And it was good of you to come home for the ceremony tomorrow.

osv. That's the least I could do for Father's memory.

MRS. ALV. And he plans to stay here for a while — that's the nicest thing of all!

MAN. Yes, I understand you intend to spend the winter here.

osv. I plan to stay here indefinitely, Mr. Manders. It's so good to be home again!

MRS. ALV. [*Beaming*] Yes, it is, isn't it, dear?

MAN. [*Looks at him sympathetically*] You were very young when you left home, my dear Osvald.

osv. A little too young, perhaps.

MRS. ALV. What nonsense! It's good for a strong healthy boy — especially an only child — to get away from home. Much better than being petted and spoiled by doting parents!

MAN. I think that is open to debate, Mrs. Alving. A home and parents are still a child's best refuge.

OSV. I'm inclined to agree with Mr. Manders there.

MAN. Take your own son here as an example — there's no harm in discussing it before him — what has been the result in his case? Here he is, twenty-three or twenty-four years old, and he has never yet known what a normal, well-regulated home can be.

OSV. I beg your pardon, Mr. Manders — you're quite wrong in that.

MAN. Really? But, I thought you'd been living exclusively in artistic circles.

OSV. So I have.

MAN. And mostly among the younger artists, I believe.

OSV. Quite right.

MAN. But surely the majority of such people are in no position to found a home and family.

OSV. Most of them are in no position to get married — that's true enough —

MAN. That's just what I say —

OSV. But that doesn't necessarily mean that they can't have homes of their *own* — and many of them have — very comfortable and well-run homes too.

[MRS. ALVING, *who has been listening attentively, nods in agreement but says nothing.*]

MAN. I'm not thinking of bachelor-establishments; when I use the word "home." I mean a family — a home where a man lives with his wife and children.

OSV. Or with his children — and their mother.

MAN. [*With a start, clasping his hands*] Good Heavens!

OSV. Well?

MAN. — lives with — with — his children's mother!

OSV. Would you rather he abandoned her?

MAN. Then you're speaking of illegal unions — dissolute relationships — !

OSV. I've never noticed anything especially dissolute in the lives these people lead.

MAN. How can any decent young man or woman possibly degrade themselves by living openly in such shameful circumstances!

OSV. Well — what do you expect them to do? A poor young artist — a poor young girl — marriage is an expensive business — what do you expect them to do?

MAN. I would expect them to resist temptation, Mr. Alving — to part before it is too late.

OSV. That's a lot to expect of young people in love, Mr. Manders.

MRS. ALV. Indeed it is!

MAN. [*Persistently*] And to think that the authorities put up with such behavior — that it should be openly tolerated. [*To* MRS. ALVING] You see how right I was to be concerned about your son. Living in circles where such rampant immorality prevails, where it's taken for granted, one might say —

OSV. Let me tell you something, Mr. Manders — I've spent many a Sunday at some of these "illegal homes" — as you call them —

MAN. On a Sunday too — !

OSV. Sunday happens to be a holiday — I've never once heard a single vulgar or indecent word — nor have I ever witnessed any behavior that could possibly be called immoral. But do you know when and where I *have* met with such behavior?

MAN. No! God forbid!

OSV. Then permit me to tell you: When some of your highly respected citizens — your model fathers and husbands from back home here — when they take a trip abroad to "see a bit of life" — when *they* condescend to honor us poor artists with their presence — then you would see "rampant immorality" if you like! These respectable gentlemen could tell us about things that we had never even dreamed of!

MAN. You dare imply that honorable men here from home — ?

OSV. You must have heard these same "honorable men" when they get safely home again, hold forth on the outrageous immorality that prevails abroad?

MAN. Of course I have.

MRS. ALV. I've heard them too —

OSV. Well you may take their word for it! They speak with true authority! [*Clutches his head in his hands*] It's an outrage that that free and beautiful life should be distorted by their filth!

MRS. ALV. Don't get so excited, Osvald. It's bad for you.

OSV. You're right, Mother. It's bad for me I know — it's just that I'm so tired. I think I'll take a little walk before dinner. Forgive me, Mr. Manders — I shouldn't have let go like that. I know you can't possibly understand my feelings. [*He goes out by the upstage door right.*]

MRS. ALV. Poor boy!

MAN. You may well say so! — That he should have sunk to this! [MRS. ALVING *looks at him in silence.* MANDERS *paces up and down.*] He called himself the Prodigal Son — Tragic! — Tragic! [MRS. ALVING *continues to look at him silently.*] And what do you say to all this?

MRS. ALV. I say Osvald was right in every word he said.

MAN. [*Stops pacing*] Right? — You mean you agree to such principles?

MRS. ALV. Living here alone all these years, I've come to the same conclusions — but I've never put my thoughts into words — Well — now my boy can speak for me.

MAN. You are greatly to be pitied, Mrs. Alving! — I have always had your best interests at heart; for many years I have advised you in business matters; for many years I have been your friend and your late husband's friend; as your spiritual adviser I once saved you from a reckless and foolhardy action; and it is as your spiritual adviser that I now feel it my duty to talk to you with the utmost solemnity.

MRS. ALV. And what have you to say to me, as my "spiritual adviser," Mr. Manders?

MAN. Look back over the years — it's appropriate that you should do so today, for tomorrow is the tenth anniversary of your husband's death and his Memorial will be unveiled; tomorrow I shall speak to the crowd assembled in his honor — but today I must speak to you alone.

MRS. ALV. I'm listening.

MAN. You had been married scarcely a year when you took the step that might have wrecked your life: You left house and home and ran away from your husband — yes, Mrs. Alving, ran away — and refused to go back to him in spite of all his entreaties.

MRS. ALV. I was miserably unhappy that first year — don't forget that.

MAN. What right have we to expect happiness in this life? It is the sign of a rebellious spirit — No! Mrs. Alving, we are here to do our duty, and it was your duty to stay with the man you had chosen and to whom you were bound in Holy Matrimony.

MRS. ALV. You know the kind of life Alving led in those days; his dissipation — his excesses —

MAN. It's true, I heard many rumors about him — and had those rumors been true, I should have been the first to condemn his conduct at that time; but it is not a wife's place to judge her husband; your duty was to resign yourself and bear your cross with true humility. But you rebelled against it and instead of giving your husband the help and support he needed, you deserted him, and by so doing jeopardized your own good name and reputation — and that of others too.

MRS. ALV. Of "others"? Of *one*, you mean.

MAN. It was highly imprudent to come to me, of all people, for help.

MRS. ALV. But why? Weren't you our "spiritual adviser" as well as our friend?

MAN. All the more reason. You should go down on your knees and thank God that I found the necessary strength of mind to dissuade you from your reckless purpose, to guide you back to the path of duty, and home to your husband.

MRS. ALV. Yes, Mr. Manders — that was certainly your doing.

MAN. I was merely an instrument in God's hand. And, as I had foreseen — once you had returned to your duties, and humbled your spirit in obedience — you were repaid an hundredfold. Alving reformed entirely, and remained a good and loving husband to the end of his days. He became a real benefactor to this whole community, and he allowed you to share, as his fellow-worker, in all his enterprises — and a very able fellow-worker too — I am aware of that, Mrs. Alving — I must pay you that tribute; but now I come to the second great error of your life.

MRS. ALV. What do you mean by that?

MAN. You first betrayed your duty as a wife — you later betrayed your duty as a mother.

MRS. ALV. Ah — !

MAN. All your life you have been possessed by a willful, rebellious spirit. Your natural inclinations always led you toward the undisciplined and lawless. You could never tolerate the slightest restraint; you have always disregarded any responsibility — carelessly and unscrupulously — as though it were a burden you had a right to cast aside. It no longer suited you to be a wife — so you left your husband. The cares of motherhood were too much for you — so you sent your child away to be brought up by strangers.

MRS. ALV. That's true — I did do that.

MAN. And for that reason you are now a stranger to him.

MRS. ALV. No! No! I'm not!

MAN. Of course you are! How could you be otherwise? And now you see the result of your conduct. You have much to atone for; you were guilty as a wife, Mrs. Alving, you failed your husband miserably — you are seeking to atone for that by raising this Memorial in his honor; how are you going to atone for your failure towards your son? It may not be too late to save him: by redeeming yourself — you may still help him to redemption! I warn you! [*With raised forefinger*] You are guilty as a mother, Mrs. Alving. I felt it my duty to tell you this.

[*Pause.*]

MRS. ALV. [*Slowly, with great control*] I have listened to you talk, Mr. Manders. Tomorrow you will be making speeches in my husband's honor; I shall not make any speeches tomorrow; but now I intend to talk to you — just as frankly — just as brutally — as you have talked to me!

MAN. Of course — it's natural that you should try and justify your conduct.

MRS. ALV. No — I only want to make a few things clear to you.

MAN. Well?

MRS. ALV. You've just talked a great deal about my married life after you — as you put it — "led me back to the path of duty." What do you really know about it? From that day on you never set foot inside our house — you who had been our closest friend —

MAN. But, you and your husband left town, immediately afterwards —

MRS. ALV. And you never once came out here to see us during my husband's lifetime. It wasn't until this Orphanage business, that you felt compelled to visit me.

MAN. [*In a low uncertain tone*] If that is meant as a reproach, my dear Helene, I beg you to consider —

MRS. ALV. — that in your position you had to protect your reputation! After all — I was a wife who had tried to leave her husband! One can't be too careful with such disreputable women!

MAN. My dear! — Mrs. Alving — what a gross exaggeration!

MRS. ALV. Well — never mind about that — the point is this: your opinions of my married life are based on nothing but hearsay.

MAN. That may be so — what then?

MRS. ALV. Just this: that now, Manders, I am going to tell you the truth! I swore to myself that one day I would tell it to you — to you alone!

MAN. Well? And what is the truth?

MRS. ALV. The truth is this: My husband continued to be a depraved profligate to the day of his death.

MAN. [*Feeling for a chair*] What did you say?

MRS. ALV. After nineteen years of marriage — just as depraved, just as dissolute — as he was the day you married us.

MAN. How can you use such words — !

MRS. ALV. They are the words our doctor used.

MAN. I don't understand you.

MRS. ALV. It's not necessary that you should.

MAN. I can't take it in. You mean — that this seemingly happy marriage — those long years of comradeship — all that was only a pretense — to cover up this hideous abyss?

MRS. ALV. That is just exactly what it was — nothing else.

MAN. But — it's inconceivable — I can't grasp it! How was it possible to — ? How could the truth remain concealed?

MRS. ALV. My life became one long fight to that end: After Osvald was born, Alving seemed to me a little better — but it didn't last long! And then I had to fight for my son as well: I was determined that no living soul should ever know the kind of father my boy had — As a matter of fact, you know how charming Alving could be — it was hard for people to think ill of him. He was one of those fortunate men whose private lives never seem to damage their public reputation. But then, Manders — I want you to know the whole story — then the most horrible thing of all happened.

MAN. How could anything be worse than — ?

MRS. ALV. I knew well enough all that was going on — and I put up with it as long as I didn't have to see it — but, when I was faced with it here — in my own home — !

MAN. Here?

MRS. ALV. Yes — in this very house. The first time I became aware of it, I was in there — [*Points to the downstage door right*] in the dining room — I was busy with something, and the door was ajar — then I heard the maid come up from the garden with water for the plants —

MAN. Yes?

MRS. ALV. In a few moments, I heard Alving come in after her — he said something to her in a low voice — and then I heard — [*With a short laugh*] it still rings in my ears — it was so horrible, and yet somehow so ludicrous — I heard my own servant-girl whisper: "Let me go, Mr. Alving! — Leave me alone!"

MAN. But he couldn't have meant anything by it, Mrs. Alving — believe me — I'm sure he didn't — !

MRS. ALV. I soon found out what to believe: My husband had his way with the girl, and there were — consequences, Mr. Manders.

MAN. [*As though turned to stone*] To think — that in this house — !

MRS. ALV. I had been through a lot in this house! Night after night — in order to keep him home — I sat up in his study with him — pretending to join him in his private drinking-bouts. I sat there alone with him for hours on end listening to his obscene, senseless talk — I had to struggle with him — fight with sheer brute force — in order to drag him to his bed.

MAN. [*Shaken*] How were you able to endure all this?

MRS. ALV. I had to endure it — I had my little boy to think of. But when I discovered this final outrage — with a servant — in our own house — ! That was the end. From that day on I became master here. I took full control — over him and over everything. Alving didn't dare say a word — he knew he was in my power. It was then I decided to send Osvald away. He was nearly seven and was beginning to notice things and ask questions, as children do. This I could not endure, Manders. I felt the child would be poisoned in this sordid, degraded home. That's why I sent him away. Now perhaps you understand why I never let him set foot in this house as long as his father was alive. What you could never understand — is what agony it was to have to do it!

MAN. To think of all you have been through — !

MRS. ALV. I could never have stood it if I hadn't had my work. For I can honestly say I have worked! Alving received all the praise — all the credit — but don't imagine he had anything to do with it! The increase in the value of our property — the improvements — all those fine enterprises you spoke of — all that was *my* work. All he did was to sprawl on the sofa in his study reading old newspapers. In his few lucid moments I did try to spur him to some effort — but it was no use. He sank back again into his old habits and then spent days in a maudlin state of penitence and self-pity.

MAN. And you're building a Memorial to such a man — ?

MRS. ALV. That's what comes of having a bad conscience.

MAN. A bad — ? What do you mean?

MRS. ALV. It seemed to me inevitable that the truth must come out, and that people would believe it; so I decided to dedicate this Orphanage to Alving — in order to dispel once and for all any possible rumors — any possible doubts.

MAN. You've fully succeeded in that.

MRS. ALV. But I had another reason: I didn't want my son to inherit anything whatsoever from his father.

MAN. I see — so you used Alving's money to — ?

MRS. ALV. Precisely. The money that has gone into the Orphanage amounts to the exact sum — I've calculated it very carefully — to the exact sum of the fortune, that once made people consider Lt. Alving a good match.

MAN. I understand you.

MRS. ALV. I sold myself for that sum. I don't want Osvald to touch a penny of it. Everything he has will come from me — everything!

[OSVALD *enters from the door upstage right. He has left his hat and coat outside.*]

MRS. ALV. [*Goes toward him*] Back already, dear?

OSV. Yes — what can one do — out in this everlasting rain! But I hear dinner's nearly ready — splendid!

[REGINE *enters from the dining room carrying a small parcel.*]

REG. This parcel just came for you, Mrs. Alving. [*Hands her the parcel.*]

MRS. ALV. [*With a glance at* MANDERS] Ah! The songs for tomorrow's ceremony, I expect.

MAN. Hm —

REG. And dinner is served, Mrs. Alving.

MRS. ALV. Good; we'll be there in a moment. I just want to see —

REG. [*To* OSVALD] Would you like red or white wine, Mr. Alving?

OSV. Both, by all means, Miss Engstrand.

REG. Bien — Very good, Mr. Alving. [*Exits into dining room.*]

OSV. Let me help you uncork it — [*Follows her into the dining room, half closing the door.*]

MRS. ALV. [*Who has opened the parcel*] Yes — just as I thought — the songs for tomorrow, Mr. Manders.

MAN. [*Clasping his hands*] How I shall ever have the courage to make my speech tomorrow — !

MRS. ALV. You'll manage — somehow.

MAN. [*Softly, so as not to be heard in the dining room*] It would never do to arouse suspicion —

MRS. ALV. [*Quietly but firmly*] No — And from tomorrow on, I shall be free at last — the long, hideous farce will be over — I shall forget that such a person as Alving ever lived in this house — there'll be no one here but my son and me.

[*The noise of a chair being overturned is heard from the dining room — at the same time* REGINE's *voice.*]

REG.'s VOICE. [*In a sharp whisper*] Osvald! — Are you mad? — Let me go!

MRS. ALV. [*Stiffens with horror*] Ah — !

[*She gazes distractedly at the half-open door.* OSVALD *is heard coughing and humming a tune — then the sound of a bottle being uncorked.*]

MAN. [*In agitation*] But what *is* all this? What's the *matter*, Mrs. Alving?

MRS. ALV. [*Hoarsely*] Ghosts — Those two in the conservatory — Ghosts — They've come to life again!

MAN. What do you mean? Regine — ? Is *she* — ?

MRS. ALV. Yes — Come — Not a word!

[*She takes* MANDERS' *arm and goes falteringly towards the dining room.*]

CURTAIN

Act II

SCENE. *The same room. The landscape is still shrouded in rain and mist.* MANDERS *and* MRS. ALVING *enter from the dining room.*

MRS. ALV. [*In the doorway, calls back into the dining room*] Aren't you coming too, Osvald?

OSV. [*Off stage*] No, thanks; I think I'll go out for a bit.

MRS. ALV. Yes, do, dear; I think it's cleared up a little. [*She closes the dining room door, crosses to the hall door and calls.*] Regine!

REG. [*Off stage*] Yes, Mrs. Alving?

MRS. ALV. Go down to the laundry and help them with the wreaths.

REG. Very well, Mrs. Alving.

[MRS. ALVING *makes sure that* REGINE *has gone and then closes the door.*]

MAN. You're sure he can't hear us in there?

MRS. ALV. Not with the door shut — besides, he's going out.

MAN. I'm still so overcome. I don't know how I managed to eat a morsel of that delicious food.

MRS. ALV. [*In suppressed anguish, pacing up and down*] No — Well — what's to be done?

MAN. What's to be done indeed? I wish I knew what to suggest — I don't feel competent to deal with a crisis of this sort.

MRS. ALV. One thing I'm convinced of — that, so far, nothing serious has happened.

MAN. God forbid! — But it's a shameful business all the same.

MRS. ALV. It's just a foolish whim on Osvald's part; I'm sure of that.

MAN. As I said before — I have no experience in such things — but I can't help thinking —

MRS. ALV. One thing's clear: she must leave this house at once — before it's too late.

MAN. That goes without saying.

MRS. ALV. But where can she go? We certainly wouldn't be justified in —

MAN. She must go home to her father, of course.

MRS. ALV. To whom — did you say?

MAN. To her — But of course. Engstrand isn't her — Good Heavens, Mrs. Alving — all this is impossible — there must be some mistake!

MRS. ALV. I'm afraid there is no mistake, Manders. The girl confessed to me herself. And Alving didn't deny it; so the only thing we could do was to try and hush the matter up.

MAN. Yes — I suppose so.

MRS. ALV. The girl left my service at once and was given a handsome sum to keep her mouth shut. She then took matters into her own hands — went back to town and renewed an old friendship with the carpenter, Engstrand. She hinted that she had money — told him some cock-and-bull story about a foreigner with a yacht — the outcome of all this was, that they were married in great haste. You married them yourself, I believe.

MAN. But — I can't understand it! I remember distinctly Engstrand coming to arrange about the wedding: He was overcome with confusion — and kept reproaching himself bitterly for his and his fiancée's shameless behavior.

MRS. ALV. Well — I suppose he had to take the blame on himself.

MAN. I certainly never would have believed Jakob Engstrand capable of such duplicity — and to me of all people! I shall have to teach him a good les-son, I can see that — The immorality of such a marriage — and for money too! How much did the girl receive?

MRS. ALV. Three hundred dollars.

MAN. It's almost unbelievable — for a paltry three hundred dollars — consenting to marry a loose woman.

MRS. ALV. What about me? Didn't I marry a " loose " man?

MAN. What on earth are you talking about!

MRS. ALV. Was Alving any better when he married me, than the girl Johanna was when she married Engstrand?

MAN. But — good Heavens — the two cases are utterly different —

MRS. ALV. Perhaps not so very different, after all. There was a colossal difference in the price — that's true enough! A paltry three hundred dollars as against a large fortune.

MAN. But there *can* be no comparison in this instance! Your decision was based on the advice of relatives and friends — as well as the promptings of your heart.

MRS. ALV. [*Without looking at him*] My heart, as you call it, was involved elsewhere at the time — as I thought you knew.

MAN. [*In a reserved tone*] Had I known any such thing, I should not have been a constant visitor in your husband's house.

MRS. ALV. One thing is certain; I never really consulted my own feelings in the matter.

MAN. Perhaps not — but you consulted your mother — your two aunts — all those nearest to you — as was only right.

MRS. ALV. Yes — those three! They were the ones that settled the whole business for me. As I look back on it, it seems incredible. They pointed out, in the most forceful terms, that it would be nothing short of folly to refuse an offer of such magnificence! Poor Mother. If she only knew what that " magnificence " has led to.

MAN. No one can be held responsible for the outcome — The fact remains, that your marriage in every way conformed to the strictest rules of law and order.

MRS. ALV. [*At the window*] All this talk about law and order! — I often think all the suffering in the world is due to that.

MAN. That is a very wicked thing to say, Mrs. Alving.

MRS. ALV. That may be; but I will not be bound by these responsibilities, these hypocritical conventions any longer — I simply cannot! I must **work** my way through to freedom.

MAN. What do you mean by that?

MRS. ALV. [*Drumming on the windowpane*] I should never have lied about Alving — but I didn't dare do anything else at the time — and it wasn't only for Osvald's sake — it was for my own sake too. What a coward I've been!

MAN. A coward?

MRS. ALV. A coward, yes — I could just hear what people would say if they found out the truth: Poor man! One can hardly blame him with a wife like that! She tried to leave him, you know!

MAN. They would have been justified to some extent.

MRS. ALV. [*Looking at him steadily*] If I'd had the strength I should have taken Osvald into my confidence; I should have said: Listen, my son, your father was a corrupt, contaminated man —

MAN. Good God — !

MRS. ALV. And then I should have told him the whole story — word for word — just as I told it to you.

MAN. You horrify me, Mrs. Alving!

MRS. ALV. I know — God, yes! — I know! — I'm horrified myself at the thought of it! — That's how much of a coward I am.

MAN. How can you call yourself a coward for doing what was merely your duty? Have you forgotten that a child should love and honor his father and mother?

MRS. ALV. Don't let us talk in generalities! Let us ask: Should Osvald love and honor Captain Alving?

MAN. You're his mother — how could you find it in your heart to shatter his ideals?

MRS. ALV. Oh — ideals, ideals! What about the Truth? — If only I weren't such a coward!

MAN. You shouldn't scoff at ideals, Mrs. Alving — they have a way of avenging themselves. God knows — Osvald doesn't seem to have many — unfortunately. But his father seems to be somewhat of an ideal to him.

MRS. ALV. Yes, that's quite true.

MAN. Your letters must be responsible for that feeling in him — you must have fostered it.

MRS. ALV. Yes. I was treading the path of duty and obedience, Mr. Manders — I therefore lied to my son, religiously, year after year. What a coward — what a coward I was!

MAN. You have fostered a happy illusion in your son's mind, Mrs. Alving — you shouldn't underestimate its value.

MRS. ALV. Its value may turn out to be dubious, who knows? But I won't tolerate any nonsense with Regine — he mustn't be allowed to get her into trouble.

MAN. Good Heavens, no — that would be unthinkable!

MRS. ALV. If I thought she would really make him happy — if he were really serious about it —

MAN. What do you mean?

MRS. ALV. Oh, but he couldn't be — Regine could never be enough for him —

MAN. What are you talking about?

MRS. ALV. If I weren't such a miserable coward I'd say to him: marry her — come to any arrangement you like with her — only be honest about it!

MAN. A marriage between them — ? How could you condone anything so abominable — so unheard of!

MRS. ALV. Unheard of, you say? Why not face the truth, Manders? You know there are dozens of married couples out here in the country who are related in the same way.

MAN. I refuse to understand you.

MRS. ALV. But you *do* understand me all the same!

MAN. There may be a few instances — family life is not always as blameless as it should be, unfortunately. But in nine cases out of ten the relationship is unsuspected — or at worst, unconfirmed. Here — on the other hand — That you, a mother, should be willing to allow your son — !

MRS. ALV. But I'm *not* willing to allow it — that's just what I'm saying — I wouldn't allow it for anything in the world.

MAN. Only because you're a coward — as you express it. But if you weren't a coward — ! Such a revolting marriage — God forgive you!

MRS. ALV. We're all of us descended from that kind of marriage — so they say. And who was responsible for that arrangement, Mr. Manders?

MAN. I refuse to discuss these matters with you, Mrs. Alving — you are in no fit state to touch on such things — How you can have the effrontery to call yourself a coward for not — !

MRS. ALV. I'll tell you what I mean by that; I live in constant fear and terror, because I can't rid myself of all these ghosts that haunt me.

MAN. Ghosts, you say?

MRS. ALV. Yes — Just now, when I heard Regine and Osvald in there — I felt hemmed in by ghosts — You know, Manders, the longer I live the more convinced I am that we're all haunted in this world — not only by the things we inherit from our parents — but by the ghosts of innumerable old prejudices and beliefs — half-forgotten cruelties and betrayals — we may not even be aware of them — but they're there just the same — and we can't get rid of them. The whole world is haunted by these ghosts of the dead past; you have only to pick up a newspaper to see them weaving in and out between the lines — Ah! if we only had the courage to sweep them all out and let in the light!

MAN. So this is the result of all this reading of yours — this detestable, pernicious, free-thinking literature!

MRS. ALV. You're mistaken, my dear Manders. It

was you who first goaded me into thinking — I shall always be grateful to you for that.

MAN. I?

MRS. ALV. Yes. When you forced me to obey what you called my conscience and my duty; when you hailed as right and noble what my whole soul rebelled against as false and ugly — that's when I started to analyze your teachings; that's when I first started to *think*. And one day I saw quite clearly that all that you stand for — all that you preach — is artificial and dead — there's no life or truth in it.

MAN. [*Softly, with emotion*] So that's all I achieved by the hardest struggle of my life.

MRS. ALV. I'd call it your most ignominious defeat.

MAN. It was a victory over myself, Helene; my greatest victory.

MRS. ALV. It was a crime against us both.

MAN. The fact that by my entreaties I persuaded you to return to your lawful husband, when you came to me distracted and overwrought crying: "Here I am. Take me!" You consider that a crime?

MRS. ALV. Yes; I think it was.

MAN. There is no possible understanding between us.

MRS. ALV. Not any more, at any rate.

MAN. You have always been to me — even in my most secret thoughts — another man's wife.

MRS. ALV. You really believe that, Manders?

MAN. Helene — !

MRS. ALV. It's so easy to forget one's feelings!

MAN. I don't forget. I am exactly the same as I always was.

MRS. ALV. [*With a change of tone*] Oh, don't let's talk any more about the old days! Now you're up to your eyes in committee meetings and advisory boards — and I sit out here and battle with ghosts — the ghosts within myself and those all around me.

MAN. Those around you, I can at least help you to conquer. After the dreadful things you've said to me today, I couldn't dream of leaving a young, unprotected girl alone in your house.

MRS. ALV. I think the best thing would be to arrange a good match for her — don't you agree?

MAN. Unquestionably. It would be best for her in every respect. Regine has reached the age when — of course, I know very little about these things —

MRS. ALV. Yes — she developed early.

MAN. So it seemed to me. I remember thinking when I prepared her for Confirmation, that she was remarkably well developed for a child of her age. For the present she had better go home, under her father's care — but, of course, Engstrand isn't — How could he — *he* of all people — conceal the truth from me!

[*There is a knock at the hall door.*]

MRS. ALV. Who can *that* be? Come in!

[ENGSTRAND *appears in the doorway; he is in his Sunday clothes.*]

ENG. I most humbly beg pardon — but —

MRS. ALV. Oh, it's you, Engstrand.

ENG. None of the maids seemed to be about — so I took the liberty of knocking, Ma'am —

MRS. ALV. Oh, very well — come in. Do you wish to speak to me?

ENG. [*Coming in*] No — thank you all the same, Mrs. Alving. But — if I might have a word with the Reverend —

MAN. [*Pacing up and down*] With me — eh? So you want to talk to me, do you?

ENG. I'd be most grateful —

MAN. [*Stopping in front of him*] Well — what is it?

ENG. It's just this, Sir; we're being paid off down there — and many thanks to you, Ma'am — our work's all finished; and, I thought how nice and helpful it would be to all of us who've worked together so hard and faithfully — if we could have a few prayers this evening.

MAN. Prayers? — Down at the Orphanage?

ENG. Yes, Sir; of course if it isn't convenient to you, Sir —

MAN. Oh, it's convenient enough — but — hm —

ENG. I've taken to saying a few prayers myself down there of an evening —

MRS. ALV. *You* have?

ENG. Yes — now and then; we can all do with a little edification, I thought; but I'm just a simple, humble fellow — I'm not much good at it, God help me! But as long as the Reverend happened to be here — I thought —

MAN. Look here, Engstrand; I must first ask you a question: Are you in a proper state of mind for prayer? Have you a clear untroubled conscience?

ENG. God help me! Perhaps we'd better not talk about my conscience, Mr. Manders.

MAN. That's exactly what we must talk about. Well — answer me!

ENG. Well, Sir — of course, now and then, it does trouble me a bit —

MAN. I'm glad you admit that at least. Now — will you be so kind as to tell me honestly — what is the truth about Regine?

MRS. ALV. [*Rapidly*] Mr. Manders!

MAN. [*Calming her*] I'll handle this —

ENG. Regine! — Lord, how you frightened me! [*Gives* MRS. ALVING *a look*] There's nothing wrong with Regine, is there?

MAN. It is to be hoped not. But what I mean is this: What is your true relationship to Regine? You pretend to be her father, do you not?

ENG. [*Uncertain*] Yes — hm — well, Sir — you know all about me and poor Johanna —

MAN. No more prevarication, please! Your late wife confessed the whole truth to Mrs. Alving before she left her service.

ENG. Do you mean to say she — ? Oh, she did, did she?

MAN. Yes; so it's no use lying any longer, Engstrand.

ENG. Well! And after her swearing up and down —

MAN. Swearing, you say — ?

ENG. I mean, she gave me her solemn word, Sir.

MAN. And all these years you've kept the truth from me — from *me,* who have always had the utmost faith in you!

ENG. Yes, Sir — I'm afraid I have.

MAN. Have I deserved that, Engstrand? Haven't I always done everything in my power to help you? Answer me — haven't I?

ENG. Yes, Sir. Things would often have looked pretty black for me, if it hadn't been for Mr. Manders.

MAN. And this is how you repay me! You cause me to enter erroneous statements in the Church Register, and withhold from me for years the truth which it was your duty to impart to me. Your conduct has been inexcusable, Engstrand; from now on, I shall have nothing more to do with you.

ENG. [*With a sigh*] Yes, Sir; I suppose that's how it has to be!

MAN. I don't see how you can possibly justify your conduct.

ENG. We felt it better not to add to her shame by talking about it. Supposing you'd been in poor Johanna's place, Mr. Manders —

MAN. I!

ENG. Lord bless me! I don't mean that the way it sounds! What I mean is: suppose you had done something you were ashamed of in the eyes of the world, as they say; we men oughtn't to judge a poor woman too hard, Mr. Manders.

MAN. But I don't judge her — it's *you* I'm accusing.

ENG. Mr. Manders, would you allow me to ask you just one little question?

MAN. Very well — what is it?

ENG. Shouldn't a decent honorable man help those who've gone astray?

MAN. Well — naturally —

ENG. And isn't a man bound to keep his word of honor?

MAN. Yes, of course, but —

ENG. Well — you see, after Johanna got into trouble with that Englishman — or maybe he was American — or one of those Russians even — anyway, she came back to town. Poor thing — she'd already refused me twice; she only had eyes for the handsome fellows — and, of course, I had this deformed leg of mine. You remember, Sir, I was once rash enough to enter one of those dance halls — one of those dives where sailors spend their time drinking and carousing, as they say — I was just trying to persuade them to try another kind of life —

MRS. ALV. [*By the window*] Hm —

MAN. Yes, I know, Engstrand; those dreadful men threw you downstairs; I remember your telling me of that tragic experience; you bear your deformity with honor.

ENG. I don't mean to brag about it, Sir. Well — anyway, she came to me, and confided her whole trouble to me, with tears and lamentations — it broke my heart to listen to her —

MAN. Did it, indeed, Engstrand! Well — and then — ?

ENG. Well, then I said to her, I said: that American is wandering on the seas of the world; and you, Johanna, are a sinful fallen creature, I said. But, Jakob Engstrand, I said, stands here on two solid legs, I said; of course I only meant that in a manner of speaking, you know, Sir —

MAN. Yes, yes — I understand — go on —

ENG. Well then, Sir, I married her — I made her an honest woman — so no one would know of her reckless behavior with that foreigner —

MAN. All of that was very right and good of you, Engstrand; but I cannot condone your consenting to accept money —

ENG. Money? Me? Not a penny —

MAN. [*In a questioning tone, to* MRS. ALVING] But — ?

ENG. Oh yes — wait a bit — now I remember. Johanna did say something about some money she had — but I refused to hear anything about it! Get Thee behind me, Satan, I said; it's Mammon's gold (or bank-notes or whatever it was), we'll throw it back in the American's face, I said; but, of course, he had disappeared, Sir — disappeared over the vast ocean, you see —

MAN. Yes — I see — my dear Engstrand —

ENG. Yes, Sir; and then Johanna and I agreed that every penny of that money should go to the child's upbringing; and that's where it went, Sir; and I can account for every cent of it.

MAN. But this puts things in an entirely different light —

ENG. That's the way it was, Mr. Manders. And, though I say it myself, I've tried to be a good father to Regine — to the best of my ability, that is — you know what a weak man I am, Sir — unfortunately —

MAN. Yes, yes — I know, dear Engstrand —

ENG. I can truly say I gave the child a decent upbringing and made poor Johanna a good and loving husband; but it never would have occurred to me to go to you, Mr. Manders, and brag about it and pat myself on the back for doing a good action; I'm not made like that. And most of the time, unfortunately, I've little enough to brag about. When I go and talk to you, Sir, it's mostly to confess my sins and weaknesses. For, as I said just now, my conscience troubles me quite a bit, Mr. Manders—

MAN. Give me your hand, Jakob Engstrand.

ENG. Oh — Lord, Sir! —

MAN. Come now — no nonsense! [*Grasps his hand*] There!

ENG. I most humbly ask you to forgive me, Sir —

MAN. On the contrary — it's I who must ask your forgiveness —

ENG. Oh, no, Sir!

MAN. Most certainly — and I do so with all my heart. Forgive me, dear Engstrand, for so misjudging you. I wish I might give you some proof of my sincere regret and of the esteem in which I hold you —

ENG. You'd really like to do that, Sir?

MAN. It would give me the greatest of pleasure.

ENG. Well — it just happens — there is something you could do for me, Sir; I've managed to put by a bit of money from my earnings here, and I'm thinking of opening a kind of Seamen's Home when I get back to town, Sir —

MRS. ALV. You — *what?*

ENG. It'd be like a kind of refuge for them, you see, Ma'am. These poor sailors have so many temptations when they get to port — I thought in my house, they'd find a father's care —

MAN. What do you say to that, Mrs. Alving?

ENG. Of course, I haven't much capital to go on — and I thought if I could just find a helping hand —

MAN. I shall give it some thought. I find your scheme most interesting. But now, go and get everything ready — light the lights — and prepare for our little celebration. Now I feel sure you are in a fit state for prayer, my dear Engstrand —

ENG. Yes — I really believe I am. Well, goodbye, Mrs. Alving, and thank you for everything; be sure and take good care of Regine for me. [*Wipes away a tear*] Poor Johanna's child — it's strange how she's managed to creep into my heart — but, she has — there's no denying it! [*He bows and goes out by the hall door.*]

MAN. Well — what do you think of him now, Mrs. Alving? It certainly puts things in an entirely different light.

MRS. ALV. It does indeed!

MAN. It just shows you how careful one must be in judging one's fellow-men. And what a satisfaction to find oneself mistaken! What do you say now?

MRS. ALV. I say you're a great big baby, Manders, and always will be!

MAN. *I!*

MRS. ALV. [*Puts her hands on his shoulders*] Yes; and I say I should like very much to give you a big hug!

MAN. [*Hastily drawing back*] Good Heavens — What ideas you have!

MRS. ALV. [*With a smile*] Oh, you needn't be afraid of me!

MAN. [*By the table*] You have such an extravagant way of expressing yourself! I'll just gather up all these documents and put them in my bag. [*He does so.*] There! Keep an eye on Osvald when he returns; I'll leave you for the present — but I'll come back and see you later. [*He takes his hat and goes out through the hall door.*]

MRS. ALV. [*Gives a sigh, glances out of the window, straightens up one or two things in the room and is about to go into the dining room but stops in the doorway and gives a low exclamation.*] Osvald — are you still there?

OSV. [*From the dining room*] I'm just finishing my cigar.

MRS. ALV. I thought you'd gone out for a walk.

OSV. In this kind of weather?

[*Noise of a glass clinking.* MRS. ALVING *leaves the door open, and sits down on the sofa with some knitting.*]

OSV. [*Off stage*] Was that Mr. Manders who went out just now?

MRS. ALV. Yes, he went down to the Orphanage.

OSV. Hm —

[*The clinking of a bottle on a glass is heard again.*]

MRS. ALV. [*With an uneasy glance*] Osvald dear — be careful with that liqueur — it's quite strong, you know.

OSV. It'll do me good, Mother! I feel so chilly.

MRS. ALV. Wouldn't you rather come in here with me?

OSV. You don't allow smoking in there, you said.

MRS. ALV. I don't mind a cigar, dear.

OSV. Very well, then I'll come in — I'll just have another little drop — there! [*He comes in smoking a cigar. Closes the door after him. A short silence.*] Where did Mr. Manders go?

MRS. ALV. I just told you; he went down to the Orphanage.

OSV. Oh, yes — so you did.

MRS. ALV. It's not good for you to sit so long at table, Osvald, dear.

OSV. [*Holding his cigar behind his back*] But it's so cozy, Mother. [*He pats her face and caresses her.*] You don't know what it means: To be home! To sit at my mother's table — in my mother's own room — to eat my mother's delicious food — !

MRS. ALV. My dear, dear boy!

OSV. [Walks up and down impatiently] And what on earth is there to do here? I can't seem to settle to anything —

MRS. ALV. Can't you?

OSV. In this gloomy weather — never a ray of sunshine. [Paces up and down] God! Not to be able to work — !

MRS. ALV. Perhaps you shouldn't have come home, Osvald.

OSV. I had to come, Mother.

MRS. ALV. But, if you're unhappy, Osvald. You know I'd ten times rather give up the joy of having you here, than —

OSV. [Stopping by the table] Tell me honestly, Mother — is it really such a joy to you to have me home again?

MRS. ALV. How can you ask such a thing!

OSV. [Crumpling up a newspaper] I should have thought you didn't much care one way or the other.

MRS. ALV. How have you the heart to say that to me, Osvald?

OSV. After all — you managed to live without me all these years.

MRS. ALV. That's true — I've managed to live without you —

[A pause. Twilight is falling gradually. OSVALD paces up and down. He has put out his cigar. He suddenly stops in front of MRS. ALVING.]

OSV. May I sit beside you on the sofa, Mother?

MRS. ALV. [Making room for him] Of course, dear.

OSV. [Sits beside her] There's something I must tell you.

MRS. ALV. [Anxiously] Well?

OSV. [Staring in front of him] I don't think I can bear it any longer.

MRS. ALV. Bear what? What is it?

OSV. [As before] I somehow couldn't bring myself to write to you about it — and, since I've been home —

MRS. ALV. [Grips his arm] Osvald — what is it?

OSV. All day yesterday and again today, I've tried to get rid of the thought — free myself of it — but I can't —

MRS. ALV. [Rising] You must be honest with me, Osvald —

OSV. [Pulls her down on the sofa again] No, don't get up! Sit still! I'll try and tell you. I've complained a lot about being tired after my journey —

MRS. ALV. Yes — well, what of that — ?

OSV. But that isn't really what's the matter with me; this is no ordinary fatigue —

MRS. ALV. [Tries to get up] You're not ill, are you, Osvald?

OSV. [Pulling her down again] No, don't get up, Mother. Try and be calm. I'm not really ill either

— not in the usual sort of way — [Clasping his head in his hands] It's a kind of mental breakdown, Mother — I'm destroyed — I'll never be able to work again. [He hides his face in his hands, and lets his head fall into her lap — shaking with sobs.]

MRS. ALV. [Pale and trembling] Osvald! It's not true! Look at me!

OSV. [Looking up in despair] I'll never be able to work again! Never — never! I'll be like a living corpse! Mother — can you imagine anything more frightful — ?

MRS. ALV. But, my darling! How could such a dreadful thing happen to you?

OSV. [Sitting up again] That's just it — I don't know! I can't possibly imagine! I've never lived a dissipated life — not in any kind of way — you must believe that, Mother — I haven't!

MRS. ALV. I believe that, Osvald.

OSV. And yet, in spite of that — this ghastly thing has taken hold of me!

MRS. ALV. It'll come out all right, my darling. It's just overwork — believe me!

OSV. [Dully] Yes — I thought that too at first — but it's not so.

MRS. ALV. Tell me all about it.

OSV. Yes, I will.

MRS. ALV. When did you first notice anything?

OSV. It was just after I went back to Paris — after my last visit here. I started to get terrible headaches — all up the back of my head — it was as if an iron band was screwed round my head — from the neck up —

MRS. ALV. And then — ?

OSV. At first I thought it was just the usual kind of headache I'd always had — since I was a child —

MRS. ALV. Yes — ?

OSV. But it wasn't that — I soon found that out. I was no longer able to work. I'd start on a new picture and all my strength would suddenly fail me — it was as though I were paralyzed; I couldn't concentrate — and I felt sick and dizzy; it was the most ghastly sensation; at last I went to see a doctor — and then I found out the truth.

MRS. ALV. What do you mean?

OSV. He was one of the best doctors there. I described to him just how I felt — and then he started asking me all sorts of questions — questions about things that seemed to have no bearing on the case — I couldn't make out what he was driving at —

MRS. ALV. Well — ?

OSV. At last he said: your constitution has been undermined from birth; he used the word " vermoulu." [5]

MRS. ALV. [Anxiously] What did he mean by that?

OSV. I didn't know what he meant either; I asked

5. (French) worm-eaten.

him to explain. And do you know what he said —
that cynical old man — ? [*Clenching his fist*]
Oh! —

MRS. ALV. No — what?

osv. He said: the sins of the fathers are visited
upon the children.

MRS. ALV. [*Rises slowly*] The sins of the fathers — !

osv. I almost hit him in the face.

MRS. ALV. [*Pacing the floor*] The sins of the fathers —

osv. [*With a sad smile*] Can you believe it? Of
course I assured him that such a thing was out of
the question — but he paid no attention — he repeated what he'd said. I had some of your letters
with me — and I had to translate to him the parts
that referred to Father —

MRS. ALV. Yes — ?

osv. Then he had to admit he must be on the
wrong tack. And then I learned the truth — the incredible truth! The sort of life I'd been leading —
gay and carefree, but innocent enough I thought —
had been too much for my strength; I should have
been more careful. So, you see, I've brought it on
myself —

MRS. ALV. No! You mustn't believe that, Osvald!

osv. He said that was the only possible explanation. My whole life ruined — thrown away —
through my own carelessness. All that I dreamt of
achieving, of accomplishing — I dare not think of
it — I mustn't think of it! If I could only live my
life over again — if I could wipe it all out and start
afresh! [*He flings himself face downward on the
sofa. After a pause looks up, leaning on his elbows.*]
It wouldn't be so bad if it was something I'd inherited — if it were something I couldn't help. But,
deliberately — out of carelessness — out of shameful stupidity to throw away happiness, health — everything that's worthwhile in this world — my future — my whole life — !

MRS. ALV. No — no! It's impossible, Osvald — my
darling — my boy! [*Bending over him*] It's not
true — it's not as desperate as that — !

osv. [*Jumping up*] Oh, Mother, you don't know!
And to think I should bring you such unhappiness!
I've often hoped and prayed that you didn't care
much about me, after all —

MRS. ALV. Not care about you, Osvald? You're all
I have in the world — you're the only thing on
earth that matters to me —

osv. [*Takes both her hands and kisses them*]
Yes, Mother, I know; when I'm home I realize that
— and it makes it doubly hard for me. Well — now
you know all about it; don't let's discuss it any more
today; I can't bear to dwell on it too long. [*Paces
about the room*] Give me something to drink,
Mother.

MRS. ALV. To drink? What do you want, Osvald?

osv. Oh, it doesn't matter — anything! You must
have something in the house —

MRS. ALV. Yes, but Osvald — don't you think — ?

osv. Don't refuse me, Mother — be a dear! I must
have something to help me drown these agonizing
thoughts! [*He goes up to the conservatory and
looks out.*] Oh, it's so dark — so terribly dark!
[MRS. ALVING *goes to the bell-pull and rings.*] This
incessant rain! It may go on for weeks — for
months! Never a ray of sunshine! I never remember seeing any sunshine here!

MRS. ALV. You're not thinking of leaving me, Osvald?

osv. [*With a deep sigh*] I'm not thinking of anything, Mother; I'm not capable of thinking — [*In
a low voice*] I've had to give that up!

[REGINE *comes in from the dining room.*]

REG. Did you ring, Mrs. Alving?

MRS. ALV. Yes; bring in the lamp.

REG. At once, Mrs. Alving — I have it ready. [*She
goes out.*]

MRS. ALV. [*Goes to* OSVALD] Don't keep anything
from me, Osvald.

osv. I won't, Mother. [*Goes to the table*] It seems
to me I've been very frank with you.

[REGINE *brings in the lamp and puts it on the
table.*]

MRS. ALV. Oh, and Regine — you might bring us
a half bottle of champagne.

REG. Very good, Mrs. Alving. [*She goes out.*]

osv. [*Takes her face in his hands*] That's right,
Mother! I knew you wouldn't let me go thirsty!

MRS. ALV. My own poor boy! As if I could refuse
you anything!

osv. [*Eagerly*] You really mean that, Mother?

MRS. ALV. What?

osv. That you couldn't refuse me anything?

MRS. ALV. But, my dear Osvald —

osv. Sh!

[REGINE *enters with a small tray on which are a
bottle of champagne and two glasses; she sets it
down on the table.*]

REG. Shall I open it, Mrs. Alving?

osv. No thanks — I'll do it myself.

[REGINE *goes out.*]

MRS. ALV. [*Sits down at the table*] Osvald — be
honest with me — what is it you don't want me to
refuse you — ?

osv. [*Busy opening the bottle*] First, let's have a
glass of wine — [*He opens the bottle and pours out
one glass and is about to pour another.*]

MRS. ALV. [*Puts her hand over the glass*] Thanks
— not for me.

osv. For me, then! [*He empties his glass, refills
it and empties it again; he sits down at the table.*]

MRS. ALV. [*Expectantly*] Well —

osv. Mother, tell me — what was the matter with you and Mr. Manders at dinner, just now? Why were you so quiet and solemn?

mrs. alv. Oh — did you notice that?

osv. Yes. Hm — [*A pause*] Mother, what do you think of Regine?

mrs. alv. What do I think of her?

osv. Don't you think she's wonderful?

mrs. alv. You don't know her as well as I do, Osvald —

osv. Well — what of that?

mrs. alv. I should have taken charge of her sooner — I'm afraid she spent too many years at home —

osv. But she's so wonderful to look at, Mother! [*Fills up his glass.*]

mrs. alv. She has many grave faults, Osvald —

osv. As if that mattered — ! [*He drinks.*]

mrs. alv. But I'm fond of her all the same; I feel responsible for her. I wouldn't have anything happen to her for all the world.

osv. [*Jumps up*] Mother! The one thing that could save me is Regine!

mrs. alv. [*Rising*] What do you mean?

osv. I mean I can't endure this agony alone!

mrs. alv. But I'm here to help you, Osvald —

osv. Yes, I know; I thought that would be enough — that's why I came home to you; but it's no use; I see that now. My life here would be intolerable.

mrs. alv. Osvald — !

osv. I must live a different sort of life; that's why I must go away again. I don't want you to see it happening to me —

mrs. alv. But you can't go away when you're so ill, Osvald.

osv. If it were just an ordinary illness, of course I'd stay home, Mother; I know you're the best friend I have in the world —

mrs. alv. You do know that — don't you?

osv. [*Moves about the room restlessly*] But it's the anguish, the remorse, the deadly fear — oh — that terrible fear!

mrs. alv. [*Follows after him*] Fear? Fear of what?

osv. Don't ask me any more about it! I don't know — I can't describe it to you — [mrs. alving *goes to the bell-pull and rings.*] What do you want?

mrs. alv. I want my boy to be happy, that's what I want — I won't let you suffer here! [*To* regine] More champagne, Regine! A whole bottle!

[regine *goes.*]

osv. Mother!

mrs. alv. We country-people know how to live too — you'll see.

osv. Isn't she wonderful to look at? So beautifully built! So radiant with health.

mrs. alv. [*Sitting down at the table*] Sit down, Osvald; let's talk quietly for a moment —

osv. [*Sits down*] You don't know about it, Mother — but I haven't been quite fair to Regine —

mrs. alv. Not fair — ?

osv. No — it was just thoughtlessness on my part — nothing serious; but last time I was home —

mrs. alv. Yes — ?

osv. She kept on asking questions about Paris — I told her a bit about my life there — and one day I said to her, quite casually: " Perhaps you'd like to go there and see it all for yourself, Regine — "

mrs. alv. Well — ?

osv. Then she blushed and got quite excited and said she'd give anything to go; then I said, perhaps some day it might be arranged — or something of that sort —

mrs. alv. I see.

osv. Of course I'd forgotten all about it; but the other day, when I arrived, I asked her if she was glad I intended to spend such a long time here —

mrs. alv. Yes — ?

osv. And then she looked at me so strangely and said: " Then what about my trip to Paris? "

mrs. alv. Her trip — ?

osv. Yes — it seems she'd taken me quite seriously; she'd been thinking about it all this time — thinking about *me*. She'd even tried to teach herself some French —

mrs. alv. So that was why —

osv. I'd never noticed her much before, Mother — but suddenly I saw her there — so beautiful — so vital — she stood there as though waiting to come into my arms —

mrs. alv. Osvald — !

osv. I suddenly realized that she could save me; she was so full of the joy of life!

mrs. alv. [*Startled*] Joy of life — ? Is there salvation in that?

[regine *comes in with the champagne.*]

reg. Excuse me for being so long, Mrs. Alving. I had to go down to the cellar — [*Puts the bottle on the table.*]

osv. Fetch another glass.

reg. [*Looks at him surprised*] Mrs. Alving has a glass, Sir.

osv. Yes — but fetch one for yourself, Regine. [regine *starts and gives a quick frightened glance at* mrs. alving.] Well?

reg. [*Softly, with hesitation*] Do you wish me to, Mrs. Alving?

mrs. alv. Fetch the glass, Regine.

[regine *goes into the dining room.*]

osv. [*Looking after her*] Have you noticed her walk, Mother — so strong — so sure.

MRS. ALV. This can't be allowed to happen, Osvald.

OSV. But it's all settled — you must see that — there's no use forbidding it. [REGINE *comes in with an empty glass and keeps it in her hand.*] Sit down, Regine. [REGINE *looks questioningly at* MRS. ALVING.]

MRS. ALV. Sit down. [REGINE *sits on a chair by the dining room door, with the empty glass in her hand.*] Osvald — What were you saying about the joy of life?

OSV. Yes — the joy of life, Mother — you don't know much about that here at home. I could never find it here.

MRS. ALV. Not here with me?

OSV. No. Never at home. But you don't understand that.

MRS. ALV. Yes — I believe I'm beginning to understand it — now.

OSV. That — and the joy of work. They're really the same thing, you know. But of course, you don't know anything about that here either.

MRS. ALV. No; you may be right. Tell me more about it.

OSV. Well — I simply mean that here people look on work as a curse — as a kind of punishment. They look on *life* as a wretched, miserable business — to be got through as soon as possible —

MRS. ALV. I know — a " vale of tears " — we do our best to make it so —

OSV. But, you see, abroad, people don't look at it like that. They don't believe in that old-fashioned preaching any longer. The mere fact of being alive in this world seems to them joyous and marvelous. You must have noticed, Mother, everything I paint is filled with this joy of life; always and forever the joy of life! My paintings are full of light, of sunshine, of glowing happy faces. That's why I'm afraid to stay here, Mother.

MRS. ALV. Afraid? What are you afraid of — here with me?

OSV. I'm afraid that all the strongest traits in my nature would become warped here — would degenerate into ugliness.

MRS. ALV. [*Looks at him intently*] You really believe that is what would happen?

OSV. Yes — I'm convinced of it! Even if I lived the same life here as I live abroad — it still wouldn't *be* the same life.

MRS. ALV. [*Who has listened intently, rises; a thoughtful look in her eyes*] Now I see it! It's all becoming clear to me —

OSV. What do you see?

MRS. ALV. The whole pattern — for the first time, I see it — and now I can speak.

OSV. [*Rising*] I don't understand you, Mother.

REG. [*Who has risen too*] Perhaps I'd better go —

MRS. ALV. No, no — stay where you are. Now I can speak. Now you must know everything, Osvald — and then you can choose. Osvald! Regine!

OSV. Sh! Here comes Manders.

MAN. [*Enters from hall door*] Well — I must say — we've had a most edifying time —

OSV. So have we.

MAN. There can be no doubt about it — We must make it possible for Engstrand to start that seamen's home of his. Regine must go back with him; she can be most helpful —

REG. No thank you, Mr. Manders!

MAN. [*Notices her for the first time*] What — ? You in here? And with a glass in your hand?

REG. [*Hastily puts down her glass*] Pardon!

OSV. Regine is going with me, Mr. Manders.

MAN. Going with you — ?

OSV. Yes; as my wife — if she insists on that.

MAN. But — good Heavens — !

REG. It's no fault of mine, Mr. Manders —

OSV. Or if I decide to stay here — she'll stay too.

REG. [*Involuntarily*] Stay here — !

MAN. I am amazed at you, Mrs. Alving.

MRS. ALV. None of this will happen — for now I can tell the truth at last.

MAN. But you won't — you can't!

MRS. ALV. I can and I will — and nobody's ideals will be the worse for it.

OSV. Mother, what is all this — what are you hiding from me?

REG. [*Listening*] Mrs. Alving — Listen! — I hear people shouting out there. [*She goes up to the conservatory.*]

OSV. [*Going to the window stage left*] What's happening? What's that glare in the sky?

REG. [*Calls out*] It's the Orphanage — the Orphanage is on fire!

MRS. ALV. [*Going to the window*] On fire — ?

MAN. On fire — ? Impossible! I've just come from there.

OSV. Give me my hat! — Oh never mind — Father's Orphanage! [*He runs out into the garden.*]

MRS. ALV. My shawl, Regine! The whole place is in flames!

MAN. How horrible! It's a judgment, Mrs. Alving — a judgment on this house.

MRS. ALV. Yes — undoubtedly, Manders. Come, Regine.

[MRS. ALVING *and* REGINE *hurry out through the hall door.*]

MAN. [*Clasping his hands*] And to think it's not insured! [*He follows them as the curtain falls.*]

Act III

SCENE. *The room as before. All the doors stand open. The lamp is still burning on the table. It is dark out of doors; there is only a faint glow from the fire in the background to the left.*

AT RISE OF CURTAIN: MRS. ALVING, *with a shawl over her head, stands in the conservatory looking out.* REGINE, *also with a shawl on, stands a little behind her.*

MRS. ALV. Nothing left — burned to the ground!

REG. The cellar is still in flames.

MRS. ALV. Why doesn't Osvald come? — there's no hope of saving anything.

REG. Shall I take his hat down to him?

MRS. ALV. Is he out there without it?

REG. [*Pointing to the hall*] Yes — it's hanging in the hall —

MRS. ALV. No — leave it — he'll be back in a moment — I think I'll go and look for him. [*Exits to the garden.*]

MAN. [*Enters from hall*] Isn't Mrs. Alving here?

REG. She just went down to the garden.

MAN. What a night — I've never gone through anything as dreadful!

REG. It's a terrible thing, Mr. Manders!

MAN. Don't speak of it! — I can't bear the thought of it.

REG. But how could it possibly have happened?

MAN. Oh, don't ask me, Miss Engstrand — how should I know! You're not implying — ? Isn't it enough that your father should — ?

REG. What's he been up to — ?

MAN. He's driven me half mad —

ENG. [*Enters through hall*] Oh there you are, Mr. Manders —

MAN. [*Turning around with a start*] Must you follow me in here too!

ENG. Oh, Mr. Manders! — Such a terrible thing, Sir — !

MAN. [*Pacing up and down*] Yes, yes! We know! We know! —

REG. What's the meaning of this?

ENG. It was all due to the prayer meeting, you see! [*Aside to* REGINE] We've hooked the old fool now, my girl! [*Aloud*] That poor Mr. Manders should be the cause of such a calamity — and through my fault too!

MAN. But I tell you, Engstrand —

ENG. No one touched the lights but you, Sir!

MAN. [*Standing still*] That's what *you* claim — but I could swear I never went *near* the lights!

ENG. But I saw you with my own eyes, Sir — I saw you snuff one of the candles and throw the bit of wick right into a pile of shavings!

MAN. You say you *saw* this?

ENG. So help me God, Sir!

MAN. Incredible! — I'm not in the habit of snuffing candles with my fingers.

ENG. No, Sir — I thought at the time it didn't look quite like you. It'll be quite a serious thing, won't it, Sir?

MAN. [*Walks restlessly back and forth*] Don't ask me about it!

ENG. [*Follows him about*] You hadn't insured the place, had you, Sir?

MAN. [*Still pacing*] I told you I hadn't!

ENG. [*Following him*] Hadn't insured it! — And then to go and set the whole place on fire like that! Lord! What a bit of bad luck, Sir!

MAN. [*Wipes the perspiration from his brow*] You may well say so, Engstrand.

ENG. A charitable institution too! A place dedicated, you might say, to the good of the Community! — It's likely the papers won't treat you any too kindly, Mr. Manders.

MAN. That's just it! That's what I'm thinking about — all the spiteful attacks and accusations! That's the worst part of the whole business — I can't bear the thought of it!

MRS. ALV. [*Enters from the garden*] He won't come — he can't seem to tear himself away.

MAN. Oh, it's you, Mrs. Alving.

MRS. ALV. Well, Manders! You got out of making your speech after all!

MAN. I'd be only too glad to make it!

MRS. ALV. [*In a subdued tone*] It's all for the best; that poor Orphanage could never have brought good to anyone!

MAN. You really feel that?

MRS. ALV. Well — don't you?

MAN. All the same — it's a great tragedy.

MRS. ALV. Nonsense! Now — let's discuss it from a business point of view — Are you waiting for Mr. Manders, Engstrand?

ENG. [*By the hall door*] Yes, Ma'am, I am.

MRS. ALV. Well then — sit down.

ENG. I'd rather stand, thank you, Ma'am.

MRS. ALV. [*To* MANDERS] I suppose you'll be leaving by the next boat?

MAN. Yes — there's one in an hour.

MRS. ALV. Please take all the documents with you — I don't want to hear another word about it! I've other things to think about now.

MAN. Mrs. Alving —

MRS. ALV. I'll arrange to send you Power of Attorney and you can wind things up as you think best.

MAN. I'll be glad to look after it for you. Of course now, the original terms of the bequest will have to be radically altered.

MRS. ALV. Naturally —

MAN. I would suggest making the actual land over to the Parish under the circumstances; it's not without value, and could be used for many purposes. As to the interest on the capital — I feel sure I can find some worthy project in need of support — something that would prove beneficial to the life of the community.

MRS. ALV. Do anything you like with it — it makes no difference to me.

ENG. You might give a thought to my Seamen's Home, Mr. Manders.

MAN. To be sure. A good suggestion. Well worth looking into.

ENG. [*Aside*] Looking into! That's a good one!

MAN. [*With a sigh*] Of course I may not be long in charge of these affairs; public opinion may compel me to withdraw; there will naturally be an investigation to determine the cause of the fire; it all depends on the outcome of that.

MRS. ALV. What *are* you talking about, Manders?

MAN. It's impossible to tell what that outcome will be.

ENG. [*Coming closer*] Oh no it's not, Mr. Manders! Don't forget *me* — don't forget Jakob Engstrand!

MAN. But — I don't see —

ENG. [*In a low voice*] And Jakob Engstrand is not one to desert a benefactor in his hour of need — as they say!

MAN. But, my dear man — how could you possibly — ?

ENG. Jakob Engstrand won't desert you, Sir! He'll be like a guardian angel to you, Sir!

MAN. But I could never consent — !

ENG. You'll have nothing to do with it, Sir. It wouldn't be the first time I'd taken the blame for others.

MAN. Jakob! [*Wringing his hands*] You're one in a million! I'll see that you get funds for your Seamen's Home — You can count on that. [ENGSTRAND *tries to thank him but is overcome with emotion;* MANDERS *slings his traveling-bag over his shoulder.*] And now — let's be off. We'll travel together, of course.

ENG. [*At the hall door, aside to* REGINE] You'd better come with me, hussy! You'll live like a Queen!

REG. [*Tosses her head*] Merci![6] [*She fetches* MANDERS' *things from the hall.*]

MAN. Goodbye, Mrs. Alving. May the Spirit of Truth and Righteousness soon enter into this house.

MRS. ALV. Goodbye, Manders. [*She goes to meet* OSVALD *who enters from the garden.*]

ENG. [*As he and* REGINE *help* MANDERS *with his coat*] Goodbye, my dear child. And if anything

should happen to you, remember Jakob Engstrand's always there — you know where to find him. Harbor Street — you know! [*To* MRS. ALVING *and* OSVALD] My home for poor Seamen shall be called "Captain Alving's Haven" and if it turns out the way I want it, Ma'am — I humbly hope it may prove worthy of Captain Alving's memory!

MAN. [*In the doorway*] Hm — yes. Come along, my dear Engstrand. Goodbye again — goodbye! [*They exit through the hall.*]

OSV. [*Goes toward the table*] What does he mean? What "home" is he talking about?

MRS. ALV. It's some sort of a hostel he and Manders are thinking of starting.

OSV. It'll only burn down — just like this one.

MRS. ALV. Why do you say that?

OSV. Everything will be burnt. Father's memory will be wiped out. I shall soon be burnt up too.

[REGINE *looks at him in amazement.*]

MRS. ALV. Osvald! — You poor boy! You shouldn't have stayed down there so long.

OSV. [*Sits down at the table*] I expect you're right about that.

MRS. ALV. Your face is wet, Osvald; let me dry it for you. [*Wipes his face with her handkerchief.*]

OSV. [*Indifferently*] Thanks, Mother.

MRS. ALV. You must be tired, Osvald. You'd better get some sleep.

OSV. [*Apprehensively*] No! No! I don't want to sleep! I never sleep — I only pretend to — [*Dully*] I'll sleep soon enough!

MRS. ALV. [*Looking at him anxiously*] I'm afraid you're really ill, my darling!

REG. [*Intently*] Is Mr. Alving ill?

OSV. [*Impatiently*] And close the doors! — I want all the doors closed! — this terrible fear —

MRS. ALV. Close the doors, Regine.

[REGINE *closes the doors and remains standing by the one to the hall.* MRS. ALVING *takes off her shawl, and* REGINE *does likewise.*]

MRS. ALV. [*Draws up a chair and sits next to* OSVALD] There! — I'll sit here beside you.

OSV. Yes — do, Mother. And Regine must stay here too — she must never leave me. You'll be there to help me, won't you, Regine?

REG. I don't understand —

MRS. ALV. — there to help you?

OSV. Yes — when the time comes.

MRS. ALV. Can't you trust your mother to do that?

OSV. You? [*Smiles*] You'd never do it. [*With a melancholy laugh*] You! [*Looks at her gravely*] And yet you're the only one who has the right to do it. Why are you always so formal with me, Regine? Why don't you call me Osvald?

REG. [*In a low voice*] Mrs. Alving might not like it.

MRS. ALV. You may soon have a right to — so sit

6. (*French*) thank you; here used sarcastically.

down with us, Regine. [REGINE *hesitates, then sits down quietly at the far side of the table.*]And now, my darling, I'm going to free you from this torment; you won't have to bear this dreadful burden any longer.

OSV. You're going to free me, Mother?

MRS. ALV. Yes — from this remorse, this sense of guilt, this self-reproach —

OSV. — Do you think you can do that?

MRS. ALV. Yes, I believe I can now. Earlier this evening you were talking about the joy of life — and suddenly everything became clear to me; I saw my whole life in a new light.

OSV. [*Shaking his head*] I don't understand this.

MRS. ALV. You should have known your father when he was a young lieutenant. He was filled with that joy of life, I can tell you!

OSV. Yes — so I've heard.

MRS. ALV. He seemed to radiate light and warmth — he was filled with a turbulent, joyous vitality.

OSV. Well — ?

MRS. ALV. And this boy, so full of the joy of life — he was like a boy then — was cooped up in this drab little provincial town — which could offer him no real joy — only dissipation. He had no real aim in life — no work that could stimulate his mind or feed his spirit — nothing but a dull, petty, routine job. He found no one here who understood that pure joy of life that was in him; what friends he had were bent on idling their time away or drinking themselves into a stupor —

OSV. Mother — !

MRS. ALV. And so, the inevitable happened.

OSV. The inevitable?

MRS. ALV. You told me a little while ago, what would happen to you if you stayed here.

OSV. Do you mean by that — that Father — ?

MRS. ALV. Your poor father could find no outlet for that overpowering joy of life that was in him — and I'm afraid I brought him no happiness either.

OSV. Why, Mother?

MRS. ALV. All my life I'd been taught a great deal about duty — that seemed the all-important thing. Everything was reduced to a question of duty — *my* duty — *his* duty — your poor father — I'm afraid I must have made home intolerable for him, Osvald.

OSV. Why did you never write me about all this?

MRS. ALV. You were his son — I felt it would be wrong to talk to you about it; you see, I didn't see things clearly then.

OSV. How did you see them?

MRS. ALV. [*Slowly*] I was aware of one thing only; that your father was a broken, dissolute man, long before you were born.

OSV. [*A smothered cry*] Ah! [*He rises and goes to the window.*]

MRS. ALV. And day in and day out I was tormented by the thought that Regine actually had the same rights in this house that you have.

OSV. [*Turns quickly*] Regine!

REG. [*Jumps up and says in a choking voice*] I — !

MRS. ALV. Yes. Now you know everything — both of you.

OSV. Regine!

REG. [*To herself*] So Mother was — *that* sort of woman.

MRS. ALV. Your mother had many fine qualities, Regine.

REG. She was that sort all the same. There've been times when I guessed she might be — but — Mrs. Alving! Please allow me to leave at once.

MRS. ALV. You really want to go, Regine?

REG. I certainly do, Mrs. Alving.

MRS. ALV. Of course you must do as you wish, but —

OSV. [*Goes to* REGINE] Leave now? But you belong here.

REG. Merci, Mr. Alving — I suppose I can call you Osvald now — though this wasn't the way I wanted it to happen.

MRS. ALV. Regine — I haven't been honest with you —

REG. No! You certainly haven't, Mrs. Alving! If I'd known that Osvald was a sick man — And now that there can never be anything serious between us — No! I can't waste my time out here in the country looking after invalids.

OSV. Not when it's your own brother, Regine?

REG. I should say not! I'm poor — all I have is my youth — I can't afford to waste it. I don't want to be left stranded. I have some of that "joy of life" in me too, Mrs. Alving!

MRS. ALV. No doubt. But don't throw yourself away, Regine.

REG. If I do — I *do* — that's all! If Osvald takes after his father, I take after my mother, I suppose. — May I ask, Mrs. Alving, if Mr. Manders knows about all this?

MRS. ALV. Mr. Manders knows everything.

REG. [*Rapidly putting on her shawl*] Then I'd better try and catch that boat. Mr. Manders is such a kind man, he's sure to help me. It seems to me I have a right to some of that money too — a better right than that filthy old carpenter.

MRS. ALV. You're welcome to it, Regine.

REG. [*With a hard look*] And I must say, Mrs. Alving — it seems to me I also had a right to a decent upbringing — one suited to a gentleman's daughter. [*Tosses her head*] Well — what do I care! [*Casts a bitter glance at the unopened bottle*] Some day I may be drinking champagne with the best of them — who knows?

MRS. ALV. If you should ever need a home, Regine — come to me.

REG. No thank you, Mrs. Alving! Mr. Manders'll look after me I'm sure. And if the worst comes to the worst, I know of a place where I'd be quite at home.

MRS. ALV. Where do you mean?

REG. In Captain Alving's Hostel, of course!

MRS. ALV. Be careful, Regine! Don't destroy yourself!

REG. What do I care! — Well — goodbye! [*She bows to them and goes out through the hall.*]

OSV. [*Stands at the window gazing out*] Has she gone?

MRS. ALV. Yes.

OSV. [*Mutters to himself*] How stupid it all is!

MRS. ALV. [*Stands behind him and puts her hands on his shoulders*] Osvald — my dear; has it been a very great shock to you?

OSV. [*Turns his face towards her*] All that about Father, you mean?

MRS. ALV. Yes, your poor father! — I'm afraid it's been too much for you.

OSV. Why do you say that? It was a great surprise to me, I admit; but after all, it doesn't really matter.

MRS. ALV. [*Withdraws her hands*] Not matter? That your father was so unspeakably unhappy?

OSV. I feel sorry for him of course — as I would for anyone who suffered.

MRS. ALV. No more than that? — But he was your *father*, Osvald.

OSV. [*Impatiently*] Father! Father! I never *knew* my father. The only thing I remember about him is that he once made me sick!

MRS. ALV. What a dreadful thought! But surely a child must have some love for his father, in spite of everything.

OSV. Even if he owes his father nothing? Even if he never knew him? Come now, Mother! You're too broadminded to believe in that superstitious nonsense!

MRS. ALV. Superstitious nonsense — you think that's all it is?

OSV. Of course, Mother — you must see that. It's one of those old-fashioned illusions people go on clinging to —

MRS. ALV. [*Shaken*] Ghosts —

OSV. [*Paces up and down*] Yes — call them ghosts if you like.

MRS. ALV. [*In a burst of emotion*] Osvald — Then you don't love me either!

OSV. Well, at least I know *you* —

MRS. ALV. You know me — yes; but is that all?

OSV. I know how much you care for me; I should be grateful to you for that. And now that I'm ill, you can be of great help to me.

MRS. ALV. I can — can't I, Osvald? I'm almost glad you're ill — since it's brought you home to me. I understand — you don't belong to me yet — I'll have to win you.

OSV. [*Impatiently*] Oh, don't let's have a lot of phrases, Mother! You must remember I'm ill. I can't be bothered with other people; I've got to think about myself.

MRS. ALV. [*Gently*] I'll be very quiet and patient, Osvald.

OSV. And, for God's sake, *happy,* Mother!

MRS. ALV. Yes, my darling — you're right. [*Goes to him*] And you've no more doubts, no more remorse? I've freed you of all that?

OSV. Yes, Mother, you have. But who's to free me of the terror — ?

MRS. ALV. Terror!

OSV. [*Pacing up and down*] Regine would have done it, if I'd asked her.

MRS. ALV. I don't understand. What is this terror — and what has Regine to do with it?

OSV. Mother — is it very late?

MRS. ALV. It's early morning. [*She goes to the conservatory and looks out.*] The dawn is just breaking. It's going to be a lovely day, Osvald! In a little while you'll see the sun!

OSV. I'll be glad of that. Perhaps after all there are lots of things I could be glad about, Mother — lots of things I'd like to live for —

MRS. ALV. Of course there are!

OSV. And even if I'm not able to work —

MRS. ALV. You'll soon be able to work again, you'll see. Now that you're rid of all those depressing, gloomy thoughts.

OSV. Yes — it's good that you were able to wipe out that obsession. Now, if I can just get over this other — [*Sits down on the sofa*] Come here, Mother. I want to talk to you —

MRS. ALV. Yes, Osvald. [*She pushes an armchair over near the sofa and sits close to him.*]

OSV. Meanwhile the sun is rising. And now that you know — I don't feel — so afraid any more.

MRS. ALV. Now that I know — what?

OSV. [*Without listening to her*] Mother — didn't you say a little while ago that there was nothing in this world you wouldn't do for me, if I asked you?

MRS. ALV. Yes — of course I did.

OSV. And you stand by that, Mother?

MRS. ALV. You can depend on me, my darling. You're the only thing on earth I have to live for.

OSV. Well then — listen, Mother; you have a strong, gallant spirit — I know that; I want you to sit quite still while I tell you something.

MRS. ALV. What dreadful thing are you going to — ?

OSV. Don't scream or get excited, do you hear? Promise me! We'll sit here and talk it over quietly. Promise!

MRS. ALV. Yes, yes — I promise! Tell me what it is!

OSV. Well then — listen: this fatigue of mine — my inability to work — all of that is not the *essence* of my illness —

MRS. ALV. How do you mean?

OSV. You see — my illness *is* hereditary — it — [*Touches his forehead and speaks very quietly*] It is centered — *here*.

MRS. ALV. [*Almost speechless*] Osvald! No — no!

OSV. Don't scream, Mother — I can't stand it! It's lurking here — lying in wait — ready to spring at any moment.

MRS. ALV. How horrible — !

OSV. Quiet, Mother! — Now you understand the state I'm in.

MRS. ALV. [*Springing up*] It's not true, Osvald — it's impossible!

OSV. I had one attack while I was abroad — it didn't last long. But when I realized the condition I'd been in, I was filled with unspeakable terror — and I could think of nothing but getting home to you.

MRS. ALV. So that's what you mean by "the terror"!

OSV. Yes — unspeakable, sickening terror! If it had only been an ordinary illness — even a fatal one — I wouldn't have minded so much — I'm not afraid of death — though I should like to live as long as possible —

MRS. ALV. You will, Osvald — you must!

OSV. But there's something so utterly revolting about this! To become a child again — a helpless child — to have to be fed — to have to be — oh! It's too ghastly to think of!

MRS. ALV. I'll be here to look after you, Osvald.

OSV. [*Jumping up*] No, never; I won't stand it! I can't endure the thought of lingering on like that — of growing old like that — old and gray-haired like that! And you might die and I should be left alone. [*Sits down in* MRS. ALVING's *chair*] For the doctor said I might live for years, you see. He called it "Softening of the brain" or something of the sort. [*With a sad smile*] Charming expression! It makes one think of cherry-colored velvet curtains — soft and delicate to stroke —

MRS. ALV. [*Screams*] Osvald!

OSV. [*Springs up and paces up and down*] And now you've taken Regine away from me — if only I had her. She'd have been willing to help me, I know.

MRS. ALV. [*Goes to him*] What do you mean by that, my darling? — You know I'd give my life to help you —

OSV. I recovered from that attack abroad — but the doctor said that the next time — and there's bound to be a "next time" — it would be hopeless.

MRS. ALV. How could he be so brutal — !

OSV. I insisted on the truth — I made him tell me. I explained that I had certain arrangements to make [*With a cunning smile*] and so I had. [*Takes a small box from his breast pocket*] Do you see this, Mother?

MRS. ALV. What is it?

OSV. Morphine tablets —

MRS. ALV. [*Looks at him in terror*] Osvald —

OSV. I managed to save up twelve of them —

MRS. ALV. [*Snatching at it*] Give me the box, Osvald!

OSV. Not yet, Mother. [*Puts the box back in his pocket.*]

MRS. ALV. I can't endure this!

OSV. You must endure it, Mother. If only Regine were here — I'd have explained to her how matters stood; I'd have asked her to help me put an end to it; she'd have done it, I know.

MRS. ALV. Never!

OSV. Oh yes she would! If she'd seen that ghastly thing take hold of me — if she'd seen me lying there like an imbecile child — beyond help — hopelessly, irrevocably lost —

MRS. ALV. Regine would never have done it!

OSV. Oh yes! She'd have done it! Regine has such a magnificently light and buoyant nature. She wouldn't have put up long with an invalid like me!

MRS. ALV. Then I can only thank God Regine is not here!

OSV. Yes, but then you'll have to help me, Mother.

MRS. ALV. [*With a loud scream*] I!

OSV. Who has a better right?

MRS. ALV. I — your mother.

OSV. For that very reason.

MRS. ALV. I, who gave you life!

OSV. I didn't ask you for life — and what kind of a life did you give me! I don't want it — take it back again!

MRS. ALV. Help — help! [*She runs out into the hall.*]

OSV. [*Following her*] Don't leave me! Where are you going?

MRS. ALV. [*In the hall*] I must fetch a doctor, Osvald — let me out!

OSV. [*In the hall*] You shall not go out — and no one shall come in.

[*Sound of a key turning in the lock.*]

MRS. ALV. [*Re-entering the room*] Osvald — Osvald! My little one!

OSV. [*Follows her in*] Mother — if you love me — how can you bear to see me suffer this agony of fear!

MRS. ALV. [*After a moment's silence, in a firm voice*] I give you my word, Osvald.

OSV. Then, you will — ?

MRS. ALV. Yes — If it becomes necessary — but it won't become necessary! That's impossible!

OSV. Let us hope so — Meanwhile we'll live together as long as we can. Thank you, Mother. [*He sits in the armchair that* MRS. ALVING *had moved to the sofa.*]

[*Day breaks; the lamp is still burning on the table.*]

MRS. ALV. [*Approaching him cautiously*] Do you feel calmer now?

OSV. Yes.

MRS. ALV. [*Bends over him*] This has all been a nightmare, Osvald — just something you've imagined. It's been a dreadful strain, but now you're home with me and you'll be able to get some rest. I'll spoil you as I did when you were a tiny little boy — you shall have everything you want. There! The attack's over now — You see how easily it passed. It's not so serious — I was sure it couldn't be! And it's going to be such a lovely day, Osvald. Bright sunshine! Now you'll really be able to see your home.

[*She goes to the table and puts out the lamp. The sun rises. The glaciers and peaks in the background are bathed in the bright morning light.*]

OSV. [*Immovable in his armchair with his back to the view outside, suddenly speaks*] Mother — give me the sun.

MRS. ALV. [*By the table, looks at him in amazement*] What did you say?

OSV. [*Repeats in a dull toneless voice*] The sun — The sun.

MRS. ALV. [*Goes to him*] Osvald — what's the matter with you?

[OSVALD *seems to crumple up in the chair; all his muscles relax; his face is expressionless — his eyes vacant and staring.*]

MRS. ALV. [*Trembling with terror*] What is it? [*Screams*] Osvald! What's the matter with you? [*Throws herself on her knees beside him and shakes him*] Osvald! Osvald! Look at me! Don't you know me?

OSV. [*Tonelessly as before*] The sun — The sun.

MRS. ALV. [*Springs up in despair, tears at her hair with both hands and screams*] I can't bear it! [*Whispers, paralyzed with fear*] I can't bear it! Never! [*Suddenly*] Where did he put them? [*Passes her hand rapidly over his breast*] Here! [*Draws back a couple of steps and cries*] No; no; no! — Yes! No; no! [*She stands a few steps away from him, her hands clutching her hair, and stares at him in speechless terror.*]

OSV. [*Immovable as before*] The sun — The sun.

CURTAIN

The Hairy Ape

A COMEDY OF ANCIENT AND MODERN LIFE IN EIGHT SCENES

by Eugene O'Neill

YANK (ROBERT SMITH), *a ship's stoker*
PADDY (PATRICK), *another stoker, an old Irishman*
LONG, *another stoker, a Cockney*
MILDRED DOUGLAS, *a girl of twenty sailing to England, daughter of a steel magnate*

HER AUNT, *an old woman serving as her chaperon*
SECOND ENGINEER *on the ship*
GUARD *of the prison on Blackwell's Island*
SECRETARY *of an I.W.W. local*
OTHER STOKERS, LADIES, GENTLEMEN, ETC.

Scene 1

SCENE. *The firemen's forecastle* [1] *of a transatlantic liner an hour after sailing from New York for the voyage across. Tiers of narrow, steel bunks, three deep, on all sides. An entrance in rear. Benches on the floor before the bunks. The room is crowded with men, shouting, cursing, laughing, singing — a confused, inchoate uproar swelling into a sort of unity, a meaning — the bewildered, furious, baffled defiance of a beast in a cage. Nearly all the men are drunk. Many bottles are passed from hand to hand. All are dressed in dungaree pants, heavy ugly shoes. Some wear singlets, but the majority are stripped to the waist.*

The treatment of this scene, or of any other scene in the play, should by no means be naturalistic. The effect sought after is a cramped space in the bowels of a ship, imprisoned by white steel. The lines of bunks, the uprights supporting them, cross each other like the steel framework of a cage. The ceiling crushes down upon the men's heads. They cannot stand upright. This accentuates the natural stooping posture which shoveling coal and the resultant over-development of back and shoulder muscles have given them. The men themselves should resemble those pictures in which the appearance of Neanderthal Man is guessed at. All are hairy-chested, with long arms of tremendous power, and low, receding brows above their small, fierce, resentful eyes. All the civilized white races are represented, but except for the slight differentiation in color of hair, skin, eyes, all these men are alike.

The curtain rises on a tumult of sound. YANK *is seated in the foreground. He seems broader, fiercer, more truculent, more powerful, more sure of himself than the rest. They respect his superior strength — the grudging respect of fear. Then, too, he represents to them a self-expression, the very last word in what they are, their most highly developed individual.*

VOICES. Gif me trink dere, you!
   'Ave a wet!
   Salute!
   Gesundheit!
   Skoal! [2]
   Drunk as a lord, God stiffen you!
   Here's how!
   Luck!
   Pass back that bottle, damn you!
   Pourin' it down his neck!
   Ho, Froggy! Where the devil have you been?
   La Touraine.
   I hit him smash in yaw, py Gott!
   Jenkins — the First [3] — he's a rotten swine —
   And the coppers nabbed him — and I run —

1. quarters below deck in the forward part of the ship where the firemen (also called stokers) sleep and live when not on duty. During their "watch" they work in the stokehole, tending the furnace which generates the steam used to run the ship's engines.

2. These last three are drinking toasts of Italy, Germany, and Sweden, respectively. 3. the First (or the Chief) Engineer, the ship's officer in charge of the engines, of that part of the crew (including these men) that works them, and of the subordinate engineering officers (the Second, Third, and Fourth Engineers).

I like peer better. It don't pig head gif you.

A slut, I'm sayin'! She robbed me aslape —

To hell with 'em all!

You're a bloody liar!

Say dot again!

[*Commotion. Two men about to fight are pulled apart.*]

No scrappin' now!

Tonight —

See who's the best man!

Bloody Dutchman!

Tonight on the for'ard square.

I'll bet on Dutchy.

He packa da wallop, I tella you!

Shut up, Wop!

No fightin', maties. We're all chums, ain't we?

[*A voice starts bawling a song.*]

"Beer, beer, glorious beer!
Fill yourselves right up to here."

YANK. [*For the first time seeming to take notice of the uproar about him, turns around threateningly — in a tone of contemptuous authority*] Choke off dat noise! Where d'yuh get dat beer stuff? Beer, hell! Beer's for goils — and Dutchmen. Me for somep'n wit a kick to it! Gimme a drink, one of youse guys. [*Several bottles are eagerly offered. He takes a tremendous gulp at one of them; then, keeping the bottle in his hand, glares belligerently at the owner, who hastens to acquiesce in this robbery by saying —*] All righto, Yank. Keep it and have another. [YANK *contemptuously turns his back on the crowd again. For a second there is an embarrassed silence. Then—*]

VOICES. We must be passing the Hook.[4]

She's beginning to roll to it.

Six days in hell — and then Southampton.

Py Yesus, I vish somepody take my first vatch for me!

Gittin' seasick, Square-head?

Drink up and forget it!

What's in your bottle?

Gin.

Dot's nigger trink.

Absinthe? It's doped. You'll go off your chump, Froggy!

Cochon![5]

Whisky, that's the ticket!

Where's Paddy?

Going asleep.

Sing us that whisky song, Paddy.

[*They all turn to an old, wizened Irishman who is dozing, very drunk, on the benches forward. His face is extremely monkey-like with all the sad, patient pathos of that animal in his small eyes.*]

4. Sandy Hook, where New York Harbor meets the open sea.
5. (*French*) pig.

Singa da song, Caruso Pat!

He's gettin' old. The drink is too much for him.

He's too drunk.

PAD. [*Blinking about him, starts to his feet resentfully, swaying, holding on to the edge of a bunk*] I'm never too drunk to sing. 'Tis only when I'm dead to the world I'd be wishful to sing at all. [*With a sort of sad contempt*] "Whisky Johnny," ye want? A chanty, ye want? Now that's a queer wish from the ugly like of you, God help you. But no matther. [*He starts to sing in a thin, nasal, doleful tone.*]

Oh, whisky is the life of man!
Whisky! O Johnny! [*They all join in on this.*]
Oh, whisky is the life of man!
Whisky for my Johnny! [*Again chorus.*]
Oh, whisky drove my old man mad!
Whisky! O Johnny!
Oh, whisky drove my old man mad!
Whisky for my Johnny!

YANK. [*Again turning around scornfully*] Aw hell! Nix on dat old sailing ship stuff! All dat bull's dead, see? And you're dead, too, yuh damned old Harp, on'y yuh don't know it. Take it easy, see. Give us a rest. Nix on de loud noise. [*With a cynical grin*] Can't youse see I'm tryin' to t'ink?

ALL. [*Repeating the word after him as one with the same cynical amused mockery*] Think! [*The chorused word has a brazen metallic quality as if their throats were phonograph horns. It is followed by a general uproar of hard, barking laughter.*]

VOICES. Don't be cracking your head wit ut, Yank.

You gat headache, py yingo!

One thing about it — it rhymes with drink!

Ha, ha, ha!

Drink, don't think!

Drink, don't think!

Drink, don't think!

[*A whole chorus of voices has taken up this refrain, stamping on the floor, pounding on the benches with fists.*]

YANK. [*Taking a gulp from his bottle — good-naturedly*] Aw right. Can de noise. I got yuh de foist time.

[*The uproar subsides. A very drunken sentimental tenor begins to sing.*]

"Far away in Canada,
Far across the sea,
There's a lass who fondly waits
Making a home for me —"

YANK. [*Fiercely contemptuous*] Shut up, yuh lousy boob! Where d'yuh get dat tripe? Home? Home, hell! I'll make a home for yuh! I'll knock yuh dead. Home! T'hell wit home! Where d'yuh get dat tripe? Dis is home, see? What d'yuh want wit home? [*Proudly*] I runned away from mine when I was a kid. On'y too glad to beat it, dat was me. Home was lickings for me, dat's all. But yuh can bet your shoit no one ain't never licked me since! Wanter try it, any of youse? Huh! I guess not. [*In a more placated but still contemptuous tone*] Goils waitin' for yuh, huh? Aw, hell! Dat's all tripe. Dey don't wait for no one. Dey'd double-cross yuh for a nickel. Dey're all tarts, get me? Treat 'em rough, dat's me. To hell wit 'em. Tarts, dat's what, de whole bunch of 'em.

LONG. [*Very drunk, jumps on a bench excitedly, gesticulating with a bottle in his hand*] Listen 'ere, Comrades! Yank 'ere is right. 'E says this 'ere stinkin' ship is our 'ome. And 'e says as 'ome is 'ell. And 'e's right! This is 'ell. We lives in 'ell, Comrades — and right enough we'll die in it. [*Raging*] And who's ter blame, I arsks yer? We ain't. We wasn't born this rotten way. All men is born free and ekal. That's in the bleedin' Bible, maties. But what d'they care for the Bible — them lazy, bloated swine what travels first cabin? [6] Them's the ones. They dragged us down 'til we're on'y wage slaves in the bowels of a bloody ship, sweatin', burnin' up, eatin' coal dust! Hit's them's ter blame — the damned Capitalist clarss!

[*There had been a gradual murmur of contemptuous resentment rising among the men until now he is interrupted by a storm of catcalls, hisses, boos, hard laughter.*]

VOICES. Turn it off!
　　Shut up!
　　Sit down!
　　Closa da face!
　　Tamn fool! [*Etc.*]

YANK. [*Standing up and glaring at* LONG] Sit down before I knock yuh down! [LONG *makes haste to efface himself.* YANK *goes on contemptuously.*] De Bible, huh? De Cap'tlist class, huh? Aw nix on dat Salvation Army-Socialist bull. Git a soapbox! Hire a hall! Come and be saved, huh? Jerk us to Jesus, huh? Aw g'wan! I've listened to lots of guys like you, see. Yuh're all wrong. Wanter know what I t'ink? Yuh ain't no good for no one. Yuh're de bunk! Yuh ain't got no noive, get me? Yuh're yellow, dat's what. Yellow, dat's you. Say! What's dem slobs in de foist cabin got to do wit us? We're better men dan dey are, ain't we? Sure! One of us guys could clean up de whole mob wit one mit! Put one of 'em down here for one watch in de stokehole, what'd happen? Dey'd carry him off on a stretcher. Dem boids don't amount to nothin'. Dey're just baggage. Who makes dis old tub run? Ain't it us guys? Well den, we belong, don't we? We belong and dey don't. Dat's all. [*A loud chorus of approval.* YANK *goes on.*] As for dis bein' hell —

aw, nuts! Yuh lost your noive, dat's what. Dis is a man's job, get me? It belongs. It runs dis tub. No stiffs need apply. But yuh're a stiff, see? Yuh're yellow, dat's you.

VOICES. [*With a great hard pride in them*]
　　Righto!
　　A man's job!
　　Talk is cheap, Long.
　　He never could hold up his end.
　　Divil take him!
　　Yank's right. We make it go.
　　Py Gott, Yank say right ting!
　　We don't need no one cryin' over us.
　　Makin' speeches.
　　Throw him out!
　　Yellow!
　　Chuck him overboard!
　　I'll break his jaw for him!

[*They crowd around* LONG *threateningly.*]

YANK. [*Half good-natured again — contemptuously*] Aw, take it easy. Leave him alone. He ain't woith a punch. Drink up. Here's how, whoever owns dis. [*He takes a long swallow from his bottle. All drink with him. In a flash all is hilarious amiability again, back-slapping, loud talk, etc.*]

PAD. [*Who has been sitting in a blinking, melancholy daze — suddenly cries out in a voice full of old sorrow*] We belong to this, you're saying? We make the ship to go, you're saying? Yerra [7] then, that Almighty God have pity on us! [*His voice runs into the wail of a keen,*[8] *he rocks back and forth on his bench. The men stare at him, startled and impressed in spite of themselves.*] Oh, to be back in the fine days of my youth, ochone![9] Oh, there was fine beautiful ships them days — clippers wid tall masts touching the sky — fine strong men in them — men that was sons of the sea as if 'twas the mother that bore them. Oh, the clean skins of them, and the clear eyes, the straight backs and full chests of them! Brave men they was, and bold men surely! We'd be sailing out, bound down round the Horn [10] maybe. We'd be making sail in the dawn, with a fair breeze, singing a chanty song wid no care to it. And astern the land would be sinking low and dying out, but we'd give it no heed but a laugh, and never a look behind. For the day that was, was enough, for we was free men — and I'm thinking 'tis only slaves do be giving heed to the day that's gone or the day to come — until they're old like me. [*With a sort of religious exaltation*] Oh, to be scudding south again wid the power of the Trade Wind driving her on steady through the nights and the days! Full sail on her! Nights and

---

6. first class.

7. (*Irish*) verily, truly.　8. an Irish lament or dirge.　9. (*Irish*) alas.　10. Cape Horn, which is at the southern tip of South America.

days! Nights when the foam of the wake would be flaming wid fire, when the sky'd be blazing and winking wid stars. Or the full of the moon maybe. Then you'd see her driving through the gray night, her sails stretching aloft all silver and white, not a sound on the deck, the lot of us dreaming dreams, till you'd believe 'twas no real ship at all you was on but a ghost ship like the *Flying Dutchman* they say does be roaming the seas forevermore without touching a port. And there was the days, too. A warm sun on the clean decks. Sun warming the blood of you, and wind over the miles of shiny green ocean like strong drink to your lungs. Work — aye, hard work — but who'd mind that at all? Sure, you worked under the sky and 'twas work wid skill and daring to it. And wid the day done, in the dog watch,[11] smoking me pipe at ease, the lookout would be raising land maybe, and we'd see the mountains of South Americy wid the red fire of the setting sun painting their white tops and the clouds floating by them! [*His tone of exaltation ceases. He goes on mournfully.*] Yerra, what's the use of talking? 'Tis a dead man's whisper. [*To* YANK *resentfully*] 'Twas them days men belonged to ships, not now. 'Twas them days a ship was part of the sea, and a man was part of a ship, and the sea joined all together and made it one. [*Scornfully*] Is it one wid this you'd be, Yank — black smoke from the funnels smudging the sea, smudging the decks — the bloody engines pounding and throbbing and shaking — wid divil a sight of sun or a breath of clean air — choking our lungs wid coal dust — breaking our backs and hearts in the hell of the stokehole — feeding the bloody furnace — feeding our lives along wid the coal, I'm thinking — caged in by steel from a sight of the sky like bloody apes in the Zoo! [*With a harsh laugh*] Ho-ho, divil mend you! Is it to belong to that you're wishing? Is it a flesh and blood wheel of the engines you'd be?

YANK. [*Who has been listening with a contemptuous sneer, barks out the answer*] Sure ting! Dat's me. What about it?

PAD. [*As if to himself — with great sorrow*] Me time is past due. That a great wave wid sun in the heart of it may sweep me over the side sometime I'd be dreaming of the days that's gone!

YANK. Aw, yuh crazy Mick! [*He springs to his feet and advances on* PADDY *threateningly — then stops, fighting some queer struggle within himself — lets his hands fall to his sides — contemptuously.*] Aw, take it easy. Yuh're aw right at dat. Yuh're bugs, dat's all — nutty as a cuckoo. All dat tripe yuh been pullin' — Aw, dat's all right. On'y it's dead, get me? Yuh don't belong no more, see.

Yuh don't get de stuff. Yuh're too old. [*Disgustedly*] But aw say, come up for air onct in a while, can't yuh? See what's happened since yuh croaked. [*He suddenly bursts forth vehemently, growing more and more excited.*] Say! Sure! Sure I meant it! What de hell — Say, lemme talk! Hey! Hey, you old Harp! Hey, youse guys! Say, listen to me — wait a moment — I gotter talk, see. I belong and he don't. He's dead but I'm livin'. Listen to me! Sure I'm part of de engines! Why de hell not! Dey move, don't dey? Dey're speed, ain't dey! Dey smash trou, don't dey? Twenty-five knots a hour! Dat's goin' some! Dat's new stuff! Dat belongs! But him, he's too old. He gets dizzy. Say, listen. All dat crazy tripe about nights and days; all dat crazy tripe about stars and moons; all dat crazy tripe about suns and winds, fresh air and de rest of it — Aw, hell, dat's all a dope dream! Hittin' de pipe of de past, dat's what he's doin'. He's old and don't belong no more. But me, I'm young! I'm in de pink! I move wit it! It, get me! I mean de ting dat's de guts of all dis. It ploughs trou all de tripe he's been sayin'. It blows dat up! It knocks dat dead! It slams dat offen de face of de oith! It, get me! De engines and de coal and de smoke and all de rest of it! He can't breathe and swallow coal dust, but I kin, see? Dat's fresh air for me! Dat's food for me! I'm new, get me? Hell in de stokehole? Sure! It takes a man to work in hell. Hell, sure, dat's my fav'rite climate. I eat it up! I git fat on it! It's me makes it hot! It's me makes it roar! It's me makes it move! Sure, on'y for me everyting stops. It all goes dead, get me? De noise and smoke and all de engines movin' de woild, dey stop. Dere ain't nothin' no more! Dat's what I'm sayin'. Everyting else dat makes de woild move, somep'n makes it move. It can't move witout somep'n else, see? Den yuh get down to me. I'm at de bottom, get me! Dere ain't nothin' foither. I'm de end! I'm de start! I start somep'n and de woild moves! It — dat's me! — de new dat's moiderin' de old! I'm de ting in coal dat makes it boin; I'm steam and oil for de engines; I'm de ting in noise dat makes yuh hear it; I'm smoke and express trains and steamers and factory whistles; I'm de ting in gold dat makes it money! And I'm what makes iron into steel! Steel, dat stands for de whole ting! And I'm steel — steel — steel! I'm de muscles in steel, de punch behind it! [*As he says this he pounds with his fist against the steel bunks. All the men, roused to a pitch of frenzied self-glorification by his speech, do likewise. There is a deafening metallic roar, through which* YANK's *voice can be heard bellowing.*] Slaves, hell! We run de whole woiks. All de rich guys dat tink dey're somep'n, dey ain't nothin'! Dey don't belong. But us guys, we're in de move, we're at de bottom, de whole ting is us! [PADDY *from the start of* YANK's *speech has been tak-*

11. 4:00 to 8:00 P.M.

ing one gulp after another from his bottle, at first frightenedly, as if he were afraid to listen, then desperately, as if to drown his senses, but finally has achieved complete indifference, even amused, drunkenness. YANK sees his lips moving. He quells the uproar with a shout.] Hey, youse guys, take it easy! Wait a moment! De nutty Harp is sayin' somep'n.

PAD. [Is heard now — throws his head back with a mocking burst of laughter.] Ho-ho-ho-ho-ho —

YANK. [Drawing back his fist, with a snarl] Aw! Look out who yuh're givin' the bark!

PAD. [Begins to sing the "Miller of Dee" with enormous good nature]

"I care for nobody, no, not I,
And nobody cares for me."

YANK. [Good-natured himself in a flash, interrupts PADDY with a slap on the bare back like a report] Dat's de stuff! Now yuh're gettin' wise to somep'n. Care for nobody, dat's de dope! To hell wit 'em all! And nix on nobody else carin'. I kin care for myself, get me! [Eight bells sound, muffled, vibrating through the steel walls as if some enormous brazen gong were imbedded in the heart of the ship. All the men jump up mechanically, file through the door silently close upon each other's heels in what is very like a prisoners' lockstep. YANK slaps PADDY on the back.] Our watch, yuh old Harp! [Mockingly] Come on down in hell. Eat up de coal dust. Drink in de heat. It's it, see! Act like yuh liked it, yuh better — or croak yuhself.

PAD. [With jovial defiance] To the divil wid it! I'll not report this watch. Let them log me [12] and be damned. I'm no slave the like of you. I'll be sittin' here at me ease, and drinking, and thinking, and dreaming dreams.

YANK. [Contemptuously] Tinkin' and dreamin', what'll that get yuh? What's tinkin' got to do wit it? We move, don't we? Speed, ain't it? Fog, dat's all you stand for. But we drive trou dat, don't we? We split dat up and smash trou — twenty-five knots a hour! [Turns his back on PADDY scornfully] Aw, yuh make me sick! Yuh don't belong! [He strides out the door in rear. PADDY hums to himself, blinking drowsily.]   CURTAIN

Scene II

SCENE. Two days out. A section of the promenade deck. MILDRED DOUGLAS and her AUNT are discovered reclining in deck chairs. The former is a girl of twenty, slender, delicate, with a pale, pretty face marred by a self-conscious expression of disdainful superiority. She looks fretful, nervous, and discontented, bored by her own anemia. Her AUNT is a

12. record my absence.

pompous and proud — and fat — old lady. She is a type even to the point of a double chin and lorgnettes. She is dressed pretentiously, as if afraid her face alone would never indicate her position in life. MILDRED is dressed all in white.

The impression to be conveyed by this scene is one of the beautiful, vivid life of the sea all about — sunshine on the deck in a great flood, the fresh sea wind blowing across it. In the midst of this, these two incongruous, artificial figures, inert and disharmonious, the elder like a gray lump of dough touched up with rouge, the younger looking as if the vitality of her stock had been sapped before she was conceived, so that she is the expression not of its life energy but merely of the artificialities that energy had won for itself in the spending.

MILD. [Looking up with affected dreaminess] How the black smoke swirls back against the sky! Is it not beautiful?

AUNT. [Without looking up] I dislike smoke of any kind.

MILD. My great-grandmother smoked a pipe — a clay pipe.

AUNT. [Ruffling] Vulgar.

MILD. She was too distant a relative to be vulgar. Time mellows pipes.

AUNT. [Pretending boredom but irritated] Did the sociology you took up at college teach you that — to play the ghoul on every possible occasion, excavating old bones? Why not let your great-grandmother rest in her grave?

MILD. [Dreamily] With her pipe beside her — puffing in Paradise.

AUNT. [With spite] Yes, you are a natural born ghoul. You are even getting to look like one, my dear.

MILD. [In a passionless tone] I detest you, Aunt. [Looking at her critically] Do you know what you remind me of? Of a cold pork pudding against a background of linoleum tablecloth in the kitchen of a — but the possibilities are wearisome. [She closes her eyes.]

AUNT. [With a bitter laugh] Merci for your candor. But since I am and must be your chaperon — in appearance, at least — let us patch up some sort of armed truce. For my part you are quite free to indulge any pose of eccentricity that beguiles you — as long as you observe the amenities —

MILD. [Drawling] The inanities?

AUNT. [Going on as if she hadn't heard] After exhausting the morbid thrills of social service work on New York's East Side — how they must have hated you, by the way, the poor that you made so much poorer in their own eyes! — you are now bent on making your slumming international. Well, I hope Whitechapel [13] will provide the needed nerve tonic. Do not ask me to chaperon you there, however. I told your father I would not. I loathe deformity. We will hire an army of detectives and you may investigate everything — they allow you to see.

MILD. [*Protesting with a trace of genuine earnestness*] Please do not mock at my attempts to discover how the other half lives. Give me credit for some sort of groping sincerity in that at least. I would like to help them. I would like to be some use in the world. Is it my fault I don't know how? I would like to be sincere, to touch life somewhere. [*With weary bitterness*] But I'm afraid I have neither the vitality nor integrity. All that was burnt out in our stock before I was born. Grandfather's blast furnaces, flaming to the sky, melting steel, making millions — then father keeping those home fires burning, making more millions — and little me at the tail-end of it all. I'm a waste product in the Bessemer process [14] — like the millions. Or rather, I inherit the acquired trait of the by-product, wealth, but none of the energy, none of the strength of the steel that made it. I am sired by gold and damned [15] by it, as they say at the race track — damned in more ways than one. [*She laughs mirthlessly.*]

AUNT. [*Unimpressed — superciliously*] You seem to be going in for sincerity today. It isn't becoming to you, really — except as an obvious pose. Be as artificial as you are, I advise. There's a sort of sincerity in that, you know. And, after all, you must confess you like that better.

MILD. [*Again affected and bored*] Yes, I suppose I do. Pardon me for my outburst. When a leopard complains of its spots, it must sound rather grotesque. [*In a mocking tone*] Purr, little leopard. Purr, scratch, tear, kill, gorge yourself and be happy — only stay in the jungle where your spots are camouflage. In a cage they make you conspicuous.

AUNT. I don't know what you are talking about.

MILD. It would be rude to talk about anything to you. Let's just talk. [*She looks at her wrist watch.*] Well, thank goodness, it's about time for them to come for me. That ought to give me a new thrill, Aunt.

AUNT. [*Affectedly troubled*] You don't mean to say you're really going? The dirt — the heat must be frightful —

MILD. Grandfather started as a puddler. [16] I should have inherited an immunity to heat that would make a salamander shiver. It will be fun to put it to the test.

AUNT. But don't you have to have the captain's — or someone's — permission to visit the stokehole?

MILD. [*With a triumphant smile*] I have it — both his and the chief engineer's. Oh, they didn't want to at first, in spite of my social service credentials. They didn't seem a bit anxious that I should investigate how the other half lives and works on a ship. So I had to tell them that my father, the president of Nazareth Steel, chairman of the board of directors of this line, had told me it would be all right.

AUNT. He didn't.

MILD. How naïve age makes one! But I said he did, Aunt. I even said he had given me a letter to them — which I had lost. And they were afraid to take the chance that I might be lying. [*Excitedly*] So it's ho! for the stokehole. The second engineer is to escort me. [*Looking at her watch again*] It's time. And here he comes, I think.

[*The* SECOND ENGINEER *enters. He is a husky, fine-looking man of thirty-five or so. He stops before the two and tips his cap, visibly embarrassed and ill-at-ease.*]

2. ENG. Miss Douglas?

MILD. Yes. [*Throwing off her rugs and getting to her feet*] Are we all ready to start?

2. ENG. In just a second, ma'am. I'm waiting for the Fourth. He's coming along.

MILD. [*With a scornful smile*] You don't care to shoulder this responsibility alone, is that it?

2. ENG. [*Forcing a smile*] Two are better than one. [*Disturbed by her eyes, glances out to sea — blurts out*] A fine day we're having.

MILD. Is it?

2. ENG. A nice warm breeze —

MILD. It feels cold to me.

2. ENG. But it's hot enough in the sun —

MILD. Not hot enough for me. I don't like Nature. I was never athletic.

2. ENG. [*Forcing a smile*] Well, you'll find it hot enough where you're going.

MILD. Do you mean hell?

2. ENG. [*Flabbergasted, decides to laugh*] Ho-ho! No, I mean the stokehole.

MILD. My grandfather was a puddler. He played with boiling steel.

2. ENG. [*All at sea — uneasily*] Is that so? Hum, you'll excuse me, ma'am, but are you intending to wear that dress?

MILD. Why not?

2. ENG. You'll likely rub against oil and dirt. It can't be helped.

MILD. It doesn't matter. I have lots of white dresses.

13. a slum district in London, comparable to New York's lower East Side.   14. for producing steel from iron.   15. In the pedigree of a racehorse, the male parent is called the sire, the female parent the dam.   16. worker who stirs molten pig iron in a furnace to convert it into wrought iron.

2. ENG. I have an old coat you might throw over —

MILD. I have fifty dresses like this. I will throw this one into the sea when I come back. That ought to wash it clean, don't you think?

2. ENG. [*Doggedly*] There's ladders to climb down that are none too clean — and dark alleyways —

MILD. I will wear this very dress and none other.

2. ENG. No offense meant. It's none of my business. I was only warning you —

MILD. Warning? That sounds thrilling.

2. ENG. [*Looking down the deck — with a sigh of relief*] There's the Fourth now. He's waiting for us. If you'll come —

MILD. Go on. I'll follow you. [*He goes.* MILDRED *turns a mocking smile on her aunt.*] An oaf — but a handsome, virile oaf.

AUNT. [*Scornfully*] Poser!

MILD. Take care. He said there were dark alleyways —

AUNT. [*In the same tone*] Poser!

MILD. [*Biting her lips angrily*] You are right. But would that my millions were not so anemically chaste!

AUNT. Yes, for a fresh pose I have no doubt you would drag the name of Douglas in the gutter!

MILD. From which it sprang. Goodby, Aunt. Don't pray too hard that I may fall into the fiery furnace.

AUNT. Poser!

MILD. [*Viciously*] Old hag! [*She slaps her aunt insultingly across the face and walks off, laughing gayly.*]

AUNT. [*Screams after her*] I said poser!

CURTAIN

Scene III

SCENE. *The stokehole. In the rear, the dimly outlined bulks of the furnaces and boilers. High overhead one hanging electric bulb sheds just enough light through the murky air laden with coal dust to pile up masses of shadows everywhere. A line of men, stripped to the waist, is before the furnace doors. They bend over, looking neither to right nor left, handling their shovels as if they were part of their bodies, with a strange, awkward, swinging rhythm. They use the shovels to throw open the furnace doors. Then from these fiery round holes in the black a flood of terrific light and heat pours full upon the men who are outlined in silhouette in the crouching, inhuman attitudes of chained gorillas. The men shovel with a rhythmic motion, swinging as on a pivot from the coal which lies in heaps on the floor behind to hurl it into the flaming mouths before them. There is a tumult of noise — the brazen clang of the furnace doors as they are flung open or slammed shut, the grating, teeth-gritting grind of steel against steel, of crunching coal. This clash of sounds stuns one's ears with its rending dissonance. But there is order in it, rhythm, a mechanical regulated recurrence, a tempo. And rising above all, making the air hum with the quiver of liberated energy, the roar of leaping flames in the furnaces, the monotonous throbbing beat of the engines.*

As the curtain rises, the furnace doors are shut. The men are taking a breathing spell. One or two are arranging the coal behind them, pulling it into more accessible heaps. The others can be dimly made out leaning on their shovels in relaxed attitudes of exhaustion.

PAD. [*From somewhere in the line — plaintively*] Yerra, will this divil's own watch nivir end? Me back is broke. I'm destroyed entirely.

YANK. [*From the center of the line — with exuberant scorn*] Aw, yuh make me sick! Lie down and croak, why don't yuh? Always beefin', dat's you! Say, dis is a cinch! Dis was made for me! It's my meat, get me! [*A whistle is blown — a thin, shrill note from somewhere overhead in the darkness.* YANK *curses without resentment.*] Dere's de damn engineer crackin' de whip. He tinks we're loafin'.

PAD. [*Vindictively*] God stiffen him!

YANK. [*In an exultant tone of command*] Come on, youse guys! Git into de game! She's gittin' hungry! Pile some grub in her. Trow it into her belly! Come on now, all of youse! Open her up!

[*At this last all the men, who have followed his movements of getting into position, throw open their furnace doors with a deafening clang. The fiery light floods over their shoulders as they bend round for the coal. Rivulets of sooty sweat have traced maps on their backs. The enlarged muscles form bunches of high light and shadow.*]

YANK. [*Chanting a count as he shovels without seeming effort*] One — two — tree — [*His voice rising exultantly in the joy of battle*] Dat's de stuff! Let her have it! All togedder now! Sling it into her! Let her ride! Shoot de piece now! Call de toin on her! Drive her into it! Feel her move! Watch her smoke! Speed, dat's her middle name! Give her coal, youse guys! Coal, dat's her booze! Drink it up, baby! Let's see yuh sprint! Dig in and gain a lap! Dere she go-o-es. [*This last in the chanting formula of the gallery gods[17] at the six-day bike race. He slams his furnace door shut. The others do likewise with as much unison as their wearied bodies will permit. The effect is of one fiery eye after another*

---

17. the people who occupy the highest and cheapest seats in an auditorium.

being blotted out with a series of accompanying bangs.]

PAD. [*Groaning*] Me back is broke. I'm bate out — bate —

[*There is a pause. Then the inexorable whistle sounds again from the dim regions above the electric light. There is a growl of cursing rage from all sides.*]

YANK. [*Shaking his fist upward — contemptuously*] Take it easy dere, you! Who d'yuh tink's runnin' dis game, me or you? When I git ready, we move. Not before! When I git ready, get me!

VOICES. [*Approvingly*] That's the stuff!

Yank tal him, py golly!

Yank ain't afeerd.

Goot poy, Yank!

Give him hell!

Tell 'im 'e's a bloody swine!

Bloody slave-driver!

YANK. [*Contemptuously*] He ain't got no noive. He's yellow, get me? All de engineers is yellow. Dey got streaks a mile wide. Aw, to hell wit him! Let's move, youse guys. We had a rest. Come on, she needs it! Give her pep! It ain't for him. Him and his whistle, dey don't belong. But we belong, see! We gotter feed de baby! Come on! [*He turns and flings his furnace door open. They all follow his lead. At this instant the* SECOND *and* FOURTH EN-GINEERS *enter from the darkness on the left with* MILDRED *between them. She starts, turns paler, her pose is crumbling, she shivers with fright in spite of the blazing heat, but forces herself to leave the* EN-GINEERS *and take a few steps nearer the men. She is right behind* YANK. *All this happens quickly while the men have their backs turned.*]

YANK. Come on, youse guys! [*He is turning to get coal when the whistle sounds again in a peremptory, irritating note. This drives* YANK *into a sudden fury. While the other men have turned full around and stopped dumfounded by the spectacle of* MIL-DRED *standing there in her white dress,* YANK *does not turn far enough to see her. Besides, his head is thrown back, he blinks upward through the murk trying to find the owner of the whistle, he brandishes his shovel murderously over his head in one hand, pounding on his chest, gorilla-like, with the other, shouting.*] Toin off dat whistle! Come down outa dere, yuh yellow, brass-buttoned, Belfast bum, yuh! Come down and I'll knock yer brains out! Yuh lousy, stinkin', yellow mut of a Catholic-moiderin' bastard! Come down and I'll moider yuh. Pullin' dat whistle on me, huh? I'll show yuh! I'll crash yer skull in! I'll drive yer teet' down yer troat! I'll slam yer nose trou de back of yer head! I'll cut yer guts out for a nickel, yuh lousy boob, yuh dirty, crummy, muck-eatin' son of a — [*Suddenly he becomes conscious of all the other men staring at something directly behind his back. He whirls defensively with a snarling, murderous growl, crouching to spring, his lips drawn back over his teeth, his small eyes gleaming ferociously. He sees* MILDRED, *like a white apparition in the full light from the open furnace doors. He glares into her eyes, turned to stone. As for her, during his speech she has listened, paralyzed with horror, terror, her whole personality crushed, beaten in, collapsed, by the terrific impact of this unknown, abysmal brutality, naked and shameless. As she looks at his gorilla face, as his eyes bore into hers, she utters a low, choking cry and shrinks away from him, putting both hands up before her eyes to shut out the sight of his face, to protect her own. This startles* YANK *to a reaction. His mouth falls open, his eyes grow bewildered.*]

MILD. [*About to faint — to the* ENGINEERS, *who now have her one by each arm — whimperingly*] Take me away! Oh, the filthy beast! [*She faints. They carry her quickly back, disappearing in the darkness at the left, rear. An iron door clangs shut. Rage and bewildered fury rush back on* YANK. *He feels himself insulted in some unknown fashion in the very heart of his pride. He roars.*] God damn yuh! [*And hurls his shovel after them at the door which has just closed. It hits the steel bulkhead with a clang and falls clattering on the steel floor. From overhead the whistle sounds again in a long, angry, insistent command.*]

CURTAIN

Scene IV

SCENE. *The firemen's forecastle.* YANK'S *watch has just come off duty and had dinner. Their faces and bodies shine from a soap and water scrubbing but around their eyes, where a hasty dousing does not touch, the coal dust sticks like black make-up, giving them a queer, sinister expression.* YANK *has not washed either face or body. He stands out in contrast to them, a blackened, brooding figure. He is seated forward on a bench in the exact attitude of Rodin's "The Thinker."* [18] *The others, most of them smoking pipes, are staring at* YANK *half-apprehensively, as if fearing an outburst; half-amusedly, as if they saw a joke somewhere that tickled them.*

VOICES. He ain't ate nothin'.

Py golly, a fallar gat to gat grub in him.

Divil a lie.

Yank feeda da fire, no feeda da face.

Ha-ha.

18. a famous statue by the French sculptor Auguste Rodin (1849-1917), showing a powerful man sitting in deep concentration, with his right elbow resting on his knee, and his chin supported by his right hand.

He ain't even washed hisself.

He's forgot.

Hey, Yank, you forgot to wash.

YANK. [*Sullenly*] Forgot, nothin'! To hell wit washin'.

VOICES. It'll stick to you.

It'll get under your skin.

Give yer the bleedin' itch, that's wot.

It makes spots on you — like a leopard.

Like a piebald nigger, you mean.

Better wash up, Yank.

You sleep better.

Wash up, Yank.

Wash up! Wash up!

YANK. [*Resentfully*] Aw say, youse guys. Lemme alone. Can't youse see I'm tryin' to tink?

ALL. [*Repeating the word after him as one with cynical mockery*] Think! [*The word has a brazen, metallic quality as if their throats were phonograph horns. It is followed by a chorus of hard, barking laughter.*]

YANK. [*Springing to his feet and glaring at them belligerently*] Yes, tink! Tink, dat's what I said! What about it? [*They are silent, puzzled by his sudden resentment at what used to be one of his jokes.* YANK *sits down again in the same attitude of " The Thinker."*]

VOICES. Leave him alone.

He's got a grouch on.

Why wouldn't he?

PAD. [*With a wink at the others*] Sure I know what's the matter. 'Tis aisy to see. He's fallen in love, I'm telling you.

ALL. [*Repeating the word after him as one with cynical mockery*] Love! [*The word has a brazen, metallic quality as if their throats were phonograph horns. It is followed by a chorus of hard, barking laughter.*]

YANK. [*With a contemptuous snort*] Love, hell! Hate, dat's what. I've fallen in hate, get me?

PAD. [*Philosophically*] 'Twould take a wise man to tell one from the other. [*With a bitter, ironical scorn, increasing as he goes on*] But I'm telling you it's love that's in it. Sure what else but love for us poor bastes in the stokehole would be bringing a fine lady, dressed like a white quane, down a mile of ladders and steps to be havin' a look at us?

[*A growl of anger goes up from all sides.*]

LONG. [*Jumping on a bench — hectically*] Hinsultin' us! Hinsultin' us, the bloody cow! And them bloody engineers! What right 'as they got to be ex-hibitin' us 's if we was bleedin' monkeys in a menagerie? Did we sign for hinsults to our dignity as 'onest workers? Is that in the ship's articles? You kin bloody well bet it ain't! But I knows why they done it. I arsked a deck steward 'o she was and 'e

told me. 'Er old man's a bleedin' millionaire, a bloody Capitalist! 'E's got enuf bloody gold to sink this bleedin' ship! 'E makes arf the bloody steel in the world! 'E owns this bloody boat! And you and me, Comrades, we're 'is slaves! And the skipper and mates and engineers, they're 'is slaves! And she's 'is bloody daughter and we're all 'er slaves, too! And she gives 'er orders as 'ow she wants to see the bloody animals below decks and down they takes 'er!

[*There is a roar of rage from all sides.*]

YANK. [*Blinking at him bewilderedly*] Say! Wait a moment! Is all dat straight goods?

LONG. Straight as string! The bleedin' steward as waits on 'em, 'e told me about 'er. And what're we goin' ter do, I arsks yer? 'Ave we got ter swaller 'er hinsults like dogs? It ain't in the ship's articles. I tell yer we got a case. We kin go to law —

YANK. [*With abysmal contempt*] Hell! Law!

ALL. [*Repeating the word after him as one with cynical mockery*] Law! [*The word has a brazen metallic quality as if their throats were phonograph horns. It is followed by a chorus of hard, barking laughter.*]

LONG. [*Feeling the ground slipping from under his feet — desperately*] As voters and citizens we kin force the bloody governments —

YANK. [*With abysmal contempt*] Hell! Governments!

ALL. [*Repeating the word after him as one with cynical mockery*] Governments! [*The word has a brazen metallic quality as if their throats were phonograph horns. It is followed by a chorus of hard, barking laughter.*]

LONG. [*Hysterically*] We're free and equal in the sight of God —

YANK. [*With abysmal contempt*] Hell! God!

ALL. [*Repeating the word after him as one with cynical mockery*] God! [*The word has a brazen metallic quality as if their throats were phonograph horns. It is followed by a chorus of hard, barking laughter.*]

YANK. [*Witheringly*] Aw, join de Salvation Army!

ALL. Sit down! Shut up! Damn fool! Sea-lawyer! [LONG *slinks back out of sight.*]

PAD. [*Continuing the trend of his thoughts as if he had never been interrupted — bitterly*] And there she was standing behind us, and the Second pointing at us like a man you'd hear in a circus would be saying: In this cage is a queerer kind of baboon than ever you'd find in darkest Africy. We roast them in their own sweat — and be damned if you won't hear some of thim saying they like it! [*He glances scornfully at* YANK.]

YANK. [*With a bewildered uncertain growl*] Aw!

PAD. And there was Yank roarin' curses and turning round wid his shovel to brain her — and she looked at him, and him at her —

YANK. [*Slowly*] She was all white. I tought she was a ghost. Sure.

PAD. [*With heavy, biting sarcasm*] 'Twas love at first sight, divil a doubt of it! If you'd seen the endearin' look on her pale mug when she shriveled away with her hands over her eyes to shut out the sight of him! Sure, 'twas as if she'd seen a great hairy ape escaped from the Zoo!

YANK. [*Stung — with a growl of rage*] Aw!

PAD. And the loving way Yank heaved his shovel at the skull of her, only she was out the door! [*A grin breaking over his face*] 'Twas touching, I'm telling you! It put the touch of home, swate home in the stokehole.

[*There is a roar of laughter from all.*]

YANK. [*Glaring at PADDY menacingly*] Aw, choke dat off, see!

PAD. [*Not heeding him — to the others*] And her grabbin' at the Second's arm for protection. [*With a grotesque imitation of a woman's voice*] Kiss me, Engineer dear, for it's dark down here and me old man's in Wall Street making money! Hug me tight, darlin', for I'm afeerd in the dark and me mother's on deck makin' eyes at the skipper!

[*Another roar of laughter.*]

YANK. [*Threateningly*] Say! What yuh tryin' to do, kid me, yuh old Harp?

PAD. Divil a bit! Ain't I wishin' myself you'd brained her?

YANK. [*Fiercely*] I'll brain her! I'll brain her yet, wait 'n' see! [*Coming over to PADDY — slowly*] Say, is dat what she called me — a hairy ape?

PAD. She looked it at you if she didn't say the word itself.

YANK. [*Grinning horribly*] Hairy ape, huh? Sure! Dat's de way she looked at me, aw right. Hairy ape! So dat's me, huh? [*Bursting into rage — as if she were still in front of him*] Yuh skinny tart! Yuh whitefaced bum, yuh! I'll show yuh who's a ape! [*Turning to the others, bewilderment seizing him again*] Say, youse guys. I was bawlin' him out for pullin' de whistle on us. You heard me. And den I seen youse lookin' at somep'n and I tought he'd sneaked down to come up in back of me, and I hopped round to knock him dead wit de shovel. And dere she was wit de light on her! Christ, yuh coulda pushed me over with a finger! I was scared, get me? Sure! I tought she was a ghost, see? She was all in white like dey wrap around stiffs. You seen her. Kin yuh blame me? She didn't belong, dat's what. And den when I come to and seen it was a real skoit and seen de way she was lookin' at me — like Paddy said — Christ, I was sore, get me? I don't stand for dat stuff from nobody. And I flung de shovel — on'y she'd beat it. [*Furiously*] I wished it'd banged her! I wished it'd knocked her block off!

LONG. And be 'anged for murder or 'lectrocuted? She ain't bleedin' well worth it.

YANK. I don't give a damn what! I'd be square wit her, wouldn't I? Tink I wanter let her put somep'n over on me? Tink I'm goin' to let her git away wit dat stuff? Yuh don't know me! No one ain't never put nothin' over on me and got away wit it, see! — not dat kind of stuff — no guy and no skoit neither! I'll fix her! Maybe she'll come down again —

VOICE. No chance, Yank. You scared her out of a year's growth.

YANK. I scared her? Why de hell should I scare her? Who de hell is she? Ain't she de same as me? Hairy ape, huh? [*With his old confident bravado*] I'll show her I'm better'n her, if she on'y knew it. I belong and she don't, see! I move and she's dead! Twenty-five knots a hour, dat's me! Dat carries her but I make dat. She's on'y baggage. Sure! [*Again bewilderedly*] But, Christ, she was funny lookin'! Did yuh pipe [19] her hands? White and skinny. Yuh could see de bones trough 'em. And her mush,[20] dat was dead white, too. And her eyes, dey was like dey'd seen a ghost. Me, dat was! Sure! Hairy ape! Ghost, huh? Look at dat arm! [*He extends his right arm, swelling out the great muscles.*] I coulda took her wit dat, wit just my little finger even, and broke her in two. [*Again bewilderedly*] Say, who is dat skoit, huh? What is she? What's she come from? Who made her? Who give her de noive to look at me like dat? Dis ting's got my goat right. I don't get her. She's new to me. What does a skoit like her mean, huh? She don't belong, get me! I can't see her. [*With growing anger*] But one ting I'm wise to, aw right, aw right! Youse all kin bet your shoits I'll git even wit her. I'll show her if she tinks she — She grinds de organ and I'm on de string, huh? I'll fix her! Let her come down again and I'll fling her in de furnace! She'll move den! She won't shiver at nothin', den! Speed, dat'll be her! She'll belong den! [*He grins horribly.*]

PAD. She'll never come. She's had her belly-full, I'm telling you. She'll be in bed now, I'm thinking, wid ten doctors and nurses feedin' her salts to clean the fear out of her.

YANK. [*Enraged*] Yuh tink I made her sick, too, do yuh? Just lookin' at me, huh? Hairy ape, huh? [*In a frenzy of rage*] I'll fix her! I'll tell her where to git off! She'll git down on her knees and take it back or I'll bust de face offen her! [*Shaking one fist upward and beating on his chest with the other*] I'll

19. see, look at.   20. face.

find yuh! I'm comin', d'yuh hear? I'll fix yuh, God damn yuh! [*He makes a rush for the door.*]

VOICES. Stop him!
He'll get shot!
He'll murder her!
Trip him up!
Hold him!
He's gone crazy!
Gott, he's strong!
Hold him down!
Look out for a kick!
Pin his arms!

[*They have all piled on him and, after a fierce struggle, by sheer weight of numbers have borne him to the floor just inside the door.*]

PAD. [*Who has remained detached*] Kape him down till he's cooled off. [*Scornfully*] Yerra, Yank, you're a great fool. Is it payin' attention at all you are to the like of that skinny sow widout one drop of rale blood in her?

YANK. [*Frenziedly, from the bottom of the heap*] She done me doit! She done me doit, didn't she? I'll git square wit her! I'll get her some way! Git offen me, youse guys! Lemme up! I'll show her who's a ape!

CURTAIN

Scene V

SCENE. *Three weeks later. A corner of Fifth Avenue in the Fifties on a fine Sunday morning. A general atmosphere of clean, well-tidied, wide street; a flood of mellow, tempered sunshine; gentle, genteel breezes. In the rear, the show windows of two shops, a jewelry establishment on the corner, a furrier's next to it. Here the adornments of extreme wealth are tantalizingly displayed. The jeweler's window is gaudy with glittering diamonds, emeralds, rubies, pearls, etc., fashioned in ornate tiaras, crowns, necklaces, collars, etc. From each piece hangs an enormous tag from which a dollar sign and numerals in intermittent electric lights wink out incredible prices. The same in the furrier's. Rich furs of all varieties hang there bathed in a downpour of artificial light. The general effect is of a background of magnificence cheapened and made grotesque by commercialism, a background in tawdry disharmony with the clear light and sunshine on the street itself.*

Up the side street YANK *and* LONG *come swaggering.* LONG *is dressed in shore clothes, wears a black Windsor tie, cloth cap.* YANK *is in his dirty dungarees. A fireman's cap with black peak is cocked defiantly on the side of his head. He has not shaved for days and around his fierce, resentful eyes — as around those of* LONG *to a lesser degree — the black smudge of coal dust still sticks like make-up. They*

hesitate and stand together at the corner, swaggering, looking about them with a forced, defiant contempt.

LONG. [*Indicating it all with an oratorical gesture*] Well, 'ere we are. Fif' Avenoo. This 'ere's their bleedin' private lane, as yer might say. [*Bitterly*] We're trespassers 'ere. Proletarians keep orf the grass!

YANK. [*Dully*] I don't see no grass, yuh boob. [*Staring at the sidewalk*] Clean, ain't it? Yuh could eat a fried egg offen it. The white wings [21] got some job sweepin' dis up. [*Looking up and down the avenue — surlily*] Where's all de white-collar stiffs yuh said was here — and de skoits — her kind?

LONG. In church, blarst 'em! Arskin' Jesus to give 'em more money.

YANK. Choich, huh? I useter go to choich onct — sure — when I was a kid. Me old man and woman, dey made me. Dey never went demselves, dough. Always got too big a head on Sunday mornin', dat was dem. [*With a grin*] Dey was scrappers for fair, bot' of dem. On Satiday nights when dey bot' got a skinful dey could put up a bout oughter been staged at de Garden.[22] When dey got trough dere wasn't a chair or table wit a leg under it. Or else dey bot' jumped on me for somep'n. Dat was where I loined to take punishment. [*With a grin and a swagger*] I'm a chip offen de old block, get me?

LONG. Did yer old man follow the sea?

YANK. Naw. Worked along shore. I runned away when me old lady croaked wit de tremens.[23] I helped at truckin' and in de market. Den I shipped in de stokehole. Sure. Dat belongs. De rest was nothin'. [*Looking around him*] I ain't never seen dis before. De Brooklyn waterfront, dat was where I was dragged up. [*Taking a deep breath*] Dis ain't so bad at dat, huh?

LONG. Not bad? Well, we pays for it wiv our bloody sweat, if yer wants to know!

YANK. [*With sudden angry disgust*] Aw, hell! I don't see no one, see — like her. All dis gives me a pain. It don't belong. Say, ain't dere a back room around dis dump? Let's go shoot a ball.[24] All dis is too clean and quiet and dolled-up, get me! It gives me a pain.

LONG. Wait and yer'll bloody well see —

YANK. I don't wait for no one. I keep on de move. Say, what yuh drag me up here for, anyway? Tryin' to kid me, yuh simp, yuh?

LONG. Yer wants to get back at 'er, don't yer? That's what yer been sayin' every bloomin' hour since she hinsulted yer.

---

21. street cleaners, who wore white suits at this time. 22. Madison Square Garden, New York. 23. delirium tremens, a violent delirium caused by acute alcoholism. 24. play pool.

YANK. [*Vehemently*] Sure ting I do! Didn't I try to get even with her in Southampton? Didn't I sneak on de dock and wait for her by de gangplank? I was goin' to spit in her pale mug, see! Sure, right in her pop-eyes! Dat woulda made me even, see? But no chanct. Dere was a whole army of plain-clothes bulls around. Dey spotted me and gimme de bum's rush. I never seen her. But I'll git square wit her yet, you watch! [*Furiously*] De lousy tart! She tinks she kin get away wit moider — but not wit me! I'll fix her! I'll tink of a way.

LONG. [*As disgusted as he dares to be*] Ain't that why I brought yer up 'ere — to show yer? Yer been lookin' at this 'ere 'ole affair wrong. Yer been actin' an' talkin' 's if it was all a bleedin' personal matter between yer and that bloody cow. I wants to convince yer she was on'y a representative of 'er clarss. I wants to awaken yer bloody clarss consciousness. Then yer'll see it's 'er clarss yer've got to fight, not 'er alone. There's a 'ole mob of 'em like 'er, Gawd blind 'em!

YANK. [*Spitting on his hands — belligerently*] De more de merrier when I gits started. Bring on de gang!

LONG. Yer'll see 'em in arf a mo', when that church lets out. [*He turns and sees the window display in the two stores for the first time.*] Blimey! [25] Look at that, will yer? [*They both walk back and stand looking in the jeweler's.* LONG *flies into a fury.*] Just look at this 'ere bloomin' mess! Just look at it! Look at the bleedin' prices on 'em — more'n our 'ole bloody stokehole makes in ten voyages sweatin' in 'ell! And they — 'er and 'er bloody clarss — buys 'em for toys to dangle on 'em! One of these 'ere would buy scoff [26] for a starvin' family for a year!

YANK. Aw, cut de sob stuff! T' hell wit de starvin' family! Yuh'll be passin' de hat to me next. [*With naïve admiration*] Say, dem tings is pretty, huh? Bet yuh dey'd hock for a piece of change aw right. [*Then turning away, bored*] But, aw hell, what good are dey? Let her have 'em. Dey don't belong no more'n she does. [*With a gesture of sweeping the jewelers into oblivion*] All dat don't count, get me?

LONG. [*Who has moved to the furrier's — indignantly*] And I s'pose this 'ere don't count neither — skins of poor, 'armless animals slaughtered so as 'er and 'ers can keep their bleedin' noses warm!

YANK. [*Who has been staring at something inside — with queer excitement*] Take a slant at dat! Give it de once-over! Monkey fur — two t'ousand bucks! [*Bewilderedly*] Is dat straight goods — monkey fur? What de hell — ?

LONG. [*Bitterly*] It's straight enuf. [*With grim humor*] They wouldn't bloody well pay that for a 'airy ape's skin — no, nor for the 'ole livin' ape with all 'is 'ead, and body, and soul thrown in!

YANK. [*Clenching his fists, his face growing pale with rage as if the skin in the window were a personal insult*] Trowin' it up in my face! Christ! I'll fix her!

LONG. [*Excitedly*] Church is out. 'Ere they come, the bleedin' swine. [*After a glance at* YANK's *lowering face — uneasily*] Easy goes, Comrade. Keep yer bloomin' temper. Remember force defeats itself. It ain't our weapon. We must impress our demands through peaceful means — the votes of the on-marching proletarians of the bloody world!

YANK. [*With abysmal contempt*] Votes, hell! Votes is a joke, see. Votes for women! Let dem do it!

LONG. [*Still more uneasily*] Calm, now. Treat 'em wiv the proper contempt. Observe the bleedin' parasites but 'old yer 'orses.

YANK. [*Angrily*] Git away from me! Yuh're yellow, dat's what. Force, dat's me! De punch, dat's me every time, see!

[*The crowd from church enter from the right, sauntering slowly and affectedly, their heads held stiffly up, looking neither to right nor left, talking in toneless, simpering voices. The women are rouged, calcimined, dyed, over-dressed to the nth degree. The men are in Prince Alberts, high hats, spats, canes, etc. A procession of gaudy marionettes, yet with something of the relentless horror of Frankensteins in their detached, mechanical unawareness.*]

VOICES. Dear Doctor Caiaphas! [27] He is so sincere!
    What was the sermon? I dozed off.
    About the radicals, my dear — and the false doctrines that are being preached.
    We must organize a hundred per cent American bazaar.
    And let everyone contribute one one-hundredth per cent of their income tax.
    What an original idea!
    We can devote the proceeds to rehabilitating the veil of the temple. [28]
    But that has been done so many times.

YANK. [*Glaring from one to the other of them — with an insulting snort of scorn*] Huh! Huh!

[*Without seeming to see him, they make wide detours to avoid the spot where he stands in the middle of the sidewalk.*]

---

25. a Cockney exclamation (short for "God blind me!").
26. food, meals.

27. the name of the High Priest who presided at the Council of Sadducees which condemned Jesus. 28. When Jesus died the veil protecting the Ark of the Covenant in the temple of Jerusalem "was rent in twain from the top to the bottom" (Mark 15:38; cf. Matthew 27:51, Luke 23:45).

LONG. [*Frightenedly*] Keep yer bloomin' mouth shut, I tells yer.

YANK. [*Viciously*] G'wan! Tell it to Sweeney! [*He swaggers away and deliberately lurches into a top-hatted gentleman, then glares at him pugnaciously.*] Say, who d'yuh tink yuh're bumpin'? Tink yuh own de oith?

GENT. [*Coldly and affectedly*] I beg your pardon. [*He has not looked at* YANK *and passes on without a glance, leaving him bewildered.*]

LONG. [*Rushing up and grabbing* YANK's *arm*] 'Ere! Come away! This wasn't what I meant. Yer'll 'ave the bloody coppers down on us.

YANK. [*Savagely — giving him a push that sends him sprawling*] G'wan!

LONG. [*Picks himself up — hysterically*] I'll pop orf then. This ain't what I meant. And whatever 'appens, yer can't blame me. [*He slinks off left.*]

YANK. T' hell wit youse! [*He approaches a lady — with a vicious grin and a smirking wink.*] Hello, Kiddo. How's every little ting? Got anyting on for tonight? I know an old boiler down to de docks we kin crawl into. [*The lady stalks by without a look, without a change of pace.* YANK *turns to others — insultingly.*] Holy smokes, what a mug! Go hide yuhself before de horses shy at yuh. Gee, pipe de heine [29] on dat one! Say, youse, yuh look like de stoin of a ferry-boat. Paint and powder! All dolled up to kill! Yuh look like stiffs laid out for de boneyard! Aw, g'wan, de lot of youse! Yuh give me de eye-ache. Yuh don't belong, get me! Look at me, why don't youse dare? I belong, dat's me! [*Pointing to a skyscraper across the street which is in process of construction — with bravado*] See dat building goin' up dere? See de steel work? Steel, dat's me! Youse guys live on it and tink yuh're somep'n. But I'm *in* it, see! I'm de hoistin' engine dat makes it go up! I'm it — de inside and bottom of it! Sure! I'm steel and steam and smoke and de rest of it! It moves — speed — twenty-five stories up — and me at de top and bottom — movin'! Youse simps don't move. Yuh're on'y dolls I winds up to see 'em spin. Yuh're de garbage, get me — de leavin's — de ashes we dump over de side! Now, what 'a' yuh gotta say? [*But as they seem neither to see nor hear him, he flies into a fury.*] Bums! Pigs! Tarts! Bitches! [*He turns in a rage on the men, bumping viciously into them but not jarring them the least bit. Rather it is he who recoils after each collision. He keeps growling.*] Git off de oith! G'wan, yuh bum! Look where yuh're goin', can't yuh? Git outa here! Fight, why don't yuh? Put up yer mits! Don't be a dog! Fight or I'll knock yuh dead! [*But, without seeming to see him, they*

29. rump.

all answer with mechanical affected politeness.] I beg your pardon. [*Then at a cry from one of the women, they all scurry to the furrier's window.*]

THE WOMAN. [*Ecstatically, with a gasp of delight*] Monkey fur! [*The whole crowd of men and women chorus after her in the same tone of affected delight.*] Monkey fur!

YANK. [*With a jerk of his head back on his shoulders, as if he had received a punch full in the face — raging*] I see yuh, all in white! I see yuh, yuh white-faced tart, yuh! Hairy ape, huh? I'll hairy ape yuh! [*He bends down and grips at the street curbing as if to pluck it out and hurl it. Foiled in this, snarling with passion, he leaps to the lamp-post on the corner and tries to pull it up for a club. Just at that moment a bus is heard rumbling up. A fat, high-hatted, spatted gentleman runs out from the side street. He calls out plaintively.*] Bus! Bus! Stop there! [*And runs full tilt into the bending, straining* YANK, *who is bowled off his balance.*]

YANK. [*Seeing a fight — with the roar of joy as he springs to his feet*] At last! Bus, huh? I'll bust yuh! [*He lets drive a terrific swing, his fist landing full on the fat gentleman's face. But the gentleman stands unmoved as if nothing had happened.*]

GENT. I beg your pardon. [*Then irritably*] You have made me lose my bus. [*He claps his hands and begins to scream.*] Officer! Officer!

[*Many police whistles shrill out on the instant and a whole platoon of policemen rush in on* YANK *from all sides. He tries to fight but is clubbed to the pavement and fallen upon. The crowd at the window have not moved or noticed this disturbance. The clanging gong of the patrol wagon approaches with a clamoring din.*]

CURTAIN

Scene VI

SCENE. *Night of the following day. A row of cells in the prison on Blackwell's Island.* [30] *The cells extend back diagonally from right front to left rear. They do not stop, but disappear in the dark background as if they ran on, numberless, into infinity. One electric bulb from the low ceiling of the narrow corridor sheds its light through the heavy steel bars of the cell at the extreme front and reveals part of the interior.* YANK *can be seen within, crouched on the edge of his cot in the attitude of Rodin's "The Thinker." His face is spotted with black and blue bruises. A blood-stained bandage is wrapped around his head.*

30. in the East River just east of Manhattan, site of city prison (now called Welfare Island).

YANK. [*Suddenly starting as if awakening from a dream, reaches out and shakes the bars — aloud to himself, wonderingly*] Steel. Dis is de Zoo, huh? [*A burst of hard, barking laughter comes from the unseen occupants of the cells, runs back down the tier, and abruptly ceases.*]

VOICES. [*Mockingly*] The Zoo? That's a new name for this coop — a damn good name!

Steel, eh? You said a mouthful. This is the old iron house.

Who is that boob talkin'?

He's the bloke they brung in out of his head. The bulls had beat him up fierce.

YANK. [*Dully*] I musta been dreamin'. I tought I was in a cage at de Zoo — but de apes don't talk, do dey?

VOICES. [*With mocking laughter*] You're in a cage aw right.

A coop!

A pen!

A sty!

A kennel! [*Hard laughter — a pause.*]

Say, guy! Who are you? No, never mind lying. What are you?

Yes, tell us your sad story. What's your game?

What did they jug yuh for?

YANK. [*Dully*] I was a fireman — stokin' on de liners. [*Then with sudden rage, rattling his cell bars*] I'm a hairy ape, get me? And I'll bust youse all in de jaw if yuh don't lay off kiddin' me.

VOICES. Huh! You're a hard boiled duck, ain't you!

When you spit, it bounces! [*Laughter.*]

Aw, can it. He's a regular guy. Ain't you?

What did he say he was — a ape?

YANK. [*Defiantly*] Sure ting! Ain't dat what youse all are — apes? [*A silence. Then a furious rattling of bars from down the corridor.*]

A VOICE. [*Thick with rage*] I'll show yuh who's a ape, yuh bum!

VOICES. Ssshh! Nix!

Can de noise!

Piano! [31]

You'll have the guard down on us!

YANK. [*Scornfully*] De guard? Yuh mean de keeper, don't yuh? [*Angry exclamations from all the cells.*]

VOICE. [*Placatingly*] Aw, don't pay no attention to him. He's off his nut from the beatin'-up he got. Say, you guy! We're waitin' to hear what they landed you for — or ain't yuh tellin'?

YANK. Sure, I'll tell youse. Sure! Why de hell not? On'y — youse won't get me. Nobody gets me but me, see? I started to tell de Judge and all he says

was: "Toity days to tink it over." Tink it over! Christ, dat's all I been doin' for weeks! [*After a pause*] I was tryin' to git even wit someone, see? — someone dat done me doit.

VOICES. [*Cynically*] De old stuff, I bet. Your goil, huh?

Give yuh the double-cross, huh?

That's them every time!

Did yuh beat up de odder guy?

YANK. [*Disgustedly*] Aw, yuh're all wrong! Sure dere was a skoit in it — but not what youse mean, not dat old tripe. Dis was a new kind of skoit. She was dolled up all in white — in de stokehole. I tought she was a ghost. Sure. [*A pause.*]

VOICES. [*Whispering*] Gee, he's still nutty.

Let him rave. It's fun listenin'.

YANK. [*Unheeding — groping in his thoughts*] Her hands — dey was skinny and white like dey wasn't real but painted on somep'n. Dere was a million miles from me to her — twenty-five knots a hour. She was like some dead ting de cat brung in. Sure, dat's what. She didn't belong. She belonged in de window of a toy store, or on de top of a garbage can, see! Sure! [*He breaks out angrily.*] But would yuh believe it, she had de noive to do me doit. She lamped me like she was seein' somep'n broke loose from de menagerie. Christ, yuh'd oughter seen her eyes! [*He rattles the bars of his cell furiously.*] But I'll get back at her yet, you watch! And if I can't find her I'll take it out on de gang she runs wit. I'm wise to where dey hangs out now. I'll show her who belongs! I'll show her who's in de move and who ain't. You watch my smoke!

VOICES. [*Serious and joking*] Dat's de talkin'!

Take her for all she's got!

What was this dame, anyway? Who was she, eh?

YANK. I dunno. First cabin stiff. Her old man's a millionaire, dey says — name of Douglas.

VOICES. Douglas? That's the president of the Steel Trust, I bet.

Sure. I seen his mug in de papers.

He's filthy with dough.

VOICE. Hey, feller, take a tip from me. If you want to get back at that dame, you better join the Wobblies. You'll get some action then.

YANK. Wobblies? What de hell's dat?

VOICE. Ain't you ever heard of the I. W. W.? [32]

YANK. Naw. What is it?

VOICE. A gang of blokes — a tough gang. I been readin' about 'em today in the paper. The guard

31. Quiet down, watch out!

32. Industrial Workers of the World (whose members were called "Wobblies"), a socialist labor organization founded in Chicago in 1905, which disintegrated after World War I.

give me the *Sunday Times*. There's a long spiel [33] about 'em. It's from a speech made in the Senate by a guy named Senator Queen. [*He is in the cell next to* YANK's. *There is a rustling of paper.*] Wait'll I see if I got light enough and I'll read you. Listen. [*He reads.*] "There is a menace existing in this country today which threatens the vitals of our fair Republic — as foul a menace against the very life-blood of the American Eagle as was the foul conspiracy of Catiline [34] against the eagles of ancient Rome! "

VOICE. [*Disgustedly*] Aw, hell! Tell him to salt de tail of dat eagle!

VOICE. [*Reading*] "I refer to that devil's brew of rascals, jailbirds, murderers and cut-throats who libel all honest workingmen by calling themselves the Industrial Workers of the World; but in the light of their nefarious plots, I call them the Industrious *Wreckers* of the World! "

YANK. [*With vengeful satisfaction*] Wreckers, dat's de right dope! Dat belongs! Me for dem!

VOICE. Ssshh! [*Reading*] "This fiendish organization is a foul ulcer on the fair body of our Democracy — "

VOICE. Democracy, hell! Give him the boid, fellers — the raspberry! [*They do.*]

VOICE. Ssshh! [*Reading*] "Like Cato [35] I say to this Senate, the I. W. W. must be destroyed! For they represent an ever-present dagger pointed at the heart of the greatest nation the world has ever known, where all men are born free and equal, with equal opportunities to all, where the Founding Fathers have guaranteed to each one happiness, where Truth, Honor, Liberty, Justice, and the Brotherhood of Man are a religion absorbed with one's mother's milk, taught at our father's knee, sealed, signed, and stamped upon in the glorious Constitution of these United States! " [*A perfect storm of hisses, catcalls, boos, and hard laughter.*]

VOICES. [*Scornfully*] Hurrah for de Fort' of July!
Pass de hat!
Liberty!
Justice!
Honor!
Opportunity!
Brotherhood!

ALL. [*With abysmal scorn*] Aw, hell!

VOICE. Give that Queen Senator guy the bark! All togedder now — one — two — tree — [*A terrific chorus of barking and yapping.*]

33. speech.   34. Lucius Sergius Catilina, who led an unsuccessful conspiracy against the Roman republic (63–62 B.C.) which Cicero opposed in his famous orations.   35. Marcus Porcius Cato, "The Censor" (234–149 B.C.), who campaigned in the Roman Senate for war against Carthage, ending every speech with the words, "Carthage must be destroyed."

GUARD. [*From a distance*] Quiet there, youse — or I'll git the hose. [*The noise subsides.*]

YANK. [*With growling rage*] I'd like to catch that Senator guy alone for a second. I'd loin him some trute!

VOICE. Ssshh! Here's where he gits down to cases on the Wobblies. [*Reads*] "They plot with fire in one hand and dynamite in the other. They stop not before murder to gain their ends, nor at the outraging of defenseless womanhood. They would tear down society, put the lowest scum in the seats of the mighty, turn Almighty God's revealed plan for the world topsy-turvy, and make of our sweet and lovely civilization a shambles, a desolation where man, God's masterpiece, would soon degenerate back to the ape! "

VOICE. [*To* YANK] Hey, you guy. There's your ape stuff again.

YANK. [*With a growl of fury*] I got him. So dey blow up tings, do dey? Dey turn tings round, do dey? Hey, lend me dat paper, will yuh?

VOICE. Sure. Give it to him. On'y keep it to yourself, see. We don't wanter listen to no more of that slop.

VOICE. Here you are. Hide it under your mattress.

YANK. [*Reaching out*] Tanks. I can't read much but I kin manage. [*He sits, the paper in the hand at his side, in the attitude of Rodin's "The Thinker." A pause. Several snores from down the corridor. Suddenly* YANK *jumps to his feet with a furious groan as if some appalling thought had crashed on him — bewilderedly.*] Sure — her old man — president of de Steel Trust — makes half de steel in de world — steel — where I tought I belonged — drivin' trou — movin' — in dat — to make *her* — and cage me in for her to spit on! Christ! [*He shakes the bars of his cell door till the whole tier trembles. Irritated, protesting exclamations from those awakened or trying to get to sleep.*] He made dis — dis cage! Steel! *It* don't belong, dat's what! Cages, cells, locks, bolts, bars — dat's what it means! — holdin' me down wit him at de top! But I'll drive trou! Fire, dat melts it! I'll be fire — under de heap — fire dat never goes out — hot as hell — breakin' out in de night — [*While he has been saying this last he has shaken his cell door to a clanging accompaniment. As he comes to the " breakin' out " he seizes one bar with both hands and, putting his two feet up against the others so that his position is parallel to the floor like a monkey's, he gives a great wrench backwards. The bar bends like a licorice stick under his tremendous strength. Just at this moment the* PRISON GUARD *rushes in, dragging a hose behind him.*]

GUARD. [*Angrily*] I'll loin youse bums to wake me up! [*Sees* YANK] Hello, it's you, huh? Got the

D. Ts.,[36] hey? Well, I'll cure 'em. I'll drown your snakes for yuh! [*Noticing the bar*] Hell, look at dat bar bended! On'y a bug is strong enough for dat!

YANK. [*Glaring at him*] Or a hairy ape, yuh big yellow bum! Look out! Here I come! [*He grabs another bar.*]

GUARD. [*Scared now — yelling off left*] Toin de hose on, Ben! — full pressure! And call de others — and a strait jacket! [*The curtain is falling. As it hides* YANK *from view, there is a splattering smash as the stream of water hits the steel of* YANK's *cell.*]

CURTAIN

Scene VII

SCENE. *Nearly a month later. An I. W. W. local near the waterfront, showing the interior of a front room on the ground floor, and the street outside. Moonlight on the narrow street, buildings massed in black shadow. The interior of the room, which is general assembly room, office, and reading room, resembles some dingy settlement boys' club. A desk and high stool are in one corner. A table with papers, stacks of pamphlets, chairs about it, is at center. The whole is decidedly cheap, banal, commonplace, and unmysterious as a room could well be. The secretary is perched on the stool making entries in a large ledger. An eye shade casts his face into shadows. Eight or ten men, longshoremen, iron workers, and the like, are grouped about the table. Two are playing checkers. One is writing a letter. Most of them are smoking pipes. A big signboard is on the wall at the rear, "Industrial Workers of the World — Local No. 57."*

[YANK *comes down the street outside. He is dressed as in Scene V. He moves cautiously, mysteriously. He comes to a point opposite the door; tiptoes softly up to it, listens, is impressed by the silence within, knocks carefully, as if he were guessing at the password to some secret rite. Listens. No answer. Knocks again a bit louder. No answer. Knocks impatiently, much louder.*]

SECRETARY. [*Turning around on his stool*] What the hell is that — someone knocking? [*Shouts*] Come in, why don't you? [*All the men in the room look up.* YANK *opens the door slowly, gingerly, as if afraid of an ambush. He looks around for secret doors, mystery, is taken aback by the commonplaceness of the room and the men in it, thinks he may have gotten in the wrong place, then sees the signboard on the wall and is reassured.*]

36. delirium tremens, which sometimes produces hallucinations of snakes, insects, etc.

YANK. [*Blurts out*] Hello.

MEN. [*Reservedly*] Hello.

YANK. [*More easily*] I tought I'd bumped into de wrong dump.

SEC. [*Scrutinizing him carefully*] Maybe you have. Are you a member?

YANK. Naw, not yet. Dat's what I come for — to join.

SEC. That's easy. What's your job — longshore?

YANK. Naw. Fireman — stoker on de liners.

SEC. [*With satisfaction*] Welcome to our city. Glad to know you people are waking up at last. We haven't got many members in your line.

YANK. Naw. Dey're all dead to de woild.

SEC. Well, you can help to wake 'em. What's your name? I'll make out your card.

YANK. [*Confused*] Name? Lemme tink.

SEC. [*Sharply*] Don't you know your own name?

YANK. Sure; but I been just Yank for so long — Bob, dat's it — Bob Smith.

SEC. [*Writing*] Robert Smith. [*Fills out the rest of the card*] Here you are. Cost you half a dollar.

YANK. Is dat all — four bits? Dat's easy. [*Gives the* SECRETARY *the money.*]

SEC. [*Throwing it in drawer*] Thanks. Well, make yourself at home. No introductions needed. There's literature on the table. Take some of those pamphlets with you to distribute aboard ship. They may bring results. Sow the seed, only go about it right. Don't get caught and fired. We got plenty out of work. What we need is men who can hold their jobs — and work for us at the same time.

YANK. Sure. [*But he still stands, embarrassed and uneasy.*]

SEC. [*Looking at him — curiously*] What did you knock for? Think we had a coon in uniform to open doors?

YANK. Naw. I tought it was locked — and dat yuh'd wanter give me the once-over trou a peephole or somep'n to see if I was right.

SEC. [*Alert and suspicious but with an easy laugh*] Think we were running a crap game? That door is never locked. What put that in your nut?

YANK. [*With a knowing grin, convinced that this is all camouflage, a part of the secrecy*] Dis burg is full of bulls, ain't it?

SEC. [*Sharply*] What have the cops got to do with us? We're breaking no laws.

YANK. [*With a knowing wink*] Sure. Youse wouldn't for woilds. Sure. I'm wise to dat.

SEC. You seem to be wise to a lot of stuff none of us knows about.

YANK. [*With another wink*] Aw, dat's aw right, see. [*Then made a bit resentful by the suspicious glances from all sides*] Aw, can it! Youse needn't put me trou de toid degree. Can't youse see I belong? Sure! I'm reg'lar. I'll stick, get me? I'll shoot de woiks for youse. Dat's why I wanted to join in.

SEC. [*Breezily, feeling him out*] That's the right spirit. Only are you sure you understand what you've joined? It's all plain and above board; still, some guys get a wrong slant on us. [*Sharply*] What's your notion of the purpose of the I. W. W.?

YANK. Aw, I know all about it.

SEC. [*Sarcastically*] Well, give us some of your valuable information.

YANK. [*Cunningly*] I know enough not to speak outa my toin. [*Then, resentfully again*] Aw, say! I'm reg'lar. I'm wise to de game. I know yuh got to watch your step wit a stranger. For all youse know, I might be a plain-clothes dick, or somep'n, dat's what yuh're tinkin', huh? Aw, forget it! I belong, see? Ask any guy down to de docks if I don't.

SEC. Who said you didn't?

YANK. After I'm 'nitiated, I'll show yuh.

SEC. [*Astounded*] Initiated? There's no initiation.

YANK. [*Disappointed*] Ain't there no password — no grip nor nothin'?

SEC. What'd you think this is — the Elks [37] — or the Black Hand? [38]

YANK. De Elks, hell! De Black Hand, dey're a lot of yellow back-stickin' Ginees. Naw. Dis is a man's gang, ain't it?

SEC. You said it! That's why we stand on our two feet in the open. We got no secrets.

YANK. [*Surprised but admiringly*] Yuh mean to say yuh always run wide open — like dis?

SEC. Exactly.

YANK. Den yuh sure got your noive wit youse!

SEC. [*Sharply*] Just what was it made you want to join us? Come out with that straight.

YANK. Yuh call me? Well, I got noive, too! Here's my hand. Yuh wanter blow tings up, don't yuh? Well, dat's me! I belong!

SEC. [*With pretended carelessness*] You mean change the unequal conditions of society by legitimate direct action — or with dynamite?

YANK. Dynamite! Blow it offen de oith — steel — all de cages — all de factories, steamers, buildings, jails — de Steel Trust and all dat makes it go.

SEC. So — that's your idea, eh? And did you have any special job in that line you wanted to propose to us? [*He makes a sign to the men, who get up cautiously one by one and group behind* YANK.]

YANK. [*Boldly*] Sure, I'll come out wit it. I'll show youse I'm one of de gang. Dere's dat millionaire guy, Douglas —

SEC. President of the Steel Trust, you mean? Do you want to assassinate him?

YANK. Naw, dat don't get yuh nothin'. I mean blow up de factory, de woiks, where he makes de steel. Dat's what I'm after — to blow up de steel, knock all de steel in de woild up to de moon. Dat'll fix tings! [*Eagerly, with a touch of bravado*] I'll do it by me lonesome! I'll show yuh! Tell me where his woiks is, how to git there, all de dope. Gimme de stuff, de old butter — and watch me do de rest! Watch de smoke and see it move! I don't give a damn if dey nab me — long as it's done! I'll soive life for it — and give 'em de laugh! [*Half to himself*] And I'll write her a letter and tell her de hairy ape done it. Dat'll square tings.

SEC. [*Stepping away from* YANK] Very interesting. [*He gives a signal. The men, huskies all, throw themselves on* YANK *and before he knows it they have his legs and arms pinioned. But he is too flabbergasted to make a struggle, anyway. They feel him over for weapons.*]

MAN. No gat, no knife. Shall we give him what's what and put the boots to him?

SEC. No. He isn't worth the trouble we'd get into. He's too stupid. [*He comes closer and laughs mockingly in* YANK's *face.*] Ho-ho! By God, this is the biggest joke they've put up on us yet. Hey, you Joke! Who sent you — Burns or Pinkerton? [39] No, by God, you're such a bonehead I'll bet you're in the Secret Service! Well, you dirty spy, you rotten agent provocateur,[40] you can go back and tell whatever skunk is paying you blood-money for betraying your brothers that he's wasting his coin. You couldn't catch a cold. And tell him that all he'll ever get on us, or ever has got, is just his own sneaking plots that he's framed up to put us in jail. We are what our manifesto says we are, neither more nor less — and we'll give him a copy of that any time he calls. And as for you — [*He glares scornfully at* YANK, *who is sunk in an oblivious stupor.*] Oh, hell, what's the use of talking? You're a brainless ape.

YANK. [*Aroused by the word to fierce but futile struggles*] What's dat, yuh Sheeny bum, yuh!

SEC. Throw him out, boys. [*In spite of his struggles, this is done with gusto and éclat. Propelled by several parting kicks,* YANK *lands sprawling in the middle of the narrow cobbled street. With a growl he starts to get up and storm the closed door, but stops bewildered by the confusion in his brain, pathetically impotent. He sits there, brooding, in as near to the attitude of Rodin's "Thinker" as he can get in his position.*]

YANK. [*Bitterly*] So dem boids don't tink I belong, neider. Aw, to hell wit 'em! Dey're in de

---

37. a fraternal organization.   38. a secret criminal society apparently formed in Italy about 1870 and brought to America by immigrants toward the end of the century.

39. two famous private detective agencies, sometimes engaged by employers to spy on labor unions.   40. secret agent hired to incite people to some illegal action so they can be arrested.

wrong pew — de same old bull — soap boxes and
Salvation Army — no guts! Cut out an hour offen
de job a day and make me happy! Gimme a dollar
more a day and make me happy! Tree square a
day, and cauliflowers in de front yard — ekal rights
— a woman and kids — a lousy vote — and I'm all
fixed for Jesus, huh? Aw, hell! What does dat get
yuh? Dis ting's in your inside, but it ain't your
belly. Feedin' your face — sinkers and coffee — dat
don't touch it. It's way down — at de bottom. Yuh
can't grab it, and yuh can't stop it. It moves, and
everything moves. It stops and de whole woild
stops. Dat's me now — I don't tick, see? — I'm a
busted Ingersoll,[41] dat's what. Steel was me, and
I owned de woild. Now I ain't steel, and de woild
owns me. Aw, hell! I can't see — it's all dark, get
me? It's all wrong! [*He turns a bitter mocking face
up like an ape gibbering at the moon.*] Say, youse
up dere, Man in de Moon, yuh look so wise, gimme
de answer, huh? Slip me de inside dope, de information right from de stable — where do I get off
at, huh?

A POLICEMAN. [*Who has come up the street in
time to hear this last — with grim humor*] You'll
get off at the station, you boob, if you don't get up
out of that and keep movin'.

YANK. [*Looking up at him — with a hard, bitter
laugh*] Sure! Lock me up! Put me in a cage! Dat's
de on'y answer yuh know. G'wan, lock me up!

POL. What you been doin'?

YANK. Enuf to gimme life for! I was born, see?
Sure, dat's de charge. Write it in de blotter. I was
born, get me!

POL. [*Jocosely*] God pity your old woman! [*Then
matter-of-factly*] But I've no time for kidding.
You're soused. I'd run you in but it's too long a
walk to the station. Come on now, get up, or I'll
fan your ears with this club. Beat it now! [*He hauls
YANK to his feet.*]

YANK. [*In a vague mocking tone*] Say, where do
I go from here?

POL. [*Giving him a push — with a grin, indifferently*] Go to hell.

CURTAIN

Scene VIII

SCENE. *Twilight of the next day. The monkey
house at the Zoo. One spot of clear gray light falls
on the front of one cage so that the interior can be
seen. The other cages are vague, shrouded in shadow from which chatterings pitched in a conversa-
tional tone can be heard. On the one cage a sign
from which the word "Gorilla" stands out. The
gigantic animal himself is seen squatting on his*

haunches on a bench in much the same attitude as
Rodin's "Thinker." YANK *enters from the left. Immediately a chorus of angry chattering and screech-
ing breaks out. The gorilla turns his eyes but makes
no sound or move.*

YANK. [*With a hard, bitter laugh*] Welcome to
your city, huh? Hail, hail, de gang's all here! [*At
the sound of his voice the chattering dies away into
an attentive silence.* YANK *walks up to the gorilla's
cage and, leaning over the railing, stares in at its
occupant, who stares back at him, silent and motionless. There is a pause of dead stillness. Then
YANK begins to talk in a friendly confidential tone,
half-mockingly, but with a deep undercurrent of
sympathy.*] Say, yuh're some hard-lookin' guy, ain't
yuh? I seen lots of tough nuts dat de gang called
gorillas, but yuh're de foist real one I ever seen.
Some chest yuh got, and shoulders, and dem arms
and mits! I bet yuh got a punch in eider fist dat'd
knock 'em all silly! [*This with genuine admiration.
The gorilla, as if he understood, stands upright,
swelling out his chest and pounding on it with his
fists.* YANK *grins sympathetically.*] Sure, I get yuh.
Yuh challenge de whole woild, huh? Yuh got what
I was sayin' even if yuh muffed de woids. [*Then
bitterness creeping in*] And why wouldn't yuh get
me? Ain't we both members of de same club — de
Hairy Apes? [*They stare at each other — a pause
— then YANK goes on slowly and bitterly.*] So yuh're
what she seen when she looked at me, de white-
faced tart! I was you to her, get me? On'y outa de
cage — broke out — free to moider her, see? Sure!
Dat's what she tought. She wasn't wise dat I was in
a cage, too — worser'n yours — sure — a damn
sight — 'cause you got some chanct to bust loose —
but me — [*He grows confused.*] Aw, hell! It's all
wrong, ain't it? [*A pause.*] I s'pose yuh wanter
know what I'm doin' here, huh? I been warmin' a
bench down to de Battery [42] — ever since last night.
Sure. I seen de sun come up. Dat was pretty, too —
all red and pink and green. I was lookin' at de sky-
scrapers — steel — and all de ships comin' in, sailin'
out, all over de oith — and dey was steel, too. De
sun was warm, dey wasn't no clouds, and dere was
a breeze blowin'. Sure, it was great stuff. I got it aw
right — what Paddy said about dat bein' de right
dope — on'y I couldn't get *in* it, see? I couldn't belong in dat. It was over my head. And I kept
tinkin' — and den I beat it up here to see what
youse was like. And I waited till dey was all gone
to git yuh alone. Say, how d'yuh feel sittin' in dat
pen all de time, havin' to stand for 'em comin' and
starin' at yuh — de white-faced, skinny tarts and de

41. an inexpensive and popular watch.

42. a park at the southern tip of Manhattan, on upper New
York Bay.

boobs what marry 'em — makin' fun of yuh, laughin' at yuh, gittin' scared of yuh — damn 'em! [*He pounds on the rail with his fist. The gorilla rattles the bars of his cage and snarls. All the other monkeys set up an angry chattering in the darkness.* YANK *goes on excitedly.*] Sure! Dat's de way it hits me, too. On'y yuh're lucky, see? Yuh don't belong wit 'em and yuh know it. But me, I belong wit 'em — but I don't, see? Dey don't belong wit me, dat's what. Get me? Tinkin' is hard — [*He passes one hand across his forehead with a painful gesture. The gorilla growls impatiently.* YANK *goes on gropingly.*] It's dis way, what I'm drivin' at. Youse can sit and dope dream in de past, green woods, de jungle and de rest of it. Den yuh belong and dey don't. Den yuh kin laugh at 'em, see? Yuh're de champ of de woild. But me — I ain't got no past to tink in, nor nothin' dat's comin', on'y what's now — and dat don't belong. Sure, you're de best off! Yuh can't tink, can yuh? Yuh can't talk neider. But I kin make a bluff at talkin' and tinkin' — a'most git away wit it — a'most! — and dat's where de joker comes in. [*He laughs.*] I ain't on oith and I ain't in heaven, get me? I'm in de middle tryin' to separate 'em, takin' all de woist punches from bot' of 'em. Maybe dat's what dey call hell, huh? But you, yuh're at de bottom. You belong! Sure! Yuh're de on'y one in de woild dat does, yuh lucky stiff! [*The gorilla growls proudly.*] And dat's why dey gotter put yuh in a cage, see? [*The gorilla roars angrily.*] Sure! Yuh get me. It beats it when you try to tink it or talk it — it's way down — deep — behind — you 'n' me we feel it. Sure! Bot' members of dis club! [*He laughs — then in a savage tone.*] What de hell! T' hell wit it! A little action, dat's our meat! Dat belongs! Knock 'em down and keep bustin' 'em till dey croaks yuh wit a gat — wit steel! Sure! Are yuh game? Dey've looked at youse, ain't dey — in a cage? Wanter git even? Wanter wind up like a sport 'stead of croakin' slow in dere? [*The gorilla roars an emphatic affirmative.* YANK *goes on with a sort of furious exaltation.*] Sure! Yuh're reg'lar! Yuh'll stick to de finish! Me 'n' you, huh? — bot' members of dis club! We'll put up one last star

bout dat'll knock 'em offen deir seats! Dey'll have to make de cages stronger after we're trou! [*The gorilla is straining at his bars, growling, hopping from one foot to the other.* YANK *takes a jimmy from under his coat and forces the lock on the cage door. He throws this open.*] Pardon from de governor! Step out and shake hands! I'll take yuh for a walk down Fif' Avenoo. We'll knock 'em offen de oith and croak wit de band playin'. Come on, Brother. [*The gorilla scrambles gingerly out of his cage. Goes to* YANK *and stands looking at him.* YANK *keeps his mocking tone — holds out his hand.*] Shake — de secret grip of our order. [*Something, the tone of mockery, perhaps, suddenly enrages the animal. With a spring he wraps his huge arms around* YANK *in a murderous hug. There is a crackling snap of crushed ribs — a gasping cry, still mocking, from* YANK.] Hey, I didn't say kiss me! [*The gorilla lets the crushed body slip to the floor; stands over it uncertainly, considering; then picks it up, throws it in the cage, shuts the door, and shuffles off menacingly into the darkness at left. A great uproar of frightened chattering and whimpering comes from the other cages. Then* YANK *moves, groaning, opening his eyes, and there is silence. He mutters painfully.*] Say — dey oughter match him — wit Zybszko.[43] He got me, aw right. I'm trou. Even him didn't tink I belonged. [*Then, with sudden passionate despair*] Christ, where do I get off at? Where do I fit in? [*Checking himself as suddenly*] Aw, what de hell! No squawkin', see! No quittin', get me! Croak wit your boots on! [*He grabs hold of the bars of the cage and hauls himself painfully to his feet — looks around him bewilderedly — forces a mocking laugh.*] In de cage, huh? [*In the strident tones of a circus barker*] Ladies and gents, step forward and take a slant at de one and only — [*His voice weakening*] — one and original — Hairy Ape from de wilds of — [*He slips in a heap on the floor and dies. The monkeys set up a chattering, whimpering wail. And, perhaps, the Hairy Ape at last belongs.*]

CURTAIN

43. Stanislaus Zbyszko, a famous wrestler of the twenties.

Oedipus

by Lucius Annaeus Seneca

There is little evidence for dating Seneca's plays; they might have been written at any time from about 35 A.D. to 65 A.D., the year of his death. Nor is there any evidence that they were presented on the stage in his own day (although they were acted during the Renaissance). Some scholars believe they were not intended for the stage, but were written to be recited by a single reader before small literary gatherings; others dispute this.

The complete play is reprinted here, in the translation of Clarence Whittlesey Mendell, as it appears in his book Our Seneca *(New Haven:*

Yale University Press, 1941). The original was in Latin verse. The present editor has added the footnotes and, to facilitate comparison, has designated the parts of the play in the manner of the Fitts-Fitzgerald version of Sophocles' Oedipus Rex.

The cast of characters is the same as in Sophocles' play with the following exceptions: TIRESIAS *is assisted here by his daughter,* MANTO. *The messenger from Corinth is here called* SENEX *(old man). The shepherd of Laius is here called* PHORBAS.

Prologue

OED. Banishing night, the uncertain sun returns,
The dawn creeps up by squalid clouds oppressed
And, with a baleful light of ominous flame,
It shall behold homes swept by greedy pest
As day shall show destruction wrought by night.
Joys any man in power? O treacherous boon,
What ills with what fair seeming thou dost hide!
Even as the loftiest peaks ever receive
The tempests' blasts or as the surging sea
Howsoe'er mild lashes the cliff that cleaves   10
With rocky front the mighty deeps, so power
Exalted lies exposed to Destiny.
How wise I fled the throne of Polybus
My sire. An exile fearless, wandering
From care set free, by gods and heaven I swear
I stumbled upon power. And now I cherish
A fear unspeakable that by my hand
My father die: so warn the Delphic laurels°
And yet a greater crime beside they tell.

Is there then fouler than a father's murder?   20
O wretched filial love (I blush to speak
The fated word), marriage incestuous,
A bridal couch by son and mother shared
With impious torches Phoebus prophesies:
Such fear now spurs me from my father's realm.
No driven exile I, forth from my hearth,
But, trusting not myself, for safety's sake
I yielded, mighty Nature, to thy sway.
When fearsome terror rules thee thou must dread
Even what thou still believest impossible: 30
I fear all things nor trust me to myself.
  Now, now for me the Fates prepare some blow.
Else how am I to think this pestilence
That slays the race of Cadmus far and wide
Spares me alone? For what am I reserved?
Amidst the city's ruins and the deaths
Wept ever by new tears, the holocaust
Of a whole folk, I stand apart untouched,
Victim I ween of Phoebus. Could'st believe
A realm so prosperous abandoned so   40
To such dire crimes? We have stained heaven with
    guilt.

18. Delphic laurels: Delphic oracle.

No tender breeze with cooling draught revives
The hearts that breathe forth flames, no Zephyrs
    light
Blow now, but Titan° multiplies the fires
Of burning Dog Star,° pressing hard behind
The Nemean lion.° Moisture leaves the rivers,
Color the grass; Dirce° is dry, within
A tenuous stream Ismenus° flows and scarce
Moistens the shallows with its failing flood.
Darkened, from heaven Phoebus' sister° slips,   50
The world ensaddened pales 'neath clouded day.
No star shines forth in any night serene
But black and heavy vapor broods o'er earth.
The counterfeit of hell has deep disguised
The strongholds of the gods, the homes on high.
Ceres,° long pregnant, will not bring to birth
But trembles yellowing on the lofty stalks.
In withering shoots the sterile harvest dies.
Nowhere is safety from destruction: each
Sex and all ages fall alike, old men   60
And youth, fathers and sons the pestilence
Unites in fatal bond, the wedding torch
Kindles the couch of death and funeral trains
Know neither sounds of weeping nor lament.
Persistent death in such catastrophe
Has drained the eyes, the customary tears
Are dead. Here to the funeral flames a sire,
Dying himself, carries his son and there
A mother maddened carries one child, in haste
To seek another for the self-same bier.   70
Nay, from each grief another grief upsprings
And round the pyre gather new obsequies.
Bodies of dear ones burn with alien fires
Stolen by force: such misery knows no shame.
The cherished bones have not their separate tombs.
Enough to burn them — yet how much of all
Departs to ashes? — earth for the burial mounds
Is wanting and the wood for funeral pyres.
No prayers, no skill avail the stricken, those
Fall that give aid. The pest filches the cure. 80
    Prone at the altar stretch I suppliant hands
Craving swift death that I may anticipate
My falling country nor when all are gone
Die last to be my kingdom's final loss.
O gods too cruel, bitter Fate! To me
Alone of this great multitude is death,
So prompt at hand, denied? Then fly these realms
Infected with a fatal touch, desert
These tears, these deaths, stains that contaminate
The heaven, stains that thou broughtest with thee
    here.   90
Ill-fated guest, flee with all speed, begone

Even to thy parents.
    IOK.   What avails my lord
To augment with such complaint these evils sore?
This is the role of kings, methinks: to accept
Misfortunes, and, the more in doubt thy state,
The while the might of crumbling empire fails,
With foot more firmly planted brave to stand.
'Tis not the hero's part to flee from Fate.
    OED. No fault is mine of cowardice or shame;
My valor knows not timid fear. If now   100
Drawn weapons should confront me or the
    dread
Power of Mars,° against fierce giant hosts
Boldly I'd raise contending hands: not I
Did flee the Sphinx, weaving in riddling wise
Her words, but dared to face the bloody jaws
Of that foul prophetess, the scattered bones
That whitened all the ground, and when upon
Her lofty cliff, scenting the prey, she reared
Her wings, lashing her tail and lionlike
Threatening destruction, I did ask her test.   110
Above me then with dreadful din she roared,
Her jaws snapped and, impatient of delay,
She clawed the cliffside as she hoped to claw
My vitals. But the words involved wherein
She hid her prophecy, the blind deceit,
The treacherous riddle of the beast, I solved.
    IOK. Why now in madness pray too late for
    death?
Thou might'st have died. Yet here is thy reward:
The scepter that repays the Sphinx destroyed.
    OED. There, there is that which fights against us
    now,   120
The fatal ashes of that clever beast.
She now in death is Thebes' destroying pest.
One safety, only one, remains for us
If Phoebus show us yet the way to life.

Párodos

CHOR: Scion of Cadmus' home
        Fallen art thou,
        Thou and thy state alike;
        Reft is thy land of men,
        Desolate Thebes.
        Bacchus, to death a prey   130
        Falls now thy soldiery —
        Host that to farthest Ind°
        Followed thy call,
        Riding the eastern waste,
        Planting thy standards where
        Earth at her farthest stretch
        Greets the new light;
        Looked on the Arab tribes

---

44. Titan: the sun.   45. Dog Star: the bright star Sirius.   46.
Nemean lion: Leo. The sun is in the constellation Leo in July.
47. Dirce: a spring near Thebes.   48. Ismenus: a river near
Thebes.   50. sister: Phoebe, the moon.   56. Ceres: goddess
of agriculture.

102. Mars: god of war.   132. Ind: India.

Dwelling in spicy groves;
Faced the false Parthian shaft   140
Flung in retreat;°
Traversed the Red Sea° shore
Whence on his rising course
Phoebus° with nearer flame
Paints with a darker hue
Savage of Ind.

We of unconquered stock
Perish in headlong fate
While unto death still ride
Panoplies new;   150
Down to the shades beneath
Hastens our endless line
Till for the countless throng
Thebes with her seven gates
Offers no way.
Falters the long slow line,
Death makes delay for death.
Ready to strike the blow
Stood with uplifted hand
Priest of high god.   160
But ere he struck, the bull,
Bending his gilded horns,
Halted before him;
Swift fell the axe, the wound,
Gaping unsightly wide,
Stainless the weapon left;
Stumbled and fell the beast
Helpless before him.

First hath the pestilence
Stricken the feeble sheep   170
Cropping in vain the grass,
Then as they fail,
Fail too the cattle strong.
While midst the dying herds
Shepherds lie dying,
Flocks unattended stray
Into the meadows.
No more the timid deer
Flee from the ravening wolf;
Lions their roaring cease,   180
Bears lose their sullen wrath,
Serpents forget their sting,
Reft of their poison.

No more do the leafy groves
Spread shade on the mountainside,
No more are the meadows green
Or the vines bowed down with grapes:
All things have tasted our woe.

From the depths of hell have burst
The Furies with torch aflame,   190
While Phlegethon° changes his course
And Styx° is loosed from its banks.
Black death spreads her greedy jaws
And stretches o'er earth her wings,
While the aged ferryman° plies
His barque with a wearied arm —
His barque that carries the dead
Across the benighted stream —
And ever returns for more.

And the hound° of hell is loosed   200
From his bonds to roam the earth.
The deserts are filled with groans
And through the sacred groves
Go wandering shades of the dead.
The Cadmeian grove is torn
With hail and Dirce's stream
Runs blood: in the silent night
Go howling the dogs of the dead.

O death that is worse than death!
Dull languor seizes the limbs: 210
Comes a flush on the sickly skin
That is spotted and seared in death.
A breath like a fire consumes
The seat of this mortal life,
Till the cheeks are aflame with blood
And the eyes are glazed and stiff,
Till the eardrums roar and the nose
Drops blood that is black and bursts
The veins till they stand agape.
Incessant the entrails groan   220
As the fever feeds on the flesh.
In vain do they seize apace
The chill of the cold gray stone.
The happier sons of wealth
Seek springs to assuage their thirst;
The rest at the altar base
Beg death and the ready gods
Grant this as their only boon.
For now the shrines are sought
With never a thought of a vow   230
But only to sate the gods.

Scene I

OED. Who seeks the palace there with hurrying
    step?
Is Kreon come, famous in birth and deeds,
Or does my sickened mind blend false and true?

140–41. false . . . retreat: the horsemen of Parthia (south of the Caspian Sea) would pretend flight and then shoot their arrows at the pursuing enemy.   142. Red Sea: Indian Ocean.   144. Phoebus: here seen as the sun.

191. Phlegethon: burning stream in Hades, suggesting the fever brought by the plague.   192. Styx: the river surrounding Hades.   195. ferryman: Charon, who ferried the dead across the Styx.   200. hound: Cerberus, a three-headed dog, chained

CHOR. Kreon is come, sought by our common
   prayers.
OED. With dread I tremble fearful whither Fate
May lead, my fluttering heart fails me distraught
By twin emotions: when ambiguous
Joys come commingled with calamity
The uncertain mind, though eager, fears to know.
Brother of mine own wife, if aught of help   241
Thou bringest to the weary, speak with haste.
   KRE. Doubtful the oracle and puzzling sore.
   OED. Who gives but doubtful aid in woe gives
   none.
   KRE. The Delphic god is wont with riddling
   turns
To hide his secrets.
   OED.   Speak; though the riddle's dark,
Oedipus only has the gift to solve.
   KRE. That royal murder must be expiated
And Laius' death by exile be avenged,
The god decrees. Not sooner shall the day   250
Through heaven course serenely nor produce
Safe draughts of ether uncontaminate.
   OED. Who was the slayer of that famous King?
Whom Phoebus hints at, name, that he may pay
The penalty.
   KRE.   I pray that safely I
May speak things terrible to see or hear.
Dull torpor wraps my limbs, my blood congeals.
For when with suppliant foot at Phoebus' shrine
I entered duly raising reverent hands
In prayer unto the god, an ominous roar   260
Burst from Parnassus' twofold° citadel,
Snow clad, and Phoebus' laurel pendant there
Trembled and shook its leaves while suddenly
Castalia's° sacred stream stood motionless.
Straightway the Letoan° prophetess began
To shake her dreadful locks, in frenzy caught,
To receive Apollo. Ere she had reached the cave
Burst forth these words in more than human voice:
"Kindlier stars shall come to Cadmeian Thebes
If thou, O exile stranger, shalt depart   270
From Dirce, guilty of a monarch's death,
Known as thou art to Phoebus from thy birth.
For thee no lengthy joys remain from that
Slaughter most foul: nay, wars with thine own self
Thou shalt engage, and to thy sons beside
Leave other shameful wars° when thou has turned
Back in thy course to thy nativity."
   OED. What now at heaven's behest I contemplate
Is fitting tribute to a monarch slain
That none by craft may assail true royalty.   280

A king should guard the safety of a king:
No man reveres when dead whom safe he fears.
   KRE. A greater fear expelled our reverence.
   OED. Could any fear prevent the pious task?
   KRE. The Sphinx and her fierce threats of baneful
   song.
   OED. Now shall this crime by order of the gods
Be expiated. Of the immortal host
Whoever looks appeased upon our realm,
Thou in whose hands reside the eternal laws
Of swift revolving heaven, and thou the lord   290
Supreme of this bright universe that dost
With swift revolving wheel unfold the slow
Centuries, thou, too, sister to the sun
That keepest with thy brother constant tryst,
Night wandering Phoebe, thou that rulest the
   winds,
Driving thy dark blue chariot o'er the deep,
And thou that lordst it in the realms of night:°
Hearken ye all: by whoso's violence
Laius fell dead, him may no peaceful home,
No faithful hearth, no kindly welcoming land,   300
Receive in exile. Sorrowing let him mourn
His shameful wedlock and the fruit thereof;
By his own hand may he his father slay
And (what more dreadful can be prayed) commit
All that I fled — no hope for pardon then.
By this my realm I swear which now I rule,
By that I left, by all my household gods,
By thee, O father Neptune, that dost wash
On either side° mine ancient heritage
With twin floods swift recurring: come thou° too   311
As witness to my words, thou that dost stir
The pregnant words of Cirrha's prophetess:
So may old age be sweet for me, my sire
Pass his last day in rich security
Upon his lofty throne and Merope
Conceive no wedlock but with Polybus,
As I spare not through favor him that slew.
   But tell me now, where was the impious act
Committed, was it war or treachery?
   KRE. Faring to chaste Castalia's shady grove,   320
He trod a road with thickets dense beset
Where to the open fields a threefold way
Divides itself: while one road intersects
The land of Phocis, dear to Bacchus' heart,
Whence rising from the plain, soaring aloft
Parnassus rears its double head to heaven,
The second leads to where two oceans guard
The land of Sisyphus;° and still a third
Winds through a hollowed valley to attain

---

to his place, who guarded the entrance to Hades.   **261.** twofold: Mt. Parnassus had twin peaks.   **264.** Castalia: fountain
near the Delphic oracle.   **265.** Letoan: Apollo was the son of
Leto.   **276.** wars: foreshadows the warfare that broke out
after Oedipus' exile between his two sons, Eteocles and Polyneices, over their rights to the throne.

289–97. Thou . . . night: He addresses the gods in this order:
Jupiter, king of the gods; Phoebus, seen as the sun; Phoebe, the
moon; Neptune, god of the sea; and Dis, god of the underworld.
309. either side: Corinth is on an isthmus.   **310. thou:** Phoebus,
who inspired the priestess of the Delphic oracle (Cirrha's prophetess) to pronounce her revelations.   **328. Sisyphus:** founder of
Corinth.

The Olenian meadows, skirts the wandering stream,
Crossing at last fair Elis' chilling flood.   331
There as he passed secure, all unobserved,
A robber band wrought suddenly the deed.
  Now at our time of need, roused by the word
Of Phoebus, comes with slow and trembling step
The blind Tiresias led by Manto's hand.
    OED. Honored of gods, second to Phoebus' self,
Expound this word: name him whom Justice seeks.
    TIR. That slow my tongue is, seeking some delay,   339
Thou with thy generous heart canst understand.
Great share of truth lies hidden from the blind.
But where my country calls and Phoebus too
I follow: let the facts be brought to light:
If still within my veins the blood ran hot
With lusty vigor, I should welcome god
Himself within this breast.° Now to the shrine
Drive ye a bullock with a whitened back,
Likewise a heifer knowing not the yoke.
Thou, daughter, that dost teach my unseeing eyes,
Recount the unfailing signs of augury.   350
    MANTO. At the dread altar stands the victim rich.
    TIR. Call thou the gods solemnly to our rites,
Strewing the altar's top with frankincense.
    MAN. Already incense burns on the gods' hearth.
    TIR. What of the flame? Doth it burn copiously?
    MAN. Quickly it blazes bright and quickly dies.
    TIR. And is the firelight clear, does it rise pure,
Rearing its head untarnished to the sky
To wave its fiery locks to heaven's breeze?
Or creeps it low about the altar's sides   360
Uncertainly bedimmed in circling smoke?
    MAN. Not one the fashion of the flickering flame,
But, like the rainbow when the showers fall,
It takes on varying hues: where to high heaven
Its arch heralds the rain with painted bow
Till doubt assails what colors fail and what
Are there. The blue of heaven is intertwined
With saffron hues, these with blood red until
All ends in darkness; lo the battling flame
Divides and ashes of one sacrifice   370
Are made twofold; father, I dread to look;
Blood takes the place of Bacchus' offering°
And round the King's° head rolls a darkening
        smoke,
Settling more dense around his countenance,
And hides in one thick cloud the murky light;
The meaning, father, speak.
    TIR.   What can I speak,
Lost in the tumult of a mind distraught?
What shall I say? 'Tis evil, dire but dark.
The gods are wont to show their anger clear;

What may it be that so they would reveal,   380
Then would not, but conceal their dreadful wrath?
There is that shames the gods. Bring hither swift
The salted meal and on the victims' necks
Sprinkle it now. Do they with peaceful mien
Endure the sacred rites, the hands that touch?
    MAN. The bullock rears aloft his head, his face,
Turned to the rising sun, avoids the light
And trembling looks away, shunning its rays.
    TIR. And do they fall to earth each at one blow?
    MAN. The heifer yields to the sword: at the first
        stroke   390
She falls; the bull, struck for the second time,
Blunders now here now there till weariness
At length extorts his last reluctant breath.°
    TIR. Spurts forth the blood from out a narrow
        wound
Or flows more sluggish from a deeper source?
    MAN. Forth from the heifer's breast an abundant
        stream
Pours rushing out, the bullock's mightier wounds
Are stained with lesser stream, but, turning back,
The blood flows amply through the mouth and eyes.
    TIR. These portents dire augur some mighty fear.
But tell me now the entrails' certain signs.   401
    MAN. My lord, how now? Not in accustomed wise
Tremble the entrails; mightily they shake
And from the veins there leaps a fount of blood.
The heart is shriveled, hides far out of sight;
The veins show livid; sinews that should be here
Are not, the rotting liver seethes with black gall
And lo, an omen dread to tyrant's reign,
Two heads° appear rising on equal trunks
Until a slender membrane hides them both: 410
The side unfriendly, granting no hiding place
To secret members, rises in its might
Displaying seven veins° that in their turn
Are thwarted by the border set aslant.
Nature and nature's order are reversed:
No single organ holds its rightful place:
All are reversed — the lungs, that cannot hold
The breath, lie bloody on the right, the heart
Has vanished from the left, the bowels give
No passage to the body's excrements,   420
Nature herself is changed: no natural law
Controls this womb. Come, let us find the cause
That makes these entrails stiffen as they lie;
What impious horror here? An embryo calf
Within the unwedded womb, nor holds its place
Therein but fills its mother's body, groans
And weakly moves its legs that stiffly shake;

390–93. heifer . . . breath: The heifer prefigures the suicide of
Iokaste, and the bullock the self-inflicted blindness (see also
ll. 386–88, 399) and long suffering of Oedipus.   409. Two
heads: another foreshadowing of the struggle between Eteocles
and Polyneices.   413. seven veins: Polyneices gathered seven
armies to storm Thebes in this struggle.

345–46. I . . . breast: I would speak by direct inspiration (instead of by divination from the sacrifice).   372. offering: ceremonial wine.   373. King: Oedipus (this suggests his self-blinding).

The livid blood besmears the sinews black,
The empty body rears itself and strikes
With budding horn the sacrificing slaves.   430
The vitals slip from out my hand. That sound
That startles thee is not the lowing herd;
The cattle make no sound: the altar fire
It is that groans and tremblings seize the hearth.
   OED. What mean these omens of the fearful
     rite?
Expound; I hearken with no timid ear.
   TIR. You will be angry at the signs you seek.
   OED. Tell me that one thing that the gods would
     tell,
What man with royal murder stained his hands.
   TIR. Nor birds that fly high heaven on pinions
     light   440
Nor vitals torn from living breasts can tell
That name: we must explore another way.
The King himself from shades of nether night
Must be called forth from Erebus° to speak
His murderer's name. Earth must be reft in twain,
Dis the implacable invoked and all the host
Of Styx infernal summoned to our sight.
Name one to act for thee: who reigns in might
May not behold the dead.
   OED.   Kreon, to thee
This labor falls who art second in this realm.   450
   TIR. While we unloose the bolts of lowest Styx
Let all the host give voice to Bacchus' praise.

Ode I°

   CHOR. With nodding ivy wreathe your disheveled
     locks:
Seize ye° the thyrsus° — seek the Corycian
    rocks.
Thou light of heaven, come.
Thy suppliant band,
Here in thy Theban home,
Summon thee, Bacchus, from thy native
    land.

Hither in festive dance
Turn thy clear virgin glance   460
And with the starry light
Of thy bright countenance
Scatter the clouds of night,
The threats of Erebus
And Fate omnivorous.

Flowers of spring are thine to wear,
And, to crown thy ambrosial hair,
Tyrian miter is for thee
And the clinging briony.
Tresses flung to the wanton wind   470
Or with a serpent clasp confined.

So, in the fear of Juno's hate,
Thou didst grow in virgin state,
And maiden figure counterfeit
To thy saffron robe commit.
Thence thy soft luxurious ways,
Trailing robes and roundelays,
Thus, in golden chariot drawn,
Lions swept thee toward the dawn
Where the Ganges' waters flow   480
And Araxes clothed with snow.

On humble ass Silenus follows thee,
Aged, his swelling temples garlanded,
While wanton followers bear the myster-
    ies.

Following thee a maenad train
Scorned the lowlands and the plain,
Trod in joy Pangaeus' height,
O'er Thracian Pindus took their flight.

Thence to Thebes the maenad band
Led our Bacchus. Cadmus' land   490
Welcomed with its frenzied horde
India's fair Ogygian lord.

Matrons of the Theban state,
Girt with fawn skins dedicate
To Bacchus, thyrsus wielding,
Blindly to his madness yielding.

Limb from limb the Thyiad band
Tore the monarch of the land;
Then from Bacchic frenzy freed
Saw and knew not whose the deed.°   500

O'er Ocean, Bacchus' foster mother
    reigns,
Cadmeian Ino, trailed of Nereids,
And Bacchus' youthful kinsman o'er the
    waves
Shares sway, Palaemon clothed with deity.

---

444. Erebus: Hades, the underworld. **Ode I:** This ode relates
various episodes in the career of Bacchus which, since they have
nothing to do with the plot, have not been annotated extensively.
454. ye: The Chorus addresses the Bacchantic women (also
called maenads, Thyiades, and Edones), represented as wor-
shipping Bacchus in a frenzied dance, their hair disheveled.
thyrsus: staff entwined with ivy, sacred to Bacchus.

493–500. Matrons . . . deed: This episode, which occurred on
Mt. Kithaeron, is referred to several times later in the play (ll.
547–49, 697–701, 712–13, 1053–56, and 1134–37). Pentheus was
the son of Agave, daughter of Cadmus, and succeeded Cadmus
as King of Thebes. He opposed the worship of Bacchus, who, in
revenge, drove his mother, her sisters, and other Theban matrons into a Bacchic frenzy in which they tore him to pieces,
believing him to be a wild beast.

Thee a child the Tuscan band
Stole away till Nereus' power
Stilled the waves; his mighty hand
Made the salty seaways flower.

Plane trees burst to vernal green;
Laurel loved of Delphi's lord   510
Flashes twixt the branches seen;
Birds break forth with one accord;

Ivy twines about the oars,
Ivy to the masthead soars,
Indian tigers roam the stern,
By the bow a lion roars;

Pirates filled with strange alarms
Plunge beyond the ivied rail,
Rise transformed, their vanished arms
Shrunk to fins, a crescent tail   520

Cleaves the waves behind a back
Curved and shiny. Where before,
Pirates ranged o'er Neptune's track,
Dolphins follow evermore.

Thee, Pactolus, Lydia's golden stream
Bore on its wealthy waters twixt hot banks
While the blood drinking Massegete fore-
    swore
His Getic arrows and his unstrung bow.

Bacchus is lord; the realm Lycurgus
    wrought
With fierce axe-wielding hands,   530
The savage lands
Where range wild Dacian bands
Call Bacchus lord; the roaming races
    caught
By cold Maeotis flowing past,
Tribes frozen fast
By Boreas' nearer blast
Call Bacchus lord; hoardes that the years
    have taught
To seek on high
Where zenith crowns the sky
The wagons twain, the Arcadian galaxy.
Bacchus is lord.   541

Victor he o'er tribes Gelonian,
O'er the warriors Amazonian:
Squadrons from the Thermodon,
Steeds abandoned, arrows gone,
Maenads tread the rites Edonian.

For him Kithaeron's sacred earth,
   Crimsoned with stain
   Of Pentheus slain,

And Proetus' daughter reft of mirth   550
   Fled to his wood;
     While Juno helpless stood,
Argos bowed down to his miraculous
   birth.

To him the sea-girt Nasian isle
Gave for a bride the Cretan maid°
Abandoned by Athenian wile
To join with godhead unafraid.
Then from the barren stone,
Not in one stream alone,
Burst brooks of wine,   560
But fountains sprang apace
Down grassy slopes to race,
Fruit of the vine,
Thyme scented and withal
The milky streams of liquor mystical.

All heaven above
To bind that love
Followed the new-made bride,
While Phoebus sang
The age-old nuptial song,   570
A-down whose shoulders hang
The curling locks ambrosial, wondrous
   long;
Twin Cupids waving torches by his side
Light the procession.
And Jupiter, his fiery terror shed,
Disowns the thunderbolt for Bacchus wed.

So while the stars of heaven shall run their
   course
Or Ocean with his ambient stream enclose
The imprisoned earth; while the full moon
   shall still
Collect her scattered fires and Lucifer 580
Proclaim returning dawn; until the Bear
Leave heaven above to plunge in Nereus'
   flood,
We shall do homage to the Lycean lord.

Scene II

OED. Albeit thy face bespeaks a sad report,
Tell me whose life shall pacify the gods.
    KRE. Thou bidst me speak what fear would bid
    me hide.
    OED. If crumbling Thebes move thee not, yet re-
    gard
The slipping scepter of a kindred house.

---

555. maid: Ariadne, whom Theseus of Athens had deserted on
the isle of Naxos. The following lines celebrate her marriage to
Bacchus.

KRE. Thou'lt pray to know not what thou seekst
  to know.

OED. A futile cure for ills is ignorance: 590
Wouldst thou then hide the way to public weal?

KRE. When medicine is foul, one shuns the cure.

OED. Speak what thou knowest or prepare to
  know
What ill can follow from an angry king.

KRE. Kings hate the words they order men to
  speak.

OED. Thyself shalt go a scapegoat unto hell
And thou speak not thy secret utterly.

KRE. Would that I might be silent. Can a king
Be asked a lesser liberty than that?

OED. Mute liberty is oft a greater bane   600
To king and kingdom than the spoken word.

KRE. When silence is forbidden what is left?

OED. He nullifies the law who will not speak.

KRE. I pray thee hear in peace words that are
  forced.

OED. Was ever penalty when force made speech?

KRE. Far from the city wall there lies a grove,
Dark with thick ilex, Dirce's is the spot
Within a well-washed valley. Stately woods
Are guarded by a cypress and an oak,
The one forever green, the aged oak   610
Spreading wide crooked branches dry with age;
One side consuming time has stripped away,
The other, tearing loose its rotted roots,
Leans on its neighbor. Laurel trees are there
With bitter berries, quivering lindens too
And Paphian myrtle, ash that presently
Shall drive its branches through the unending sea,
And pines whose branches battle Zephyrus,
Defying Phoebus. In the very midst
Rises a mighty tree whose shade widespread   620
Covers the lesser woods, with far-flung branch
Above, it stands defender of the grove.
Darkling beneath, bereft of Phoebus' light,
The unmoving waters sense eternal chill,
A stagnant swamp that rims a sluggish spring.
  Hither the aged priest guided his step
Nor hesitated; for the spot itself
Bred night.° Into a trench new dug were hurled
Torches snatched up from funeral pyres. Himself
The priest, wrapped in his garb funereal,   630
Brandished his wand. Down to his very feet
Fell his black robe and round his hoary head
A wreath of blackest yew. So he advanced,
A downcast aged man in squalor clad.
Black° sheep and oxen black within the trench

Are driven till on their living flesh the flame
Feeds as they tremble. Thence he summons forth
The shades and thee° the ruler of the shades
And him° who guards the dark Lethean° Lake.
Magic he chants and with inspired voice   640
And threatening mien recites whatever words
Have power to appease or force the shades. He
  pours
Blood on the hearth the while he burns the beasts,
Making the trench run blood, then pours above,
Snow white, great streams of milk, with the left
  hand
Bacchus-made wine; his eyes upon the ground
A second time he chants with louder voice
Of Frenzy, calls upon the shades to come.
Then howled the host of Hecate° and thrice
The hollow vales re-echoed mournfully.   650
Earth shook to her foundations till he cried,
" They hear my words well spoken. Chaos black
Is burst asunder: to the hosts of hell
A passage opens to the upper air."
The woods drew back yet reared their foliage
In horror, mighty oaks were split, the earth
Retreated groaning as afraid to see
The piercing of the depths of Acheron,°
Or as, perforce, its framework wrecked, itself
Giving passage to the dead resoundingly.   660
Perchance 'twas Cerberus with triple head
That in his anger shook his mighty chains.
For suddenly earth yawned and opened wide.
I saw myself the sluggish lakes that lie
Amongst the shades, I saw the ghostly gods
And veritable night; the blood within
My veins stood frozen. Forth in ranks there leaped
Full-armed the serpent host,° the serried ranks
Of brothers, harvest of the dragon's teeth,
Baleful Erinys° shrieked and Madness blind,   670
Horror and all the hidden brood produced
In the eternal darkness: Grief that tore
Her locks, Disease with weary sinking head,
Old Age that hates itself, uncertain Fear
And Pestilence the greedy scourge of Thebes.
Our spirits failed us: even she° who knew
The old man's art and ritual, stood dumb.
Her sire unterrified, bold, by his curse
Summoned the bloodless troupe of dreadful Dis.
Straightway like fleecy clouds flitting they come
To breathe heaven's freedom. Eryx° scatters not
So many falling leaves, innumerable   682
They come as flowers on Hybla° in the spring
Where gather swarms of bees, more countless they

627–28. Nor . . . night: Since the place was so dark, Tiresias did
not have to wait for night (when these rites were usually performed).   635. Black: Because these rites were offered to the
infernal powers, the usual procedures were reversed (as in the
later Black Mass): the sacrificed animals were black, the priest
used his left hand, etc.

638. thee: Dis.   639. him: Cerberus.   Lethean: Lethe was a
river in Hades.   649. Hecate: a goddess of the underworld.
658. Acheron: river in Hades.   668. host: the warriors who
sprang from the dragon's teeth that Cadmus planted.   670.
Erinys: avenging deity.   676. she: Manto.   681. Eryx: mountain in Sicily.   683. Hybla: region in Sicily famous for its honey.

Than waves that shatter on the Ionian sea
Or birds in winter flying from the wrath
Of Strymon's° bitter cold cleaving the sky
To exchange the Arctic snows for the warm Nile.
So thronged the shades to hear the prophet's voice.
Eager the trembling spirits hasten toward   690
The darkling grove; first from the earth emerged,
With right hand seizing by the horns a fierce
High-spirited bull, Zethus, and after him
Amphion, lyre in hand, charming the rocks
With dulcet tones;° safe in her arrogance
Amongst her sons, head bowed, comes Tantalis°
Counting the shades. More dread than Tantalis,
Agave, fury tossed, followed by all
The band that tore to shreds their wretched king:
And after them Pentheus himself who still,   700
A mutilated Bacchant, breathed forth threats.
Then last of all, invoked incessantly,
Hanging his head in shame, cringing apart,
Seeking concealment while the priestess calls
Unceasing and repeats her Stygian prayers,
Until he shows at length his features veiled,
Comes Laius — terror seizes me to speak:
His limbs still smeared with his own blood, his hair
Squalid with dreadful filth he stands and speaks
In frenzied tones: " O cruel house of Cadmus,   710
Ever delighting in the blood of kin,
Shake high the thyrses and with hands inspired
By god tear limb from limb thy sons° — at Thebes
The crime that tops all crime is mother's love.
O country mine, no anger of the gods
But thine own guilt destroys thee. Pestilence
That comes with Auster's° leaden breath nor
      drought,
When earth under a burning blast receives
No rainfall — these are not thy bane but he,
That bloodstained king who holds the scepter as
The prize of cruel murder, occupies   721
Impiously the couch that was his sire's,
Sowing where he himself was sown, to breed
Offspring unholy in his mother's womb
And, daring what wild beasts would spurn, beget
Brothers unto himself — sin so involved,
So monstrous as to shame the very Sphinx.
A hateful progeny, yet not so cursed
The son as his own sire who bears the guilt
Of that twice outraged womb. 'Tis thou, 'tis thou,
The bloody scepter in thine hand, 'tis thou   731
That I, thy father unavenged, pursue,

Thou and thy city bringing in my train
The Fury, fit attendant o'er thy couch.
Her far-resounding blows follow me where
I shall o'erthrow this house accursed and so
With impious war obliterate its gods.
Hence from your borders drive in haste your king
An exile wheresoe'er his guilty steps
Shall lead him; let him flee the land for then,   740
Bursting to green with spring fair flowering,
It shall repair its herbage and the air
Produce once more pure breezes and the woods
Regain their ancient glory: Pestilence,
Wasting and Death, Disease and Toil and Grief
Shall fare with him, companions suitable.
Yet, though he flee our land with hurrying step,
I shall make slow his feet, holding him back,
The while he creeps uncertain of the road
Testing each cruel step with aged staff: 750
Take ye his earth from him: I'll hide his heaven."°
      OED. Through all my frame, aye to the very bones
Pierces a chilling terror. All that I feared
To do is charged as done — yet Merope
Refutes the impious charge of lawless love,
Wedded to Polybus, and Polybus
Living acquits my hands: both parents give
The lie to charge of incest or of death.
What circumstance of blame remains? Before
I e'er set foot upon Boeotian° soil   760
Thebes had long mourned her sovereign Laius
      slain.
Doth then the old man lie or is the god
Angered at Thebes? Nay, but I see the wiles,
The treacherous plot: to hide his deviltry
The prophet, making pretext of god's will,
Invents these lies to win for you my power.
      KRE. Would I expel my sister from the throne?
Did not the sacred faith of kindred hearth
Hold me contented in mine own estate?
Fortune herself, beset with constant care,   770
Would fright me from such action: couldst thysel
Cast off unscathed this load intolerable
Thou shouldst be safer in a lesser sphere.
      OED. Dost counsel me willingly to resign
Such royal power?
      KRE.   Counsel it, yes — to such
As still are free to make unfettered choice:
Thou of necessity must bear thy fate.
      OED. The surest path for him who seeks a throne
Is praise of moderation, quietude:
The turbulent soul oft counterfeits repose.   780
      KRE. Does such long loyalty avail me naught?
      OED. Loyalty gives the traitorous soul its chance.
      KRE. Free from encumbering care, I share the
      fruit
Of royal power; my home is ever filled

---

687. Strymon: river in Macedonia.   693–95. Zethus . . . tones:
Amphion conquered Thebes with the help of his brother, Zethus;
then with his music he charmed the rocks so that they moved of
their own accord and formed a wall about the city.   696.
Tantalis: Niobe, wife of Amphion, who was so proud of the
number of her sons that she aroused the indignation of Apollo,
who killed them all.   712–13. Shake . . . sons: refers to the
murder of Pentheus.   717. Auster: dry, sultry south wind (the
modern *Sirocco*).

748–51. I . . . heaven: foreshadows Oedipus' blindness.   760.
Boeotian: district of Greece in which Thebes was located.

With citizens; and each returning day
Sees favors from the throne heaped lavishly
Upon my hearth: rich vestments, ample feasts,
And succor by my favor richly given:
What may I dream is lacking in such lot?
    OED. That which indeed is lacking:° second
    place   790
Knows never satisfaction.
    KRE.   Shall I then
Fall as though guilty with my case unheard?
    OED. Did ye give reasons when ye sought my life?
Did even Tiresias hear my case? And yet
Ye deem me guilty: yours the precedent
I follow.
    KRE.   If I then be innocent?
    OED. Kings must fear doubts as certainties.
    KRE.   Who fears
Vain terrors earns the real.
    OED.   He who's at fault
And is forgiven, hates: let doubt be done.   799
    KRE. Even so are hatreds born.
    OED.   Who dreads too much
Such hatreds knows not royal power: for fear
Guards kingdoms.
    KRE.   Whoso wields with tyranny
The scepter fears even the fearful: dread
Returns against its author.
    OED.   Guard him well —
For he is guilty — in some rock-bound cave.
Myself will hie me to my palace home.

Ode II

    CHOR. Not thou° the cause of ills
        So great. Never from thee
        Found Fate excuse to attack
        Labdakus' sons.   810
        Nay, 'tis an ancient wrath
        Nursed by the gods.
        Time was Castalian shade
        Sheltered Sidonian guests;
        Settlers from Tyre° bathed
        In Dirce's stream,
        When first Agenor's son°
        Wearily searching
        Jove's victim came at last
        Weary and worn to Thebes;   820
        Sat 'neath our sacred tree,
        Bowed there in prayer,
        Heard from Apollo's self
        Bidding divine;

Followed the wandering heifer's track,
Heifer untouched of plough
Or curving share;
Ceasing at last his flight
Gave to our land a name°
From that same heifer's plight.   830

Ever since that ill day
New marvels haunt our land:
The serpent monster reared
In lowly vale to rise
Hissing beyond the height
Of oak and pine.
O'er the Chaonian heath
It reared its head,
Its body spread beneath.
Anon an armèd host° arose   840
From earth; the trumpet sang
Untaught, the curving brass
Sounded its infant note
In battle line.
Lines of embattled kin
Swarmed o'er the plain,
Worthy the dragon seed,
Spanning in single day
A lifetime whole,
Born when the stars had set,   850
Dead before evening star.
The Tyrian stranger° feared
Monsters of such surprise,
Dreaded to war with such
Till youth in combat fell
With cruel youth and earth
Received again in death her progeny.
So civil strife spread wide
And Herculaean Thebes
Learned fratricide.   860

Hence came the fate untoward
Of Cadmus' scion° when
Horns decked his head and, now
A stag, transformed he fled
From his own dogs.
Swift through the hilly woods
Actaeon fled
With agile leaps through rocky glades,
Fearing the traps
Himself had set,   870
Till in the limpid stream
He saw his horn-crowned head,

---

829. name: Boeotia, from *bous*, the Greek word for cow. **840. host:** the warriors who sprang from the dragon's teeth that Cadmus planted, and who then killed each other in a furious battle. **852. Tyrian stranger:** Cadmus. **862. scion:** Actaeon, grandson of Cadmus, while hunting on Mt. Kithaeron saw Diana (the goddess "of too stern chastity") bathing in a pool, whereupon she changed him into a stag, in which form he was chased and torn to pieces by his own hunting dogs.

---

790. That . . . lacking: royal power. **807. thou:** Oedipus. **814–15. Sidonian . . . Tyre:** Sidon and Tyre were cities of Phoenicia. **817. son:** Cadmus' father, Agenor, King of Phoenicia, sent him to find his sister, Europa, whom Jove, in the form of a bull, had abducted.

Himself a wild beast,
Where once the goddess that tradition
    hymns
Of too stern chastity,
Had bathed in perfect peace her virgin
    limbs.

Scene III

OED. My heart renews its cares, renews its fears.
The gods of heaven and hell are joined to prove
My guilt — 'twas I slew Laius: but my heart,
Nearer to me than any god, protests   880
And knows its innocence. Memory traces still
The story of a man too proud, too old,
That in his chariot drove me from the road.
I, in the flush of youth, struck with my staff
And sent him on the way to Dis. 'Twas on
The triple road of Phocis, far from Thebes.

Wife of my heart, tell me what I would know:
Was Laius broken in age or still a youth?
   IOK. Twixt youth and age but nearer age than
     youth.
   OED. And were there many followers with the
     King?   890
   IOK. The most had lost their way, a faithful few
Still followed constant by his chariot wheel.
   OED. Did any perish sharing the King's fate?
   IOK. One man whose faith and courage held him
     true.
   OED. I see it clear: the number fits, the place —
But when was this?
   IOK.   Ten years have passed since then.
   SENEX. The host of Corinth summon you to take
Your father's throne, Polybus sleeps in peace.
   OED. How cruel Fate attacks me everywhere.
Speak more and tell me how my father died.   900
   SEN. In peaceful sleep of age he breathed his last.
   OED. My father dead and by no murderous act!
Bear witness all, I now may raise to heaven
Hands pure of guilt nor fearing any crime.
And yet Fate's greater part remains to fear.
   SEN. Thy father's throne will banish every fear.
   OED. I'll seek that throne; but no, I fear my
     mother.
   SEN. Thou fearest her who waits impatient there
Thy coming?
   OED.   Piety forbids me thence.
   SEN. Wouldst leave her then bereft?
   OED.   There lies my fear.
   SEN. Speak out; what hidden fear burdens thy
     mind?   911
   OED. A mother's couch, that Delphi prophesied.
   SEN. Then cease to dread vain shadows; put aside
Base fear; thy mother was not Merope.

   OED. What profit sought she then from such pre-
     tense?
   SEN. Children bring pride of confidence to kings.
   OED. Speak out: how knowest thou secrets of her
     couch?
   SEN. These hands bestowed thee as a babe on
     them.
   OED. Thou gavest the babe to them: who gave it
     thee?
   SEN. A shepherd on Kithaeron's snowy ridge.
   OED. What chance brought thee unto Kithaeron's
     groves?   921
   SEN. Upon that mountain side I watched my
     herds.
   OED. Tell me beside, what marks prove me that
     babe?
   SEN. Thou wert already pierced by the iron goad
And from thy swollen feet didst get thy name.
   OED. And who was he that of my body made
A gift to thee?
   SEN.   He kept the royal herds,
And under him the lesser shepherds served.
   OED. Tell me his name.
   SEN.   I cannot, memory
Slips first away beneath the weight of age.   930
   OED. Couldst recognize the man by face and
     form?
   SEN. Perchance I might; often some trifling thing
Recalls a memory clouded long by time.
   OED. Unto the altars drive the royal herds,
Their shepherds with them: go ye slaves and call
Those who are masters of the royal herds.
   SEN. Whether intent or Fortune hid these things
Let what is hidden be forever dark.
Truth oft brings ill to her discoverer.
   OED. Is there aught worse to fear than what we
     know?   940
   SEN. Be sure what must be greatly sought is
     great.
Here stands the public safety, here the king's,
Full weighty both: keep thou an even hand;
Stir not — and Fate will manifest itself.
   OED. To disturb a happy state availeth naught;
Safe is't to unsettle one in extremity.
   SEN. Dost seek some nobler state than royalty?
Beware lest found thy father cause thee shame.
   OED. I shall search out my lineage though low
It be, if I may surely learn. And see,   950
The aged guardian of the royal herd,
Phorbas. Dost know the old man's name or face?
   SEN. His presence stirs my mind. Not wholly
     known
Nor yet unknown his countenance to me.
   OED. When Laius reigned wert thou his slave to
     tend
His lordly herds upon Kithaeron's slope?
   PHORBAS. Kithaeron ever with green pasturage

In summertime welcomed our roving herd.
 SEN. Dost know me?
 PHOR.   Nay, my memory hesitates. 959
 OED. Was once a child given to him by thee?
Speak. Dost thou falter? Why that paling cheek?
What wouldst thou say? Truth cannot brook delay.
 PHOR. Thou stirrest matters hidden long by time.
 OED. Confess or pain shall wring the truth from
  thee.
 PHOR. Useless the gift on him by me bestowed.
That child could never live to enjoy the light.
 SEN. May god avert the omen. Live he does.
 OED. Why sayest thou the infant could not live?
 PHOR. The iron driven through had pierced both
  feet
And bound his limbs. The wound quick festering
Consumed with fever all his childish frame. 971
 OED. Why question further? Fate approaches
  near.
Tell the child's name.
 PHOR.   My loyalty forbids.
 OED. Bring fire, ye slaves. The flame shall force
  thy faith.
 PHOR. Shall truth be sought through bloody means
  like this?
Forgive I pray.
 OED.   If cruel I seem to thee,
Tyrannical, thy vengeance lies at hand.
Speak out the truth. Who was he, who his sire?
Who gave him birth?
 PHOR.   He was thine own wife's son.
 OED. Yawn earth, and thou great monarch of the
  dark, 980
Thou ruler of the shades, to lowest hell
Receive a scion worthy of its stock;
Ye citizens upon this guilty head
Heap rocks; slay me with weapons; with the sword
Let every father seek my life, each son
Worthy the name; let husbands arm themselves
Against me, brothers too and let the sick
Pest-ridden populace from funeral pyres
Seize brands to hurl at me. I am become
The guilty curse of all our age, a thing 990
Detestable to gods and ruinous
To all that's sacred; on that very day
Whereon I breathed the first crude breath of life,
Worthy of death. Up, rouse thy courage now,
Dare again something worthy of thy crimes.
Begone and swiftly seek the palace there,
Congratulate thy mother on her brood.

Ode III

 CHOR. If Fate were mine to guide
  As I should choose,
  Only to Zephyr's breeze 1000

My sails I'd loose,
Lest 'neath the sterner gale
The sheets should fail.

Ever may gentle airs
That mildly float
Nor threaten ill, conduct
My unfearing boat.
From life's safe middle way
I would not stray.

Fearing the Cretan king, 1010
In mad career
Seeking a starry course,
With new-found arts
Striving to emulate
Birds of the air,
Trusting too much to wings
Fashioned by craft,
Icarus to the sea
Gave his lost name.

Daedalus, warily 1020
Finding his way
Through the more lowly clouds
Midway to heaven,
Like an old hawk his brood,
Watched for his son
Till from the sea he saw
Hands stretched for help:°
All that betrays excess
Stands insecure.

But what is this? The door 1030
Creaks and a royal slave
Downcast with shaking head
Comes forth.
Tell us what news thou hast.

Scene IV

 MESS. When Oedipus had learned the will of fate
And his own origin and had condemned
Himself guilty of crime unspeakable,
Seeking the palace furious he came
With hastened step within that hated home,
Like Libyan lion raging o'er the plain 1040
Shaking its tawny mane with threatening head.
His face was grim with fury; flashing his eyes,
With a deep roar he groaned and down his limbs

1010–27. Fearing...help: Daedalus, the famous craftsman, made waxen wings for himself and his son, Icarus, with which to escape from Minos, King of Crete. But Icarus flew so high that the sun melted his wings and he plunged into the sea (subsequently given his name, the Icarian Sea), whereas Daedalus. flying lower, arrived safely in Italy.

The cold sweat ran, foam flecked his lips, he
    breathed
Dire threats, his mighty passion overflowed.
In rage he plans some great catastrophe
Fit for his fate. "Why hesitate," he shouts.
"Let whoso will pierce with the sword this breast
Dishonored or with kindled flame or rock
O'erwhelm me. Is there no cruel tigress then   1050
Or bird ill-omened that shall feast upon
My vitals? Thou Kithaeron that dost hold
Crimes all uncounted, send thy cruel beasts
Against me, send thy maddened hounds, let come
Once more Agave. Soul, dost fear to die?
Death only saves the innocent from Fate."
So did he speak and put his impious hand
Swift to the hilt and drew his sword. "Is't so?
Canst pay such short-lived penalty for crimes
So mighty? Thou shalt die and satisfy   1060
Thy father, what of thy mother then and what
Of thy most ill-begotten children, what
Sufficient ruin to requite thyself
And thy great guilt; what of thy country's wrong?
Thou canst not pay: Nature that ratified
New laws for Oedipus, devising strange
And unknown ways of birth, shall be herself
Deviser of his punishment: were I
To live and die again, by constant birth
To pay fresh penalty — come wretched soul,   1070
Bestir thy mind; what may not be but once
May be protracted; seek some lingering death.
Find out some means whereby, though not yet
    dead,
Thou yet mayst linger here bereft of life.
Die must thou but beyond thy father's realm.
Dost hesitate, my soul?" A sudden storm
Of tears drenched both his cheeks. "Is it enough
To weep," he cried; "Is such an innocent flood
Enough? Nay, let my battered eyes themselves
Follow these tears: ye gods of married love,   1080
Is this enough? I'll gouge these eyes." He spake
And raged in fury, cheeks aflame with fire
And eyes that scarce retained their wonted seat.
His face transformed with anger, like one mad,
He groaned and with a roar assailed his eyes,
While they in turn flashing with fell intent
Leaped forth to meet the hand that wounded
    them —
Hands like to talons that laid hold of them
And tore them pitiless from their very roots.
Then impotent explored the hollow space   1090
Tearing the sockets where the eyes had been
And raged incontinent in fury vain.
  At last he tried the light, raising his head,
And from his empty hollows searched the sky
Finding but night. The last mangled remains
Of what were eyes he sweeps aside and shouts
Victorious to the gods: "Spare ye, I pray,

My Fatherland; I have made good the debt
Of punishment and for my marriage couch
Found worthy night." The foul descending flood
Watered his face, the wounded head belched
    forth   1101
From severed vein abundant streams of gore.

Ode IV

CHOR. By Fate we are compelled — yield ye to
    Fate:
    No anxious thought
    Can change the fabric wrought
    Upon the loom of Fate;
    All that befalls this race of mortal man,
    All that we do began
    Within the clouded past.
    For Lachesis° with hand that may not stay
    Without regret   1111
    Preserves the pattern set.
    As all things move by Fate's predestined
      way,
    So Earth's first revolution fixed the last.
    Not god himself may turn
    From its appointed course
    Aught that by precept stern
    Must hold to the order of its ancient
      source.
    Many in futile hate
    Have wrecked their lives — or soon or late
    Seeking to outwit destiny have met their
      fate.   1121

    The doors are opening — lo, the King
      himself
    Sightless, abandoned, makes his way alone.

Éxodos

OED. 'Tis well, 'tis finished; unto my father's
    spirit
I have performed the rites decreed. This dark
Delights me. Pray what god at length appeased
Spreads o'er my head this cloud of blackness.
    Who
Gives recompense to crime — I have escaped
The witness of the day — yet, parricide,
Thou owest naught to thy right hand — the light
Fled thee — that face disfigured suits thee well.
  CHOR. Look you, Iokaste comes with maddened
    heart   1132
And maddened leaping step like that bemused
And frenzied mother° of the Cadmeian house

1110. Lachesis: one of the Fates.   1134. mother: Agave again.

When she had torn away her own son's head —
And knew what she had done. She would address
The sufferer; she halts in fear; till shame
Overcomes sorrow. Yet the words half formed
Stumble upon her lips.

ＩＯＫ.　　　　　What shall I call thee?
Son? For thou art my son. Dost hesitate　　1140
In shame before that name? Nay, speak,
My son, even against thy wishes. Why
Avert thy head, that empty countenance?

ＯＥＤ. Who now forbids me to enjoy the dark,
Giving me back my eyes? My mother's voice.
All, all in vain. We may no longer meet.
Our impious selves let the deep sea divide,
The depths of earth or if beneath our earth
There be another facing other stars
And wandering sun — let it take one of us.　　1150

ＩＯＫ. Fate's is the blame: no man can sin by
　　Fate.

ＯＥＤ. Ah mother, spare these words and spare
　　mine ears,
I beg you by this body's torn remains,
And by the ill-omened issue of my blood,
By all that's foul or noble in our name.

ＩＯＫ. Why dost thou sleep, my soul, why dost re-
　　fuse
To pay the common penalty of crime?
Through thee, incestuous, all humanity
Hath lost its honor. Die thou then, destroy
Thy guilty life. Not if the omnipotent　　1160
Father of all the gods himself should hurl
Through shaken universe his thunderbolt,
Would he exact from me full punishment
To fit my crimes, foul mother that I am.
Death is my will, now find the way of death.
Come, and thou art a parricide, now give
Thy hand to help thy mother; only this

Is left for thy fulfilment. Seize the sword.
By that blade fell my husband; nay, not so:
The father of my husband. Shall I plunge　　1170
The blade into my breast or sheathe it deep,
Deep in my throat? Thou canst not choose the
　　place?
Hither, right hand, strike here the ample womb
That bare my husband and my husband's sons.

ＣＨＯＲ. She lies there dead. Within the very wound
Her hand succumbs; the gushing flow of blood
Spews out the knife.

ＯＥＤ.　　　　　O, god of prophecy,°
God of the shrine of Truth, to thee I speak.
My father only did the Fates demand:
Twice parricide, more guilty than I feared,　　1180
I killed my mother too: 'tis by my crime
That she is dead. O lying god of light,°
I have outdone the impious Fates foredoomed.
Trembling my step, I follow darkling ways;
And with uncertain foot and quavering hand
Master the unseeing night. Go, wanderer,
Hasten thy steps unsure, begone — Yet stay:
Step not upon thy mother.

　　　　　　　　　All that be
Weary in body, with disease oppressed,
Disheartened unto death — behold I go.　　1190
Lift up your heads: a kindlier heaven shows
Behind me as I flee. Let whosoe'er
Clings to a failing life breath, draw again
Deep draughts that vivify. Go bear to those
Abandoned unto death some timely aid.
The ills of all the world I take with me.
Ye Fates of Violence, fell Pestilence,
Wasting and frenzied Grief and dread Disease:
Come ye with me, with me. Such be my guides.

1177. **god of prophecy:** Phoebus, patron of the Delphic oracle
(the "shrine of Truth"). 　1182. **god of light:** also Phoebus.

THE SOURCE OF

Othello

The source of the plot of Othello *is the " Tale of the Moor of Venice," which appeared as the seventh novella in the third decade of the* Heca-tommithi *(Hundred Tales), a collection of stories by Gianbattista Giraldi Cinthio, published in Venice in 1565. We do not know whether Shakespeare read this story in the Italian, or in a French translation written by Gabriel Chappuys* *in 1584, or in some English version which has not survived. The complete story is reprinted here in the translation of John Edward Taylor, as it appears in Taylor's* The Moor of Venice: Cinthio's Tale and Shakespere's Tragedy *(London: Chapman and Hall, 1855). Taylor's footnotes have been omitted, and the footnote which appears here is the present editor's.*

There once lived in Venice a Moor, who was very valiant, and of a handsome person; and having given proofs in war of great skill and prudence, he was highly esteemed by the Signoria of the Republic, who in rewarding deeds of valour advanced the interests of the State.

It happened that a virtuous lady, of marvellous beauty, named Disdemona, fell in love with the Moor, moved thereto by his valour; and he, vanquished by the beauty and the noble character of Disdemona, returned her love; and their affection was so mutual, that, although the parents of the lady strove all they could to induce her to take another husband, she consented to marry the Moor; and they lived in such harmony and peace in Venice, that no word ever passed between them that was not affectionate and kind. /15/

Now it happened at this time that the Signoria of Venice made a change in the troops whom they used to maintain in Cyprus, and they appointed the Moor commander of the soldiers whom they despatched thither. Joyful as was the Moor at the honour proffered him — such dignity being only conferred on men of noble rank and well-tried faith, and who had displayed bravery in arms — yet his pleasure was lessened when he reflected on the length and dangers of the voyage, fearing that Disdemona would be pained at his absence. But Disdemona, who had no other happiness in the world than the Moor, and who rejoiced to witness the testimony of his valour her husband had received from so powerful and noble a Republic, was all impatient that he should embark with his troops, and longed to accompany him to so honourable a post. And all the more it vexed her to see the Moor so troubled; and not knowing what could be the reason, one day, when they were at dinner, she said to him, "How is it, O Moor, that when so honourable a post has been conferred on you by the Signoria, you are thus melancholy?"

The Moor answered Disdemona, "My pleasure at the honour I have received is disturbed by the love I bear you; for I see that of necessity one of two things must happen; either that I take you with me, to encounter the perils of the sea, or, to save you from this danger, I must leave you here /16/ in Venice. The first could not be otherwise than serious to me, for all the

toil you would have to bear, and every danger that might befall you, would cause me extreme anxiety and pain. Yet, were I to leave you behind me, I should be hateful to myself, since in parting from you I should part from my own life."

Disdemona, on hearing this, replied, "My husband, what thoughts are these that wander through your mind? Why let such things disturb you? I will accompany you whithersoe'er you go, were it to pass through fire, as now to cross the water in a safe and well-provided ship: if indeed there are toils and perils to encounter, I will share them with you. And in truth I should think you loved me little, were you to leave me here in Venice, denying me to bear you company, or could believe that I would liefer bide in safety here, than share the dangers that await you. Prepare then for the voyage, with all the readiness which the dignity of the post you hold deserves."

The Moor, in the fulness of his joy, threw his arms around his wife's neck, and with an affectionate and tender kiss exclaimed, "God keep you long in such love, dear wife!" Then speedily donning his armour, and having prepared everything for his expedition, he embarked on board the galley, with his wife and all his troops; and /17/ setting sail, they pursued their voyage, and with a perfectly tranquil sea arrived safely at Cyprus.

Now amongst the soldiery there was an Ensign, a man of handsome figure, but of the most depraved nature in the world. This man was in great favour with the Moor, who had not the slightest idea of his wickedness; for despite the malice lurking in his heart, he cloaked with proud and valourous speech, and with a specious presence, the villainy of his soul, with such art, that he was to all outward show another Hector or Achilles. This man had likewise taken with him his wife to Cyprus, a young, and fair, and virtuous lady; and being of Italian birth, she was much loved by Disdemona, who spent the greater part of every day with her.

In the same Company there was a certain Captain of a troop, to whom the Moor was much affectioned. And Disdemona, for this cause, knowing how much her husband valued him, showed him proofs of the greatest kindness, which was all very grateful to the Moor. Now the wicked Ensign, regardless of the faith that he had pledged his wife, no less than of the friendship, fidelity, and obligation which he owed the Moor, fell passionately in love with Disdemona, and bent all his thoughts to achieve his conquest; yet he dared not to declare his passion openly, fearing that, should the Moor perceive it, he would at once kill /*18*/ him. He therefore sought in various ways, and with secret guile, to betray his passion to the lady. But she, whose every wish was centred in the Moor, had no thought for this Ensign more than for any other man; and all the means he tried to gain her love, had no more effect than if he had not tried them. But the Ensign imagined that the cause of his ill success was that Disdemona loved the Captain of the troop; and he pondered how to remove him from her sight. The love which he had borne the lady now changed into the bitterest hate; and, having failed in his purposes, he devoted all his thoughts to plot the death of the Captain of the troop, and to divert the affection of the Moor from Disdemona. After revolving in his mind various schemes, all alike wicked, he at length resolved to accuse her of unfaithfulness to her husband, and to represent the Captain as her paramour. But knowing the singular love the Moor bore to Disdemona, and the friendship which he had for the Captain, he was well aware that, unless he practised an artful fraud upon the Moor, it were impossible to make him give ear to either accusation: wherefore he resolved to wait, until time and circumstance should open a path for him to engage in his foul project.

Not long afterwards, it happened that the Captain, having drawn his sword upon a soldier of the guard, and struck him, the Moor deprived him of /*19*/ his rank; whereat Disdemona was deeply grieved, and endeavoured again and again to reconcile her husband to the man. This the Moor told to the wicked Ensign, and how his wife importuned him so much about the Captain, that he feared he should be forced at last to receive him back to service. Upon this hint the Ensign resolved to act, and began to work his web of intrigue; " Perchance," said he, " the lady Disdemona may have good reason to look kindly on him."

" And wherefore? " said the Moor.

" Nay, I would not step 'twixt man and wife," replied the Ensign; " but let your eyes be witness to themselves."

In vain the Moor went on to question the officer — he would proceed no further; nevertheless his words left a sharp stinging thorn in the Moor's heart, who could think of nothing else, trying to guess their meaning, and lost in melancholy. And one day, when his wife had been endeavouring to pacify his anger toward the Captain, and praying him not to be unmindful of ancient services and friendship, for one small fault, especially since peace had been made between the Captain and the soldier he had struck, the Moor was angered, and exclaimed, " Great cause have you, Disdemona, to care so anxiously about this man! Is he a brother, or your kinsman, that he should be so near your heart? " /*20*/

The lady, with all gentleness and humility, replied, " Be not angered, my dear lord; I have no other cause to bid me speak, than sorrow that I see you lose so dear a friend as, by your own words, this Captain has been to you: nor has he done so grave a fault, that you should bear him so much enmity. Nay, but you Moors are of so hot a nature, that every little trifle moves you to anger and revenge."

Still more enraged at these words, the Moor replied, " I could bring proofs — by heaven it mocks belief! but for the wrongs I have endured, revenge must satisfy my wrath."

Disdemona, in astonishment and fright, seeing her husband's anger kindled against her, so contrary to his wont, said humbly and with timidity, " None save a good intent has led me thus to speak with you, my lord; but to give cause no longer for offence, I'll never speak a word more on the subject."

The Moor, observing the earnestness with which his wife again pleaded for the Captain, began to guess the meaning of the Ensign's words; and in deep melancholy he went to seek that villain, and induce him to speak more openly of what he knew. Then the Ensign, who was bent upon injuring the unhappy lady, after feigning at first great reluctance to say aught that might displease the Moor, at length pretended to yield to his entreaties, and /*21*/ said, " I can't deny, it pains me to the soul to be thus forced to say what needs must be more hard to hear than any other grief; but since you will it so, and that the regard I owe your honour compels me to confess the truth, I will no longer refuse to satisfy your questions and my duty.

Know then, that for no other reason is your lady vext to see the Captain in disfavour, than for the pleasure that she has in his company whenever he comes to your house, and all the more since she has taken an aversion to your blackness."

These words went straight to the Moor's heart; but in order to hear more (now that he believed true all that the Ensign had told him), he replied, with a fierce glance, " By heavens, I scarce can hold this hand from plucking out that tongue of thine, so bold, which dares to speak such slander of my wife! "

" Captain," replied the Ensign, " I looked for such reward, for these my faithful offices — none else; but since my duty, and the jealous care I bear your honour, have carried me thus far, I do repeat, so stands the truth, as you have heard it from these lips: and if the lady Disdemona hath, with a false show of love for you, blinded your eyes to /22/ what you should have seen, this is no argument but that I speak the truth. Nay, this same Captain told it me himself, like one whose happiness is incomplete until he can declare it to another: and, but that I feared your anger, I should have given him, when he told it me, his merited reward, and slain him. But since informing you, of what concerns more you than any other man, brings me so undeserved a recompense, would I had held my peace, since silence might have spared me your displeasure."

Then the Moor, burning with indignation and anguish, said, " Make thou these eyes self-witnesses of what thou tell'st, or on thy life I'll make thee wish thou hadst been born without a tongue."

" An easy task it would have been," replied the villain, " when he was used to visit at your house; but now, that you have banished him, not for just cause, but for more frivolous pretext, it will be hard to prove the truth. Still I do not forgo the hope, to make you witness of that which you will not credit from my lips."

Thus they parted. The wretched Moor, struck to the heart as by a barbed dart, returned to his home, and awaited the day when the Ensign should disclose to him the truth which was to make him miserable to the end of his days. But the evil-minded Ensign was, on his part, not less troubled by the chastity which he knew the lady Disdemona /23/ observed inviolate; and it

seemed to him impossible to discover a means of making the Moor believe what he had falsely told him; and turning the matter over in his thoughts, in various ways, the villain resolved on a new deed of guilt.

Disdemona often used to go, as I have already said, to visit the Ensign's wife, and remained with her a good part of the day. Now the Ensign observed, that she carried about with her a handkerchief, which he knew the Moor had given her, finely embroidered in the Moorish fashion, and which was precious to Disdemona, nor less so to the Moor. Then he conceived the plan, of taking this kerchief from her secretly, and thus laying the snare for her final ruin. The Ensign had a little daughter, a child three years of age who was much loved by Disdemona; and one day, when the unhappy lady had gone to pay a visit at the house of this vile man, he took the little child up in his arms, and carried her to Disdemona, who took her, and pressed her to her bosom; whilst at the same instant this traitor, who had extreme dexterity of hand, drew the kerchief from her sash so cunningly, that she did not notice him, and overjoyed he took his leave of her.

Disdemona, ignorant of what had happened, /24/ returned home, and, busied with other thoughts, forgot the handkerchief. But a few days afterwards looking for it, and not finding it, she was in alarm, lest the Moor should ask her for it, as he oft was wont to do. Meanwhile the wicked Ensign, seizing a fit opportunity, went to the Captain of the troop, and with crafty malice left the handkerchief at the head of his bed, without his discovering the trick; until the following morning, when, on his getting out of bed, the handkerchief fell upon the floor, and he set his foot upon it. And not being able to imagine how it had come into his house, knowing that it belonged to Disdemona, he resolved to give it her; and waiting until the Moor had gone from home, he went to the back door, and knocked. It seemed as if fate conspired with the Ensign to work the death of the unhappy Disdemona. Just at that time the Moor returned home, and hearing a knocking at the back door, he went to the window, and in a rage exclaimed, " Who knocks there? " The Captain, hearing the Moor's voice, and fearing lest he should come downstairs and attack him, took to flight without answering a word. The

Moor went down, and opening the door, hastened into the street, and looked about, but in vain. Then returning into the house, in great anger, he demanded of his wife who it was that had knocked at the door. Disdemona replied, as was true, that she did not /25/ know: but the Moor said, "It seemed to me the Captain."

"I know not," answered Disdemona, "whether it was he, or another person."

The Moor restrained his fury, great as it was, wishing to do nothing before consulting the Ensign, to whom he hastened instantly, and told him all that had passed, praying him to gather from the Captain all he could respecting the affair. The Ensign, overjoyed at the occurrence, promised the Moor to do as he requested; and one day he took occasion to speak with the Captain, when the Moor was so placed that he could see and hear them as they conversed. And whilst talking to him of every other subject than of Disdemona, he kept laughing all the time aloud; and feigning astonishment, he made various movements with his head and hands, as if listening to some tale of marvel. As soon as the Moor saw the Captain depart, he went up to the Ensign, to hear what he had said to him. And the Ensign, after long entreaty, at length said, "He has hidden from me nothing, and has told me that he has been used to visit your wife whenever you went from home, and that on the last occasion she gave him this handkerchief, which you presented to her when you married her."

The Moor thanked the Ensign, and it seemed now clear to him that, should he find Disdemona not to have the handkerchief, it was all true that /26/ the Ensign had told to him. One day, therefore, after dinner, in conversation with his wife on various subjects, he asked her for the kerchief. The unhappy lady, who had been in great fear of this, grew red as fire at this demand; and to hide the scarlet of her cheeks, which was closely noted by the Moor, she ran to a chest, and pretended to seek the handkerchief: and after hunting for it a long time, she said, "I know not how it is — I cannot find it — can you perchance have taken it?"

"If I had taken it," said the Moor, "why should I ask it of you? but you will look better another time."

On leaving the room, the Moor fell to meditating how he should put his wife to death, and likewise the Captain of the troop, so that their death should not be laid to his charge. And as he ruminated over this day and night, he could not prevent his wife's observing that he was not the same toward her as he had been wont; and she said to him again and again, "What is the matter? what troubles you? how comes it that you, who were the most light-hearted man in the world, are now so melancholy?"

The Moor feigned various reasons in reply to his wife's questioning, but she was not satisfied; and, although conscious that she had given the Moor no cause, by act or deed, to be so troubled, yet she feared that he might have grown wearied of her; /27/ and she would say to the Ensign's wife, "I know not what to say of the Moor; he used to be all love toward me; but within these few days he has become another man; and much I fear, that I shall prove a warning to young girls not to marry against the wishes of their parents, and that the Italian ladies may learn from me not to wed a man whom nature and habitude of life estrange from us. But as I know the Moor is on such terms of friendship with your husband, and communicates to him all his affairs, I pray you, if you have heard from him aught that you may tell me of, fail not to befriend me." And as she said this, she wept bitterly.

The Ensign's wife, who knew the whole truth (her husband wishing to make use of her to compass the death of Disdemona), but could never consent to such a project, dared not, from fear of her husband, disclose a single circumstance: all she said was, "Beware lest you give any cause of suspicion to your husband, and show to him by every means your fidelity and love."

"Indeed I do so," replied Disdemona; "but it is all of no avail." /28/

Meanwhile the Moor sought in every way to convince himself of what he fain would have found untrue; and he prayed the Ensign to contrive that he might see the handkerchief in the possession of the Captain. This was a difficult matter to the wicked Ensign, nevertheless he promised to use every means to satisfy the Moor of the truth of what he said.

Now the Captain had a wife [1] at home, who

---

1. This may be a mistranslation for "woman." Shakespeare has combined her and the courtesan of the following paragraph in the character of Bianca; but see *Othello*, I.i.21.

worked the most marvellous embroidery upon lawn; and seeing the handkerchief which belonged to the Moor's wife, she resolved, before it was returned to her, to work one like it. As she was engaged in this task, the Ensign observed her standing at a window, where she could be seen by all passers-by in the street; and he pointed her out to the Moor, who was now perfectly convinced of his wife's guilt. Then he arranged with the Ensign to slay Disdemona, and the Captain of the troop, treating them as it seemed they both deserved. And the Moor prayed the Ensign that he would kill the Captain, promising eternal gratitude /29/ to him. But the Ensign at first refused to undertake so dangerous a task, the Captain being a man of equal skill and courage; until at length, after much entreating, and being richly paid, the Moor prevailed on him to promise to attempt the deed.

Having formed this resolution, the Ensign, going out one dark night, sword in hand, met the Captain, on his way to visit a courtesan, and struck him a blow on his right thigh, which cut off his leg, and felled him to the earth. Then the Ensign was on the point of putting an end to his life, when the Captain, who was a courageous man, and used to the sight of blood and death, drew his sword, and, wounded as he was, kept on his defence, exclaiming with a loud voice, "I'm murdered!" Thereupon the Ensign, hearing the people come running up, with some of the soldiers who were lodged thereabouts, took to his heels, to escape being caught; then turning about again, he joined the crowd, pretending to have been attracted by the noise. And when he saw the Captain's leg cut off, he judged that, if not already dead, the blow must at all events end his life; and whilst in /30/ his heart he was rejoiced at this, he yet feigned to compassionate the Captain as he had been his brother.

The next morning the tidings of this affair spread through the whole city, and reached the ears of Disdemona; whereat she, who was kind-hearted and little dreamed that any ill would betide her, evinced the greatest grief at the calamity. This served but to confirm the Moor's suspicions, and he went to seek for the Ensign, and said to him, "Do you know, that ass my wife is in such grief at the Captain's accident, that she is well-nigh gone mad."

"And what could you expect, seeing he is her very soul?" replied the Ensign.

"Ay, soul forsooth!" exclaimed the Moor; "I'll draw the soul from out her body: call me no man, if that I fail to shut the world upon this wretch."

Then they consulted of one means and another — poison and daggers — to kill poor Disdemona, but could resolve on nothing. At length the Ensign said, "A plan comes to my mind, which will give you satisfaction, and raise cause for no suspicion — it is this: the house in which you live is very old, and the ceiling of your chamber has many cracks; I propose we take a stocking, filled with sand, and beat Disdemona with it till she dies; thus will her body bear no signs of violence. When she is dead, we can pull down a portion of the /31/ ceiling, and thus make it seem as if a rafter falling on her head had killed the lady. Suspicion can not rest on you, since all men will impute her death to accident."

This cruel counsel pleased the Moor, and he only waited for a fitting time to execute the plot. One night, when he and Disdemona had retired to bed, the Ensign, whom the Moor had concealed in a closet which opened into the chamber, raised a noise in the closet, according to a concerted plan; whereat the Moor said to his wife, "Did you not hear that noise?"

"Indeed I heard it," she replied.

"Rise," said the Moor, "and see what 'tis."

The unhappy Disdemona rose from bed, and the instant she approached the closet, out rushed the Ensign, and being strong and of stout nerve, he beat her cruelly with the bag of sand across her back; upon which Disdemona fell to the ground, scarce able to draw her breath: but with the little voice she had left, she called upon the Moor for aid. But the Moor, leaping from bed, exclaimed, "Thou wickedest of women, thus has thy falseness found its just reward — the recompense to wives, who counterfeiting love, place horns upon their husbands' brows."

The wretched lady, hearing these words, and feeling that she was near her end (for the Ensign had given her another blow), appealed to the /32/ justice of Heaven, since justice here had failed her, in proof of her fidelity and truth; and as she was thus calling Heaven to witness, the wicked Ensign inflicted a third blow, under which she sank lifeless on the floor.

Then the Ensign and the Moor, laying Disdemona on the bed, and wounding her head, pulled down part of the ceiling of the chamber, as they had arranged; whereupon the Moor began to call aloud for help, exclaiming that the house was falling. Hearing this uproar, the neighbors all came running up, and there found Disdemona lying dead beneath a rafter — a sight which, from the good life of that poor lady, did fill all hearts with sorrow.

On the following day Disdemona was buried, followed to the grave by the universal grief of the people. But Heaven, the just regarder of all hearts, willed not that so wicked a deed should go unpunished. Ere long the Moor, whom Disdemona had loved more than her own life, began to feel such sorrow at her loss, that he went wandering about, as one bereft of reason, searching in every part of the house. And reflecting in his thoughts that the Ensign had been the cause that he had lost, with Disdemona, all joy in life, he conceived so deep a hatred to that wicked man, he could not bear to set eyes on him; and had it not been for his fear of the inviolable justice of the Signoria /33/ of Venice, he would have slain him openly. But being unable to do this with safety, he deprived him of his rank, and would not allow him to remain in his Company; whereat such an enmity arose between the two, that no greater or more deadly can be imagined.

The Ensign, that wickedest of all bad men, now turned his thoughts to injuring the Moor; and seeking out the Captain, whose wound was by this time healed, and who went about with a wooden leg, in place of the one that had been cut off, he said to him, " 'Tis time you should be avenged for your lost limb; and if you will come with me to Venice, I'll tell you who the malefactor is, whom I dare not mention to you here, for many reasons, and I will bring you proofs."

The Captain of the troop, whose anger returned fiercely, but without knowing why, thanked the Ensign, and went with him to Venice. On arriving there, the Ensign told him that it was the Moor who had cut off his leg, on account of the suspicion he had formed of Disdemona's conduct with him; and for that reason he had slain her, and then spread the report that the ceiling had fallen and killed her. Upon hearing which, the Captain accused the Moor to the Signoria, both of having cut off his leg and killed his wife, and called the Ensign to witness the truth of what he said. The Ensign declared both charges to be /34/ true, for that the Moor had disclosed to him the whole plot, and had tried to persuade him to perpetrate both crimes; and that having afterwards killed his wife, out of jealousy he had conceived, he had narrated to him the manner in which he had perpetrated her death.

The Signori of Venice, when they heard of the cruelty inflicted by a barbarian upon a lady of their city, commanded that the Moor's arms should be pinioned in Cyprus, and he be brought to Venice, where with many tortures they sought to draw from him the truth. But the Moor, bearing with unyielding courage all the torment, denied the whole charge so resolutely, that no confession could be drawn from him. But although, by his constancy and firmness, he escaped death, he was, after being confined for several days in prison, condemned to perpetual banishment, in which he was eventually slain by the kinsfolk of Disdemona, as he merited. The Ensign returned to his own country, and following up his wonted villainy, he accused one of his companions of having sought to persuade him to kill an enemy of his, who was a man of noble rank; whereupon this person was arrested, and put to the torture; but when he denied the truth of what his accuser had declared, the Ensign himself was likewise tortured, to make him prove the truth of his accusation; and he was tortured so that his body ruptured, upon which he /35/ was removed from prison and taken home, where he died a miserable death. Thus did Heaven avenge the innocence of Disdemona; and all these events were narrated by the Ensign's wife, who was privy to the whole, after his death, as I have told them here. /36/

IBSEN ON

Ghosts

Ibsen's notes

These are all the surviving notes or memoranda that Ibsen wrote while working on Ghosts *during the years 1880–1881. Each of the five notes is independent and complete; they do not appear to be arranged in any significant order. The translation is by A. G. Chater and is taken from the Viking Edition of* The Works of Henrik Ibsen *(N.Y.: Scribner's, 1917), Vol. XII, From Ibsen's Workshop.*

[1] The play is to be like a picture of life. Belief undermined. But it does not do to say so. "The Orphanage"—for the sake of others. They are to be happy—but this too is only an appearance—Everything is ghosts.—

A leading point: She has been a believer and romantic—this is not entirely obliterated by the standpoint reached later—"Everything is ghosts."

Marriage for external reasons, even when these are religious or moral, brings a Nemesis upon the offspring.

She, the illegitimate child, can be saved by being married to—the son—but then—?

[2] He was dissipated and his health was shattered in his youth; then she appeared, the religious enthusiast; she saved him; she was rich. He was going to marry a girl who was considered unworthy. He had a son by his wife, then he went back to the girl; a daughter.—

[3] These women of the present day, ill-used as daughters, as sisters, as wives, not educated according to their gifts, prevented from following their inclination, deprived of their inheritance, embittered in temper—it is these who furnish the mothers of the new generation. What is the result?

[4] The key-note is to be: The prolific growth of our intellectual life, in literature, art, etc.— and in contrast to this: the whole of mankind gone astray. /185/

The complete human being is no longer a product of nature, he is an artificial product like corn, and fruit-trees, and the Creole race and thoroughbred horses and dogs, the vine, etc.—

The fault lies in that all mankind has failed. If a man claims to live and develop in a human way, it is megalomania. All mankind, and especially the Christian part of it, suffers from megalomania.

[5] Among us, monuments are erected to the *dead,* since we have a duty towards them; we allow lepers to marry; but their offspring—? The unborn—? /186/

An early draft of Ghosts

This is the longest fragment that has been preserved of an early draft of Ghosts. *Ibsen's final version can be seen on page 69 of this edition. The translation is by A. G. Chater, and is taken from the same volume as the notes on* Ghosts.

MAN. That is a very disputable point, Mrs. Alving. A child's proper place is, and must be, the home.

OSW. There I think you're quite right, Pastor Manders.

MAN. Ah, you can hardly have any idea of what a home should be—

OSW. Oh, but anyhow I have seen other people's homes.

MAN. I thought, however, that over there, especially in artistic circles, the life was a somewhat homeless one—

OSW. Well, most of the young men are forced to live so; they have no money, and besides they don't want to give up their precious freedom— they live frugally, I can tell you, a slice of ham and a bottle of wine.

MAN. But in what company?

OSW. In very pleasant company, Pastor Manders. Sometimes a few models join them and then, as likely as not, there's dancing. /187/

MAN. Models—? What do you mean by that?

OSW. We painters and sculptors require models, I suppose. Otherwise how could we reproduce the tension of the muscles and the reflected lights on the skin — and all that sort of thing?

MAN. But you don't mean to say that there are women who —

osw. Who sit to us artists; yes, I can assure you there are.

MAN. And such immorality is tolerated by the authorities?

osw. The authorities tolerate worse kinds of immorality than that, Pastor, as you are doubtless not unaware —

MAN. Alas, alas, that is only too true; but as to these models, it is even worse, for it takes place openly and is spoken about —

osw. Yes, it would never occur to us to do otherwise. Oh, I can assure you, there are many fine figures among the models one doesn't often see here.

MAN. Is it in such society you have been living abroad?

osw. Sometimes too I visit my friends at their homes; one has to see what their domestic circle is like, play a little with the children.

MAN. But you said most of the artists were not married.

osw. Oh, that was a mistake — I meant wedded.

MAN. But, good heavens —

osw. But, my dear Pastor Manders, what are they to do? A poor painter, a poor girl; they can't afford to marry, it costs a great deal. What are they to do?

MAN. I will tell you, Mr. Alving; they should remain apart.

osw. That doctrine will scarcely go down with /188/ warm-blooded young people, full of the joy of life. Oh, the glorious free life out there.

MAN. And, to make matters worse, such freedom is to be signalised as praiseworthy —

osw. Let me tell you, sir, you may visit many of these irregular homes and you will never hear an offensive word there. And let me tell you another thing: I have never come across immorality among our artists over there — but do you know where I have found it — ?

MAN. No, I'm happy to say —

osw. Well, then, I'm afraid I must inform you. I have met with it in many a pattern husband and father who has come to Paris to have a look round on his own account, one of these gentlemen with a heavy gold chain outside his waistcoat; do you know what is the first thing these gentlemen do? Why, they hunt up some poor artist or other, get on familiar terms with him, ask him to supper at a smart restaurant, make the champagne flow freely — and then take his arm and propose that they shall make a night of it — and then we artists hear of places we never knew of before, and see things we never dreamed of — But these are the respectable men, Pastor Manders, and on their return you can hear their praises of the pure morals of home in contrast to the corruption abroad — oh yes — these men know what's what — they have a right to be heard.

MRS. ALV. But, my dear Oswald, you mustn't get excited.

osw. No, you're right; it's bad for me — I shall go for a little turn before dinner. Excuse me, Pastor, I know you can't take my point of view; but I had to speak out for once.

[*He goes out by the second door to the right.*]

MAN. Then this is what he has come to! /189/

Ibsen's letter to Schandorph

This is a letter that Ibsen wrote to Sophus Schandorph, a Danish novelist, shortly after the publication of Ghosts. *The complete letter is reprinted here (except for a postscript) as it appears in* Letters of Henrik Ibsen, *translated by John N. Laurvik and Mary Morison (N.Y.: Fox, Duffield, 1905).*

Rome, 6th January 1882.

HONOURED SIR:

Accept my sincere thanks for the letter which you were good enough to write me, and excuse my not having found time to answer it until today. It came as a very welcome Christmas greeting at the time when my new play was being subjected to all kinds of misrepresentation and foolish criticism at home.

I was quite prepared for the hubbub. If certain of our Scandinavian reviewers have no talent for anything else, they have an unquestionable talent for thoroughly misunderstanding and misinterpreting those authors whose books they undertake to judge.

Is it, however, really nothing but misunderstanding? Have not many of these misrepresentations and distortions been presented to the public by writers fully aware of their being such? I can hardly think otherwise.

They endeavour to make me responsible for the opinions which certain of the personages of my drama express. And /351/ yet there is not in the whole book a single opinion, a single utterance, which can be laid to the account of the author. I took good care to avoid this. The method, the technique of the construction in itself entirely precludes the author's appearing in the speeches. My intention was to produce the impression in the mind of the reader that he was witnessing something real. Now, nothing would more effectually prevent such an impression than the insertion of the author's private opinions in the dialogue. Do they imagine at home that I have not enough of the dramatic instinct to be aware of this? Of course I am aware of it, and act accordingly. And in no other play which I have written is the author such an outsider, so entirely absent, as in this last one.

Then they say that the book preaches nihilism. It does not. It preaches nothing at all. It merely points out that there is a ferment of nihilism under the surface, at home as elsewhere. And this is inevitable. A Pastor Manders will always rouse some Mrs. Alving to revolt. And just because she is a woman, she will, once she has begun, go to great extremes.

I hope that George Brandes's article in the *Morgenblad* will be of great assistance in producing a more correct impression of the play. The *Morgenblad* has on several occasions evidenced goodwill towards me; and I trust you will be good enough to convey to the editors the assurance of my gratitude.

Your letter was both a pleasure and an honour; and it has begun an acquaintance which I have long desired. Your writings have given much enjoyment to me and my more immediate circle; and I have followed you on your different literary and critical campaigns, with great pleasure and interest.

I hope that a meeting, somewhere or other, is in store for us. — Believe me, Yours very respectfully and sincerely,

HENRIK IBSEN /352/

Ibsen's reply to Archer

This is a report of a conversation Ibsen had with William Archer, a British drama critic who greatly admired Ibsen and translated his plays. It is taken from Halvdan Koht's The Life of Ibsen, *translated by Ruth L. McMahon and Hanna A. Larsen (N.Y.: Norton, 1931), Vol. II.*

Immediately after the play was published, William Archer asked him outright how he himself imagined the conclusion. Would Mrs. Alving give her son poison, or not? Ibsen smiled and said thoughtfully: " I don't know. Each one must find that out for himself. I should never dream of deciding so delicate a question. But what is your opinion? " Archer answered that if she did not " come to the rescue " it must be because there still dwelt in her a " ghost," a specter of former times — that is if it were granted that the disease was absolutely incurable. Yes, said Ibsen, that was perhaps the solution — that the mother would always wait and put off " coming to the rescue " with the excuse that as long as there was life there was hope. /167/

O'NEILL ON

The Hairy Ape

This is an excerpt from Mary B. Mullett's interview with O'Neill, published as " The Extraordinary Story of Eugene O'Neill " in the November 1922 issue of the American Magazine, *Vol. XCIV, No. 5.*

" Take the fo'c'sle scenes in *The Hairy Ape,* for instance. People think I am giving an exact picture of the reality. They don't understand that the whole play is expressionistic.

" Yank is really yourself, and myself. He is

every human being. But, apparently, very few people seem to get this. They have written, picking out one thing or another in the play and saying 'how true' it is. But no one has said: 'I am Yank! Yank is my own self!'

"Yet that was what I meant him to be. His struggle to 'belong,' to find the thread that will make him a part of the fabric of Life — we are all struggling to do just that. One idea I had in writing the play was to show that the missing thread, literally 'the tie that binds,' is understanding of one another.

"In the scene where the bell rings for the stokers to go on duty, you remember that they all stand up, come to attention, then go out in a lockstep file. Some people think even that is an actual custom aboard ship! But it is only symbolic of the regimentation of men who are the slaves of machinery. In a larger sense, it applies to all of us, because we all are more or less the slaves of convention, or of discipline, or of a rigid formula of some sort." /118/

The following paragraphs are taken from the report of an anonymous interview with O'Neill which appeared in the New York Herald Tribune *on November 16, 1924, Section VII–VIII.*

"Many of the characters in my plays were suggested to me by people in real life, especially the sea characters. In special pleading I do not believe. Gorki's *A Night's Lodging*,[1] the great proletarian revolutionary play, is really more wonderful propaganda for the submerged than any other play ever written, simply because it contains no propaganda, but simply shows humanity as it is — truth in terms of human life. As soon as an author slips propaganda into a play everyone feels it and the play becomes simply an argument.

"*The Hairy Ape* was propaganda in the sense that it was a symbol of man, who has lost his old harmony with nature, the harmony which he used to have as an animal and has not /p. 14, col. 1/ yet acquired in a spiritual way. Thus, not being able to find it on earth nor in heaven, he's in the middle, trying to make peace, taking the 'woist punches from bot' of 'em.' This idea was expressed in Yank's speech. The public saw just the stoker, not the symbol, and the symbol makes the play either important or just another play. Yank can't go forward, and so he tries to go back. This is what his shaking hands with the gorilla meant. But he can't go back to 'belonging' either. The gorilla kills him. The subject here is the same ancient one that always was and always will be the one subject for drama, and that is man and his struggle with his own fate. The struggle used to be with the gods, but is now with himself, his own past, his attempt 'to belong.'" /p. 14, col. 2/.

This paragraph is from a brief "Note to this Edition" written by O'Neill for the Wilderness Edition of The Plays of Eugene O'Neill *(N.Y.: Scribner's, 1935), Vol. V.*

It was at Jimmy the Priest's[2] that I knew Driscoll, a Liverpool Irishman who was a stoker on a transatlantic liner. Shortly afterwards I learned that he had committed suicide by jumping overboard in mid-ocean. Why? The search for an explanation of why Driscoll, proud of his animal superiority and in complete harmony with his limited conception of the universe, should kill himself provided the germ of the idea for *The Hairy Ape*. Whether *The Hairy Ape,* written in Provincetown in December 1921 and produced by the Provincetown Players on March 9, 1922, is to be classified as an Expressionist play or not is of little consequence. Its manner is inseparable from its matter, and it found its form as a direct descendant from *The Emperor Jones*.[3] /xi/

---

1. first produced in Moscow in 1902. The title is more commonly translated as *The Lower Depths*.

2. a waterfront dive in New York City.
3. written by O'Neill in 1920, shortly before *The Hairy Ape.*

3. Some Theories of Tragedy

from the *Poetics*

by Aristotle

The Poetics *was written about 330* B.C., *approximately seventy years after the deaths of Sophocles and Euripides brought to an end the greatest period of Greek tragedy. The selection here is from the translation by Ingram Bywater and consists of the complete text from the beginning through the first half of Chapter 19, and those later passages which should be most relevant to modern students of tragedy, including all references to* Oedipus *and to Sophocles. It is taken from* The Student's Oxford Aristotle *(N.Y.: Oxford University Press, 1942), Vol. VI, published under the general editorship of W. D. Ross. Bywater's footnotes have been omitted and those which appear here are the present editor's.*

1. Our subject being Poetry, I propose to speak not only of the art in general but also of its species and their respective capacities; of the structure of plot required for a good poem; of the number and nature of the constituent parts of a poem; and likewise of any other matters in the same line of inquiry. Let us follow the natural order and begin with the primary facts.

Epic poetry and Tragedy, as also Comedy, Dithyrambic poetry,[1] and most flute-playing and lyre-playing, are all, viewed as a whole, modes of imitation. But at the same time they differ from one another in three ways, either by a difference of kind in their means, or by differences in the objects, or in the manner of their imitations.

Just as colour and form are used as means by some, who (whether by art or constant practice) imitate and portray many things by their aid, and the voice is used by others; so also in the above-mentioned group of arts, the means with them as a whole are rhythm, language, and harmony — used, however, either singly or in certain combinations. A combination of harmony and rhythm alone is the means in flute-playing and lyre-playing, and any other arts there may be of the same description, e.g., imitative piping. Rhythm alone, without harmony, is the means in the dancer's imitations; for even he, by the rhythms of his attitudes, may represent men's characters, as well as what they do and suffer. There is further an art which imitates by language alone, without harmony, in prose or in verse, and if in verse, either in some one or in a plurality of metres. This form of imitation is to this day without a name. We have no common name for a mime of Sophron or Xenarchus and a Socratic Conversation;[2] and we should still be without one even if the imitation in the two instances were in trimeters or elegiacs or some other kind of verse — though it is the way with people to tack on " poet " to the name of a metre, and talk of elegiac-poets and epic-poets, thinking that they call them poets not by reason of the imitative nature of their work, but indiscriminately by reason of the metre they write in. Even if a theory of medicine or physical philosophy be put forth in a metrical form, it is usual to describe the writer in this way; Homer and Em-

1. choral hymns sung at the festivals of Dionysos, out of which Greek tragedy evolved (see Chapter 4).

2. The most famous of these were Plato's *Dialogues*.

pedocles, however, have really nothing in common apart from their metre; so that, if the one is to be called a poet, the other should be termed a physicist rather than a poet. We should be in the same position also, if the imitation in these instances were in all the metres, like the *Centaur* (a rhapsody in a medley of all metres) of Chaeremon; and Chaeremon one has to recognize as a poet. So much, then, as to these arts. There are, lastly, certain other arts, which combine all the means enumerated, rhythm, melody, and verse, e.g., Dithyrambic and Nomic [3] poetry, Tragedy and Comedy; with this difference, however, that the three kinds of means are in some of them all employed together, and in others brought in separately, one after the other. These elements of difference in the above arts I term the means of their imitation.

2. The objects the imitator represents are actions, with agents who are necessarily either good men or bad — the diversities of human character being nearly always derivative from this primary distinction, since the line between virtue and vice is one dividing the whole of mankind. It follows, therefore, that the agents represented must be either above our own level of goodness, or beneath it, or just such as we are; in the same way as, with the painters, the personages of Polygnotus are better than we are, those of Pauson worse, and those of Dionysius just like ourselves. It is clear that each of the above-mentioned arts will admit of these differences, and that it will become a separate art by representing objects with this point of difference. Even in dancing, flute-playing, and lyre-playing such diversities are possible; and they are also possible in the nameless art that uses language, prose or verse without harmony, as its means; Homer's personages, for instance, are better than we are; Cleophon's are on our own level; and those of Hegemon of Thasos, the first writer of parodies, and Nicochares, the author of the *Diliad,* are beneath it. The same is true of the Dithyramb and the Nome: the personages may be presented in them with the difference exemplified in the . . . of . . .[4] and Argas, and in the Cyclopses of Timotheus and Philoxenus. This difference it is that distinguishes Tragedy and Comedy also; the one would make its personages worse, and the other better, than the men of the present day.

3. A third difference in these arts is in the manner in which each kind of object is represented. Given both the same means and the same kind of object for imitation, one may either (1) speak at one moment in narrative and at another in an assumed character, as Homer does; or (2) one may remain the same throughout, without any such change; or (3) the imitators may represent the whole story dramatically, as though they were actually doing the things described.

As we said at the beginning, therefore, the differences in the imitation of these arts come under three heads, their means, their objects, and their manner.

So that as an imitator Sophocles will be on one side akin to Homer, both portraying good men; and on another to Aristophanes,[5] since both present their personages as acting and doing. This in fact, according to some, is the reason for plays being termed dramas, because in a play the personages act the story.[6] Hence too both Tragedy and Comedy are claimed by the Dorians as their discoveries; Comedy by the Megarians — by those in Greece as having arisen when Megara became a democracy, and by the Sicilian Megarians on the ground that the poet Epicharmus was of their country, and a good deal earlier than Chionides and Magnes; even Tragedy also is claimed by certain of the Peloponnesian Dorians. In support of this claim they point to the words "comedy" and "drama." Their word for the outlying hamlets, they say, is *comae,* whereas Athenians call them *demes* — thus assuming that comedians got the name not from their *comoe* or revels, but from their strolling from hamlet to hamlet, lack of appreciation keeping them out of the city. Their word also for "to act," they say, is *dran,* whereas Athenians use *prattein.*

So much, then, as to the number and nature of the points of difference in the imitation of these arts.

4. It is clear that the general origin of poetry was due to two causes, each of them part of hu-

---

3. Nomes were poems sung by a single voice to the accompaniment of a stringed instrument.
4. The ellipses indicate something missing in the original text.

5. the greatest comic dramatist of the preceding age.
6. The Greek words for "drama" and "action" are related (see the end of this paragraph).

man nature. Imitation is natural to man from childhood, one of his advantages over the lower animals being this, that he is the most imitative creature in the world, and learns at first by imitation. And it is also natural for all to delight in works of imitation. The truth of this second point is shown by experience: though the objects themselves may be painful to see, we delight to view the most realistic representations of them in art, the forms for example of the lowest animals and of dead bodies. The explanation is to be found in a further fact: to be learning something is the greatest of pleasures not only to the philosopher but also to the rest of mankind, however small their capacity for it; the reason of the delight in seeing the picture is that one is at the same time learning — gathering the meaning of things, e.g., that the man there is so-and-so; for if one has not seen the thing before, one's pleasure will not be in the picture as an imitation of it, but will be due to the execution or colouring or some similar cause. Imitation, then, being natural to us — as also the sense of harmony and rhythm, the metres being obviously species of rhythms — it was through their original aptitude, and by a series of improvements for the most part gradual on their first efforts, that they created poetry out of their improvisations.

Poetry, however, soon broke up into two kinds according to the differences of character in the individual poets; for the graver among them would represent noble actions, and those of noble personages; and the meaner sort the actions of the ignoble. The latter class produced invectives at first, just as others did hymns and panegyrics. We know of no such poem by any of the pre-Homeric poets, though there were probably many such writers among them; instances, however, may be found from Homer downwards, e.g., his *Margites,* and the similar poems of others. In this poetry of invective its natural fitness brought an iambic metre into use; hence our present term " iambic," because it was the metre of their " iambs " or invectives against one another. The result was that the old poets became some of them writers of heroic and others of iambic verse. Homer's position, however, is peculiar: just as he was in the serious style the poet of poets, standing alone not only through the literary excellence, but also through the dramatic character of his imitations, so too he was

the first to outline for us the general forms of Comedy by producing not a dramatic invective, but a dramatic picture of the Ridiculous; his *Margites* in fact stands in the same relation to our comedies as the *Iliad* and *Odyssey* to our tragedies. As soon, however, as Tragedy and Comedy appeared in the field, those naturally drawn to the one line of poetry became writers of comedies instead of iambs, and those naturally drawn to the other, writers of tragedies instead of epics, because these new modes of art were grander and of more esteem than the old.

If it be asked whether Tragedy is now all that it need be in its formative elements, to consider that, and decide it theoretically and in relation to the theatres, is a matter for another inquiry.

It certainly began in improvisations — as did also Comedy; the one originating with the authors of the Dithyramb, the other with those of the phallic songs, which still survive as institutions in many of our cities. And its advance after that was little by little, through their improving on whatever they had before them at each stage. It was in fact only after a long series of changes that the movement of Tragedy stopped on its attaining to its natural form. (1) The number of actors was first increased to two by Aeschylus, who curtailed the business of the Chorus, and made the dialogue, or spoken portion, take the leading part in the play. (2) A third actor and scenery were due to Sophocles. (3) Tragedy acquired also its magnitude. Discarding short stories and a ludicrous diction, through its passing out of its satyric stage, it assumed, though only at a late point in its progress, a tone of dignity; and its metre changed then from trochaic to iambic. The reason for their original use of the trochaic tetrameter was that their poetry was satyric and more connected with dancing than it now is. As soon, however, as a spoken part came in, nature herself found the appropriate metre. The iambic, we know, is the most speakable of metres, as is shown by the fact that we very often fall into it in conversation, whereas we rarely talk hexameters, and only when we depart from the speaking tone of voice. (4) Another change was a plurality of episodes or acts. As for the remaining matters, the superadded embellishments and the account of their introduction, these must be taken as said, as it would probably be a long piece of work to go through the details.

5. As for Comedy, it is (as has been observed) an imitation of men worse than the average; worse, however, not as regards any and every sort of fault, but only as regards one particular kind, the Ridiculous, which is a species of the Ugly. The Ridiculous may be defined as a mistake or deformity not productive of pain or harm to others; the mask, for instance, that excites laughter, is something ugly and distorted without causing pain.

Though the successive changes in Tragedy and their authors are not unknown, we cannot say the same of Comedy; its early stages passed unnoticed, because it was not as yet taken up in a serious way. It was only at a late point in its progress that a chorus of comedians was officially granted by the archon;[7] they used to be mere volunteers. It had also already certain definite forms at the time when the record of those termed comic poets begins. Who it was who supplied it with masks, or prologues, or a plurality of actors and the like, has remained unknown. The invented Fable, or Plot, however, originated in Sicily with Epicharmus and Phormis; of Athenian poets Crates was the first to drop the Comedy of invective and frame stories of a general and non-personal nature, in other words, Fables or Plots.

Epic poetry, then, has been seen to agree with Tragedy to this extent, that of being an imitation of serious subjects in a grand kind of verse. It differs from it, however, (1) in that it is in one kind of verse and in narrative form; and (2) in its length — which is due to its action having no fixed limit of time, whereas Tragedy endeavours to keep as far as possible within a single circuit of the sun, or something near that. This, I say, is another point of difference between them, though at first the practice in this respect was just the same in tragedies as in epic poems. They differ also (3) in their constituents, some being common to both and others peculiar to Tragedy — hence a judge of good and bad in Tragedy is a judge of that in epic poetry also. All the parts of an epic are included in Tragedy; but those of Tragedy are not all of them to be found in the Epic.

6. Reserving hexameter poetry and Comedy for consideration hereafter,[8] let us proceed now to the discussion of Tragedy; before doing so, however, we must gather up the definition resulting from what has been said. A tragedy, then, is the imitation of an action that is serious and also, as having magnitude, complete in itself; in language with pleasurable accessories, each kind brought in separately in the parts of the work; in a dramatic, not in a narrative form; with incidents arousing pity and fear, wherewith to accomplish its catharsis of such emotions. Here by "language with pleasurable accessories" I mean that with rhythm and harmony or song superadded; and by "the kinds separately" I mean that some portions are worked out with verse only, and others in turn with song.

As they act the stories, it follows that in the first place the Spectacle (or stage-appearance of the actors) must be some part of the whole; and in the second Melody and Diction, these two being the means of their imitation. Here by "Diction" I mean merely this, the composition of the verses; and by "Melody," what is too completely understood to require explanation. But further: the subject represented also is an action; and the action involves agents, who must necessarily have their distinctive qualities both of character and thought, since it is from these that we ascribe certain qualities to their actions. There are in the natural order of things, therefore, two causes, Thought and Character, of their actions, and consequently of their success or failure in their lives. Now the action (that which was done) is represented in the play by the Fable or Plot. The Fable, in our present sense of the term, is simply this, the combination of the incidents, or things done in the story; whereas Character is what makes us ascribe certain moral qualities to the agents; and Thought is shown in all they say when proving a particular point or, it may be, enunciating a general truth. There are six parts consequently of every tragedy, as a whole (that is) of such or such quality, viz., a Fable or Plot, Characters, Diction, Thought, Spectacle, and Melody; two of them arising from the means, one from the manner, and three from the objects of the dramatic imitation; and there is

---

7. The archon was a high civic official. Choruses, trained at the expense of the wealthy citizens, were granted by the government to the Athenian dramatists for use in their plays.

8. Hexameter poetry is the Epic, discussed in Chapters 23–24. The section on Comedy has been lost.

nothing else besides these six. Of these, its formative elements, then, not a few of the dramatists have made due use, as every play, one may say, admits of Spectacle, Character, Fable, Diction, Melody, and Thought.

The most important of the six is the combination of the incidents of the story. Tragedy is essentially an imitation not of persons but of action and life, of happiness and misery. All human happiness or misery takes the form of action; the end for which we live is a certain kind of activity, not a quality. Character gives us qualities, but it is in our actions — what we do — that we are happy or the reverse. In a play accordingly they do not act in order to portray the Characters; they include the Characters for the sake of the action. So that it is the action in it, i.e., its Fable or Plot, that is the end and purpose of the tragedy; and the end is everywhere the chief thing. Besides this, a tragedy is impossible without action, but there may be one without Character. The tragedies of most of the moderns are characterless — a defect common among poets of all kinds, and with its counterpart in painting in Zeuxis as compared with Polygnotus; for whereas the latter is strong in character, the work of Zeuxis is devoid of it. And again: one may string together a series of characteristic speeches of the utmost finish as regards Diction and Thought, and yet fail to produce the true tragic effect; but one will have much better success with a tragedy which, however inferior in these respects, has a Plot, a combination of incidents, in it. And again: the most powerful elements of attraction in Tragedy, the Peripeties [9] and Discoveries, are parts of the Plot. A further proof is in the fact that beginners succeed earlier with the Diction and Characters than with the construction of a story; and the same may be said of nearly all the early dramatists. We maintain, therefore, that the first essential, the life and soul, so to speak, of Tragedy is the Plot; and that the Characters come second — compare the parallel in painting, where the most beautiful colours laid on without order will not give one the same pleasure as a simple black-and-white sketch of a portrait. We maintain that Tragedy is primarily an imitation of action, and that it is mainly for the sake of the action that it imitates the personal agents. Third comes the element of Thought, i.e., the power of saying whatever can be said, or what is appropriate to the occasion. This is what, in the speeches in Tragedy, falls under the arts of Politics and Rhetoric; for the older poets make their personages discourse like statesmen, and the modern like rhetoricians. One must not confuse it with Character. Character in a play is that which reveals the moral purpose of the agents, i.e., the sort of thing they seek or avoid, where that is not obvious — hence there is no room for Character in a speech on a purely indifferent subject. Thought, on the other hand, is shown in all they say when proving or disproving some particular point, or enunciating some universal proposition. Fourth among the literary elements is the Diction of the personages, i.e., as before explained, the expression of their thoughts in words, which is practically the same thing with verse as with prose. As for the two remaining parts, the Melody is the greatest of the pleasurable accessories of Tragedy. The Spectacle, though an attraction, is the least artistic of all the parts, and has least to do with the art of poetry. The tragic effect is quite possible without a public performance and actors; and besides, the getting-up of the Spectacle is more a matter for the costumier than the poet.

7. Having thus distinguished the parts, let us now consider the proper construction of the Fable or Plot, as that is at once the first and the most important thing in Tragedy. We have laid it down that a tragedy is an imitation of an action that is complete in itself, as a whole of some magnitude; for a whole may be of no magnitude to speak of. Now a whole is that which has beginning, middle, and end. A beginning is that which is not itself necessarily after anything else, and which has naturally something else after it; an end is that which is naturally after something itself, either as its necessary or usual consequent, and with nothing else after it; and a middle, that which is by nature after one thing and has also another after it. A well-constructed Plot, therefore, cannot either begin or end at any point one likes; beginning and end in it must be of the forms just described. Again: to be beautiful, a living creature, and every whole made up of parts, must not only present a certain order in its arrangement of parts, but also be of a certain

9. Peripeties are "reversals." They are explained, along with Discoveries, in Chapter 11.

definite magnitude. Beauty is a matter of size and order, and therefore impossible either (1) in a very minute creature, since our perception becomes indistinct as it approaches instantaneity; or (2) in a creature of vast size — one, say, 1,000 miles long — as in that case, instead of the object being seen all at once, the unity and wholeness of it is lost to the beholder. Just in the same way, then, as a beautiful whole made up of parts, or a beautiful living creature, must be of some size, but a size to be taken in by the eye, so a story or Plot must be of some length, but of a length to be taken in by the memory. As for the limit of its length, so far as that is relative to public performances and spectators, it does not fall within the theory of poetry. If they had to perform a hundred tragedies, they would be timed by water-clocks, as they are said to have been at one period. The limit, however, set by the actual nature of the thing is this: the longer the story, consistently with its being comprehensible as a whole, the finer it is by reason of its magnitude. As a rough general formula, " a length which allows of the hero passing by a series of probable or necessary stages from misfortune to happiness, or from happiness to misfortune," may suffice as a limit for the magnitude of the story.

8. The Unity of a Plot does not consist, as some suppose, in its having one man as its subject. An infinity of things befall that one man, some of which it is impossible to reduce to unity; and in like manner there are many actions of one man which cannot be made to form one action. One sees, therefore, the mistake of all the poets who have written a *Heracleid*, a *Theseid*,[10] or similar poems; they suppose that, because Heracles was one man, the story also of Heracles must be one story. Homer, however, evidently understood this point quite well, whether by art or instinct, just in the same way as he excels the rest in every other respect. In writing an *Odyssey*, he did not make the poem cover all that ever befell his hero — it befell him, for instance, to get wounded on Parnassus and also to feign madness at the time of the call to arms, but the two incidents had no necessary or probable connexion with one another — instead of doing that, he took as the subject of the *Odyssey*, as also of the *Iliad*, an action with a Unity of the kind we are describing. The truth is that, just as

in the other imitative arts one imitation is always of one thing, so in poetry the story, as an imitation of action, must represent one action, a complete whole, with its several incidents so closely connected that the transposal or withdrawal of any one of them will disjoin and dislocate the whole. For that which makes no perceptible difference by its presence or absence is no real part of the whole.

9. From what we have said it will be seen that the poet's function is to describe, not the thing that has happened, but a kind of thing that might happen, i.e., what is possible as being probable or necessary. The distinction between historian and poet is not in the one writing prose and the other verse — you might put the work of Herodotus into verse, and it would still be a species of history; it consists really in this, that the one describes the thing that has been, and the other a kind of thing that might be. Hence poetry is something more philosophic and of graver import than history, since its statements are of the nature rather of universals, whereas those of history are singulars. By a universal statement I mean one as to what such or such a kind of man will probably or necessarily say or do — which is the aim of poetry, though it affixes proper names to the characters; by a singular statement, one as to what, say, Alcibiades did or had done to him. In Comedy this has become clear by this time; it is only when their plot is already made up of probable incidents that they give it a basis of proper names, choosing for the purpose any names that may occur to them, instead of writing like the old iambic poets about particular persons. In Tragedy, however, they still adhere to the historic names; and for this reason: what convinces is the possible; now whereas we are not yet sure as to the possibility of that which has not happened, that which has happened is manifestly possible, else it would not have come to pass. Nevertheless even in Tragedy there are some plays with but one or two known names in them, the rest being inventions; and there are some without a single known name, e.g., Agathon's *Antheus*,[11] in which both incidents and names are of the poet's invention; and it is no less delightful on that account. So that one must not aim at a rigid adherence to the traditional stories on which trag-

---

10. that is, a *Life of Heracles* or a *Life of Theseus*.

11. This play is lost.

edies are based. It would be absurd, in fact, to do so, as even the known stories are only known to a few, though they are a delight none the less to all.

It is evident from the above that the poet must be more the poet of his stories or Plots than of his verses, inasmuch as he is a poet by virtue of the imitative element in his work, and it is actions that he imitates. And if he should come to take a subject from actual history, he is none the less a poet for that; since some historic occurrences may very well be in the probable and possible order of things; and it is in that aspect of them that he is their poet.

Of simple Plots and actions the episodic are the worst. I call a Plot episodic when there is neither probability nor necessity in the sequence of its episodes. Actions of this sort bad poets construct through their own fault, and good ones on account of the players. His work being for public performance, a good poet often stretches out a Plot beyond its capabilities, and is thus obliged to twist the sequence of incident.

Tragedy, however, is an imitation not only of a complete action, but also of incidents arousing pity and fear. Such incidents have the very greatest effect on the mind when they occur unexpectedly and at the same time in consequence of one another; there is more of the marvellous in them then than if they happened of themselves or by mere chance. Even matters of chance seem most marvellous if there is an appearance of design as it were in them; as for instance the statue of Mitys at Argos killed the author of Mitys' death by falling down on him when a looker-on at a public spectacle; for incidents like that we think to be not without a meaning. A Plot, therefore, of this sort is necessarily finer than others.

10. Plots are either simple or complex, since the actions they represent are naturally of this twofold description. The action, proceeding in the way defined, as one continuous whole, I call simple, when the change in the hero's fortunes takes place without Peripety or Discovery; and complex, when it involves one or the other, or both. These should each of them arise out of the structure of the Plot itself, so as to be the consequence, necessary or probable, of the antecedents. There is a great difference between a thing happening *propter hoc* and *post hoc*.[12]

11. A Peripety is the change of the kind described from one state of things within the play to its opposite, and that too in the way we are saying, in the probable or necessary sequence of events; as it is for instance in *Oedipus:* here the opposite state of things is produced by the Messenger, who, coming to gladden Oedipus and to remove his fears as to his mother, reveals the secret of his birth. And in *Lynceus:*[13] just as he is being led off for execution, with Danaus at his side to put him to death, the incidents preceding this bring it about that he is saved and Danaus put to death. A Discovery is, as the very word implies, a change from ignorance to knowledge, and thus to either love or hate, in the personages marked for good or evil fortune. The finest form of Discovery is one attended by Peripeties, like that which goes with the Discovery in *Oedipus.* There are no doubt other forms of it; what we have said may happen in a way in reference to inanimate things, even things of a very casual kind; and it is also possible to discover whether some one has done or not done something. But the form most directly connected with the Plot and the action of the piece is the first-mentioned. This, with a Peripety, will arouse either pity or fear — actions of that nature being what Tragedy is assumed to represent; and it will also serve to bring about the happy or unhappy ending. The Discovery, then, being of persons, it may be that of one party only to the other, the latter being already known; or both the parties may have to discover themselves. Iphigenia, for instance, was discovered to Orestes by sending the letter; and another Discovery was required to reveal him to Iphigenia.[14]

Two parts of the Plot, then, Peripety and Discovery, are on matters of this sort. A third part is Suffering; which we may define as an action of a destructive or painful nature, such as murders on the stage, tortures, woundings, and the like. The other two have been already explained.

12. The parts of Tragedy to be treated as formative elements in the whole were mentioned in a previous Chapter. From the point of view, however, of its quantity, i.e., the separate sections into which it is divided, a tragedy has the

---

12. between a thing happening *because* of the preceding events and a thing merely happening *after* them.

13. This play is lost.

14. In Euripides' *Iphigenia in Tauris*, Iphigenia and Orestes are brother and sister (children of Agamemnon and Clytemnestra) who have been separated for many years and do not recognize each other. See Aristotle's summary of the plot in Chapter 17.

following parts: Prologue, Episode, Exode, and a choral portion, distinguished into Parode and Stasimon; these two are common to all tragedies, whereas songs from the stage and *Commoe* are only found in some. The Prologue is all that precedes the Parode of the chorus; an Episode all that comes in between two whole choral songs; the Exode all that follows after the last choral song. In the choral portion the Parode is the whole first statement of the chorus; a Stasimon, a song of the chorus without anapaests or trochees; a *Commos,* a lamentation sung by chorus and actor in concert. The parts of Tragedy to be used as formative elements in the whole we have already mentioned; the above are its parts from the point of view of its quantity, or the separate sections into which it is divided.

13. The next points after what we have said above will be these: (1) What is the poet to aim at, and what is he to avoid, in constructing his Plots? and (2) What are the conditions on which the tragic effect depends?

We assume that, for the finest form of Tragedy, the Plot must be not simple but complex; and further, that it must imitate actions arousing fear and pity, since that is the distinctive function of this kind of imitation. It follows, therefore, that there are three forms of Plot to be avoided. (1) A good man must not be seen passing from happiness to misery, or (2) a bad man from misery to happiness. The first situation is not fear-inspiring or piteous, but simply odious to us. The second is the most untragic that can be; it has no one of the requisites of Tragedy; it does not appeal either to the human feeling in us, or to our pity, or to our fears. Nor, on the other hand, should (3) an extremely bad man be seen falling from happiness into misery. Such a story may arouse the human feeling in us, but it will not move us to either pity or fear; pity is occasioned by undeserved misfortune, and fear by that of one like ourselves; so that there will be nothing either piteous or fear-inspiring in the situation. There remains, then, the intermediate kind of personage, a man not pre-eminently virtuous and just, whose misfortune, however, is brought upon him not by vice and depravity but by some error of judgment, of the number of those in the enjoyment of great reputation and prosperity; e.g., Oedipus, Thyestes, and the men of note of similar families. The

perfect Plot, accordingly, must have a single, and not (as some tell us) a double issue; the change in the hero's fortunes must be not from misery to happiness, but on the contrary from happiness to misery; and the cause of it must lie not in any depravity, but in some great error on his part; the man himself being either such as we have described, or better, not worse, than that. Fact also confirms our theory. Though the poets began by accepting any tragic story that came to hand, in these days the finest tragedies are always on the story of some few houses, on that of Alcmeon, Oedipus, Orestes, Meleager, Thyestes, Telephus, or any others that may have been involved, as either agents or sufferers, in some deed of horror. The theoretically best tragedy, then, has a Plot of this description. The critics, therefore, are wrong who blame Euripides for taking this line in his tragedies, and giving many of them an unhappy ending. It is, as we have said, the right line to take. The best proof is this: on the stage, and in the public performances, such plays, properly worked out, are seen to be the most truly tragic; and Euripides, even if his execution be faulty in every other point, is seen to be nevertheless the most tragic certainly of the dramatists. After this comes the construction of Plot which some rank first, one with a double story (like the *Odyssey*) and an opposite issue for the good and the bad personages. It is ranked as first only through the weakness of the audiences; the poets merely follow their public, writing as its wishes dictate. But the pleasure here is not that of Tragedy. It belongs rather to Comedy, where the bitterest enemies in the piece (e.g., Orestes and Aegisthus [15]) walk off good friends at the end, with no slaying of any one by any one.

14. The tragic fear and pity may be aroused by the Spectacle; but they may also be aroused by the very structure and incidents of the play — which is the better way and shows the better poet. The Plot in fact should be so framed that, even without seeing the things take place, he who simply hears the account of them shall be filled with horror and pity at the incidents;

15. Aegisthus, the lover of Clytemnestra, took part with her in the murder of her husband, Agamemnon. Two of Agamemnon's children, Orestes and Electra, revenged his death by killing Aegisthus and their mother. The story is the basis of Aeschylus' *Oresteia,* Sophocles' *Electra,* and Euripides' *Electra* and his *Orestes.* There was, of course, no play in which they walked off good friends.

which is just the effect that the mere recital of the story in *Oedipus* would have on one. To produce this same effect by means of the Spectacle is less artistic, and requires extraneous aid. Those, however, who make use of the Spectacle to put before us that which is merely monstrous and not productive of fear, are wholly out of touch with Tragedy; not every kind of pleasure should be required of a tragedy, but only its own proper pleasure.

The tragic pleasure is that of pity and fear, and the poet has to produce it by a work of imitation; it is clear, therefore, that the causes should be included in the incidents of his story. Let us see, then, what kinds of incident strike one as horrible, or rather as piteous. In a deed of this description the parties must necessarily be either friends, or enemies, or indifferent to one another. Now when enemy does it on enemy, there is nothing to move us to pity either in his doing or in his meditating the deed, except so far as the actual pain of the sufferer is concerned; and the same is true when the parties are indifferent to one another. Whenever the tragic deed, however, is done within the family — when murder or the like is done or meditated by brother on brother, by son on father, by mother on son, or son on mother — these are the situations the poet should seek after. The traditional stories, accordingly, must be kept as they are, e.g., the murder of Clytaemnestra by Orestes and of Eriphyle by Alcmeon.[16] At the same time even with these there is something left to the poet himself; it is for him to devise the right way of treating them. Let us explain more clearly what we mean by "the right way." The deed of horror may be done by the doer knowingly and consciously, as in the old poets, and in Medea's murder of her children in Euripides.[17] Or he may do it, but in ignorance of his relationship, and discover that afterwards, as does the Oedipus in Sophocles. Here the deed is outside the play; but it may be within it, like the act of the Alcmeon in Astydamas, or that of the Telegonus in *Ulysses Wounded*. A third possibility is for one meditating some deadly injury to another, in ignorance of his relationship, to make the dis-

covery in time to draw back. These exhaust the possibilities, since the deed must necessarily be either done or not done, and either knowingly or unknowingly.

The worst situation is when the personage is with full knowledge on the point of doing the deed, and leaves it undone. It is odious and also (through the absence of suffering) untragic; hence it is that no one is made to act thus except in some few instances, e.g., Haemon and Creon in *Antigone*.[18] Next after this comes the actual perpetration of the deed meditated. A better situation than that, however, is for the deed to be done in ignorance, and the relationship discovered afterwards, since there is nothing odious in it, and the Discovery will serve to astound us. But the best of all is the last; what we have in *Cresphontes,* for example, where Merope, on the point of slaying her son, recognizes him in time; in *Iphigenia,* where sister and brother are in a like position; and in *Helle,* where the son recognizes his mother, when on the point of giving her up to her enemy.[19]

This will explain why our tragedies are restricted (as we said just now) to such a small number of families. It was accident rather than art that led the poets in quest of subjects to embody this kind of incident in their Plots. They are still obliged, accordingly, to have recourse to the families in which such horrors have occurred.

On the construction of the Plot, and the kind of Plot required for Tragedy, enough has now been said.

15. In the Characters there are four points to aim at. First and foremost, that they shall be good. There will be an element of character in the play, if (as has been observed) what a personage says or does reveals a certain moral purpose; and a good element of character, if the purpose so revealed is good. Such goodness is possible in every type of personage, even in a woman or a slave, though the one is perhaps an

---

16. Alcmeon killed his mother, Eriphyle. No play on this subject has survived.

17. In Euripides' *Medea*, Medea deliberately kills her children to punish her husband, who has deserted her. The play by Astydamas and *Ulysses Wounded*, mentioned here, have not survived.

18. In Sophocles' *Antigone*, Antigone commits suicide after Creon (the same Creon as in *Oedipus Rex*) sentences her to be buried alive. When Creon's son Haemon, who loved Antigone, discovers this, he draws his sword to kill his father but then decides to kill himself instead.

19. The *Cresphontes* is lost, but from another version of the story we learn that Merope was about to kill a sleeping boy whom she thought had slain her son when, just in time, she recognized that he was her son himself. In Euripides' *Iphigenia in Tauris*, Iphigenia is about to sacrifice her brother, Orestes, and then discovers who he is. *Helle* is another lost play.

inferior, and the other a wholly worthless being. The second point is to make them appropriate. The Character before us may be, say,
manly; but it is not appropriate in a female
Character to be manly, or clever. The third is
to make them like the reality, which is not the
same as their being good and appropriate, in
our sense of the term. The fourth is to make
them consistent and the same throughout; even
if inconsistency be part of the man before one
for imitation as presenting that form of character, he should still be consistently inconsistent.
We have an instance of baseness of character,
not required for the story, in the Menelaus in
Orestes; of the incongruous and unbefitting in
the lamentation of Ulysses in *Scylla,* and in the
(clever) speech of Melanippe; and of inconsistency in *Iphigenia at Aulis,* where Iphigenia the
suppliant is utterly unlike the later Iphigenia.[20]
The right thing, however, is in the Characters
just as in the incidents of the play to endeavour
always after the necessary or the probable; so
that whenever such-and-such a personage says
or does such-and-such a thing, it shall be the
necessary or probable outcome of his character;
and whenever this incident follows on that, it
shall be either the necessary or the probable consequence of it. From this one sees (to digress for
a moment) that the Dénouement also should
arise out of the plot itself, and not depend on a
stage-artifice, as in *Medea,* or in the story of the
(arrested) departure of the Greeks in the *Iliad*.[21]
The artifice must be reserved for matters outside the play—for past events beyond human
knowledge, or events yet to come, which require to be foretold or announced; since it is
the privilege of the Gods to know everything.
There should be nothing improbable among the
actual incidents. If it be unavoidable, however,
it should be outside the tragedy, like the improbability in the *Oedipus* of Sophocles.[22] But
to return to the Characters. As Tragedy is an imitation of personages better than the ordinary
man, we in our way should follow the example
of good portrait-painters, who reproduce the distinctive features of a man, and at the same time,
without losing the likeness, make him hand-
somer than he is. The poet in like manner, in
portraying men quick or slow to anger, or with
similar infirmities of character, must know how
to represent them as such, and at the same time
as good men, as Agathon and Homer have represented Achilles.

All these rules one must keep in mind
throughout, and, further, those also for such
points of stage-effect as directly depend on the
art of the poet, since in these too one may often
make mistakes. Enough, however, has been said
on the subject in one of our published writings.[23]

16. Discovery in general has been explained
already. As for the species of Discovery, the first
to be noted is (1) the least artistic form of it, of
which the poets make most use through mere
lack of invention, Discovery by signs or marks.
Of these signs some are congenital, like the
"lance-head which the Earth-born have on
them," or "stars," such as Carcinus brings in his
Thyestes; others acquired after birth—these latter being either marks on the body, e.g., scars,
or external tokens, like necklaces, or (to take
another sort of instance) the ark in the Discovery in *Tyro.* Even these, however, admit of two
uses, a better and a worse; the scar of Ulysses is
an instance; the Discovery of him through it is
made in one way by the nurse and in another
by the swineherds.[24] A Discovery using signs as
a means of assurance is less artistic, as indeed
are all such as imply reflection; whereas one
bringing them in all of a sudden, as in the
Bath-story, is of a better order. Next after these
are (2) Discoveries made directly by the poet;
which are inartistic for that very reason; e.g.,
Orestes' Discovery of himself in *Iphigenia:*
whereas his sister reveals who she is by the letter, Orestes is made to say himself what the poet

---

20. *Orestes* and *Iphigenia at Aulis* are tragedies by Euripides;
the other works referred to here have been lost.

21. At the end of Euripides' play, Medea escapes in a magic
chariot after killing her children. In Book II of the *Iliad* the
goddess Athene intervenes to prevent the Greeks from abandoning the war against Troy. By "stage-artifice" Aristotle probably
means the special machine (some sort of hoist) used to carry
Medea off or, in other plays, to lower a god onto the stage so
that he can solve the difficulties of the characters (the source of
the expression *deus ex machina*).

22. Presumably, the improbability is Oedipus' ignorance of
the circumstances of Laius' death, which is what Aristotle
specifies in Chapter 24, Paragraph 6.

23. This treatise has been lost.

24. The "lance-head" was a birthmark found on the descendants of the men ("the Earth-born") who sprouted from the
dragon's teeth sown by Kadmos, the ancestor of Oedipus, at
the founding of Thebes. The "star" was a mark on the shoulders
of the men of Thyestes' family. The *Tyro* is lost, but apparently
in it a child was identified by some object found in a boat in
which he had been cast adrift. In the *Odyssey,* Ulysses shows
his scar to the swineherds to prove his identity; earlier, in the
"Bath-story," the nurse sees the scar by accident and recognizes
him when he wishes to remain unknown.

rather than the story demands. This, therefore, is not far removed from the first-mentioned fault, since he might have presented certain tokens as well. Another instance is the "shuttle's voice" in the *Tereus* of Sophocles.[25] (3) A third species is Discovery through memory, from a man's consciousness being awakened by something seen. Thus in *The Cyprioe* of Dicaeogenes, the sight of the picture makes the man burst into tears; and in the *Tale of Alcinous,* hearing the harper Ulysses is reminded of the past and weeps; [26] the Discovery of them being the result. (4) A fourth kind is Discovery through reasoning; e.g., in *The Choephoroe;* "One like me is here; there is no one like me but Orestes; he, therefore, must be here." [27] Or that which Polyidus the Sophist suggested for *Iphigenia;* since it was natural for Orestes to reflect: "My sister was sacrificed, and I am to be sacrificed like her." [28] Or that in the *Tydeus* of Theodectes: "I came to find a son, and am to die myself." Or that in *The Phinidae*: on seeing the place the women inferred their fate, that they were to die there, since they had also been exposed there. (5) There is, too, a composite Discovery arising from bad reasoning on the side of the other party. An instance of it is in *Ulysses the False Messenger:* [29]

he said he should know the bow — which he had not seen; but to suppose from that that he would know it again (as though he had once seen it) was bad reasoning. (6) The best of all Discoveries, however, is that arising from the incidents themselves, when the great surprise comes about through a probable incident, like that in the *Oedipus* of Sophocles; and also in *Iphigenia;* for it was not improbable that she should wish to have a letter taken home. These last are the only Discoveries independent of the artifice of signs and necklaces. Next after them come Discoveries through reasoning.

17. At the time when he is constructing his Plots, and engaged on the Diction in which they are worked out, the poet should remember (1) to put the actual scenes as far as possible before his eyes. In this way, seeing everything with the vividness of an eye-witness as it were, he will devise what is appropriate, and be least likely to overlook incongruities. This is shown by what was censured in Carcinus, the return of Amphiaraus from the sanctuary; it would have passed unnoticed, if it had not been actually seen by the audience; but on the stage his play failed, the incongruity of the incident offending the spectators. (2) As far as may be, too, the poet should even act his story with the very gestures of his personages. Given the same natural qualifications, he who feels the emotions to be described will be the most convincing; distress and anger, for instance, are portrayed most truthfully by one who is feeling them at the moment. Hence it is that poetry demands a man with a special gift for it, or else one with a touch of madness in him; the former can easily assume the required mood, and the latter may be actually beside himself with emotion. (3) His story, again, whether already made or of his own making, he should first simplify and reduce to a universal form, before proceeding to lengthen it out by the insertion of episodes. The following will show how the universal element in *Iphigenia,* for instance, may be viewed: A certain maiden having been offered in sacrifice, and spirited away from her sacrifices into another land, where the custom was to sacrifice all strangers to the Goddess, she was made there the priestess of this rite. Long after that the brother of the priestess happened to come; the fact, however, of the oracle having for a certain reason bidden him go thither, and his

25. In Euripides' *Iphigenia in Tauris*, Orestes proves his identity to Iphigenia by describing some objects in their parents' house. His earlier recognition of her, on the other hand, is the unintended result of her attempt to send a letter home, and this Aristotle regards as superior (see the end of this chapter). In the lost *Tereus*, Philomela was raped by Tereus, who cut out her tongue so she could not reveal his crime; but with her shuttle she wove a tapestry that told the whole story.

26. In this incident in the *Odyssey*, Ulysses hears a minstrel sing of the Trojan War and weeps in memory of his comrades, which causes Alcinous to ask him who he is. *The Cyprioe* is lost.

27. *The Choephoroe* is the second play of the *Oresteia*, Aeschylus' trilogy based on the murder of Agamemnon and its consequences. The reasoner is Electra; she discovers a lock of hair and a footprint like hers and concludes from this that her brother, Orestes, has returned (he was taken away when their father was murdered and has come back now after many years to avenge his death).

28. That is, Orestes would say this and Iphigenia, overhearing him, would realize he is her brother. (Iphigenia had been sacrificed by her father, Agamemnon, many years previous at Aulis in order to secure a favorable wind to take the Greeks to Troy; this is the subject of Euripides' *Iphigenia at Aulis*. But, in this version of the story, the goddess Artemis has secretly spirited her away to Tauris, where she is required to take part in the sacrifice of all strangers who land there. See the plot summary in the following chapter.) Apparently Polyidus suggested this as an improvement upon the device Euripides actually uses to have Orestes reveal himself to Iphigenia (described in note 25).

29. *Tydeus, The Phinidae,* and *Ulysses the False Messenger* are lost, as is the play about Amphiaraus discussed at the beginning of the next chapter.

object in going, are outside the Plot of the play. On his coming he was arrested, and about to be sacrificed, when he revealed who he was — either as Euripides puts it, or (as suggested by Polyidus) by the not improbable exclamation, " So I too am doomed to be sacrificed, as my sister was "; and the disclosure led to his salvation. This done, the next thing, after the proper names have been fixed as a basis for the story, is to work in episodes or accessory incidents. One must mind, however, that the episodes are appropriate, like the fit of madness in Orestes, which led to his arrest, and the purifying, which brought about his salvation. In plays, then, the episodes are short; in epic poetry they serve to lengthen out the poem. The argument of the *Odyssey* is not a long one. A certain man has been abroad many years; Poseidon is ever on the watch for him, and he is all alone. Matters at home too have come to this, that his substance is being wasted and his son's death plotted by suitors to his wife. Then he arrives there himself after his grievous sufferings; reveals himself, and falls on his enemies; and the end is his salvation and their death. This being all that is proper to the *Odyssey,* everything else in it is episode.

18. (4) There is a further point to be borne in mind. Every tragedy is in part Complication and in part Dénouement; the incidents before the opening scene, and often certain also of those within the play, forming the Complication; and the rest the Dénouement. By Complication I mean all from the beginning of the story to the point just before the change in the hero's fortunes; by Dénouement, all from the beginning of the change to the end. In the *Lynceus* of Theodectes, for instance, the Complication includes, together with the presupposed incidents, the seizure of the child and that in turn of the parents; and the Dénouement all from the indictment for the murder to the end. Now it is right, when one speaks of a tragedy as the same or not the same as another, to do so on the ground before all else of their Plot, i.e., as having the same or not the same Complication and Dénouement. Yet there are many dramatists who, after a good Complication, fail in the Dénouement. But it is necessary for both points of construction to be always duly mastered. (5) There are four distinct species of Tragedy — that being the number of the constituents also that have been men-

tioned: first, the complex Tragedy, which is all Peripety and Discovery; second, the Tragedy of suffering, e.g., the *Ajaxes* and *Ixions;* third, the Tragedy of character, e.g., *The Phthiotides* and *Peleus.* The fourth constituent is that of " Spectacle," exemplified in *The Phorcides,* in *Prometheus,*[30] and in all plays with the scene laid in the nether world. The poet's aim, then, should be to combine every element of interest, if possible, or else the more important and the major part of them. This is now especially necessary owing to the unfair criticism to which the poet is subjected in these days. Just because there have been poets before him strong in the several species of tragedy, the critics now expect the one man to surpass that which was the strong point of each one of his predecessors. (6) One should also remember what has been said more than once, and not write a tragedy on an epic body of incident (i.e., one with a plurality of stories in it), by attempting to dramatize, for instance, the entire story of the *Iliad*. In the epic owing to its scale every part is treated at proper length; with a drama, however, on the same story the result is very disappointing. This is shown by the fact that all who have dramatized the fall of Ilium in its entirety, and not part by part, like Euripides, or the whole of the Niobe story, instead of a portion, like Aeschylus, either fail utterly or have but ill success on the stage; for that and that alone was enough to ruin even a play by Agathon. Yet in their Peripeties, as also in their simple plots, the poets I mean show wonderful skill in aiming at the kind of effect they desire — a tragic situation that arouses the human feeling in one, like the clever villain (e.g., Sisyphus) deceived, or the brave wrongdoer worsted. This is probable, however, only in Agathon's sense, when he speaks of the probability of even improbabilities coming to pass. (7) The Chorus too should be regarded as one of the actors; it should be an integral part of the whole, and take a share in the action — that which it has in Sophocles, rather than in Euripides. With the later poets, however, the songs in a play of theirs have no more to do with the Plot of that than of any other tragedy. Hence it is that they are now singing intercalary pieces, a practice first introduced by Agathon. And yet what real dif-

30. An *Ajax* by Sophocles and a *Prometheus Bound* by Aeschylus are extant. No plays bearing the other four titles in this section have come down to us.

ference is there between singing such intercalary pieces, and attempting to fit in a speech, or even a whole act, from one play into another?

19. The Plot and Characters having been discussed, it remains to consider the Diction and Thought. As for the Thought, we may assume what is said of it in our Art of Rhetoric,[31] as it belongs more properly to that department of inquiry. The Thought of the personages is shown in everything to be effected by their language — in every effort to prove or disprove, to arouse emotion (pity, fear, anger, and the like), or to maximize or minimize things. It is clear, also, that their mental procedure must be on the same lines in their actions likewise, whenever they wish them to arouse pity or horror, or to have a look of importance or probability. The only difference is that with the act the impression has to be made without explanation; whereas with the spoken word it has to be produced by the speaker, and result from his language. What, indeed, would be the good of the speaker, if things appeared in the required light even apart from anything he says?

The second half of Chapter 19 and all of Chapters 20–22 are devoted to Diction, concluding Aristotle's discussion of the formative elements of Tragedy. In Chapters 23–24 he takes up the Epic; in Chapter 25 he examines possible criticisms of an epic or tragedy and the answers to them; and in Chapter 26, the final chapter, he compares Tragedy and the Epic. The following passages appear in this final portion of the treatise. Each paragraph is numbered to indicate its place in the chapter from which it is taken.

FROM CHAPTER 22

[1] The perfection of Diction is for it to be at once clear and not mean. The clearest indeed is that made up of the ordinary words for things, but it is mean, as is shown by the poetry of Cleophon and Sthenelus. On the other hand the Diction becomes distinguished and non-prosaic by the use of unfamiliar terms, i.e., strange words, metaphors, lengthened forms, and everything that deviates from the ordinary modes of speech. But a whole statement in such terms will be either a riddle or a barbarism, a riddle, if made up of metaphors, a barbarism, if made up of strange

words. . . . — A certain admixture, accordingly, of unfamiliar terms is necessary. These, the strange word, the metaphor, the ornamental equivalent, etc., will save the language from seeming mean and prosaic, while the ordinary words in it will secure the requisite clearness. . . . A too apparent use of these licences has certainly a ludicrous effect, but they are not alone in that; the rule of moderation applies to all the constituents of the poetic vocabulary; even with metaphors, strange words, and the rest, the effect will be the same, if one uses them improperly and with a view to provoking laughter. The proper use of them is a very different thing. . . . It is a great thing, indeed, to make a proper use of these poetical forms, as also of compounds and strange words. But the greatest thing by far is to be a master of metaphor. It is the one thing that cannot be learnt from others; and it is also a sign of genius, since a good metaphor implies an intuitive perception of the similarity in dissimilars.

FROM CHAPTER 24

[6] A likely impossibility is always preferable to an unconvincing possibility. The story should never be made up of improbable incidents; there should be nothing of the sort in it. If, however, such incidents are unavoidable, they should be outside the piece, like the hero's ignorance in *Oedipus* of the circumstances of Laius' death; not within it. . . . So that it is ridiculous to say that one's Plot would have been spoilt without them, since it is fundamentally wrong to make up such Plots. If the poet has taken such a Plot, however, and one sees that he might have put it in a more probable form, he is guilty of absurdity as well as a fault of art. . . .

FROM CHAPTER 25

[1] As regards Problems and their Solutions, one may see the number and nature of the assumptions on which they proceed by viewing the matter in the following way. (1) The poet being an imitator just like the painter or other maker of likenesses, he must necessarily in all instances represent things in one or other of three aspects, either as they were or are, or as they are said or thought to be or to have been, or as they ought to be. (2) All this he does in language, with an admixture, it may be, of strange words and metaphors, as also of the various modified forms of words, since the use

of these is conceded in poetry. (3) It is to be remembered, too, that there is not the same kind of correctness in poetry as in politics, or indeed any other art. There is, however, within the limits of poetry itself a possibility of two kinds of error, the one directly, the other only accidentally connected with the art. If the poet meant to describe the thing correctly, and failed through lack of power of expression, his art itself is at fault. But if it was through his having meant to describe it in some incorrect way (e.g., to make the horse in movement have both right legs thrown forward) that the technical error (one in a matter of, say, medicine or some other special science), or impossibilities of whatever kind they may be, have got into his description, his error in that case is not in the essentials of the poetic art. These, therefore, must be the premisses of the Solutions in answer to the criticisms involved in the Problems.

[2] As to the criticisms relating to the poet's art itself. Any impossibilities there may be in his descriptions of things are faults. But from another point of view, they are justifiable, if they serve the end of poetry itself — if (to assume what we have said of that end) they make the effect of either that very portion of the work or some other portion more astounding. . . . If, however, the poetic end might have been as well or better attained without sacrifice of technical correctness in such matters, the impossibility is not to be justified, since the description should be, if it can, entirely free from error. . . .

[3] If the poet's description be criticized as not true to fact, one may urge perhaps that the object ought to be as described — an answer like that of Sophocles, who said that he drew men as they ought to be, and Euripides as they were. If the description, however, be neither true nor of the thing as it ought to be, the answer must be then, that it is in accordance with opinion. . . .

[5] Speaking generally, one has to justify (1) the Impossible by reference to the requirements of poetry, or to the better, or to opinion. For the purposes of poetry a convincing impossibility is preferable to an unconvincing possibility; and if men such as Zeuxis depicted be impossible, the answer is that it is better they should be like that, as the artist ought to improve on his model. (2) The Improbable one has to justify either by showing it to be in accordance with opinion, or by urging that at times it is not improbable; for there is a probability of things happening also against probability. (3) The contradictions found in the poet's language one should first test as one does an opponent's confutation in a dialectical argument, so as to see whether he means the same thing, in the same relation, and in the same sense, before admitting that he has contradicted either something he has said himself or what a man of sound sense assumes as true. But there is no possible apology for improbability of Plot or depravity of character, when they are not necessary and no use is made of them. . . .

FROM CHAPTER 26

[3] . . . one must remember (1) that Tragedy has everything that the Epic has (even the epic metre being admissible), together with a not inconsiderable addition in the shape of the Music (a very real factor in the pleasure of the drama) and the Spectacle. (2) That its reality of presentation is felt in the play as read, as well as in the play as acted. (3) That the tragic imitation requires less space for the attainment of its end; which is a great advantage, since the more concentrated effect is more pleasurable than one with a large admixture of time to dilute it — consider the *Oedipus* of Sophocles, for instance, and the effect of expanding it into the number of lines of the *Iliad*. (4) That there is less unity in the imitation of the epic poets, as is proved by the fact that any one work of theirs supplies matter for several tragedies; the result being that, if they take what is really a single story, it seems curt when briefly told, and thin and waterish when on the scale of length usual with their verse. In saying that there is less unity in an epic, I mean an epic made up of a plurality of actions, in the same way as the *Iliad* and *Odyssey* have many such parts, each one of them in itself of some magnitude; yet the structure of the two Homeric poems is as perfect as can be, and the action in them is as nearly as possible one action. If, then, Tragedy is superior in these respects, and also, besides these, in its poetic effect (since the two forms of poetry should give us, not any or every pleasure, but the very special kind we have mentioned), it is clear that, as attaining the poetic effect better than the Epic, it will be the higher form of art.

Of Tragedy

by David Hume

The complete essay, first published in London in 1757, is reprinted here as it appears in Hume's Essays and Treatises on Several Subjects (*Edinburgh, 1809*), *Vol. I, " Essays, Moral, Political, and Literary," Part I. Spelling and punctuation have been modernized. Hume's footnotes have been omitted and those which appear here are the present editor's.*

It seems an unaccountable pleasure, which the spectators of a well-written tragedy receive from sorrow, terror, anxiety, and other passions that are in themselves disagreeable and uneasy. The more they are touched and affected, the more are they delighted with the spectacle; and as soon as the uneasy passions cease to operate, the piece is at an end. One scene of full joy and contentment and security is the utmost that any composition of this kind can bear; and it is sure always to be the concluding one. If in the texture of the piece there be interwoven any scenes of satisfaction, they afford only faint gleams of pleasure, which are thrown in by way of variety, and in order to plunge the actors into deeper distress by means of that contrast and disappointment. The whole art of the poet is employed in rousing and supporting the compassion and indignation, the anxiety and resentment, of his audience. They are pleased in proportion as they are afflicted, and never are so happy as when they employ tears, sobs, and cries, to give vent to their sorrow, and relieve their heart, swollen with the tenderest sympathy and compassion. /231/

The few critics who have had some tincture of philosophy have remarked this singular phenomenon, and have endeavored to account for it.

L'Abbé Dubos, in his reflections on poetry and painting,[1] asserts that nothing is in general so disagreeable to the mind as the languid, listless state of indolence into which it falls upon the removal of all passion and occupation. To

[1]. Abbé Jean Baptiste Dubos, *Réflexions critiques sur la poésie et sur la peinture* (1719).

get rid of this painful situation, it seeks every amusement and pursuit: business, gaming, shows, executions; whatever will rouse the passions and take its attention from itself. No matter what the passion is: let it be disagreeable, afflicting, melancholy, disordered; it is still better than that insipid languor, which arises from perfect tranquillity and repose.

It is impossible not to admit this account as being, at least in part, satisfactory. You may observe, when there are several tables of gaming, that all the company run to those where the deepest play is, even though they find not there the best players. The view, or, at least, imagination of high passions, arising from great loss or gain, affects the spectator by sympathy, gives him some touches of the same passions, and serves him for a momentary entertainment. It makes the time pass the easier with him, and is some relief to that oppression under which men commonly labor when left entirely to their own thoughts and meditations.

We find that common liars always magnify, in their narrations, all kinds of danger, pain, distress, sickness, deaths, murders, and cruelties, as well as joy, beauty, mirth, and magnificence. It is an absurd secret which they have for pleasing their company, fixing their attention, and attaching them to such marvelous relations by the passions and emotions which they excite. /232/

There is, however, a difficulty in applying to the present subject, in its full extent, this solution, however ingenious and satisfactory it may appear. It is certain that the same object of distress which pleases in a tragedy, were it really set before us, would give the most unfeigned uneasiness; though it be then the most effectual cure to languor and indolence. Monsieur Fontenelle seems to have been sensible of this difficulty, and accordingly attempts another solution of the phenomenon; at least makes some addition to the theory above mentioned.

" Pleasure and pain," says he, " which are two

sentiments so different in themselves, differ not so much in their cause. From the instance of tickling, it appears, that the movement of pleasure, pushed a little too far, becomes pain; and that the movement of pain, a little moderate, becomes pleasure. Hence it proceeds that there is such a thing as a sorrow, soft and agreeable; it is a pain weakened and diminished. The heart likes naturally to be moved and affected. Melancholy objects suit it, and even disastrous and sorrowful, provided they are softened by some circumstance. It is certain that, on the theatre, the representation has almost the effect of reality; yet it has not altogether that effect. However we may be hurried away by the spectacle, whatever dominion the senses and imagination may usurp over the reason, there still lurks at the bottom a certain idea of falsehood in the whole of what we see. This idea, though weak and disguised, suffices to diminish the pain which we suffer from the misfortunes of those whom we love, and to reduce that affliction to such a pitch as converts it into a pleasure. We weep for the misfortune of a /233/ hero to whom we are attached. In the same instant we comfort ourselves by reflecting that it is nothing but a fiction; and it is precisely that mixture of sentiments which composes an agreeable sorrow and tears that delight us. But as that affliction which is caused by exterior and sensible objects is stronger than the consolation which arises from an internal reflection, they are the effects and symptoms of sorrow that ought to predominate in the composition." [2]

This solution seems just and convincing; but perhaps it wants still some new addition, in order to make it answer fully the phenomenon which we here examine. All the passions, excited by eloquence, are agreeable in the highest degree, as well as those which are moved by painting and the theatre. The epilogues of Cicero are, on this account chiefly, the delight of every reader of taste; and it is difficult to read some of them without the deepest sympathy and sorrow. His merit as an orator, no doubt, depends much on his success in this particular. When he had raised tears in his judges and all his audience, they were then the most highly delighted, and expressed the greatest satisfaction with the pleader. The pathetic description of

the butchery made by Verres of the Sicilian captains is a masterpiece of this kind; but I believe none will affirm that the being present at a melancholy scene of that nature would afford any entertainment. Neither is the sorrow here softened by fiction, for the audience were convinced of the reality of every circumstance. What is it, then, which in this case raises a pleasure from the bosom of uneasiness, so to speak, and a pleasure which still retains all the features and outward symptoms of distress and sorrow?

I answer: This extraordinary effect proceeds from that very eloquence with which the melancholy scene /234/ is represented. The genius required to paint objects in a lively manner, the art employed in collecting all the pathetic circumstances, the judgment displayed in disposing them — the exercise, I say, of these noble talents, together with the force of expression, and beauty of oratorial numbers, diffuse the highest satisfaction on the audience, and excite the most delightful movements. By this means, the uneasiness of the melancholy passions is not only overpowered and effaced by something stronger of an opposite kind; but the whole impulse of those passions is converted into pleasure and swells the delight which the eloquence raises in us. The same force of oratory, employed on an uninteresting subject, would not please half so much, or rather would appear altogether ridiculous; and the mind, being left in absolute calmness and indifference, would relish none of those beauties of imagination or expression, which, if joined to passion, give it such exquisite entertainment. The impulse or vehemence arising from sorrow, compassion, indignation, receives a new direction from the sentiments of beauty. The latter, being the predominant motion, seize the whole mind, and convert the former into themselves, at least tincture them so strongly as totally to alter their nature. And the soul, being at the same time roused by passion and charmed by eloquence, feels on the whole a strong movement which is altogether delightful.

The same principle takes place in tragedy, with this addition, that tragedy is an imitation, and imitation is always of itself agreeable. This circumstance serves still further to smooth the motions of passion, and convert the whole feeling into one uniform and strong enjoyment. Objects of the greatest terror and distress please in painting, and please more than the most beauti-

2. Bernard le Bovier de Fontenelle, *Réflexions sur la poétique* (written *ca.* 1695, published 1742), Section 36.

ful objects /235/ that appear calm and indifferent. The affection, rousing the mind, excites a large stock of spirit and vehemence, which is all transformed into pleasure by the force of the prevailing movement. It is thus the fiction of tragedy softens the passion, by an infusion of a new feeling, not merely by weakening or diminishing the sorrow. You may by degrees weaken a real sorrow, till it totally disappears; yet in none of its gradations will it ever give pleasure, except, perhaps, by accident, to a man sunk under lethargic indolence, whom it rouses from that languid state.

To confirm this theory, it will be sufficient to produce other instances, where the subordinate movement is converted into the predominant, and gives force to it, though of a different, and even sometimes though of a contrary nature.

Novelty naturally rouses the mind, and attracts our attention; and the movements which it causes are always converted into any passion belonging to the object, and join their force to it. Whether an event excite joy or sorrow, pride or shame, anger or good will, it is sure to produce a stronger affection, when new or unusual. And though novelty of itself be agreeable, it fortifies the painful, as well as agreeable, passions.

Had you any intention to move a person extremely by the narration of any event, the best method of increasing its effect would be artfully to delay informing him of it, and first to excite his curiosity and impatience before you let him into the secret. This is the artifice practiced by Iago in the famous scene of Shakespeare; and every spectator is sensible that Othello's jealousy acquires additional /236/ force from his preceding impatience, and that the subordinate passion is here readily transformed into the predominant one.

Difficulties increase passions of every kind; and by rousing our attention, and exciting our active powers, they produce an emotion which nourishes the prevailing affection.

Parents commonly love that child most whose sickly infirm frame of body has occasioned them the greatest pains, trouble, and anxiety, in rearing him. The agreeable sentiment of affection here acquires force from sentiments of uneasiness.

Nothing endears so much a friend as sorrow for his death. The pleasure of his company has

not so powerful an influence.

Jealousy is a painful passion; yet without some share of it, the agreeable affection of love has difficulty to subsist in its full force and violence. Absence is also a great source of complaint among lovers, and gives them the greatest uneasiness; yet nothing is more favorable to their mutual passion than short intervals of that kind. And if long intervals often prove fatal, it is only because, through time, men are accustomed to them, and they cease to give uneasiness. Jealousy and absence in love compose the *dolce piccante*[3] of the Italians, which they suppose so essential to all pleasure.

There is a fine observation of the elder Pliny, which illustrates the principle here insisted on. " It is very remarkable," says he, " that the last works of celebrated artists, which they left imperfect, are always the most prized, such as the *Iris* of Aristides, the *Tyndarides* of Nicomachus, the *Medea* of Timomachus, and the *Venus* of Apelles. These are valued even above their finished productions. The broken lineaments of the piece, and the /237/ half-formed idea of the painter, are carefully studied; and our very grief for that curious hand, which had been stopped by death, is an additional increase to our pleasure." [4]

These instances (and many more might be collected) are sufficient to afford us some insight into the analogy of nature, and to show us that the pleasure which poets, orators, and musicians give us, by exciting grief, sorrow, indignation, compassion, is not so extraordinary or paradoxical as it may at first sight appear. The force of imagination, the energy of expression, the power of numbers, the charms of imitation — all these are naturally, of themselves, delightful to the mind. And when the object presented lays hold also of some affection, the pleasure still rises upon us, by the conversion of this subordinate movement into that which is predominant. The passion, though perhaps naturally and when excited by the simple appearance of a real object it may be painful, yet is so smoothed, and softened, and mollified, when raised by the finer arts, that it affords the highest entertainment.

To confirm this reasoning, we may observe that if the movements of the imagination be not

3. piquant sweetness, sweetness enhanced by a sharp or biting quality, roughly similar to our "bittersweet."
4. C. Plinius Secundus (Pliny the Elder), *Historia Naturalis* (*Natural History*), Book XXXV, Chapter 40, p. 145.

predominant above those of the passion, a contrary effect follows; and the former, being now subordinate, is converted into the latter, and still further increases the pain and affliction of the sufferer.

Who could ever think of it as a good expedient for comforting an afflicted parent, to exaggerate, with all the force /238/ of elocution, the irreparable loss which he has met with by the death of a favorite child? The more power of imagination and expression you here employ, the more you increase his despair and affliction.

The shame, confusion, and terror of Verres, no doubt, rose in proportion to the noble eloquence and vehemence of Cicero; so also did his pain and uneasiness. These former passions were too strong for the pleasure arising from the beauties of elocution, and operated, though from the same principle, yet in a contrary manner, to the sympathy, compassion, and indignation of the audience.

Lord Clarendon, when he approaches towards the catastrophe of the royal party, supposes that his narration must then become infinitely disagreeable; and he hurries over the king's death without giving us one circumstance of it.[5] He considers it as too horrid a scene to be contemplated with any satisfaction, or even without the utmost pain and aversion. He himself, as well as the readers of that age, were too deeply concerned in the events, and felt a pain from subjects which an historian and a reader of another age would regard as the most pathetic and most interesting, and, by consequence, the most agreeable.

An action represented in tragedy may be too bloody and atrocious. It may excite such movements of horror as will not soften into pleasure; and the greatest energy of expression, bestowed on descriptions of that nature, serves only to augment our uneasiness. Such is that action represented in the *Ambitious Stepmother*,[6] where a

venerable old man, raised to the height of fury and despair, rushes against a pillar and, striking his head upon it, besmears it all over with mingled brains and gore. The English theatre abounds too much with such shocking images.

Even the common sentiments of compassion require to be softened by some agreeable affection, in order to give /239/ a thorough satisfaction to the audience. The mere suffering of plaintive virtue, under the triumphant tyranny and oppression of vice, forms a disagreeable spectacle, and is carefully avoided by all masters of the drama. In order to dismiss the audience with entire satisfaction and contentment, the virtue must either convert itself into a noble courageous despair, or the vice receive its proper punishment.

Most painters appear in this light to have been very unhappy in their subjects. As they wrought much for churches and convents, they have chiefly represented such horrible subjects as crucifixions and martyrdoms, where nothing appears but tortures, wounds, executions, and passive suffering, without any action or affection. When they turned their pencil from this ghastly mythology, they had commonly recourse to Ovid, whose fictions, though passionate and agreeable, are scarcely natural or probable enough for painting.

The same inversion of that principle, which is here insisted on, displays itself in common life, as in the effects of oratory and poetry. Raise so the subordinate passion that it becomes the predominant, it swallows up that affection which it before nourished and increased. Too much jealousy extinguishes love; too much difficulty renders us indifferent; too much sickness and infirmity disgusts a selfish and unkind parent.

What so disagreeable as the dismal, gloomy, disastrous stories, with which melancholy people entertain their companions? The uneasy passion being there raised alone, unaccompanied with any spirit, genius, or eloquence, conveys a pure uneasiness, and is attended with nothing that can soften it into pleasure or satisfaction. /240/

---

5. Edward Hyde, Earl of Clarendon, *The True Historical Narrative of the Rebellion and Civil Wars in England* (commonly known as *The History of the Rebellion*), published posthumously 1702–1704. The king is Charles I, who was executed by the Parliamentary forces in 1649.

6. a tragedy by Nicholas Rowe (1700).

The Substance of Shakespearean Tragedy

by Andrew Cecil Bradley

Bradley developed this essay from his lectures at several British universities and published it in its present form in 1904 as the first chapter (or "lecture") of Shakespearean Tragedy. *The complete chapter is reprinted here, as it appears in A. C. Bradley,* Shakespearean Tragedy *(N.Y.: Meridian Books, 1955). Some of Bradley's footnotes have been omitted, and those which appear here are followed by his name and their original number. All notes not followed by Bradley's name are the present editor's.*

The question we are to consider in this lecture may be stated in a variety of ways. We may put it thus: What is the substance of a Shakespearean tragedy, taken in abstraction both from its form and from the differences in point of substance between one tragedy and another? Or thus: What is the nature of the tragic aspect of life as represented by Shakespeare? What is the general fact shown now in this tragedy and now in that? And we are putting the same question when we ask: What is Shakespeare's tragic conception, or conception of tragedy?

These expressions, it should be observed, do not imply that Shakespeare himself ever asked or answered such a question; that he set himself to reflect on the tragic aspects of life, that he framed a tragic conception, and still less that, like Aristotle or Corneille,[1] he had a theory of the kind of poetry called tragedy. These things are all possible; how far any one of them is probable we need not discuss; but none of them is presupposed by the question we are going to consider. This question implies only that, as a matter of fact, Shakespeare in writing tragedy did represent a certain aspect of life in a certain way, and that through examination of his writings we ought to be able, to some extent, to describe this aspect and way in terms addressed to the understanding. Such a description, so far as it is true and adequate, may, after these explana-

tions, be called indifferently an account of the substance of Shakespearean /15/ tragedy, or an account of Shakespeare's conception of tragedy or view of the tragic fact.

Two further warnings may be required. In the first place, we must remember that the tragic aspect of life is only one aspect. We cannot arrive at Shakespeare's whole dramatic way of looking at the world from his tragedies alone, as we can arrive at Milton's way of regarding things, or at Wordsworth's or at Shelley's, by examining almost any one of their important works. Speaking very broadly, one may say that these poets at their best always look at things in one light; but *Hamlet* and *Henry IV.* and *Cymbeline* reflect things from quite distinct positions, and Shakespeare's whole dramatic view is not to be identified with any one of these reflections. And, in the second place, I may repeat that in these lectures, at any rate for the most part, we are to be content with his *dramatic* view, and are not to ask whether it corresponded exactly with his opinions or creed outside his poetry — the opinions or creed of the being whom we sometimes oddly call "Shakespeare the man." It does not seem likely that outside his poetry he was a very simple-minded Catholic or Protestant or Atheist, as some have maintained; but we cannot be sure, as with those other poets we can, that in his works he expressed his deepest and most cherished convictions on ultimate questions, or even that he had any. And in his dramatic conceptions there is enough to occupy us.

I

In approaching our subject it will be best, without attempting to shorten the path by referring to famous theories of the drama, to start directly from the facts, and to collect from them gradually an idea of Shakespearean Tragedy. And first, to begin from the outside, such a tragedy brings before us a considerable number of persons (many more than the persons in a Greek play, unless the members of the Chorus

---

1. Pierre Corneille, a French playwright of the seventeenth century who also wrote some essays on the theory of tragedy.

are reckoned among them); but it is pre-eminently the story of one person, the "hero,"[2] or at most of two, the "hero" and "heroine." Moreover, it is only in the love-tragedies, *Romeo and Juliet* and *Antony and Cleopatra,* that the heroine is as much the centre of the action as the hero. The rest, including *Macbeth,* are /16/ single stars. So that, having noticed the peculiarity of these two dramas, we may henceforth, for the sake of brevity, ignore it, and may speak of the tragic story as being concerned primarily with one person.

The story, next, leads up to, and includes, the *death* of the hero. On the one hand (whatever may be true of tragedy elsewhere), no play at the end of which the hero remains alive is, in the full Shakespearean sense, a tragedy; and we no longer class *Troilus and Cressida* or *Cymbeline* as such, as did the editors of the Folio.[3] On the other hand, the story depicts also the troubled part of the hero's life which precedes and leads up to his death; and an instantaneous death occurring by "accident" in the midst of prosperity would not suffice for it. It is, in fact, essentially a tale of suffering and calamity conducting to death.

The suffering and calamity are, moreover, exceptional. They befall a conspicuous person. They are themselves of some striking kind. They are also, as a rule, unexpected, and contrasted with previous happiness or glory. A tale, for example, of a man slowly worn to death by disease, poverty, little cares, sordid vices, petty persecutions, however piteous or dreadful it might be, would not be tragic in the Shakespearean sense.

Such exceptional suffering and calamity, then, affecting the hero, and — we must now add — generally extending far and wide beyond him, so as to make the whole scene a scene of woe, are an essential ingredient in tragedy, and a chief source of the tragic emotions, and especially of pity. But the proportions of this ingredient, and the direction taken by tragic pity, will naturally vary greatly. Pity, for example, has a

much larger part in *King Lear* than in *Macbeth,* and is directed in the one case chiefly to the hero, in the other chiefly to minor characters.

Let us now pause for a moment on the ideas we have so far reached. They would more than suffice to describe the whole tragic fact as it presented itself to the mediaeval mind. To the mediaeval mind a tragedy meant a narrative rather than a play, and its notion of the matter of this narrative may readily be gathered from Dante or, still better, from Chaucer. Chaucer's *Monk's Tale* is a series of what he calls "tragedies"; and this means in fact a series of tales *de Casibus Illustrium Virorum* — /17/ stories of the Falls of Illustrious Men, such as Lucifer, Adam, Hercules and Nebuchadnezzar. And the Monk ends the tale of Croesus thus:

Anhanged was Cresus, the proudè kyng;
His roial tronè myghte hym nat availle.
Tragédie is noon oother maner thyng,
Ne kan in syngyng criè ne biwaille
But for that Fortune alwey wole assaile
With unwar strook the regnès that been proude;
For whan men trusteth hire, thanne wol she faille,
And covere hire brightè facè with a clowde.[4]

A total reverse of fortune, coming unawares upon a man who "stood in high degree," happy and apparently secure — such was the tragic fact to the mediaeval mind. It appealed strongly to common human sympathy and pity; it startled also another feeling, that of fear. It frightened men and awed them. It made them feel that man is blind and helpless, the plaything of an inscrutable power, called by the name of Fortune or some other name — a power which appears to smile on him for a little, and then on a sudden strikes him down in his pride.

Shakespeare's idea of the tragic fact is larger than this idea and goes beyond it; but it includes it, and it is worth while to observe the identity of the two in a certain point which is often ignored. Tragedy with Shakespeare is concerned always with persons of "high degree"; often with kings or princes; if not, with leaders

---

2. *Julius Caesar* is not an exception to this rule. Caesar, whose murder comes in the Third Act, is in a sense the dominating figure in the story, but Brutus is the "hero." [Bradley's footnote 1]

3. In the Folio of 1623, which was the first collected edition of Shakespeare's works, his plays were grouped into three categories: Comedies, Histories, and Tragedies. *Troilus and Cressida* and *Cymbeline* were included in the group of Tragedies.

4. freely rendered in modern English: Croesus, the proud king (of ancient Lydia) was hanged; his royal power could not help him. Tragedy is no other sort of thing, and this is the only theme the tragic poet can lament or bewail in his song: that Fortune always will assail with an unexpected stroke those rulers who have been proud; for when men trust Fortune, then she will fail them and cover her bright face with a cloud.

in the state like Coriolanus, Brutus, Antony; at the least, as in *Romeo and Juliet,* with members of great houses, whose quarrels are of public moment. There is a decided difference here between *Othello* and our three other tragedies,[5] but it is not a difference of kind. Othello himself is no mere private person; he is the General of the Republic. At the beginning we see him in the Council-Chamber of the Senate. The consciousness of his high position never leaves him. At the end, when he is determined to live no longer, he is as anxious as Hamlet not to be misjudged by the great world, and his last speech begins,

Soft you; a word or two before you go.
I have done the state some service, and they
know it. /18/

And this characteristic of Shakespeare's tragedies, though not the most vital, is neither external nor unimportant. The saying that every death-bed is the scene of the fifth act of a tragedy has its meaning, but it would not be true if the word "tragedy" bore its dramatic sense. The pangs of despised love and the anguish of remorse, we say, are the same in a peasant and a prince; but, not to insist that they cannot be so when the prince is really a prince, the story of the prince, the triumvir,[6] or the general, has a greatness and dignity of its own. His fate affects the welfare of a whole nation or empire; and when he falls suddenly from the height of earthly greatness to the dust, his fall produces a sense of contrast, of the powerlessness of man, and of the omnipotence — perhaps the caprice — of Fortune or Fate, which no tale of private life can possibly rival.

Such feelings are constantly evoked by Shakespeare's tragedies — again in varying degrees. Perhaps they are the very strongest of the emotions awakened by the early tragedy of *Richard II.,* where they receive a concentrated expression in Richard's famous speech about the antic Death, who sits in the hollow crown

That rounds the mortal temples of a king,

grinning at his pomp, watching till his vanity and his fancied security have wholly encased him round, and then coming and boring with a little pin through his castle wall. And these feelings, though their predominance is subdued in the mightiest tragedies, remain powerful there. In the figure of the maddened Lear we see

A sight most pitiful in the meanest wretch,
Past speaking of in a king;

and if we would realise the truth in this matter we cannot do better than compare with the effect of *King Lear* the effect of Tourgénief's parallel and remarkable tale of peasant life, *A King Lear of the Steppes.*

II

A Shakespearean tragedy as so far considered may be called a story of exceptional calamity leading to the death of a man in /19/ high estate. But it is clearly much more than this, and we have now to regard it from another side. No amount of calamity which merely befell a man, descending from the clouds like lightning, or stealing from the darkness like pestilence, could alone provide the substance of its story. Job was the greatest of all the children of the east, and his afflictions were well-nigh more than he could bear; but even if we imagined them wearing him to death, that would not make his story tragic. Nor yet would it become so, in the Shakespearean sense, if the fire, and the great wind from the wilderness, and the torments of his flesh were conceived as sent by a supernatural power, whether just or malignant. The calamities of tragedy do not simply happen, nor are they sent; they proceed mainly from actions, and those the actions of men.

We see a number of human beings placed in certain circumstances; and we see, arising from the cooperation of their characters in these circumstances, certain actions. These actions beget others, and these others beget others again, until this series of interconnected deeds leads by an apparently inevitable sequence to a catastrophe. The effect of such a series on imagination is to make us regard the sufferings which accompany it, and the catastrophe in which it ends, not only or chiefly as something which happens to the persons concerned, but equally as something which is caused by them. This at least may be

---

5. The other three tragedies are *Hamlet, King Lear,* and *Macbeth,* which, with *Othello,* are the central concern of the remainder of the book following Lecture II.

6. a member of one of the triumvirates (coalitions of three men) that ruled Rome at two periods in her history just before the collapse of the Republic: the first triumvirate included Julius Caesar, Pompey, and Crassus; the second, Mark Antony, Octavius Caesar, and Lepidus.

said of the principal persons, and, among them, of the hero, who always contributes in some measure to the disaster in which he perishes.

This second aspect of tragedy evidently differs greatly from the first. Men, from this point of view, appear to us primarily as agents, "themselves the authors of their proper woe"; and our fear and pity, though they will not cease or diminish, will be modified accordingly. We are now to consider this second aspect, remembering that it too is only one aspect, and additional to the first, not a substitute for it.

The "story" or "action" of a Shakespearean tragedy does not consist, of course, solely of human actions or deeds; but the deeds are the predominant factor. And these deeds are, for the most part, actions in the full sense of the word; not things done "'tween asleep and wake," but acts or omissions thoroughly /20/ expressive of the doer — characteristic deeds. The centre of the tragedy, therefore, may be said with equal truth to lie in action issuing from character, or in character issuing in action.

Shakespeare's main interest lay here. To say that it lay in *mere* character, or was a psychological interest, would be a great mistake, for he was dramatic to the tips of his fingers. It is possible to find places where he has given a certain indulgence to his love of poetry, and even to his turn for general reflections; but it would be very difficult, and in his later tragedies perhaps impossible, to detect passages where he has allowed such freedom to the interest in character apart from action. But for the opposite extreme, for the abstraction of mere "plot" (which is a very different thing from the tragic "action"), for the kind of interest which predominates in a novel like *The Woman in White*,[7] it is clear that he cared even less. I do not mean that this interest is absent from his dramas; but it is subordinate to others, and is so interwoven with them that we are rarely conscious of it apart, and rarely feel in any great strength the half-intellectual, half-nervous excitement of following an ingenious complication. What we do feel strongly, as a tragedy advances to its close, is that the calamities and catastrophe follow inevitably from the deeds of men, and that the main source of these deeds is character. The dictum that, with Shakespeare, "character is des-

7. a novel by Wilkie Collins, published in 1860, a forerunner of the modern suspense tale or mystery thriller.

tiny" is no doubt an exaggeration, and one that may mislead (for many of his tragic personages, if they had not met with peculiar circumstances, would have escaped a tragic end, and might even have lived fairly untroubled lives); but it is the exaggeration of a vital truth.

This truth, with some of its qualifications, will appear more clearly, if we now go on to ask what elements are to be found in the "story" or "action," occasionally or frequently, beside the characteristic deeds, and the sufferings and circumstances, of the persons. I will refer to three of these additional factors.

(*a*) Shakespeare, occasionally and for reasons which need not be discussed here, represents abnormal conditions of mind; insanity, for example, somnambulism, hallucinations. And deeds issuing from these are certainly not what we called deeds in the fullest sense, deeds expressive of character. No; but these abnormal conditions are never introduced as the origin of deeds /21/ of any dramatic moment. Lady Macbeth's sleepwalking has no influence whatever on the events that follow it. Macbeth did not murder Duncan because he saw a dagger in the air: he saw the dagger because he was about to murder Duncan. Lear's insanity is not the cause of a tragic conflict any more than Ophelia's; it is, like Ophelia's, the result of a conflict; and in both cases the effect is mainly pathetic. If Lear were really mad when he divided his kingdom, if Hamlet were really mad at any time in the story, they would cease to be tragic characters.

(*b*) Shakespeare also introduces the supernatural into some of his tragedies; he introduces ghosts, and witches who have supernatural knowledge. This supernatural element certainly cannot in most cases, if in any, be explained away as an illusion in the mind of one of the characters. And further, it does contribute to the action, and is in more than one instance an indispensable part of it: so that to describe human character, with circumstances, as always the *sole* motive force in this action would be a serious error. But the supernatural is always placed in the closest relation with character. It gives a confirmation and a distinct form to inward movements already present and exerting an influence; to the sense of failure in Brutus, to the stifled workings of conscience in Richard, to the half-formed thought or the horrified memory of guilt in Macbeth, to suspicion in Hamlet.

Moreover, its influence is never of a compulsive kind. It forms no more than an element, however important, in the problem which the hero has to face; and we are never allowed to feel that it has removed his capacity or responsibility for dealing with this problem. So far indeed are we from feeling this, that many readers run to the opposite extreme, and openly or privately regard the supernatural as having nothing to do with the real interest of the play.

(c) Shakespeare, lastly, in most of his tragedies allows to " chance " or " accident " an appreciable influence at some point in the action. Chance or accident here will be found, I think, to mean any occurrence (not supernatural, of course) which enters the dramatic sequence neither from the agency of a character, nor from the obvious surrounding circumstances.[8] It may be called an accident, in this sense, that Romeo never got the Friar's message about the potion, and that Juliet did not awake /22/ from her long sleep a minute sooner; an accident that Edgar arrived at the prison just too late to save Cordelia's life; an accident that Desdemona dropped her handkerchief at the most fatal of moments; an accident that the pirate ship attacked Hamlet's ship, so that he was able to return forthwith to Denmark. Now this operation of accident is a fact, and a prominent fact, of human life. To exclude it *wholly* from tragedy, therefore, would be, we may say, to fail in truth. And, besides, it is not merely a fact. That men may start a course of events but can neither calculate nor control it, is a *tragic* fact. The dramatist may use accident so as to make us feel this; and there are also other dramatic uses to which it may be put. Shakespeare accordingly admits it. On the other hand, any *large* admission of chance into the tragic sequence would certainly weaken, and might destroy, the sense of the causal connection of character, deed, and catastrophe. And Shakespeare really uses it very sparingly. We seldom find ourselves exclaiming, " What an unlucky accident! " I believe most readers would have to search painfully for instances. It is, further, frequently easy to see the dramatic intention of an accident; and some things which look like accidents have really a connection with character,

and are therefore not in the full sense accidents. Finally, I believe it will be found that almost all the prominent accidents occur when the action is well advanced and the impression of the causal sequence is too firmly fixed to be impaired.

Thus it appears that these three elements in the " action " are subordinate, while the dominant factor consists in deeds which issue from character. So that, by way of summary, we may now alter our first statement, " A tragedy is a story of exceptional calamity leading to the death of a man in high estate," and we may say instead (what in its turn is one-sided, though less so), that the story is one of human actions producing exceptional calamity and ending in the death of such a man.[9]

Before we leave the " action," however, there is another question that may usefully be asked. Can we define this " action " further by describing it as a conflict?

The frequent use of this idea in discussions on tragedy is ultimately due, I suppose, to the influence of Hegel's theory on /23/ the subject, certainly the most important theory since Aristotle's. But Hegel's view of the tragic conflict is not only unfamiliar to English readers and difficult to expound shortly, but it had its origin in reflections on Greek tragedy and, as Hegel was well aware, applies only imperfectly to the works of Shakespeare.[10] I shall, therefore, confine myself to the idea of conflict in its more general form. In this form it is obviously suitable to Shakespearean tragedy; but it is vague, and I will try to make it more precise by putting the question, Who are the combatants in this conflict?

Not seldom the conflict may quite naturally be conceived as lying between two persons, of

8. Even a deed would, I think, be counted an "accident," if it were the deed of a very minor person whose character had not been indicated; because such a deed would not issue from the little world to which the dramatist had confined our attention. [Bradley's footnote 3]

9. It may be observed that the influence of the three elements just considered is to strengthen the tendency, produced by the sufferings considered first, to regard the tragic persons as passive rather than as agents. [Bradley's footnote 5]

10. Hegel's theory is developed in the final section of his *Aesthetik*. His view, briefly stated, is that Greek tragedy presents a conflict between two ethical principles (in Sophocles' *Antigone*, which he takes as his model, the conflict is between the dictates of family obligation espoused by Antigone and of political obligation espoused by Creon), each of which is valid in itself but becomes destructive when asserted to the exclusion of the opposing principle. In his lecture, "Hegel's Theory of Tragedy" (published in his *Oxford Lectures on Poetry*, 1909), Bradley suggests some modifications in Hegel's position which would bring it very close to the theory he is developing here.

whom the hero is one; or, more fully, as lying between two parties or groups, in one of which the hero is the leading figure. Or if we prefer to speak (as we may quite well do if we know what we are about) of the passions, tendencies, ideas, principles, forces, which animate these persons or groups, we may say that two of such passions or ideas, regarded as animating two persons or groups, are the combatants. The love of Romeo and Juliet is in conflict with the hatred of their houses, represented by various other characters. The cause of Brutus and Cassius struggles with that of Julius, Octavius and Antony. In *Richard II.* the King stands on one side, Bolingbroke and his party on the other. In *Macbeth* the hero and heroine are opposed to the representatives of Duncan. In all these cases the great majority of the *dramatis personae* fall without difficulty into antagonistic groups, and the conflict between these groups ends with the defeat of the hero.

Yet one cannot help feeling that in at least one of these cases, *Macbeth,* there is something a little external in this way of looking at the action. And when we come to some other plays this feeling increases. No doubt most of the characters in *Hamlet, King Lear, Othello,* or *Antony and Cleopatra* can be arranged in opposed groups;[11] and no doubt there is a conflict; and yet it seems misleading to describe this conflict as one *between these groups.* It cannot be simply this. For though Hamlet and the King are mortal foes, yet that which engrosses our interest and dwells in our memory at least as much as the conflict between them, is the conflict *within* one of them. And so it is, though not in the same degree, with *Antony and Cleopatra* /24/ and even with *Othello;* and, in fact, in a certain measure, it is so with nearly all the tragedies. There is an outward conflict of persons and groups, there is also a conflict of forces in the hero's soul; and even in *Julius Caesar* and

Macbeth the interest of the former can hardly be said to exceed that of the latter.

The truth is, that the type of tragedy in which the hero opposes to a hostile force an undivided soul, is not the Shakespearean type. The souls of those who contend with the hero may be thus undivided; they generally are; but, as a rule, the hero, though he pursues his fated way, is, at least at some point in the action, and sometimes at many, torn by an inward struggle; and it is frequently at such points that Shakespeare shows his most extraordinary power. If further we compare the earlier tragedies with the later, we find that it is in the latter, the maturest works, that this inward struggle is most emphasised. In the last of them, *Coriolanus,* its interest completely eclipses towards the close of the play that of the outward conflict. *Romeo and Juliet, Richard III., Richard II.,* where the hero contends with an outward force, but comparatively little with himself, are all early plays.

If we are to include the outer and the inner struggle in a conception more definite than that of conflict in general, we must employ some such phrase as " spiritual force." This will mean whatever forces act in the human spirit, whether good or evil, whether personal passion or impersonal principle; doubts, desires, scruples, ideas — whatever can animate, shake, possess, and drive a man's soul. In a Shakespearean tragedy some such forces are shown in conflict. They are shown acting in men and generating strife between them. They are also shown, less universally, but quite as characteristically, generating disturbance and even conflict in the soul of the hero. Treasonous ambition in Macbeth collides with loyalty and patriotism in Macduff and Malcolm: here is the outward conflict. But these powers or principles equally collide in the soul of Macbeth himself: here is the inner. And neither by itself could make the tragedy.[12]

We shall see later the importance of this idea. Here we need only observe that the notion of tragedy as a conflict emphasises the fact that

---

11. The reader, however, will find considerable difficulty in placing some very important characters in these and other plays. I will give only two or three illustrations. Edgar is clearly not on the same side as Edmund, and yet it seems awkward to range him on Gloster's side when Gloster wishes to put him to death. Ophelia is in love with Hamlet, but how can she be said to be of Hamlet's party against the King and Polonius, or of their party against Hamlet? Desdemona worships Othello, yet it sounds odd to say that Othello is on the same side with a person whom he insults, strikes and murders. [Bradley's footnote 7]

12. I have given names to the "spiritual forces" in *Macbeth* merely to illustrate the idea, and without any pretension to adequacy. Perhaps, in view of some interpretation of Shakespeare's plays, it will be as well to add that I do not dream of suggesting that in any of his dramas Shakespeare imagined two abstract principles or passions conflicting, and incorporated them in persons; or that there is any necessity for a reader to define for himself the particular forces which conflict in a given case. [Bradley's footnote 8]

action is the centre of the story, while the concentration of interest, in the greater plays, on the inward struggle /25/ emphasises the fact that this action is essentially the expression of character.

III

Let us now turn from the "action" to the central figure in it; and, ignoring the characteristics which distinguish the heroes from one another, let us ask whether they have any common qualities which appear to be essential to the tragic effect.

One they certainly have. They are exceptional beings. We have seen already that the hero, with Shakespeare, is a person of high degree or of public importance, and that his actions or sufferings are of an unusual kind. But this is not all. His nature also is exceptional, and generally raises him in some respect much above the average level of humanity. This does not mean that he is an eccentric or a paragon. Shakespeare never drew monstrosities of virtue; some of his heroes are far from being "good"; and if he drew eccentrics he gave them a subordinate position in the plot. His tragic characters are made of the stuff we find within ourselves and within the persons who surround them. But, by an intensification of the life which they share with others, they are raised above them; and the greatest are raised so far that, if we fully realise all that is implied in their words and actions, we become conscious that in real life we have known scarcely any one resembling them. Some, like Hamlet and Cleopatra, have genius. Others, like Othello, Lear, Macbeth, Coriolanus, are built on the grand scale; and desire, passion, or will attains in them a terrible force. In almost all we observe a marked one-sidedness, a predisposition in some particular direction; a total incapacity, in certain circumstances, of resisting the force which draws in this direction; a fatal tendency to identify the whole being with one interest, object, passion, or habit of mind. This, it would seem, is, for Shakespeare, the fundamental tragic trait. It is present in his early heroes, Romeo and Richard II., infatuated men, who otherwise rise comparatively little above the ordinary level. It is a fatal gift, but it carries with it a touch of greatness; and when there is joined to it nobility of mind, or genius, or immense force, we realise the full power and reach of the soul, and the conflict in which it engages acquires that magnitude which /26/ stirs not only sympathy and pity, but admiration, terror, and awe.

The easiest way to bring home to oneself the nature of the tragic character is to compare it with a character of another kind. Dramas like *Cymbeline* and the *Winter's Tale,* which might seem destined to end tragically, but actually end otherwise, owe their happy ending largely to the fact that the principal characters fail to reach tragic dimensions. And, conversely, if these persons were put in the place of the tragic heroes, the dramas in which they appeared would cease to be tragedies. Posthumus would never have acted as Othello did; Othello, on his side, would have met Iachimo's challenge with something more than words. If, like Posthumus, he had remained convinced of his wife's infidelity, he would not have repented her execution; if, like Leontes, he had come to believe that by an unjust accusation he had caused her death, he would never have lived on, like Leontes. In the same way the villain Iachimo has no touch of tragic greatness. But Iago comes nearer to it, and if Iago had slandered Imogen and had supposed his slanders to have led to her death, he certainly would not have turned melancholy and wished to die. One reason why the end of the *Merchant of Venice* fails to satisfy us is that Shylock is a tragic character, and that we cannot believe in his accepting his defeat and the conditions imposed on him. This was a case where Shakespeare's imagination ran away with him, so that he drew a figure with which the destined pleasant ending would not harmonise.

In the circumstances where we see the hero placed, his tragic trait, which is also his greatness, is fatal to him. To meet these circumstances something is required which a smaller man might have given, but which the hero cannot give. He errs, by action or omission; and his error, joining with other causes, brings on him ruin. This is always so with Shakespeare. As we have seen, the idea of the tragic hero as a being destroyed simply and solely by external forces is quite alien to him; and not less so is the idea of the hero as contributing to his destruction only by acts in which we see no flaw. But the fatal imperfection or error, which is never absent, is of different kinds and degrees. At one extreme stands the excess and precipitancy of Romeo, /27/ which scarcely, if at all, diminish our regard for him; at the other the murderous ambition of Richard III. In most cases the tragic error involves no conscious breach of right; in some (*e.g.*, that of Brutus or Othello) it is accompanied by a full conviction of right. In Hamlet there is a painful consciousness that duty is being neglected; in Antony a clear knowledge that the worse of two courses is being pursued; but Richard and Macbeth are the only heroes who do what they themselves recognise to be villainous. It is important to observe that Shakespeare does admit such heroes,[13] and also that he appears to feel, and exerts himself to meet, the difficulty that arises from their admission. The difficulty is that the spectator must desire their defeat and even their destruction; and yet this desire, and the satisfaction of it, are not tragic feelings. Shakespeare gives to Richard therefore a power which excites astonishment, and a courage which extorts admiration. He gives to Macbeth a similar, though less extraordinary, greatness, and adds to it a conscience so terrifying in its warnings and so maddening in its reproaches that the spectacle of inward torment compels a horrified sympathy and awe which balance, at the least, the desire for the hero's ruin.

The tragic hero with Shakespeare, then, need not be " good," though generally he is " good " and therefore at once wins sympathy in his error. But it is necessary that he should have so much of greatness that in his error and fall we may be vividly conscious of the possibilities of human nature. Hence, in the first place, a Shakespearean tragedy is never, like some miscalled tragedies, depressing. No one ever closes the book with the feeling that man is a poor mean creature. He may be wretched and he may be awful, but he is not small. His lot may be heart-rending and mysterious, but it is not contemptible. The most confirmed of cynics ceases to be a cynic while he reads these plays. And with this greatness of the tragic hero (which is not always confined to him) is connected, secondly, what I venture to describe as the centre of the tragic impression. This central feeling is the impression of waste. With Shakespeare, at any rate, the pity and fear which are stirred by the tragic story

13. Aristotle apparently would exclude them. [Bradley's footnote 9]

seem to unite with, and even to merge in, a profound sense of sadness and mystery, which is due to this impression of waste. " What a piece of work is man," we cry; " so much more beautiful and so /28/ much more terrible than we knew! Why should he be so if this beauty and greatness only tortures itself and throws itself away? " We seem to have before us a type of the mystery of the whole world, the tragic fact which extends far beyond the limits of tragedy. Everywhere, from the crushed rocks beneath our feet to the soul of man, we see power, intelligence, life and glory, which astound us and seem to call for our worship. And everywhere we see them perishing, devouring one another and destroying themselves, often with dreadful pain, as though they came into being for no other end. Tragedy is the typical form of this mystery, because that greatness of soul which it exhibits oppressed, conflicting and destroyed, is the highest existence in our view. It forces the mystery upon us, and it makes us realise so vividly the worth of that which is wasted that we cannot possibly seek comfort in the reflection that all is vanity.

IV

In this tragic world, then, where individuals, however great they may be and however decisive their actions may appear, are so evidently not the ultimate power, what is this power? What account can we give of it which will correspond with the imaginative impressions we receive? This will be our final question.

The variety of the answers given to this question shows how difficult it is. And the difficulty has many sources. Most people, even among those who know Shakespeare well and come into real contact with his mind, are inclined to isolate and exaggerate some one aspect of the tragic fact. Some are so much influenced by their own habitual beliefs that they import them more or less into their interpretation of every author who is " sympathetic " to them. And even where neither of these causes of error appears to operate, another is present from which it is probably impossible wholly to escape. What I mean is this. Any answer we give to the question proposed ought to correspond with, or to represent in terms of the understanding, our imaginative and emotional experience in reading the tragedies. We have, of course, to do our best by study and effort to make this experience true to Shakespeare; but, that done to the best of our ability, the experience is the matter to be interpreted, and the test by which the interpretation must be tried. But it is /29/ extremely hard to make out exactly what this experience is, because, in the very effort to make it out, our reflecting mind, full of everyday ideas, is always tending to transform it by the application of these ideas, and so to elicit a result which, instead of representing the fact, conventionalises it. And the consequence is not only mistaken theories; it is that many a man will declare that he feels in reading a tragedy what he never really felt, while he fails to recognise what he actually did feel. It is not likely that we shall escape all these dangers in our effort to find an answer to the question regarding the tragic world and the ultimate power in it.

It will be agreed, however, first, that this question must not be answered in " religious " language. For although this or that *dramatis persona* may speak of gods or of God, of evil spirits or of Satan, of heaven and of hell, and although the poet may show us ghosts from another world, these ideas do not materially influence his representation of life, nor are they used to throw light on the mystery of its tragedy. The Elizabethan drama was almost wholly secular; and while Shakespeare was writing he practically confined his view to the world of nontheological observation and thought, so that he represents it substantially in one and the same way whether the period of the story is pre-Christian or Christian. He looked at this " secular " world most intently and seriously; and he painted it, we cannot but conclude, with entire fidelity, without the wish to enforce an opinion of his own, and, in essentials, without regard to anyone's hopes, fears, or beliefs. His greatness is largely due to this fidelity in a mind of extraordinary power; and if, as a private person, he had a religious faith, his tragic view can hardly have been in contradiction with this faith, but must have been included in it, and supplemented, not abolished, by additional ideas.

Two statements, next, may at once be made regarding the tragic fact as he represents it: one, that it is and remains to us something piteous, fearful and mysterious; the other, that the representation of it does not leave us crushed, rebellious or desperate. These statements will be accepted, I believe, by any reader who is in touch with Shakespeare's mind and can observe /30/ his own. Indeed such a reader is rather likely to complain that they are painfully obvious. But if they are true as well as obvious, something follows from them in regard to our present question.

From the first it follows that the ultimate power in the tragic world is not adequately described as a law or order which we can see to be just and benevolent — as, in that sense, a " moral order ": for in that case the spectacle of suffering and waste could not seem to us so fearful and mysterious as it does. And from the second it follows that this ultimate power is not adequately described as a fate, whether malicious and cruel, or blind and indifferent to human happiness and goodness: for in that case the spectacle would leave us desperate or rebellious. Yet one or other of these two ideas will be found to govern most accounts of Shakespeare's tragic view or world. These accounts isolate and exaggerate single aspects, either the aspect of action or that of suffering; either the close and unbroken connection of character, will, deed and catastrophe, which, taken alone, shows the individual simply as sinning against, or failing to conform to, the moral order and drawing his just doom on his own head; or else that pressure of outward forces, that sway of accident, and those blind and agonised struggles, which, taken alone, show him as the mere victim of some power which cares neither for his sins nor for his pain. Such views contradict one another, and no third view can unite them; but the several aspects from whose isolation and exaggeration they spring are both present in the fact, and a view which would be true to the fact and to the whole of our imaginative experience must in some way combine these aspects.

Let us begin, then, with the idea of fatality and glance at some of the impressions which give rise to it, without asking at present whether this idea is their natural or fitting expression. There can be no doubt that they do arise and that they ought to arise. If we do not feel at times that the hero is, in some sense, a doomed man; that he and others drift struggling to destruction like helpless creatures borne on an irresistible flood towards a cataract; that, faulty as they may be, their fault is far from being the sole or sufficient cause of all they suffer; and /31/ that the power from which they cannot escape is relentless and immovable, we have failed to receive an essential part of the full tragic effect.

The sources of these impressions are various, and I will refer only to a few. One of them is put into words by Shakespeare himself when he makes the player-king in *Hamlet* say:

Our thoughts are ours, their ends none of our own;

"their ends" are the issues or outcomes of our thoughts, and these, says the speaker, are not our own. The tragic world is a world of action, and action is the translation of thought into reality. We see men and women confidently attempting it. They strike into the existing order of things in pursuance of their ideas. But what they achieve is not what they intended; it is terribly unlike it. They understand nothing, we say to ourselves, of the world on which they operate. They fight blindly in the dark, and the power that works through them makes them the instrument of a design which is not theirs. They act freely, and yet their action binds them hand and foot. And it makes no difference whether they meant well or ill. No one could mean better than Brutus, but he contrives misery for his country and death for himself. No one could mean worse than Iago, and he too is caught in the web he spins for others. Hamlet, recoiling from the rough duty of revenge, is pushed into blood-guiltiness he never dreamed of, and forced at last on the revenge he could not will. His adversary's murders, and no less his adversary's remorse, bring about the opposite of what they sought. Lear follows an old man's whim, half generous, half selfish; and in a moment it looses all the powers of darkness upon him. Othello agonises over an empty fiction, and, meaning to execute solemn justice, butchers innocence and strangles love. They understand themselves no better than the world about them. Coriolanus thinks that his heart is iron, and it melts like snow before a fire. Lady Macbeth, who thought she could dash out her own child's brains, finds herself hounded to death by the smell of a stranger's blood. Her husband thinks that to gain a crown he would jump the life to come, and finds that the crown has brought him all the horrors of that life. Everywhere, in this tragic world, man's thought, translated into act, is transformed /32/ into the opposite of itself. His act, the movement of a few ounces of matter in a moment of time, becomes a monstrous flood which spreads over a kingdom. And whatsoever he dreams of doing, he achieves that which he least dreamed of, his own destruction.

All this makes us feel the blindness and helplessness of man. Yet by itself it would hardly suggest the idea of fate, because it shows man as in some degree, however slight, the cause of his own undoing. But other impressions come to aid it. It is aided by everything which makes us feel that a man is, as we say, terribly unlucky; and of this there is, even in Shakespeare, not a little. Here come in some of the accidents already considered: Juliet's waking from her trance a minute too late, Desdemona's loss of her handkerchief at the only moment when the loss would have mattered, that insignificant delay which cost Cordelia's life. Again, men act, no doubt, in accordance with their characters; but what is it that brings them just the one problem which is fatal to them and would be easy to another, and sometimes brings it to them just when they are least fitted to face it? How is it that Othello comes to be the companion of the one man in the world who is at once able enough, brave enough, and vile enough to ensnare him? By what strange fatality does it happen that Lear has such daughters and Cordelia such sisters? Even character itself contributes to these feelings of fatality. How could men escape, we cry, such vehement propensities as drive Romeo, Antony, Coriolanus, to their doom? And why is it that a man's virtues help to destroy him, and that his weakness or defect is so intertwined with everything that is admirable in him that we can hardly separate them even in imagination?

If we find in Shakespeare's tragedies the source of impressions like these, it is important, on the other hand, to notice what we do *not* find there. We find practically no trace of fatalism in its more primitive, crude and obvious forms. Nothing, again, makes us think of the actions and sufferings of the persons as somewhat arbitrarily fixed beforehand without regard to their feelings, thoughts and resolutions. Nor, I believe, are the facts ever so presented that it seems to us as if the supreme power, whatever it may be, had a special spite against a family /33/ or an individual. Neither, lastly, do we receive the impression (which, it must be observed, is not purely fatalistic) that a family, owing to some hideous crime or impiety in early days, is doomed in later days to continue a career of portentous calamities and sins. Shakespeare, indeed, does not appear to have taken much interest in heredity, or to have attached much importance to it.

What, then, is this "fate" which the impressions already considered lead us to describe as the ultimate power in the tragic world? It appears to be a mythological expression for the whole system or order, of which the individual characters form an inconsiderable and feeble part; which seems to determine, far more than they, their native dispositions and their circumstances, and, through these, their action; which is so vast and complex that they can scarcely at all understand it or control its workings; and which has a nature so definite and fixed that whatever changes take place in it produce other changes inevitably and without regard to men's desires and regrets. And whether this system or order is best called by the name of fate or no,[14] it can hardly be denied that it does appear as the ultimate power in the tragic world, and that it has such characteristics as these. But the name "fate" may be intended to imply something more — to imply that this order is a blank necessity, totally regardless alike of human weal and of the difference between good and evil or right and wrong. And such an implication many readers would at once reject. They would maintain, on the contrary, that this order shows characteristics of quite another kind from those which made us give it the name of fate, characteristics which certainly should not induce us to forget those others, but which would lead us to describe it as a moral order and its necessity as a moral necessity.

---

14. I have raised no objection to the use of the idea of fate, because it occurs so often both in conversation and in books about Shakespeare's tragedies that I must suppose it to be natural to many readers. Yet I doubt whether it would be so if Greek tragedy had never been written; and I must in candour confess that to me it does not often occur while I am reading, or when I have just read, a tragedy of Shakespeare. Wordsworth's lines, for example, about

> poor humanity's afflicted will
> Struggling in vain with ruthless destiny

do not represent the impression I receive; much less do images which compare man to a puny creature helpless in the claws of a bird of prey. The reader should examine himself closely on this matter. [Bradley's footnote 12]

V

Let us turn, then, to this idea. It brings into the light those aspects of the tragic fact which the idea of fate throws into the shade. And the argument which leads to it in its simplest form may be stated briefly thus: " Whatever may be said of accidents, circumstances and the like, human action is, after all, presented to us as the central fact in tragedy, and also as the main cause /34/ of the catastrophe. That necessity which so much impresses us is, after all, chiefly the necessary connection of actions and consequences. For these actions we, without even raising a question on the subject, hold the agents responsible; and the tragedy would disappear for us if we did not. The critical action is, in greater or less degree, wrong or bad. The catastrophe is, in the main, the return of this action on the head of the agent. It is an example of justice; and that order which, present alike within the agents and outside them, infallibly brings it about, is therefore just. The rigour of its justice is terrible, no doubt, for a tragedy is a terrible story; but, in spite of fear and pity, we acquiesce, because our sense of justice is satisfied."

Now, if this view is to hold good, the "justice" of which it speaks must be at once distinguished from what is called "poetic justice." "Poetic justice" means that prosperity and adversity are distributed in proportion to the merits of the agents. Such "poetic justice" is in flagrant contradiction with the facts of life, and it is absent from Shakespeare's tragic picture of life; indeed, this very absence is a ground of constant complaint on the part of Dr. Johnson.[15] Δράσαντι παθεῖν, " the doer must suffer " — this we find in Shakespeare. We also find that villainy never remains victorious and prosperous at the last. But an assignment of amounts of happiness and misery, an assignment even of life and death, in proportion to merit, we do not find. No one who thinks of Desdemona and Cordelia; or who remembers that one end awaits Richard III. and Brutus, Macbeth and Hamlet; or who asks himself which suffered most, Othello or Iago; will ever accuse Shakespeare of representing the ultimate power as " poetically " just.

And we must go further. I venture to say that it is a mistake to use at all these terms of justice

---

15. Samuel Johnson, one of the foremost literary critics of the eighteenth century, who edited Shakespeare's works.

and merit or desert. And this for two reasons. In the first place, essential as it is to recognise the connection between act and consequence, and natural as it may seem in some cases (*e.g.,* Macbeth's) to say that the doer only gets what he deserves, yet in very many cases to say this would be quite unnatural. We might not object to the statement that Lear deserved to suffer for his folly, selfishness and tyranny; but to assert that he deserved to suffer what he did suffer is to do violence not merely to language but to any /35/ healthy moral sense. It is, moreover, to obscure the tragic fact that the consequences of action cannot be limited to that which would appear to us to follow "justly" from them. And, this being so, when we call the order of the tragic world just, we are either using the word in some vague and unexplained sense, or we are going beyond what is shown us of this order, and are appealing to faith.

But, in the second place, the ideas of justice and desert are, it seems to me, in *all* cases — even those of Richard III. and of Macbeth and Lady Macbeth — untrue to our imaginative experience. When we are immersed in a tragedy, we feel towards dispositions, actions, and persons such emotions as attraction and repulsion, pity, wonder, fear, horror, perhaps hatred; but we do not *judge*. This is a point of view which emerges only when, in reading a play, we slip, by our own fault or the dramatist's, from the tragic position, or when, in thinking about the play afterwards, we fall back on our everyday legal and moral notions. But tragedy does not belong, any more than religion belongs, to the sphere of these notions; neither does the imaginative attitude in presence of it. While we are in its world we watch what is, seeing that so it happened and must have happened, feeling that it is piteous, dreadful, awful, mysterious, but neither passing sentence on the agents, nor asking whether the behaviour of the ultimate power towards them is just. And, therefore, the use of such language in attempts to render our imaginative experience in terms of the understanding is, to say the least, full of danger.[16]

Let us attempt then to restate the idea that the ultimate power in the tragic world is a moral order. Let us put aside the ideas of justice and merit, and speak simply of good and evil. Let us understand by these words, primarily, moral good and evil, but also everything else in human beings which we take to be excellent or the reverse. Let us understand the statement that the ultimate power or order is "moral" to mean that it does not show itself indifferent to good and evil, or equally favourable or unfavourable to both, but shows itself akin to good and alien from evil. And, understanding the statement thus, let us ask what grounds it has in the tragic fact as presented by Shakespeare.

Here, as in dealing with the grounds on which the idea of /36/ fate rests, I choose only two or three out of many. And the most important is this. In Shakespearean tragedy the main source of the convulsion which produces suffering and death is never good: good contributes to this convulsion only from its tragic implication with its opposite in one and the same character. The main source, on the contrary, is in every case evil; and, what is more (though this seems to have been little noticed), it is in almost every case evil in the fullest sense, not mere imperfection but plain moral evil. The love of Romeo and Juliet conducts them to death only because of the senseless hatred of their houses. Guilty ambition, seconded by diabolic malice and issuing in murder, open the action in *Macbeth*. Iago is the main source of the convulsion in *Othello;* Goneril, Regan and Edmund in *King Lear*. Even when this plain moral evil is not the obviously prime source within the play, it lies behind it: the situation with which Hamlet has to deal has been formed by adultery and murder. *Julius Caesar* is the only tragedy in which one is even tempted to find an exception to this rule. And the inference is obvious. If it is chiefly evil that violently disturbs the order of the world, this order cannot be friendly to evil or indifferent between evil and good, any more than a body which is convulsed by poison is friendly to it or indifferent to the distinction between poison and food.

16. It is dangerous, I think, in reference to all really good tragedies, but I am dealing here only with Shakespeare's. In not a few Greek tragedies it is almost inevitable that we should think of justice and retribution, not only because the *dramatis personae* often speak of them, but also because there is something casuistical about the tragic problem itself. The poet treats the story in such a way that the question, Is the hero doing right or wrong? is almost forced upon us. But this is not so with Shakespeare. *Julius Caesar* is probably the only one of his tragedies in which the question suggests itself to us, and this is one of the reasons why that play has something of a classic air. Even here, if we ask the question, we have no doubt at all about the answer. [Bradley's footnote 13]

Again, if we confine our attention to the hero, and to those cases where the gross and palpable evil is not in him but elsewhere, we find that the comparatively innocent hero still shows some marked imperfection or defect — irresolution, precipitancy, pride, credulousness, excessive simplicity, excessive susceptibility to sexual emotions, and the like. These defects or imperfections are certainly, in the wide sense of the word, evil, and they contribute decisively to the conflict and catastrophe. And the inference is again obvious. The ultimate power which shows itself disturbed by this evil and reacts against it, must have a nature alien to it. Indeed its reaction is so vehement and " relentless " that it would seem to be bent on nothing short of good in perfection, and to be ruthless in its demand for it.

To this must be added another fact, or another aspect of the same fact. Evil exhibits itself everywhere as something negative, barren, weakening, destructive, a principle of death. It /37/ isolates, disunites, and tends to annihilate not only its opposite but itself. That which keeps the evil man [17] prosperous, makes him succeed, even permits him to exist, is the good in him (I do not mean only the obviously " moral " good). When the evil in him masters the good and has its way, it destroys other people through him, but it also destroys *him*. At the close of the struggle he has vanished, and has left behind him nothing that can stand. What remains is a family, a city, a country, exhausted, pale and feeble, but alive through the principle of good which animates it; and, within it, individuals who, if they have not the brilliance or greatness of the tragic character, still have won our respect and confidence. And the inference would seem clear. If existence in an order depends on good, and if the presence of evil is hostile to such existence, the inner being or soul of this order must be akin to good.

These are aspects of the tragic world at least as clearly marked as those which, taken alone, suggest the idea of fate. And the idea which they in their turn, when taken alone, may suggest, is that of an order which does not indeed award " poetic justice," but which reacts through

the necessity of its own " moral " nature both against attacks made upon it and against failure to conform to it. Tragedy, on this view, is the exhibition of that convulsive reaction; and the fact that the spectacle does not leave us rebellious or desperate is due to a more or less distinct perception that the tragic suffering and death arise from collision, not with a fate or blank power, but with a moral power, a power akin to all that we admire and revere in the characters themselves. This perception produces something like a feeling of acquiescence in the catastrophe, though it neither leads us to pass judgment on the characters nor diminishes the pity, the fear, and the sense of waste, which their struggle, suffering and fall evoke. And, finally, this view seems quite able to do justice to those aspects of the tragic fact which give rise to the idea of fate. They would appear as various expressions of the fact that the moral order acts not capriciously or like a human being, but from the necessity of its nature, or, if we prefer the phrase, by general laws — a necessity or law which of course knows no exception and is as " ruthless " as fate. /38/

It is impossible to deny to this view a large measure of truth. And yet without some amendment it can hardly satisfy. For it does not include the whole of the facts, and therefore does not wholly correspond with the impressions they produce. Let it be granted that the system or order which shows itself omnipotent against individuals is, in the sense explained, moral. Still — at any rate for the eye of sight — the evil against which it asserts itself, and the persons whom this evil inhabits, are not really something outside the order, so that they can attack it or fail to conform to it; they are within it and a part of it. It itself produces them — produces Iago as well as Desdemona, Iago's cruelty as well as Iago's courage. It is not poisoned, it poisons itself. Doubtless it shows by its violent reaction that the poison *is* poison, and that its health lies in good. But one significant fact cannot remove another, and the spectacle we witness scarcely warrants the assertion that the order is responsible for the good in Desdemona, but Iago for the evil in Iago. If we make this assertion we make it on grounds other than the facts as presented in Shakespeare's tragedies.

Nor does the idea of a moral order asserting itself against attack or want of conformity an-

17. It is most essential to remember that an evil man is much more than the evil in him. I may add that in this paragraph I have, for the sake of clearness, considered evil in its most pronounced form; but what is said would apply, *mutatis mutandis*, to evil as imperfection, etc. [Bradley's footnote 14]

swer in full to our feelings regarding the tragic character. We do not think of Hamlet merely as failing to meet its demand, of Antony as merely sinning against it, or even of Macbeth as simply attacking it. What we feel corresponds quite as much to the idea that they are *its* parts, expressions, products; that in their defect or evil *it* is untrue to its soul of goodness, and falls into conflict and collision with itself; that, in making them suffer and waste themselves, *it* suffers and wastes itself; and that when, to save its life and regain peace from this intestinal struggle, it casts them out, it has lost a part of its own substance — a part more dangerous and unquiet, but far more valuable and nearer to its heart, than that which remains — a Fortinbras, a Malcolm, an Octavius. There is no tragedy in its expulsion of evil: the tragedy is that this involves the waste of good.

Thus we are left at last with an idea showing two sides or aspects which we can neither separate nor reconcile. The whole or order against which the individual part shows itself powerless seems to be animated by a passion for perfection: we /39/ cannot otherwise explain its behaviour towards evil. Yet it appears to engender this evil within itself, and in its effort to overcome and expel it it is agonised with pain, and driven to mutilate its own substance and to lose not only evil but priceless good. That this idea, though very different from the idea of a blank fate, is no solution of the riddle of life is obvious; but why should we expect it to be such a solution? Shakespeare was not attempting to justify the ways of God to men, or to show the universe as a Divine Comedy.[18] He was writing

18. Early in *Paradise Lost* Milton states that his purpose is to "assert Eternal Providence,/And justify the ways of God to men" (ll. 25–26). (See Krutch's essay, p. 85.) Dante is the poet Bradley has in mind who showed the universe as a Divine Comedy.

tragedy, and tragedy would not be tragedy if it were not a painful mystery. Nor can he be said even to point distinctly, like some writers of tragedy, in any direction where a solution might lie. We find a few references to gods or God, to the influence of the stars, to another life: some of them certainly, all of them perhaps, merely dramatic — appropriate to the person from whose lips they fall. A ghost comes from Purgatory to impart a secret out of the reach of its hearer — who presently meditates on the question whether the sleep of death is dreamless. Accidents once or twice remind us strangely of the words, "There's a divinity that shapes our ends." More important are other impressions. Sometimes from the very furnace of affliction a conviction seems borne to us that somehow, if we could see it, this agony counts as nothing against the heroism and love which appear in it and thrill our hearts. Sometimes we are driven to cry out that these mighty or heavenly spirits who perish are too great for the little space in which they move, and that they vanish not into nothingness but into freedom. Sometimes from these sources and from others comes a presentiment, formless but haunting and even profound, that all the fury of conflict, with its waste and woe, is less than half the truth, even an illusion, "such stuff as dreams are made on." But these faint and scattered intimations that the tragic world, being but a fragment of a whole beyond our vision, must needs be a contradiction and no ultimate truth, avail nothing to interpret the mystery. We remain confronted with the inexplicable fact, or the no less inexplicable appearance, of a world travailing for perfection, but bringing to birth, together with glorious good, an evil which it is able to overcome only by self-torture and self-waste. And this fact or appearance is tragedy. /40/

The Tragic Fallacy

by Joseph Wood Krutch

This essay first appeared in a slightly different version in the Atlantic Monthly, *November 1928, and was then published in its present form in 1929 as Chapter 5 of Krutch's* The Modern Temper: A Study and a Confession. *The complete chapter is reprinted here from the Harvest Books edition of* The Modern Temper (*N.Y.: Harcourt, Brace, 1956*). *The footnotes which appear here are the present editor's.*

I

Through the legacy of their art the great ages have transmitted to us a dim image of their glorious vitality. When we turn the pages of a Sophoclean or a Shakespearean tragedy we participate faintly in the experience which created it and we sometimes presumptuously say that we "understand" the spirit of these works. But the truth is that we see them, even at best and in the moments when our souls expand most nearly to their dimensions, through a glass darkly.

It is so much easier to appreciate than to create that an age too feeble to reach the heights achieved by the members of a preceding one can still see those heights towering above its impotence, and so it is that, when we perceive a Sophocles or a Shakespeare soaring in an air which we can never hope to breathe, we say that we can "appreciate" them. But what we mean is that we are just able to wonder, and we can never hope to participate in the glorious vision of human life out of which they were created — not even to the extent of those humbler persons for whom they were written; for while to us the triumphant voices come from far away and tell of a heroic world which no longer exists, to them they spoke of immediate realities and revealed the inner meaning of events amidst which they still lived.

When the life has entirely gone out of a work of art come down to us from the past, when we read it /79/ without any emotional comprehension whatsoever and can no longer even imag-ine why the people for whom it was intended found it absorbing and satisfying, then, of course, it has ceased to be a work of art at all and has dwindled into one of those deceptive "documents" from which we get a false sense of comprehending through the intellect things which cannot be comprehended at all except by means of a kinship of feeling. And though all works from a past age have begun in this way to fade there are some, like the great Greek or Elizabethan tragedies, which are still halfway between the work of art and the document. They no longer can have for us the immediacy which they had for those to whom they originally belonged, but they have not yet eluded us entirely. We no longer live in the world which they represent, but we can half imagine it and we can measure the distance which we have moved away. We write no tragedies today, but we can still talk about the tragic spirit of which we would, perhaps, have no conception were it not for the works in question.

An age which could really "appreciate" Shakespeare or Sophocles would have something comparable to put beside them — something like them, not necessarily in form, or spirit, but at least in magnitude — some vision of life which would be, however different, equally ample and passionate. But when we move to put a modern masterpiece beside them, when we seek to compare them with, let us say, a *Ghosts* or a *Weavers*,[1] we shrink as from the impulse to commit some folly and we feel as though we were about to superimpose Bowling Green upon the Great Prairies in order to ascertain which is the larger. The question, we see, is not primarily one of art but of the two worlds which two minds inhabited. No increased powers of expression, no greater gift for words, could have transformed Ibsen into Shakespeare. The materials out of which the latter created his works — his concep-

1. Gerhart Hauptmann's *The Weavers* (*Die Weber*, 1892), a famous landmark in the development of the modern "realistic" stage, dealt with the revolt of the Silesian weavers in 1844.

tion of human dignity, /80/ his sense of the importance of human passions, his vision of the amplitude of human life — simply did not and could not exist for Ibsen, as they did not and could not exist for his contemporaries. God and Man and Nature had all somehow dwindled in the course of the intervening centuries, not because the realistic creed of modern art led us to seek out mean people, but because this meanness of human life was somehow thrust upon us by the operation of that same process which led to the development of realistic theories of art by which our vision could be justified.

Hence, though we still apply, sometimes, the adjective "tragic" to one or another of those modern works of literature which describe human misery and which end more sadly even than they begin, the term is a misnomer since it is obvious that the works in question have nothing in common with the classical examples of the genre and produce in the reader a sense of depression which is the exact opposite of that elation generated when the spirit of a Shakespeare rises joyously superior to the outward calamities which he recounts and celebrates the greatness of the human spirit whose travail he describes. Tragedies, in that only sense of the word which has any distinctive meaning, are no longer written in either the dramatic or any other form, and the fact is not to be accounted for in any merely literary terms. It is not the result of any fashion in literature or of any deliberation to write about human nature or character under different aspects, any more than it is of either any greater sensitiveness of feeling which would make us shrink from the contemplation of the suffering of Medea or Othello or of any greater optimism which would make us more likely to see life in more cheerful terms. It is, on the contrary, the result of one of those enfeeblements of the human spirit not unlike that described in the previous chapter of this essay,[2] and a further illustration of that gradual weakening of man's confidence in his ability to /81/ impose upon the phenomenon of life an interpretation acceptable to his desires which is the subject of the whole of the present discussion.

To explain that fact and to make clear how the creation of classical tragedy did consist in the successful effort to impose such a satisfactory interpretation will require, perhaps, the special section which follows, although the truth of the fact that it does impose such an interpretation must be evident to any one who has ever risen from the reading of *Oedipus* or *Lear* with that feeling of exultation which comes when we have been able, by rare good fortune, to enter into its spirit as completely as it is possible for us of a remoter and emotionally enfeebled age to enter it. Meanwhile one anticipatory remark may be ventured. If the plays and the novels of today deal with littler people and less mighty emotions it is not because we have become interested in commonplace souls and their unglamorous adventures but because we have come, willy-nilly, to see the soul of man as commonplace and its emotions as mean.

II

Tragedy, said Aristotle, is the "imitation of noble actions," and though it is some twenty-five hundred years since the dictum was uttered there is only one respect in which we are inclined to modify it. To us "imitation" seems a rather naïve word to apply to that process by which observation is turned into art, and we seek one which would define or at least imply the nature of that interposition of the personality of the artist between the object and the beholder which constitutes his function and by means of which he transmits a modified version, rather than a mere imitation, of the thing which he has contemplated.

In the search for this word the aestheticians of romanticism invented the term "expression" to describe the artistic purpose to which apparent imitation was /82/ subservient. Psychologists, on the other hand, feeling that the artistic process was primarily one by which reality is modified in such a way as to render it more acceptable to the desires of the artist, employed various terms in the effort to describe that distortion which the wish may produce in vision. And though many of the newer critics reject both romanticism and psychology, even they insist upon the fundamental fact that in art we are concerned, not with mere imitation, but with the imposition of some form upon the material which it would not have if it were merely copied as a camera copies.

Tragedy is not, then, as Aristotle said, the *imitation* of noble actions, for, indeed, no one knows what a *noble* action is or whether or not

2. The previous chapter discussed the decline of love as a value in modern civilization.

such a thing as nobility exists in nature apart from the mind of man. Certainly the action of Achilles in dragging the dead body of Hector around the walls of Troy and under the eyes of Andromache, who had begged to be allowed to give it decent burial, is not to us a noble action, though it was such to Homer, who made it the subject of a noble passage in a noble poem.[3] Certainly, too, the same action might conceivably be made the subject of a tragedy and the subject of a farce, depending upon the way in which it was treated; so that to say that tragedy is the *imitation* of a *noble* action is to be guilty of assuming, first, that art and photography are the same and, second, that there may be something inherently noble in an act as distinguished from the motives which prompted it or from the point of view from which it is regarded.

And yet, nevertheless, the idea of nobility is inseparable from the idea of tragedy, which cannot exist without it. If tragedy is not the imitation or even the modified representation of noble actions it is certainly a representation of actions *considered* as noble, and herein lies its essential nature, since no man can conceive it unless he is capable of believing in the /83/ greatness and importance of man. Its action is usually, if not always, calamitous, because it is only in calamity that the human spirit has the opportunity to reveal itself triumphant over the outward universe which fails to conquer it; but this calamity in tragedy is only a means to an end and the essential thing which distinguishes real tragedy from those distressing modern works sometimes called by its name is the fact that it is in the former alone that the artist has found himself capable of considering and of making us consider that his people and his actions have that amplitude and importance which make them noble. Tragedy arises then when, as in Periclean Greece or Elizabethan England, a people fully aware of the calamities of life is nevertheless serenely confident of the greatness of man, whose mighty passions and supreme fortitude are revealed when one of these calamities overtakes him.

To those who mistakenly think of it as something gloomy or depressing, who are incapable of recognizing the elation which its celebration of human greatness inspires, and who, therefore, confuse it with things merely miserable or pa-

thetic, it must be a paradox that the happiest, most vigorous, and most confident ages which the world has ever known — the Periclean and the Elizabethan — should be exactly those which created and which most relished the mightiest tragedies; but the paradox is, of course, resolved by the fact that tragedy is essentially an expression, not of despair, but of the triumph over despair and of confidence in the value of human life. If Shakespeare himself ever had that " dark period " which his critics and biographers have imagined for him, it was at least no darkness like that bleak and arid despair which sometimes settles over modern spirits. In the midst of it he created both the elemental grandeur of Othello and the pensive majesty of Hamlet and, holding them up to his contemporaries, he said in the words of his own Miranda, " Oh, rare new world that hath *such* creatures in it." [4] /84/

All works of art which deserve their name have a happy end. This is indeed the thing which constitutes them art and through which they perform their function. Whatever the character of the events, fortunate or unfortunate, which they recount, they so mold or arrange or interpret them that we accept gladly the conclusion which they reach and would not have it otherwise. They may conduct us into the realm of pure fancy where wish and fact are identical and the world is remade exactly after the fashion of the heart's desire or they may yield some greater or less allegiance to fact; but they must always reconcile us in one way or another to the representation which they make and the distinctions between the genres are simply the distinctions between the means by which this reconciliation is effected.

Comedy laughs the minor mishaps of its characters away; drama solves all the difficulties which it allows to arise; and melodrama, separating good from evil by simple lines, distributes its rewards and punishments in accordance with the principles of a naïve justice which satisfies the simple souls of its audience, which are neither philosophical enough to question its primitive ethics nor critical enough to object to the way in which its neat events violate the laws of probability. Tragedy, the greatest and the most difficult of the arts, can adopt none of these methods; and yet it must reach its own happy end in its own way. Though its conclusion must

---

3. These events occur toward the end of the *Iliad*.

4. in Shakespeare's *The Tempest*, V. i. 183–84.

be, by its premise, outwardly calamitous, though it must speak to those who know that the good man is cut off and that the fairest things are the first to perish, yet it must leave them, as *Othello* does, content that this is so. We must be and we are glad that Juliet dies and glad that Lear is turned out into the storm.

Milton set out, he said, to justify the ways of God to man,[5] and his phrase, if it be interpreted broadly enough, may be taken as describing the function of all /85/ art, which must, in some way or other, make the life which it seems to represent satisfactory to those who see its reflection in the magic mirror, and it must gratify or at least reconcile the desires of the beholder, not necessarily, as the naïver exponents of Freudian psychology maintain, by gratifying individual and often eccentric wishes, but at least by satisfying the universally human desire to find in the world some justice, some meaning, or, at the very least, some recognizable order. Hence it is that every real tragedy, however tremendous it may be, is an affirmation of faith in life, a declaration that even if God is not in his Heaven, then at least Man is in his world.

We accept gladly the outward defeats which it describes for the sake of the inward victories which it reveals. Juliet died, but not before she had shown how great and resplendent a thing love could be; Othello plunged the dagger into his own breast, but not before he had revealed that greatness of soul which makes his death seem unimportant. Had he died in the instant when he struck the blow, had he perished still believing that the world was as completely black as he saw it before the innocence of Desdemona was revealed to him, then, for him at least, the world would have been merely damnable, but Shakespeare kept him alive long enough to allow him to learn his error and hence to die, not in despair, but in the full acceptance of the tragic reconciliation to life. Perhaps it would be pleasanter if men could believe what the child is taught — that the good are happy and that things turn out as they should — but it is far more important to be able to believe, as Shakespeare did, that however much things in the outward world may go awry, man has, nevertheless, splendors of his own and that, in a word, Love and Honor and Glory are not words but realities.

Thus for the great ages tragedy is not an ex-

5. See the selection by Bradley, footnote 18.

pression of despair but the means by which they saved themselves from it. It is a profession of faith, and a sort of /86/ religion; a way of looking at life by virtue of which it is robbed of its pain. The sturdy soul of the tragic author seizes upon suffering and uses it only as a means by which joy may be wrung out of existence, but it is not to be forgotten that he is enabled to do so only because of his belief in the greatness of human nature and because, though he has lost the child's faith in life, he has not lost his far more important faith in human nature. A tragic writer does not have to believe in God, but he must believe in man.

And if, then, the Tragic Spirit is in reality the product of a religious faith in which, sometimes at least, faith in the greatness of God is replaced by faith in the greatness of man, it serves, of course, to perform the function of religion, to make life tolerable for those who participate in its beneficent illusion. It purges the souls of those who might otherwise despair and it makes endurable the realization that the events of the outward world do not correspond with the desires of the heart, and thus, in its own particular way, it does what all religions do, for it gives a rationality, a meaning, and a justification to the universe. But if it has the strength it has also the weakness of all faiths, since it may — nay, it must — be ultimately lost as reality, encroaching further and further into the realm of imagination, leaving less and less room in which that imagination can build its refuge.

III

It is, indeed, only at a certain stage in the development of the realistic intelligence of a people that the tragic faith can exist. A naïve people may have, as the ancient men of the north had, a body of legends which are essentially tragic, or it may have only (and need only) its happy and childlike mythology which arrives inevitably at its happy end, where the only ones who suffer " deserve " to do so and in which, therefore, life is represented as directly and easily acceptable. A too /87/ sophisticated society on the other hand — one which, like ours, has outgrown not merely the simple optimism of the child but also that vigorous, one might almost say adolescent, faith in the nobility of man which marks a Sophocles or a Shakespeare — has neither fairy tales to assure it that all is always right in the end nor tragedies to make it believe that it rises superior in soul to the outward calamities which befall it.

Distrusting its thought, despising its passions, realizing its impotent unimportance in the universe, it can tell itself no stories except those which make it still more acutely aware of its trivial miseries. When its heroes (sad misnomer for the pitiful creatures who people contemporary fiction) are struck down it is not, like Oedipus, by the gods that they are struck but only, like Oswald Alving, by syphilis, for they know that the gods, even if they existed, would not trouble with them and they cannot attribute to themselves in art an importance in which they do not believe. Their so-called tragedies do not and cannot end with one of those splendid calamities which in Shakespeare seem to reverberate through the universe, because they cannot believe that the universe trembles when their love is, like Romeo's, cut off or when the place where they (small as they are) have gathered up their trivial treasure is, like Othello's sanctuary, defiled. Instead, mean misery piles on mean misery, petty misfortune follows petty misfortune, and despair becomes intolerable because it is no longer even significant or important.

Ibsen once made one of his characters say that he did not read much because he found reading " irrelevant," and the adjective was brilliantly chosen because it held implications even beyond those of which Ibsen was consciously aware. What is it that made the classics irrelevant to him and to us? Is it not just exactly those to him impossible premises which make tragedy what it is, those assumptions that the soul of man is great, that the universe (together with /88/ whatever gods may be) concerns itself with him and that he is, in a word, noble? Ibsen turned to village politics for exactly the same reason that his contemporaries and his successors have, each in his own way, sought out some aspect of the common man and his common life — because, that is to say, here was at least something small enough for him to be able to believe.

Bearing this fact in mind, let us compare a modern " tragedy " with one of the great works of a happy age, not in order to judge of their relative technical merits but in order to determine to what extent the former deserves its name by achieving a tragic solution capable of purging the soul or of reconciling the emotions

to the life which it pictures. And in order to make the comparison as fruitful as possible let us choose *Hamlet* on the one hand and on the other a play like *Ghosts* which was not only written by perhaps the most powerful as well as the most typical of modern writers but which is, in addition, the one of his works which seems most nearly to escape that triviality which cannot be entirely escaped by anyone who feels, as all contemporary minds do, that man is relatively trivial.

In *Hamlet* a prince (" in understanding, how like a god! ") has thrust upon him from the unseen world a duty to redress a wrong which concerns not merely him, his mother, and his uncle, but the moral order of the universe. Erasing all trivial fond records from his mind, abandoning at once both his studies and his romance because it has been his good fortune to be called upon to take part in an action of cosmic importance, he plunges (at first) not into action but into thought, weighing the claims which are made upon him and contemplating the grandiose complexities of the universe. And when the time comes at last for him to die he dies, not as a failure, but as a success. Not only has the universe regained the balance which had been upset by what *seemed* the monstrous crime /89/ of the guilty pair (" there is nothing either good nor ill but thinking makes it so "), but in the process by which that readjustment is made a mighty mind has been given the opportunity, first to contemplate the magnificent scheme of which it is a part and then to demonstrate the greatness of its spirit by playing a rôle in the grand style which it called for. We do not need to despair in *such* a world if it has *such* creatures in it.

Turn now to *Ghosts* — look upon this picture and upon that. A young man has inherited syphilis from his father. Struck by a to him mysterious malady he returns to his northern village, learns the hopeless truth about himself, and persuades his mother to poison him. The incidents prove, perhaps, that pastors should not endeavor to keep a husband and wife together unless they know what they are doing. But what a world is this in which a great writer can deduce nothing more than that from his greatest work and how are we to be purged or reconciled when we see it acted? Not only is the failure utter, but it is trivial and meaningless as well.

Yet the journey from Elsinore to Skien[6] is precisely the journey which the human spirit has made, exchanging in the process princes for invalids and gods for disease. We say, as Ibsen would say, that the problems of Oswald Alving are more "relevant" to our life than the problems of Hamlet, that the play in which he appears is more "real" than the other more glamorous one, but it is exactly because we find it so that we are condemned. We can believe in Oswald but we cannot believe in Hamlet, and a light has gone out in the universe. Shakespeare justifies the ways of God to man, but in Ibsen there is no such happy end and with him tragedy, so called, has become merely an expression of our despair at finding that such justification is no longer possible.

Modern critics have sometimes been puzzled to /90/ account for the fact that the concern of ancient tragedy is almost exclusively with kings and courts. They have been tempted to accuse even Aristotle of a certain naïveté in assuming (as he seems to assume) that the "nobility" of which he speaks as necessary to a tragedy implies a nobility of rank as well as of soul, and they have sometimes regretted that Shakespeare did not devote himself more than he did to the serious consideration of those common woes of the common man which subsequent writers have exploited with increasing pertinacity. Yet the tendency to lay the scene of a tragedy at the court of a king is not the result of any arbitrary convention but of the fact that the tragic writers believed easily in greatness just as we believe easily in meanness. To Shakespeare, robes and crowns and jewels are the garments most appropriate to man because they are the fitting outward manifestation of his inward majesty, but to us they seem absurd because the man who bears them has, in our estimation, so pitifully shrunk. We do not write about kings because we do not believe that any man is worthy to be one and we do not write about courts because hovels seem to us to be dwellings more appropriate to the creatures who inhabit them. Any modern attempt to dress characters in robes ends only by making us aware of a comic incongruity and any modern attempt to furnish them with a language resplendent like Shakespeare's ends only in bombast.

True tragedy capable of performing its function and of purging the soul by reconciling man to his woes can exist only by virtue of a certain pathetic fallacy[7] far more inclusive than that to which the name is commonly given. The romantics, feeble descendants of the tragic writers to whom they are linked by their effort to see life and nature in grandiose terms, loved to imagine that the sea or the sky had a way of according itself with their moods, of storming when they stormed and smiling when they smiled. But the tragic /91/ spirit sustains itself by an assumption much more far-reaching and no more justified. Man as it sees him lives in a world which he may not dominate but which is always aware of him. Occupying the exact center of a universe which would have no meaning except for him and being so little below the angels that, if he believes in God, he has no hesitation in imagining Him formed as he is formed and crowned with a crown like that which he or one of his fellows wears, he assumes that each of his acts reverberates through the universe. His passions are important to him because he believes them important throughout all time and all space; the very fact that he can sin (no modern can) means that this universe is watching his acts; and though he may perish, a God leans out from infinity to strike him down. And it is exactly because an Ibsen cannot think of man in any such terms as these that his persons have so shrunk and that his "tragedy" has lost that power which real tragedy always has of making that infinitely ambitious creature called man content to accept his misery if only he can be made to feel great enough and important enough. An Oswald is not a Hamlet chiefly because he has lost that tie with the natural and supernatural world which the latter had. No ghost will leave the other world to warn or encourage him, there is no virtue and no vice which he can possibly have which can be really important, and when he dies neither his death nor the manner of it will be, outside the circle of two or three people as unnecessary as himself, any more important than that of a rat behind the arras.

---

6. The action of *Hamlet* takes place in Elsinore. Skien was Ibsen's birthplace, and is perhaps the locale he had in mind for *Ghosts*.

7. The common meaning of the "pathetic fallacy," explained here, derives from John Ruskin's famous discussion of it in *Modern Painters*, Vol. III (1856).

Perhaps we may dub the illusion upon which the tragic spirit is nourished the Tragic, as opposed to the Pathetic, Fallacy, but fallacy though it is, upon its existence depends not merely the writing of tragedy but the existence of that religious feeling of which tragedy is an expression and by means of which a people aware of the dissonances of life manages /92/ nevertheless to hear them as harmony. Without it neither man nor his passions can seem great enough or important enough to justify the sufferings which they entail, and literature, expressing the mood of a people, begins to despair where once it had exulted. Like the belief in love and like most of the other mighty illusions by means of which human life has been given a value, the Tragic Fallacy depends ultimately upon the assumption which man so readily makes that something outside his own being, some " spirit not himself " — be it God, Nature, or that still vaguer thing called a Moral Order — joins him in the emphasis which he places upon this or that and confirms him in his feeling that his passions and his opinions are important. When his instinctive faith in that correspondence between the outer and the inner world fades, his grasp upon the faith that sustained him fades also, and Love or Tragedy or what not ceases to be the reality which it was because he is never strong enough in his own insignificant self to stand alone in a universe which snubs him with its indifference.

In both the modern and the ancient worlds tragedy was dead long before writers were aware of the fact. Seneca wrote his frigid melodramas under the impression that he was following in the footsteps of Sophocles, and Dryden probably thought that his *All for Love* was an improvement upon Shakespeare,[8] but in time we awoke to the fact that no amount of rhetorical bombast could conceal the fact that grandeur was not to be counterfeited when the belief in its possibility was dead, and turning from the hero to the common man we inaugurated the era of realism. For us no choice remains except that between mere rhetoric and the frank consideration of our fellow men, who may be the highest of the anthropoids but who are certainly too far below

the angels to imagine either that these angels can concern themselves with them or that they can catch any glimpse of even the soles of angelic /93/ feet. We can no longer tell tales of the fall of noble men because we do not believe that noble men exist. The best that we can achieve is pathos and the most that we can do is to feel sorry for ourselves. Man has put off his royal robes and it is only in sceptered pomp that tragedy can come sweeping by.

IV

Nietzsche was the last of the great philosophers to attempt a tragic justification of life. His central and famous dogma — " Life is good *because* it is painful " — sums up in a few words the desperate and almost meaningless paradox to which he was driven in his effort to reduce to rational terms the far more imaginative conception which is everywhere present but everywhere unanalyzed in a Sophocles or a Shakespeare and by means of which they rise triumphant over the manifold miseries of life. But the very fact that Nietzsche could not even attempt to state in any except intellectual terms an attitude which is primarily unintellectual and to which, indeed, intellectual analysis is inevitably fatal is proof of the distance which he had been carried (by the rationalizing tendencies of the human mind) from the possibility of the tragic solution which he sought; and the confused, half-insane violence of his work will reveal, by the contrast which it affords with the serenity of the tragic writers whom he admired, how great was his failure.

Fundamentally this failure was, moreover, conditioned by exactly the same thing which has conditioned the failure of all modern attempts to achieve what he attempted — by the fact, that is to say, that tragedy must have a hero if it is not to be merely an accusation against, instead of a justification of, the world in which it occurs. Tragedy is, as Aristotle said, an imitation of noble actions, and Nietzsche, for all his enthusiasm for the Greek tragic writers, was palsied by the universally modern incapacity to conceive /94/ man as noble. Out of this dilemma, out of his need to find a hero who could give to life as he saw it the only possible justification, was born the idea of the Superman, but the Superman is, after all, only a hypothetical being, destined to

---

8. Apparently all of Seneca's plays were derived from the Greek drama. John Dryden's *All for Love; or, The World Well Lost* (1676) is a tragedy based on the same material as Shakespeare's *Antony and Cleopatra*.

become what man actually was in the eyes of the great tragic writers — a creature (as Hamlet said) " how infinite in capacities, in understanding how like a god." Thus Nietzsche lived half in the past through his literary enthusiasms and half in the future through his grandiose dreams, but for all his professed determination to justify existence he was no more able than the rest of us to find the present acceptable. Life, he said in effect, is not a Tragedy now but perhaps it will be when the Ape-man has been transformed into a hero (the *Übermensch*), and trying to find that sufficient, he went mad.

He failed, as all moderns must fail when they attempt, like him, to embrace the tragic spirit as a religious faith, because the resurgence of that faith is not an intellectual but a vital phenomenon, something not achieved by taking thought but born, on the contrary, out of an instinctive confidence in life which is nearer to the animal's unquestioning allegiance to the scheme of nature than it is to that critical intelligence characteristic of a fully developed humanism. And like other faiths it is not to be recaptured merely by reaching an intellectual conviction that it would be desirable to do so.

Modern psychology has discovered (or at least strongly emphasized) the fact that under certain conditions desire produces belief, and having discovered also that the more primitive a given mentality the more completely are its opinions determined by its wishes, modern psychology has concluded that the best mind is that which most resists the tendency to believe a thing simply because it would be pleasant or advantageous to do so. But justified as this /95/ conclusion may be from the intellectual point of view, it fails to take into account the fact that in a universe as badly adapted as this one to human as distinguished from animal needs, this ability to will a belief may bestow an enormous vital advantage as it did, for instance, in the case at present under discussion where it made possible for Shakespeare the compensations of a tragic faith completely inaccessible to Nietzsche. Pure intelligence, incapable of being influenced by desire and therefore also incapable of choosing one opinion rather than another simply because the one chosen is the more fruitful or beneficent, is doubtless a relatively perfect instrument for the pursuit of truth, but the question (likely, it would seem, to be answered in the negative) is simply whether or not the spirit of man can endure the literal and inhuman truth.

Certain ages and simple people have conceived of the action which passes upon the stage of the universe as of something in the nature of a Divine Comedy, as something, that is to say, which will reach its end with the words " and they lived happily ever after." Others, less naïve and therefore more aware of those maladjustments whose reality, at least so far as outward events are concerned, they could not escape, have imposed upon it another artistic form and called it a Divine Tragedy, accepting its catastrophe as we accept the catastrophe of an *Othello,* because of its grandeur. But a Tragedy, Divine or otherwise, must, it may again be repeated, have a hero, and from the universe as we see it both the Glory of God and the Glory of Man have departed. Our cosmos may be farcical or it may be pathetic but it has not the dignity of tragedy and we cannot accept it as such.

Yet our need for the consolations of tragedy has not passed with the passing of our ability to conceive it. Indeed, the dissonances which it was tragedy's function to resolve grow more insistent instead of /96/ diminishing. Our passions, our disappointments, and our sufferings remain important to us though important to nothing else and they thrust themselves upon us with an urgency which makes it impossible for us to dismiss them as the mere trivialities which, so our intellects tell us, they are. And yet, in the absence of tragic faith or the possibility of achieving it, we have no way in which we may succeed in giving them the dignity which would not only render them tolerable but transform them as they were transformed by the great ages into joys. The death of tragedy is, like the death of love, one of those emotional fatalities as the result of which the human as distinguished from the natural world grows more and more a desert.

Poetry, said Santayana in his famous phrase, is " religion which is no longer believed," but it depends, nevertheless, upon its power to revive in us a sort of temporary or provisional credence and the nearer it can come to producing an illusion of belief the greater is its power as poetry. Once the Tragic Spirit was a living faith and out of it tragedies were written. Today these great expressions of a great faith have declined, not merely into poetry, but into a kind of poetry whose premises are so far from any we can really accept that we can only partially and dimly grasp its meaning.

We read but we do not write tragedies. The tragic solution of the problem of existence, the reconciliation to life by means of the tragic spirit is, that is to say, now only a fiction surviving in art. When that art itself has become, as it probably will, completely meaningless, when we have ceased not only to write but to *read* tragic works, then it will be lost and in all real senses forgotten, since the devolution from Religion to Art to Document will be complete. /97/

Tragedy and the Common Man

by Arthur Miller

The complete article (except for the subheadings) is included here as it appeared in the New York Times, *February 27, 1949, Section II. (It was subsequently reprinted in the March 1951 issue of* Theatre Arts, *Vol. XXXV, No. 3.)*

In this age few tragedies are written. It has often been held that the lack is due to a paucity of heroes among us, or else that modern man has had the blood drawn out of his organs of belief by the skepticism of science, and the heroic attack on life cannot feed on an attitude of reserve and circumspection. For one reason or another, we are often held to be below tragedy — or tragedy above us. The inevitable conclusion is, of course, that the tragic mode is archaic, fit only for the very highly placed, the kings or the kingly, and where this admission is not made in so many words it is most often implied.

I believe that the common man is as apt a subject for tragedy in its highest sense as kings were. On the face of it this ought to be obvious in the light of modern psychiatry, which bases its analysis upon classific formulations, such as the Oedipus and Orestes complexes, for instance, which were enacted by royal beings, but which apply to everyone in similar emotional situations.

More simply, when the question of tragedy in art is not at issue, we never hesitate to attribute to the well-placed and the exalted the very same mental processes as the lowly. And finally, if the exaltation of tragic action were truly a property of the high-bred character alone, it is inconceivable that the mass of mankind should cherish tragedy above all other forms, let alone be capable of understanding it.

As a general rule, to which there may be exceptions unknown to me, I think the tragic feeling is evoked in us when we are in the /p. 1, col. 5/ presence of a character who is ready to lay down his life, if need be, to secure one thing — his sense of personal dignity. From Orestes to Hamlet, Medea to Macbeth, the underlying struggle is that of the individual attempting to gain his " rightful " position in his society.

Sometimes he is one who has been displaced from it, sometimes one who seeks to attain it for the first time, but the fateful wound from which the inevitable events spiral is the wound of indignity, and its dominant force is indignation. Tragedy, then, is the consequence of a man's total compulsion to evaluate himself justly.

In the sense of having been initiated by the hero himself, the tale always reveals what has been called his " tragic flaw," a failing that is not peculiar to grand or elevated characters. Nor is it necessarily a weakness. The flaw, or crack in the character, is really nothing — and need be nothing — but his inherent unwillingness to remain passive in the face of what he conceives to be a challenge to his dignity, his image of his rightful status. Only the passive, only those who accept their lot without active retaliation, are "flawless." Most of us are in that category.

But there are among us today, as there always have been, those who act against the scheme of things that degrades them, and in the process of action everything we have accepted out of fear or insensitivity or ignorance is shaken before us and examined, and from this total onslaught by an individual against the seemingly stable cosmos surrounding us — from this total examination of the "unchangeable" environment — comes the terror and the fear that is classically associated with tragedy.

More important, from this total questioning of what has been previously unquestioned, we learn. And /p. 1, col. 6/ such a process is not beyond the common man. In revolutions around the world, these past thirty years, he has demonstrated again and again this inner dynamic of all tragedy.

Insistence upon the rank of the tragic hero, or the so-called nobility of his character, is really but a clinging to the outward forms of tragedy. If rank or nobility of character was indispensable, then it would follow that the problems of those with rank were the particular problems of tragedy. But surely the right of one monarch to capture the domain from another no longer raises our passions, nor are our concepts of justice what they were to the mind of an Elizabethan king.

The quality in such plays that does shake us, however, derives from the underlying fear of being displaced, the disaster inherent in being torn away from our chosen image of what and who we are in this world. Among us today this fear is as strong, and perhaps stronger, than it ever was. In fact, it is the common man who knows this fear best.

Now, if it is true that tragedy is the consequence of a man's total compulsion to evaluate himself justly, his destruction in the attempt posits a wrong or an evil in his environment. And this is precisely the morality of tragedy and its lesson. The discovery of the moral law, which is what the enlightenment of tragedy consists of, is not the discovery of some abstract or metaphysical quantity.

The tragic right is a condition of life, a condition in which the human personality is able to flower and realize itself. The wrong is the condition which suppresses man, perverts the flowing out of his love and creative instinct. Tragedy /p. 1, col. 7/ enlightens — and it must, in that it points the heroic finger at the enemy of man's freedom. The thrust for freedom is the quality in tragedy which exalts. The revolutionary questioning of the stable environment is what terrifies. In no way is the common man debarred from such thoughts or such actions.

Seen in this light, our lack of tragedy may be partially accounted for by the turn which modern literature has taken toward the purely psychiatric view of life, or the purely sociological. If all our miseries, our indignities, are born and bred within our minds, then all action, let alone the heroic action, is obviously impossible.

And if society alone is responsible for the cramping of our lives, then the protagonist must needs be so pure and faultless as to force us to deny his validity as a character. From neither of these views can tragedy derive, simply because neither represents a balanced concept of life. Above all else, tragedy /p. 3, col. 3/ requires the finest appreciation by the writer of cause and effect.

No tragedy can therefore come about when its author fears to question absolutely everything, when he regards any institution, habit or custom as being either everlasting, immutable or inevitable. In the tragic view the need of man to wholly realize himself is the only fixed star, and whatever it is that hedges his nature and lowers it is ripe for attack and examination. Which is not to say that tragedy must preach revolution.

The Greeks could probe the very heavenly origin of their ways and return to confirm the rightness of laws. And Job could face God in anger, demanding his right, and end in submission. But for a moment everything is in suspension, nothing is accepted, and in this stretching and tearing apart of the cosmos, in the very action of so doing, the character gains "size," the tragic stature which is spuriously attached to the royal or the high born in our minds. The /p. 3, col. 4/ commonest of men may take on that stature to the extent of his willingness to throw all he has into the contest, the battle to secure his rightful place in his world.

There is a misconception of tragedy with which I have been struck in review after review, and in many conversations with writers and readers alike. It is the idea that tragedy is of necessity allied to pessimism. Even the dictionary says nothing more about the word than that it means a story with a sad or unhappy ending. This impression is so firmly fixed that I almost hesitate to claim that in truth tragedy implies more optimism in its author than does comedy, and that its final result ought to be the reinforcement of the onlooker's brightest opinions of the human animal.

For, if it is true to say that in essence the tragic hero is intent upon claiming his whole due as a personality, and if this struggle must be total and without reservation, then it automatically demonstrates the indestructible will /*p. 3, col. 5*/ of man to achieve his humanity.

The possibility of victory must be there in tragedy. Where pathos rules, where pathos is finally derived, a character has fought a battle he could not possibly have won. The pathetic is achieved when the protagonist is, by virtue of his witlessness, his insensitivity, or the very air he gives off, incapable of grappling with a much superior force.

Pathos truly is the mode for the pessimist. But tragedy requires a nicer balance between what is possible and what is impossible. And it is curious, although edifying, that the plays we revere, century after century, are the tragedies. In them, and in them alone, lies the belief — optimistic, if you will — in the perfectibility of man.

It is time, I think, that we who are without kings, took up this bright thread of our history and followed it to the only place it can possibly lead in our time — the heart and spirit of the average man. /*p. 3, col. 6*/

The Tragic Form

by Richard B. Sewall

This article, which is reprinted here in its entirety, is taken from the October 1954 issue of Essays in Criticism, *Vol. IV, No. 4, a journal published by Basil Blackwell in Oxford, England. (Much of this material subsequently appeared in a different form in Sewall's* The Vision of Tragedy [*New Haven: Yale University Press, 1959*].) *All of the footnotes are Sewall's.*

A discussion of tragedy is confronted at the outset with the strenuous objections of Croce, who would have no truck with the genres. " Art is one," he wrote in his famous *Britannica* article,[1] " and cannot be divided." For convenience, he would allow the division of Shakespeare's plays into tragedies, comedies, and histories, but he warned of the dogmatism that lay in any further refining of distinctions. He made a special point of tragedy, which as usual was the fighting

P. 345: 1. eleventh edition, article "Aesthetics."

issue. No artist, he said, will submit to the servitude of the traditional definition: that a tragedy must have a subject of a certain kind, characters of a certain kind, and a plot of a certain kind and length. Each work of art is a world in itself, " a creation, not a reflection, a monument, not a document." The concepts of aesthetics do not exist " in a transcendent region " but only in innumerable specific works. To ask of a given work " is it a tragedy? " or " does it obey the laws of tragedy? " is irrelevant and impertinent.

Although this may be substituting one dogmatism for another, there is sense in it. Nothing is more dreary than the textbook categories; and their tendency, if carried too far, would rationalize art out of existence. The dilemma is one of critical means, not ends: Croce would preserve tragedy by insuring the autonomy of the artist; the schoolmen would preserve it by insuring the autonomy of the form.

But the dilemma is not insurmountable, as Eliot and a number of others have pointed out. There is a life-giving relationship between tradition and the individual talent, a " wooing /345/ both ways " (in R. P. Blackmur's phrase) between the form which the artist inherits and the new content he brings to it. This wooing both ways has been especially true of the development of tragedy, where values have been incremental, where (for instance) each new tragic protagonist is in some degree a lesser Job and each new tragic work owes an indispensable element to the Greek idea of the chorus. So I should say that, provided we can get beyond the stereotypes Croce seems to have had in mind, we should continue to talk about tragedy, to make it grow in meaning, impel more artists, and attract a greater and more discerning audience.

But we must first get a suitable idea of form. Blackmur's article [1] from which I have just quoted provides, I think, a useful suggestion. It is the concept of " theoretic form," which he distinguishes from technical or " executive " form. " Technical form," he writes, " is our means of getting at . . . and then making something of, what we feel the form of life itself is: the tensions, the stresses, the deep relations and the terrible disrelations that inhabit them . . . This is the form that underlies the forms we merely practice . . ." This (and here Croce's full concept of form is more adequately represented) is " what Croce means by theoretic form for feeling, intuition, insight, what I mean by the theoretic form of life itself." Discussion of the " form " of tragedy in this sense need be neither prescriptive nor inhibiting, but it may define a little more precisely a vital area of thought and feeling.

Here is the kind of situation in which such a discussion might be helpful: Two years ago, in *Essays in Criticism* (October 1952), Miss K. M. Burton defended what she called the " political tragedies " of Ben Jonson and George Chapman as legitimate tragedies, although non-Aristotelian. *Sejanus* was perhaps the clearest case in point. Herford and Simpson, in their commentary, had set the play down as at best " the tragedy of a satirist," a " proximate " tragedy, with no tragic hero and with no cathartic effect. " Whatever effect [Jonson] aimed at," they wrote, " it was not the purifying pity excited by the fatal errors of a noble /346/ nature." Miss Burton's reply lay in her concept of political tragedy. She saw Jonson's tragic theme as " the manner in which evil penetrates the political structure." The " flaw " that concerned him lay " within the social order," and whatever purifying pity we feel would come from contemplating the ordeal of society, not the fatal errors of a noble nature. The play for her had " tragic intensity "; it was both " dramatic, and a tragedy."

Whether one agrees with her or not, the question, despite Croce, is out: " Is the play a tragedy? " And many others follow. Can there be a tragedy without a tragic hero? Can " the social order " play his traditional role? Is catharsis the first, or only, or even a reliable test? In a recent article, Professor Pottle wrote, " I shall be told Aristotle settled all that." And added, " I wish he had." The disagreement on *Sejanus* is symptomatic. F. L. Lucas once pointed out that (on much the same issues) Hegel thought only the Greeks wrote true tragedy; and I. A. Richards, only Shakespeare. Joseph Wood Krutch ruled out the moderns, like Hardy, Ibsen and O'Neill; and Mark Harris ruled them in.[1] The question arises about every new " serious " play or novel; we seem to care a great deal about whether it is, or is not, a tragedy.

I have little hope of settling all this, but I am persuaded that progress lies in the direction of theoretic form, as Blackmur uses the term. Is it not possible to bring the dominant feelings, intuitions, insights that we meet in so-called tragic writings into some coherent relationship to which the word " form " could be applied without too great violence? This is not to tell artists what to do, nor to set up strict *a priori* formulae, nor to legislate among the major genres. The problem of evaluating the total excellence of a given work involves much more than determining its status as a tragedy, or as a " proximate " tragedy, or as a nontragedy. It involves, among other things, the verbal management within the work and the ordering of the parts. Furthermore, our discussion need not imply the superi-

P. **346**: 1. "The Loose and Baggy Monsters of Henry James: Notes on the Underlying Classic Form in the Novel," *Accent*, Summer, 1951; see also Eliseo Vivas, "Literature and Knowledge," *Sewanee Review*, Autumn, 1952.

P. **347**: 1. F. A. Pottle, "Catharsis," *Yale Review*, Summer, 1951; F. L. Lucas, *Tragedy in Relation to Aristotle's Poetics*, N.Y., 1928; Joseph Wood Krutch, *The Modern Temper*, N.Y., 1929; Mark Harris, *The Case for Tragedy*, N.Y., 1932.

ority of tragedy over comedy (certainly not as Dante conceived of comedy) or over epic, although, if we look upon these major /347/ forms as presenting total interpretations of life, the less inclusive forms (lyric, satire) would seem to occupy inferior categories. But as we enter the world of any play or novel to which the term tragedy is at all applicable, we may well judge it by what we know about the possibilities of the form, without insisting that our judgment is absolute. If, set against the full dimensions of the tragic form, Jonson's *Sejanus* or Hemingway's *A Farewell to Arms* (for instance) reveal undeveloped possibilities or contrary elements, we can still respect their particular modes of expression.

In indicating these dimensions of tragedy, I shall be mindful of Unamuno's warning [1] that tragedy is not a matter, ultimately, to be systematized. He speaks truly, I think, about "the tragic sense of life." He describes it as a subphilosophy, "more or less formulated, more or less conscious," reaching deep down into temperament, not so much "flowing from ideas as determining them." It is the sense of ancient evil, of the mystery of human suffering, of the gulf between aspiration and achievement. It colours the tragic artist's vision of life (his theoretic form) and gives his works their peculiar shade and tone. It speaks, not the language of systematic thought, but through symbolic action, symbol and figure, diction and image, sound and rhythm. Such a recognition should precede any attempt to talk "systematically" about tragedy, while not denying the value of the attempt itself.

Two more comments remain to be made about method. The first is the problem of circular evidence,[2] the use of tragedies to define tragedy. I am assuming that we can talk meaningfully about a body of literature which reveals certain generic qualities and which can be distinguished from the body of literature called comedy, epic, satire, or the literature of pathos. My purpose is to isolate these qualities and to refer to the works themselves as illustrations rather than proof.

The second comment involves the problem of affectivism, which is the problem of catharsis: "This play is a tragedy because it makes me feel

thus and so." As Max Scheler puts it, /348/ this method would bring us ultimately to the contemplation of our own ego. Thus, I would reverse the order of F. L. Lucas's discussion, which assumes that we must know what tragedy does before we can tell what it is: "We cannot fully discuss the means," Lucas wrote, "until we are clear about the ends." It is true that the usual or "scientific" way is to define natures by effects, which are observable. But rather than found a definition of tragedy on the infinite variables of an audience's reactions, I would consider first the works themselves as the "effects" and look in them for evidences of an efficient cause: a worldview, a form that "underlies the forms we merely practice." What are the generic qualities of these effects? Do they comprise a "form"? I think they do; and for convenience I shall use the term from the start as if I had already proved its legitimacy.

Basic to the tragic form is its recognition of the inevitability of paradox, of unresolved tensions and ambiguities, of opposites in precarious balance. Like the arch, tragedy never rests — or never comes to rest, with all losses restored and sorrows ended. Problems are put and pressed, but not solved. An occasional "happy ending," as in *The Oresteia* or *Crime and Punishment,* does not mean a full resolution. Though there may be intermittences, there is no ultimate discharge in that war. Although this suggests formlessness, as it must in contrast with certain types of religious orthodoxy or philosophical system, it would seem the essence of the tragic form. Surely it is more form than chaos. For out of all these tensions and paradoxes, these feelings, intuitions, insights, there emerges a fairly coherent attitude towards the universe and man. Tragedy makes certain distinguishable and characteristic affirmations, as well as denials, about (I) the cosmos and man's relation to it; (II) the nature of the individual and his relation to himself; (III) the individual in society.

(I) *The tragic cosmos.* In using the term cosmos to signify a theory of the universe and man's relation to it, I have, of course, made a statement about tragedy: that tragedy affirms a cosmos of which man is a meaningful part. To be sure, the characteristic locale of tragedy is not the empyrean. Tragedy is primarily humanistic. Its focus is an event in this world; it is uncom-

<hr>

P. 348: 1. *The Tragic Sense of Life,* tr. J. E. C. Flitch, London, 1921, pp. 17–18.

2. Cf. Max Scheler, "On the Tragic," *Cross Currents,* Winter, 1954. This is a selection from Scheler's *Vom Umsturz der Werte,* Vol. I (1923), tr. Bernard Stambler.

mitted /349/ as to questions of ultimate destiny, and it is nonreligious in its attitude toward revelation. But it speaks, however vaguely or variously, of an order that transcends time, space and matter.[1] It assumes man's connection with some supersensory or supernatural, or metaphysical being or principle, whether it be the Olympians, Job's Jehovah or the Christian God; Fate, Fortune's Wheel, the "elements" that Lear invoked, or Koestler's "oceanic sense," which comes in so tentatively (and pathetically) at the end of *Darkness at Noon*. The first thing that tragedy says about the cosmos is that, for good or ill, it *is;* and in this respect tragedy's theoretic opposite is naturalism or mechanism. Tragedy is witness (secondly) to the cosmic mystery, to the "wonderful" surrounding our lives; and in literature the opposite of tragedy is not only writing based upon naturalistic theory but also upon the four-square, "probable"[2] world of satire and rationalistic comedy. Finally, what distinguishes tragedy from other forms which bespeak this cosmic sense — for tragedy of course is not unique in this — is its peculiar and intense preoccupation with the *evil* in the universe, whatever it is in the stars that compels, harasses, and bears man down. Tragedy wrestles with the evil of the mystery — and the mystery of the evil. And the contest never ends.

But, paradoxically, its view of the cosmos is what sustains tragedy. Tragedy discerns a principle of goodness that coexists with the evil. This principle need be nothing so pat as The Moral Order, the "armies of unalterable law," and it is nothing so sure as the orthodox Christian God. It is nearer the folk sense that justice exists somewhere in the universe, or what Nietzsche describes as the orgiastic, mystical sense of oneness, of life as "indestructibly powerful and pleasurable." It may be a vision of some transcendent beauty and dignity against which the present evil may be seen as evil and the welter as welter. This is what keeps tragedy from giving up the whole human experiment, and in this respect its opposite is not comedy or satire but cynicism and nihilism, as in Schopenhauer's theory of /350/ resignation. The "prob-

lem of the good" plays as vital a part in tragedy as the "problem of evil." It provides the living tension without which tragedy ceases to exist.

Thus tragedy contemplates a universe in which man is not the measure of all things. It confronts a mystery. W. Macneile Dixon[1] pointed out that tragedy started as "an affair with the gods"; and the extent to which literature has become "secularized and humanized," he wrote, is a sign of its departure from (to use our present term) the tragic form. While agreeing with him as to the tendency, one may question the wholesale verdict which he implies. The affair with the gods has not, in the minds of all our artists, been reduced to an affair with the social order, or the environment, or the glands. But certainly where it becomes so, the muse of tragedy walks out; the universe loses its mystery and (to invoke catharsis for a moment) its terror.

The terms "pessimism" and "optimism" in the view of the universe as conceived in the tragic form, do not suggest adequate categories, as Nietzsche first pointed out.[2] Tragedy contains them both, goes beyond both, illuminates both, but comes to no conclusion. Tragedy could, it is true, be called pessimistic in its view of the evil in the universe as unremitting and irremediable, the blight man was born for, the necessary condition of existence. It is pessimistic, also, in its view of the overwhelming proportion of evil to good and in its awareness of the mystery of why this should be — the "unfathomable element" in which Ahab foundered. But it is optimistic in what might be called its vitalism, which is in some sense mystical, not earth-bound; in its faith in a cosmic good; in its vision, /351/ however

P. 350: 1. Cf. Susan Taubes, "The Nature of Tragedy," *Review of Metaphysics*, December 1953.

2. The "wonderful" and the "probable" are the basic categories in Albert Cook's distinction between tragedy and comedy (*The Dark Voyage and the Golden Mean*, Cambridge, Mass., 1949, Chap. 1).

P. 351: 1. *Tragedy*, London, 1924. The extent of my indebtedness to this book, and to the other discussions of tragedy mentioned in this paper, is poorly indicated by such passing references as this. Since observations on tragedy and the theory of tragedy appear in innumerable discussions of particular authors, eras, and related critical problems, a complete list would be far too cumbersome. Among them would be, surely, the standard work of A. C. Bradley and Willard Farnham on Shakespearean tragedy; C. M. Bowra and Cedric Whitman on Sophocles; W. L. Courtney, *The Idea of Tragedy*, London, 1900; Maxwell Anderson, *The Essence of Tragedy*, Washington, 1939; Northrop Frye, "The Archetypes of Literature," *Kenyon Review*, Winter, 1951; Moody Prior, *The Language of Tragedy*, N.Y., 1947; and Herbert Weisinger, *Tragedy and the Paradox of the Fortunate Fall*, Michigan State College Press, 1953, which makes rich use of the archaeological and mythographic studies of the origin of tragedy (Cornford, Harrison, Murray). I am indebted, also, to my colleague Laurence Michel for frequent conversations and helpful criticism.

2. See also Reinhold Niebuhr, *Beyond Tragedy*, London, 1938.

fleeting, of a world in which all questions could be answered.

(II) *Tragic man.* If the tragic form asserts a cosmos, some order behind the immediate disorder, what does it assert about the nature of man, other than that he is a being capable of cosmic affinities? What is tragic man as he lives and moves on this earth? Can he be distinguished meaningfully from the man of comedy, satire, epic or lyric? How does he differ from "pathetic man" or "religious man"? or from man as conceived by the materialistic psychologies? Tragic man shares some qualities, of course, with each of these. I shall stress differences in the appropriate contexts.

Like the cosmos which he views, tragic man is a paradox and a mystery. He is no child of God; yet he feels himself more than a child of earth. He is not the plaything of Fate, but he is not entirely free. He is "both creature and creator" (in Niebuhr's phrase) — "fatefully free and freely fated" (in George Schrader's). He recognizes "the fact of guilt" while cherishing the "dream of innocence" (Fiedler), and he never fully abandons either position. He is plagued by the ambiguity of his own nature and of the world he lives in. He is torn between the sense in common sense (which is the norm of satire and rationalistic, or corrective, comedy) and his own uncommon sense. Aware of the just but irreconcilable claims within and without, he is conscious of the immorality of his own morality and suffers in the knowledge of his own recalcitrance.

The dynamic of this recalcitrance is pride. It sustains his belief, however humbled he may become by later experience, in his own freedom, in his innocence, and in his uncommon sense. Tragic man is man at his most prideful and independent, man glorying in his humanity. Tragic pride, like everything else about tragedy, is ambiguous; it can be tainted with arrogance and have its petty side; but it is not to be equated with sin or weakness. The Greeks feared it when it threatened the gods or slipped into arrogance, but they honoured it and even worshipped it in their heroes. It was the common folk, the chorus, who had no pride, or were "flawless."[1] The chorus invariably /352/ argue against pride, urging caution and moderation,

because they know it leads to suffering; but tragedy as such does not prejudge it.

While many of these things, again, might be said of other than tragic man, it is in the peculiar nature of his suffering, and in his capacity for suffering and appropriating his suffering, that his distinguishing quality lies. For instance (to ring changes on the Cartesian formula), tragic man would not define himself, like the man of corrective comedy or satire: "I think, therefore I am"; nor like the man of achievement (epic): "I act, or conquer, therefore I am"; nor like the man of sensibility (lyric): "I feel, therefore I am"; nor like the religious man: "I believe, therefore I am." Although he has all these qualities (of thought, achievement, sensibility, and belief) in various forms and degrees, the essence of his nature is brought out by suffering: "I suffer, I will to suffer, I learn by suffering; therefore I am." The classic statement, of course, is Aeschylus's: "Wisdom comes alone through suffering" (Lattimore's translation); perhaps the most radical is Dostoevski's: "Suffering is the sole origin of consciousness."[1]

This is not to say that only tragic man suffers or that he who suffers is tragic. Saints and martyrs suffer and learn by suffering; Odysseus suffered and learned; Dante suffered and learned on his journey with Virgil. But tragic man, I think, is distinguishable from these others in the nature of his suffering as conditioned by its source and locus, in its characteristic course and consequences (that is, the ultimate disaster and the "knowledge" it leads to), and in his intense preoccupation with his own suffering.

But to consider these matters in turn and to illustrate them briefly:

I have already suggested the main sources and locus of tragic man's suffering. He suffers because he is more than usually sensitive to the "terrible disrelations" he sees about him and experiences in himself. He is more than usually aware of the mighty opposites in the universe and in man, of the gulf between desire and fulfilment, between what is and what should be. This kind of suffering is suffering on a high level, beyond /353/ the reach of the immature or brutish, and for ever closed to the extreme optimist, the extreme pessimist,[1] or the merely

P. 353: 1. *Notes from Underground,* tr. B. G. Guerney.

P. 352: 1. Cf. Arthur Miller, "Tragedy and the Common Man," New York *Times,* February 27th, 1949.

P. 354: 1. Cf. William Van O'Connor, *Climates of Tragedy,* Baton Rouge, La., 1943.

indifferent. It was Job on the ash-heap, the proto-
type of tragic man, who was first struck by the
incongruity between Jehovah's nature and His
actions, between desert and reward in this life;
and it was he who first asked, not so much for a
release from physical suffering as a reasonable
explanation of it. But above all, the source of
tragic suffering is the sense, in the consciousness
of tragic man, of simultaneous guilt and guilt-
lessness. Tillich called tragedy "a mixture of
guilt and necessity." If tragic man could say,
"I sinned, therefore I suffer" or "He (or They
or God) sinned, therefore I suffer," his problem
would be resolved, and the peculiar poignancy
of his suffering would be removed. If he felt
himself entirely free or entirely determined, he
would cease to be tragic. But he is neither — he
is, in short, a paradox and mystery, the "riddle
of the world."

To draw further distinctions: The element of
guilt in tragic suffering distinguishes it from
the pathetic suffering of the guiltless and from
the suffering of the sentimentalist's bleeding
heart. On the other hand, tragic man's sense of
fate, and of the mystery of fate, distinguishes his
suffering from the suffering (which is little more
than embarrassment) of the man of corrective
comedy and satire. The suffering of the epic hero
has little of the element of bafflement or
enigma; it is not, characteristically, spiritual
suffering. The Christian in his suffering can confess *total* guilt and look to the promise of redemption through grace.[2] The martyr seeks suffering, accepts it gladly, "glories in tribulation."
Tragic man knows nothing of grace and never
glories in his suffering. Although he may come
to acquiesce in it partly and "learn" from it (a
stage I shall discuss below), his characteristic
mood is resentment and dogged endurance. He
has not the stoic's patience, although this may
be part of what he learns. Characteristically, he
is restless, intense, probing and questioning the
universe and his own soul (Job, Lear, Ahab). It
is true that, from Greek tragedy to tragedy written in the Christian era (Shakespeare and beyond) emphasis shifts from /354/ the universe
to the soul, from the cosmic to the psychological.
But Prometheus had an inner life; Antigone, for
all her composure, suffered an ultimate doubt;
Oedipus suffered spiritually as he grew to un-

derstand the dark ambiguities in his own nature.
And we should be mistaken if we tried to interpret the divine powers in the plays of Shakespeare simply as "allegorical symbols for psychological realities."[1]

Tragic man, then, placed in a universe of ir-
reconcilables, acting in a situation in which he is
both innocent and guilty, and peculiarly sensitive to the "cursèd spite" of his condition, suffers. What in the tragic view is the characteristic
course of this suffering and what further aspects
of tragic man are revealed by it? The tragic
form develops, not only the partial outlines of a
cosmology and a psychology, but of an ethic.

(III) *Tragic man and society.* The tragic sufferer may now be viewed in his social and moral
relationships. In the tragic world there are several alternatives. A man can default from the
human condition — "Curse God and die" —
and bring his suffering to an end; he can endure
and be silent; he can turn cynic. Tragic man understands these alternatives, feels their attractions, but chooses a different way. Rising in his
pride, he protests: he pits himself in some way
against whatever, in the heavens above and in
the earth beneath, seems to him to be wrong,
oppressive, or personally thwarting. This is the
hero's commitment, made early or late, but involving him necessarily in society and in action — with Prometheus and Antigone early,
with Hamlet late. What to the orthodox mind
would appear to be the wisdom or folly, the
goodness or badness, of the commitment is not,
in the beginning, the essence of the matter. In
the first phase of his course of suffering, the
hero's position may be anarchic, individual, romantic. Herein tragedy tests all norms — as, by
contrast, satire,[2] comedy, or epic tend to confirm them. The commitment may even be expressed in what society knows as a crime, but,
as with tragic pride (of which the commitment
is in part the expression), tragedy does not prejudge it. Thus it is said that tragedy studies "the
great offenders," and Dostoevski sought among
criminals and outcasts for his greatest spiritual
/355/ discoveries. But the commitment must
grow in meaning to include the more-than-
personal. Ultimately, and ideally, the tragic hero
stands as universal man, speaking for all men.

P. 354: 2. Cf. Karl Jaspers, *Tragedy Is Not Enough,* tr. Reiche,
Moore, Deutsch; Boston, 1952.

P. 355: 1. Susan Taubes, *op. cit.,* p. 196.
2. Cf. Maynard Mack, "The Muse of Satire," *Yale Review,*
Spring, 1952.

The tragic sufferer, emerging from his early stage of lament or rebellion (Job's opening speech; the first scenes of Prometheus; Lear's early bursts of temper), moves beyond the "intermittences" of his own heart and makes a "pact with the world that is unremitting and sealed." [1]

Since the commitment cannot lead in the direction of escape or compromise, it must involve head-on collision with the forces that would oppress or frustrate. Conscious of the ambiguities without and within, which are the source of his peculiar suffering, tragic man accepts the conflict. It is horrible to do it, he says, but it is more horrible to leave it undone. He is now in the main phase of his suffering — the "passion." [2]

In his passion he differs from the rebel, who would merely smash; or the romantic hero, who is not conscious of guilt; or the epic hero, who deals with emergencies rather than dilemmas. Odysseus and Aeneas, to be sure, face moral problems, but they proceed in a clear ethical light. Their social norms are secure. But the tragic hero sees a sudden, unexpected evil at the heart of things that infects all things. His secure and settled world has gone wrong, and he must oppose his own ambiguous nature against what he loves. Doing so involves total risk, as the chorus and his friends remind him. He may brood and pause, like Hamlet, or he may proceed with Ahab's fury; but proceed he must.

He proceeds, suffers, and in his suffering "learns." This is the phase of "perception." Although it often culminates in a single apocalyptic scene, a moment of "recognition," as in *Oedipus* and *Othello,* it need not be separate in time from the passion phase. Rather, perception is all that can be summed up in the spiritual and moral change that the hero undergoes from first to last and in the similar change wrought by his actions or by his example in those about him. /356/

For the hero, perception may involve an all-but-complete transformation in character, as with Lear and Oedipus; or a gradual development in poise and self-mastery (Prometheus,

Hamlet); or the softening and humanizing of the hard outlines of a character like Antigone's. It may appear in the hero's change from moody isolation and self-pity to a sense of his sharing in the general human condition, of his responsibility for it and to it. This was one stage in Lear's pilgrimage ("I have ta'en too little care of this") and as far as Dostoevski's Dmitri Karamazov ever got. In all the manifestations of this perception there is an element of Hamlet's "readiness," of an acceptance of destiny that is not merely resignation. At its most luminous it is Lear's and Oedipus's hard-won humility and new understanding of love. It may transform or merely inform, but a change there must be.

And it is more, of course, than merely a moral change, just as the hero's problem is always more than a moral one. His affair is still with the gods. In taking up arms against the ancient cosmic evil, he transcends the human situation, mediating between the human and the divine. It was Orestes's suffering that, in the end, made the heavens more just. In the defeat or death which is the usual lot of the tragic hero, he becomes a citizen of a larger city, still defiant but in a new mood, a "calm of mind," a partial acquiescence. Having at first resented his destiny, he has lived it out, found unexpected meanings in it, carried his case to a more-than-human tribunal. He sees his own destiny, and man's destiny, in its ultimate perspective.

But the perception which completes the tragic form is not dramatized solely through the hero's change, although his pilgrimage provides the traditional tragic structure.[1] The full /357/ nature and extent of the new vision is measured also by what happens to the other figures in the

---

P. 356: 1. Wallace Fowlie, "Swann and Hamlet: A Note on the Contemporary Hero," *Partisan Review,* 1942.

2. Cf. Francis Fergusson, *The Idea of a Theatre,* Princeton, N.J., 1949, Chap. 1, "The Tragic Rhythm of Action." Fergusson translates Kenneth Burke's formulation "*Poiema, Pathema, Mathema*" into "Purpose, Passion, Perception." (See *A Grammar of Motives,* pp. 38 ff.) Cf. also Susan Taubes, *op. cit.,* p. 199.

P. 357: 1. Indeed, it has been pointed out that, in an age when the symbol of the hero as the dominating centre of the play seems to have lost its validity with artist and audience, the role is taken over by the artist himself, who is his own tragic hero. That is, "perception" is conveyed more generally, in the total movement of the piece and through all the parts. The "pact with the world" and the suffering are not objectified in a hero's ordeal but seem peculiarly the author's. This quality has been noted in Joyce's *Ulysses;* Berdiaev saw it in Dostoevski; Hardy, Conrad, Faulkner are examples that come to mind. At any rate, the distinction may be useful in determining matters of tone, although it is not clear cut, as distinctions in tone seldom are. But it is one way of pointing to the difference between the tragic tone and the Olympian distance of Meredithian comedy, the harmony of the final phase of Dantesque comedy, or the ironic detachment of satire. Nietzsche spoke of the difference between the Dionysian (or tragic) artist and "the poet of the dramatized epos... the calm, unmoved embodiment of Contemplation, whose wide eyes see the picture before them" (*Birth of Tragedy* in *Works,* ed. O. Levy, Edinburgh and London, 1909, III, p. 96).

total symbolic situation — to the hero's antagonists (King Creon, Claudius, Iago); to his opposites (the trimmers and hangers-on, the Osrics); to his approximates (Ismene, Horatio, Kent, the Chorus). Some he moves, some do not change at all. But his suffering must make a difference somewhere outside himself. After Antigone's death the community (even Creon) reforms around her; the "new acquist" at the end of *Samson Agonistes* is the common note, also, at the end of the Shakespearean tragedies. For the lookers-on there is no sudden rending of the veil of clay, no triumphant assertion of The Moral Order. There has been suffering and disaster, ultimate and irredeemable loss, and there is promise of more to come. But all who are involved have been witness to new revelations about human existence, the evil of evil and the goodness of good. They are more "ready." The same old paradoxes and ambiguities remain, but for the moment they are transcended in the higher vision. /358/

4. Criticism of the Plays

OEDIPUS REX AS THE IDEAL TRAGIC HERO
OF ARISTOTLE by Marjorie Barstow

This essay, which is reprinted here in its entirety, was written while Miss Barstow was a sophomore at Cornell University (1909–1910), and appeared in the October 5, 1912, issue of the Classical Weekly, *Vol. VI, No. 1, a journal published by the Classical Association of the Atlantic States, and known since October 1957 as the* Classical World. (*A revised version of this essay,* "Oedipus Rex: A Typical Greek Tragedy," *was subsequently included in Lane Cooper's* The Greek Genius and Its Influence [*New Haven: Yale University Press, 1917*].)

If we give ourselves up to a full sympathy with the hero, there is no question that the *Oedipus Rex* fulfils the function of a tragedy, and arouses fear and pity in the highest degree. But the modern reader, coming to the classic drama not entirely for the purpose of enjoyment, will not always surrender himself to the emotional effect. He is apt to worry about Greek " fatalism " and the justice of the downfall of Oedipus, and, finding no satisfactory solution for these intellectual difficulties, loses half the pleasure that the drama was intended to produce. Perhaps we trouble ourselves too much concerning the Greek notions of fate in human life. We are inclined to regard them with a lively antiquarian interest, as if they were something remote and peculiar; yet in reality the essential difference between these notions and the more familiar ideas of a later time is so slight that it need not concern the naïve and sympathetic reader. After all, the fundamental aim of the poet is not to teach us about these matters, but to construct a tragedy which shall completely fulfil its proper function. Nevertheless, for the student of literature who feels bound to solve the twofold problem, " How is the tragedy of Oedipus to be reconciled with a rational conception of life? " and " How does Oedipus himself comply with the Aristotelian requirements for a tragic hero? " there is a simple answer in the ethical teaching of the great philosopher in whose eyes the *Oedipus Rex* appears to have been well-nigh a perfect tragedy. In other words, let us compare the ideal of the *Ethics* with the ideal of the *Poetics*.

Aristotle finds the end of human endeavor to be happiness, that is, an unhampered activity of the soul in accordance with true reason, throughout a complete lifetime. This happiness, as Aristotle discovered by careful observation during the length of his thoughtful life, does not result principally from the gifts of fortune, but rather from a steady and comprehensive intellectual vision which views life steadily and distinguishes in every action the result to be attained. By the light of this vision the wise man preserves a just balance among his natural impulses, and firmly and consistently directs his will and emotions toward the supreme end which reason approves. He has, therefore, an inward happiness which cannot be shaken save by great and numerous outward calamities, and, moreover, he attains an adequate external prosperity, since, other things being equal, the most sensible people are the most successful, and misfortune is due, in large measure, to lack of knowledge or lack of prudence. Even if he is crushed beneath an overwhelming catastrophe from without, the ideal character of the *Ethics* is not an object of fear and pity, for " the truly good and sensible man bears all the chances of life with decorum, and always does what is noblest in the circumstances, as a good general uses the forces at his command to the best advantage in war."

Such is the ideal character, the man who is best fitted to attain happiness in the world of men. On the other hand, the tragic hero is a man who fails to attain happiness, and fails in such a way that his career excites, not blame, but fear and pity in the highest degree. In the *Poetics,* he is described as not eminently good and just, not completely under the guidance of true reason, but as falling through some great error or flaw of character, rather than through vice or depravity. Moreover, in order that his downfall may be as striking as possible, he must be, as was Oedipus, of an illustrious family, highly renowned, and prosperous. /2/

When we analyze the character of Oedipus, we discover that, in spite of much natural greatness of soul, he is, in one vital respect, the exact antithesis of Aristotle's ideal man. He has no clear vision which enables him to examine every side of a matter with unclouded eyes, and to see all things in due perspective; nor has he a calm wisdom which is always master of his passions. Oedipus can see but one side of a matter — too often he sees that wrongly — and it is his fashion immediately to act upon such half-knowledge, at the dictates, not of his reason at all, but of the first feeling which happens to come uppermost. His is no deliberate vice, no choice of a wrong purpose. His purposes are good. His emotions, his thoughts, even his errors, have an ardent generosity which stirs our deepest sympathy. But his nature is plainly imperfect, as Aristotle says the nature of a tragic hero should be, and from the beginning he was not likely to attain perfect happiness.

When the drama opens, the thoughtless energy of Oedipus has already harnessed him to the "yoke of Fate unbending." Once at a feast in Corinth, a man heated with wine had taunted him with not being the true son of Polybus. These idle words of a man in his cups so affected the excitable nature of Oedipus that he, characteristically, could think of nothing else. Day and night the saying rankled in his heart. At last, too energetic to remain in the ignorance which might have been his safety, he eagerly hastened to the sacred oracle at Delphi to learn the truth. The only response he heard was the prophecy that he should kill his father and marry his mother. Absorbed in this new suggestion, he failed to consider its bearing upon his question, and, wholly forgetting his former suspicion, he determined never to return to Corinth where his supposed father and mother dwelt,

and hurried off in the direction of Thebes. Thus his disposition to act without thinking started him headlong on the way to ruin. At a place where three roads met, all unawares he encountered his real father, Laïus, King of Thebes. When the old man insolently accosted him, Oedipus, with his usual misguided promptness, knocked him from the chariot, and slew all but one of his attendants. Thus, by an unreasonable act of passion, Oedipus fulfilled the first part of his prophetic destiny.

But in the crisis in which he found the city of Thebes, his energy and directness served him well. By the flashing quickness of thought and imagination which, when blinded by some egoistic passion, so often hurried him to wrong conclusions, he guessed the riddle of the Sphinx. Then he married the widowed queen, seized the reins of government, and generously did his best to bring peace and prosperity back to the troubled land. In this way he was raised, by the very qualities that ultimately wrought his ruin, to the height from which he fell. And yet, admirable as these performances were, he displayed in them none of the wisdom with which Aristotle endows his happy man. A thoughtful person, one who acted in accordance with true reason, and not merely with generous impulse, might have put two and two together. Adding the fact that he had killed a man to the Delphic prophecy and the old suspicion concerning his birth, he might have arrived at the truth which would have guided the rest of his life aright. But it never was the habit of Oedipus to do more thinking than seemed necessary to the particular action upon which all the power of his impetuous nature was concentrated. His lack of the "intellectual virtues" of Aristotle is only paralleled by his inability to keep the "mean" in the "moral virtues."

Between his accession to the throne of Thebes and the opening of the drama there intervened a long period of time in which Oedipus had prospered, and, as it seemed to the Chorus, had been quite happy. The play of Sophocles is concerned with the complication of the rash hero's mistakes; this complication, which is suddenly untangled by the words of the old Herdsman, forms the last chapter in the tragic career of Oedipus. In the first scene the land is blasted by a great dearth. Old men, young men, and children have come as suppliants to the king, seeking deliverance from this great evil. Oedipus appears, generous, high-minded, and prompt to act, as ever. When Creon brings the message of Apollo, that the slayer of Laïus must be cast out of the land, he immediately invokes a mighty curse upon the murderer, and we thrill with pity and fear as we see the noble king calling down upon his own head a doom so terrible. His unthinking haste furnishes the first thread in the complication which the dramatist so closely weaves. Teiresias enters. When Oedipus has forced from his unwilling lips the dreadful words, "Thou art the accursed defiler of the land," he forgets everything else in his anger at what he deems a taunt of the old prophet, and entangles a second thread of misunderstanding with the first. Still a third is added a moment later, when he indignantly accuses Creon of bribing Teiresias to speak those words. In his conversation with Jocasta the tendency of Oedipus to jump at conclusions does for one moment show him half the truth. He is possessed with the fear that it was he who killed Laïus, but here again he can think of only one thing at a time, and, again absorbed in a new thought, he forgets his wife's mention of a child of Laïus, forgets the old story concerning his birth, and misses the truth.

Then comes the message from Corinth. After his first joy in learning that his supposed father did not die by his hand, Oedipus loses all remembrance of the oracle concerning his birth, and all fear concerning the death of Laïus, in a new interest and a new fear — the fear that he may be base-born. Eagerly /3/ following up the latest train of thought, he at last comes upon the truth in a form which even he can grasp at once, and, in his agony at that vision, to which for the first time in his life he has now attained, he cries out: "Oh, Oh! All brought to pass — all true! Thou light, may I now look my last upon thee — I who have been found accursed in birth, accursed in wedlock, accursed in the shedding of blood." In a final act of mad energy, he puts out the eyes which could not see, and demands the execution upon himself of the doom which he alone had decreed. In the representation of Sophocles, this is the end of a great-souled man, endowed with all the gifts of nature, but heedless of the true reason in accordance with which the magnanimous man of Aristotle finds his way to perfect virtue or happiness.

Perhaps we are not entirely reconciled to the fate of Oedipus. Perhaps the downfall of a tragic hero never wholly satisfies the individual reader's sense of justice, for the poet, by the necessity of his art, is bound to make the particular embodiment of a universal truth as terrible and as pitiful as he can. Surely this result is attained in the *Oedipus Rex*. Every sympathetic reader will agree with Aristotle that, " even without the aid of the eye, he who hears the tale told will thrill with horror and melt to pity at what takes place." Whatever " fatalism " there may be in the drama — in the oracles, for instance, and in the performance of the prophesied crimes by Oedipus in ignorance of circumstances — directly increases the tragic effect. Aristotle himself mentions crimes committed in ignorance of particulars as deeds which especially arouse pity. The oracles, such a source of trouble to those who muddle their heads with Greek " fatalism," have a threefold function. They have a large share in the dramatic irony for which *Oedipus Rex* is so famous, and which is a powerful instrument for arousing tragic fear. They serve as a stimulus to set the hero's own nature in motion without determining whether the direction of the motion shall be right or wrong. And lastly, they point out in clear and impressive language the course of the story. Shakespeare in *Macbeth* and *Hamlet* introduces less simple and probable forms of the supernatural, for similar purposes. The oracles of Sophocles, like the ghosts and witches of Shakespeare, are but necessary means for attaining an end. The representation of their effect upon the action of the characters is not the end of the drama, and must not be so regarded. They embody the final teaching of the poet as little as the words of particular dramatic characters, in particular circumstances, express the poet's own unbiased thought and feeling.

The central conception of the *Oedipus Rex* is plainly no more fatalistic than the philosophy of Aristotle. If any reader finds the doctrine hard, he may remember that Sophocles himself completed it somewhat as the Christian Church completed Aristotle, and, in the representation of the death of Oedipus at Colonus, crowned the law with grace. Nevertheless, for the understanding not only of Sophocles, but of the great " master of those who know " the laws of life and art, it seems important to recognize the relation be-

tween these two ideal conceptions — the magnanimous man of the *Ethics,* ideal for life, the
tragic hero of the *Poetics,* ideal for death. According to Aristotle, the man who attains perfect happiness in the world is the wise man who
sees in all their aspects the facts or the forces
with which he is dealing, and can balance and
direct his own impulses in accordance with reason. In the *Oedipus Rex* Sophocles had already
shown the reverse. The man who sees but one
side of a matter, and straightway, driven on by
his uncontrolled emotions, acts in accordance
with that imperfect vision, meets a fate most

pitiful and terrible, in accordance with the great
laws which the gods have made.

This philosophy of Aristotle and Sophocles is
clearly expressed in the drama itself. " May destiny still find me," sings the Chorus, " winning
the praise of reverent purity in all words and
deeds sanctioned by those laws of range sublime,
called into life throughout the high, clear heaven,
whose father is Olympus alone; their parent was
no race of mortal men, no, nor shall oblivion
ever lay them to sleep: the god is mighty in
them and grows not old." /4/

from SOPHOCLEAN TRAGEDY
by Cecil Maurice Bowra

*These passages are taken from Chapter 5 of
Bowra's* Sophoclean Tragedy *(Oxford: Clarendon Press, 1945). Bowra's footnotes have been
omitted; and the line numbers of the Fitts-Fitzgerald version of* Oedipus Rex *have been inserted
in brackets following Bowra's quotations from
the play and his line references to the Greek
text. The footnotes which appear here are the
present editor's.*

The view that Oedipus is punished for insolent pride can, however, be stated and defended
in a different way. It can be claimed that he is
punished not for the single act of killing Laius
but for being in general proud and aggressive,
as he certainly shows himself in the scenes with
Teiresias and Creon. This is more persuasive
and brings positive advantages. For in these
scenes Oedipus transgresses the Mean and is almost swept away in a blind frenzy of pride
when he accuses Teiresias of fomenting conspiracy (380 ff.) [ll. 366 ff.] or wishes to kill
Creon on a baseless suspicion (623) [l. 590].
Moreover, the Chorus are distressed by Oedipus
and afraid that he may prove to be a tyrant.
They express their fears in guarded and general
terms, but when they sing

> Insolence it is that breeds
> A tyrant [l. 831]

it is easy to conclude that they have Oedipus in
mind. He may not yet be a full-fledged tyrant,

but he shows the signs. Yet despite this, we may
doubt whether Sophocles intended his Oedipus
to be punished for aggressive insolence. Even
Teiresias does not speak of his coming woes as
if they were a punishment; the Chorus do not
return to their suspicion but form a different
view of Oedipus' fall when it comes; Oedipus
himself, in the horror of his humiliation, does
not think that it is a punishment for pride. . . .
/165/ Proud he may be, but pride is not the direct cause of his fall.

More subtle and more persuasive than any of
these theories is Aristotle's, that Oedipus falls
through a mistake.[1] He does not say that he
means Sophocles' Oedipus, but his admiration
for the play is so great that it is hard not to think
that he does. The question is what he means by
mistake. If he means simply an intellectual mistake, an error of judgement, his own views
would lead to Oedipus' acquittal. For he says
that such mistakes originate not in vice or depravity but in ignorance of fact or circumstance,
are not voluntary, and should be forgiven.[2] Now
it is perfectly true that when Oedipus kills Laius
he makes a mistake of this kind. He acts in ignorance that Laius is his father, and this is the
beginning of his downfall. For it leads to the
plague, the curse, the discovery of the truth, and
Oedipus' blinding of himself. Because of his mistake Oedipus changes from good to bad fortune.

1. *Poetics,* Chapter 13.
2. Aristotle's *Nicomachean Ethics,* III, i–v; V, viii.

It is, however, possible that Aristotle means a different kind of mistake, something more like a fault of character which leads a man to see things wrongly. He does not say this, but it is possible that he meant it. If so, he came very near to the truth. For Oedipus' character is undeniably connected with the form that his downfall takes. But even this is not quite adequate. Neither interpretation of Aristotle's view of a tragic mistake meets all the facts of the play. Whichever we prefer, Aristotle still missed one vitally important element in *King Oedipus*. He says nothing about the part taken by the gods in the rise and fall of Oedipus. His omission /166/ is understandable since he was, apparently, not interested in this aspect of tragedy and did not discuss it in his *Poetics*. But it seriously impairs his view. For though Oedipus' mistake in killing his father leads to other disasters, it is itself foreordained by the gods. The tragic career of Oedipus does not begin with it. His doom is fixed before his birth.

The activity of the gods is an essential part of *King Oedipus*. Oedipus is their victim. They have ordained a life of horror for him, and they see that he gets it. He is even the instrument by which their plans are fulfilled. The prophecy that he will kill his father and marry his mother leaves him no escape. He fulfils it in ignorance of what he is doing, but he must fulfil it. . . . /167/

That Sophocles intended to show the gods at work is seen not only by the part which they take in events but by the dramatic effects which the poet secures by displaying the futility of Jocasta's and Oedipus' scepticism. It is Jocasta's disbelief which leads to Oedipus' discovery that he may be the slayer of Laius (707 ff.) [ll. 667 ff.], his own dismissal of the oracles (971–72) [ll. 926–27] which precedes the revelation of his true origin, his wild hope that he is the son of Luck (1080 ff.) [ll. 1026 ff.] which comes just before the final shattering truth. The play shows the power of the gods at every important turn in its development and leaves no doubt about the poet's theological intention.

King Oedipus shows the humbling of a great and prosperous man by the gods. This humbling is not deserved; it is not a punishment for insolence, nor in the last resort is it due to any fault of judgement or character in the man. The gods display their power because they will. But since they display it, man may draw a salutary lesson. This is kept till the end of the play when the Chorus, or perhaps Oedipus himself, point to the extent of his fall, and comment [*Bowra quotes here the last four lines of the play*]. /175/ . . . Its lesson is that men must be modest in prosperity and remember that at any moment the gods may destroy it. It is a warning not so much against pride as against any confidence or sense of security. To drive this warning home the gods have made an example of Oedipus. From the very beginning he has been chosen to show by his misfortunes the need for modesty in times of success.

Such, reduced to its most abstract and impersonal form, is the theological scheme in *King Oedipus.* . . . it naturally raises questions about the justice of the gods, who treat Oedipus simply as a means to enforce a lesson on others. It is not like this that we expect the gods to act. Sophocles, perhaps, might not have felt our qualms, but he sees the difficulties of his theological scheme and does something to answer possible critics. When the gods humiliate Oedipus they create a situation of great complexity in which much is concerned beside the general main lesson. There is above all the individual problem of Oedipus himself. If they force him to break their own laws, as he does when he kills his father and marries his mother, they should provide means of reconciliation by which he, polluted as he is, can make his peace with them and restore the breach in the divine order which he has made. Sophocles was conscious of this need and took steps to meet it. /176/ The play shows not only the crisis which humbles Oedipus and reveals to him that he is polluted but also the first steps by which he begins to overcome the gulf between himself and the gods, to find again a place in the ordered system of things. In this the gods help him.

This reconciliation is the meaning of Oedipus' action in blinding himself. . . . /177/ . . . when Oedipus blinds himself, he is prompted and guided by a *daimôn*, a divine spirit which rules his actions for him. The word has no exact equivalent in English and is variously translated "fate," "destiny," "god," and "spirit." It has something of all these in it. It is a supernatural power which is inferior to a true god and is closely concerned with an individual man's fortunes. . . . /179/ [*Bowra then cites the passages where the term* daimôn *occurs: these are ll. 788–89, 1137–38, 1211, 1213, 1253, 1265, 1285, and 1458 in the Fitts-Fitzgerald version. He claims (p. 181) the* daimôn *"is a kind of supernatural power, and it is assumed by the Messenger, the Chorus, and Oedipus himself to be at work at least when he blinds himself, and probably also throughout his life." He then says that Sophocles* "makes the *daimôn* an instrument of the gods to carry out their demands," *and continues:*]

Sophocles hints this at first vaguely, when Oedipus realizes that he has killed Laius and breaks out in the terrible words:

O Zeus, what is it thou wilt do to me? [l. 697]

Here he ascribes to Zeus the fate which later he ascribes to a cruel *daimôn*. This by itself carries little weight, but later Oedipus makes the position clearer. In the first moment after his appearance from the palace he claims that Apollo is really responsible for what has happened:

> Apollo! 'Twas Apollo, friends,
> Willed the evil, willed, and brought the agony
>   to pass!
> And yet the hand that struck was mine, mine
>   only, wretched. [ll. 1287–90] /181/

The hand that works the destruction is that of Oedipus, but the power behind the action is Apollo. This does not contradict the part assigned elsewhere to the *daimôn*. The *daimôn* bridges the gulf between Apollo who decides and dictates and the human agent Oedipus who carries out the decision. . . . /182/

Oedipus blinds himself because of his curse. He does it both deliberately and by divine prompting. The Greeks would make no real distinction between the two and would certainly praise /184/ Oedipus for acting as the gods desire and see that the *daimôn's* pressure on him was part of their scheme. As a parricide and incestuous he will exile himself from Thebes which he pollutes and from human society with which he can have no normal relations. To carry out his curse he inflicts a fearful injury on himself. The curse has still to finish its course. Oedipus knows this, makes no attempt to resist it, rather does his best to help it. There is no question of guilt and its punishment, but once pollution has been incurred, once the powers of heav-

en have been invoked with such solemnity, they cannot be countermanded. . . .

The gods have chosen Oedipus for this fate. In so far as he is to be an example to others it is enough that he is a great king. But the lesson that he himself has to learn must be suited to his own nature. The man who is to be taught his own utter insignificance must be endowed with special gifts of character and intellect; for only in such conditions is the lesson worth learning. Such Oedipus undeniably is. . . . But the same characteristics which brought him to success make his downfall more tragic and are almost instruments to it. It is because he is such a superior being, angry when attacked, capable of brief and brilliant action, self-confident and /185/ rapid in decision, that his discovery of the truth takes so tragic a turn. His fated life is his own life. It is his character, his typical actions, that make his mistakes so intelligible and fit so naturally into the god's plan to humble him. . . . /186/

Yet, just because Oedipus is a great king, he is exposed to great perils both from the gods and from himself. Because he is after all a monarch who acknowledges no mortal superior and no law above himself, he is liable to presumption and pride. He illustrates the question which Herodotus makes Otanes ask: " How can monarchy be a well-adjusted thing when it allows a man to do what he likes without being answerable? " [3] All is well with his character so long as he prospers, but when his will is thwarted, his kingly temper verges on the tyrannical. Both with Teiresias and with Creon he steps far beyond the bounds of decency and humanity, blusters, abuses, and threatens. His threats fail. Teiresias departs unharmed, having said the last, most deadly word; Creon is saved by the intervention of Jocasta and shows later that he bears no malice. But the great and good king shows how small is the barrier between royalty and tyranny, between authority and pride. He has lost some of his nobility, forfeited some of our admiration. He has even come nearer to Aristotle's tragic hero who is not pre-eminently virtuous or just. Consequently his sufferings stir compassion but do not awake an intolerable indignation against the gods as /188/ they might if he had shown no human faults. And for him these outbursts of unbridled tem-

3. Herodotus, *The Persian Wars*, III, lxxx.

per add to the horror of his collapse. Because he is furious with Teiresias, he is unable to grasp the seer's message and fails to see that he himself has killed Laius, so that the revelation of the truth is postponed and comes with all the greater effect when it finally breaks on him. . . .

Oedipus' high position has been given to him by the gods, and what the gods have given, they can take away. He is insufficiently aware of this. The Priest modestly says to him:

> Your own wit, touched by some god,
> Men say and think, raised us and gave us life.
> [ll. 41–42]

Oedipus himself admits no such divine help; in his view he answered the Sphinx by his own unprompted intelligence:

> I, the fool,
> Ignorant Oedipus — no birds to teach me —
> Must come, and hit the truth, and stop the song.
> [ll. 382–84] /189/

To the audience this confidence and this power would certainly seem fraught with danger. They would know that anyone so highly placed was liable to fall, and that it was a bad sign in Oedipus to be unconscious of his risks.

Oedipus' royal gifts are a source of danger to him. The same may be said of his intelligence. He solved the riddle of the Sphinx. On his own claim, he did it through his wits (398) [l. 384], but whether the gods helped him or not, he succeeded where others failed. So Sophocles makes him a man of powerful intelligence and shows that it is of the kind to solve problems. Just as he must have answered the Sphinx by a sudden stroke of insight, so now the gift of reaching rapidly the answer to a problem, of asking pertinent questions, of finding his own answers to them, is still with him. His energy in looking for the murderer of Laius, his courageous and unflinching desire to know the truth about himself, belong to his vigorous mental equipment. But by a hideous irony, this time the answers are all wrong. They are based on some kind of evidence; they sound plausible. But they do not touch the truth. . . . /190/

The predominant quality of Sophocles' Oedipus is his high temper, his θυμός. This was an ambiguous quality. On the one side it worked for good and made men active and enduring. So Plato gave it a prominent place in his psychol-

ogy and made it the ally of the reason against the appetites. As the self-assertive principle whose object is honour it is part of the mental equipment of any active man and especially of a king and leader like Oedipus. In his earlier career he has shown it in full measure, and it is no less strong when he sets to work to stop the plague by finding the murderer of Laius. But it had another side. It was not necessarily nor always allied to reason. As Plato saw, it could have a destructive side when it was allied to unreasoning violence. So in Oedipus, his high spirit and temper, admirable when the end is good, are liable to get out of control and to do damage. . . . /192/

Such anger is not kingly but tyrannical, and can do Oedipus no good. Nor is there any justification for it. Neither Teiresias nor Creon is really plotting against Oedipus. He accuses them unjustly because he is angry and finds it hard to abandon his suspicions. His whole behaviour is dominated by his high temper both for better and for worse. It is the clue to his actions, and to his mistakes. In the past it has not harmed him; it has even served him well. But now it turns on him, spoils his character, and adds to his troubles. It has blunted his insight and encouraged what there is of the bully in him. We might apply to him Heraclitus' saying, "It is hard to fight against anger; for whatsoever it wishes, it buys at the cost of the soul." [4] When Oedipus indulges his angry temper, he pays for it with the loss of judgement and decency. But the intellectual aspects of the struggle are more important than the moral. For the play what counts is that Oedipus' tendency to anger prevents him from seeing the truth, even when it is told him, and induces a state of illusion in which he lives until reality is forced upon him. . . . /194/

By modern standards the gods who decide on Oedipus' fate before he is born and then inflict it on him without mercy treat him cruelly. But this is not a view that Sophocles would have held or admitted. He would more probably hold that men cannot judge the gods and might even agree with Heraclitus that "For God all things are beautiful and good and just, but men think some things unjust and others just." For he states emphatically that the gods must be hon-

4. Heraclitus was an early Greek philosopher who flourished about 510 B.C.

oured, and shows that their word must be believed. Nor is it legitimate to argue that their word is sometimes hard to understand. That, too, arises from the ignorance and blindness in which man lives. He can only do his best to understand the gods by what means he possesses, to recognize that his own judgement may be wrong. The gods, who know everything, are right. Nor may man complain of them. He must humble himself before them and admit that he is nothing and that he knows nothing. This is the lesson of *King Oedipus* . . . /209/

The gods humble Oedipus as a lesson to men not to trust in their happiness or their knowledge. The horror of his fate and his fall is foreordained that others may learn from it. But though this plan determines all that happens, the actual events follow a pattern which is tragic and Sophoclean. When Oedipus kills his father and marries his mother the inviolable laws of the gods are broken and the divine order of things sustains a grievous wound. The wound must be healed, the order restored. Before this can be done, the evil that has been, albeit uncon-

sciously, committed, must show its full force. This it does in the growth of Oedipus' illusions when the plague forces a crisis on him. From illusions he moves to dangerous acts. His fits of fury, his moments of scepticism, his certainty that he is right, are the natural products of his state. Such a condition cannot last, and it is broken by the events which follow the death of Polybus. As Oedipus comes to see the truth and to punish himself for his past actions, he makes his peace with the gods. He does what is right, accepts his position, knows the truth. Through resignation and suffering the rightful harmony of things is restored. By divine standards Oedipus at the end of the play is a better man than at the beginning. His humiliation is a lesson both to others and to him. Democritus' words, "the foolish learn modesty in misfortune," [5] may be applied to Oedipus, who has indeed been foolish in his mistakes and illusions and has been /210/ taught modesty through suffering. /211/

5. Democritus (*ca.* 460–361 B.C.) was a Greek philosopher.

---

from UNDERSTANDING DRAMA by Cleanth Brooks and Robert B. Heilman

This passage is taken from the last two sections of the discussion of Oedipus Rex *in Brooks and Heilman's* Understanding Drama *(N.Y.: Henry Holt, 1948). The section headings have been retained, even where the complete section has not been reprinted. The footnotes which appear here are the present editor's.*

5. The problem of Oedipus's guilt

. . . Yet, as we have remarked, the modern reader may remain dissatisfied with the meaning of the play. He tends to ask what Oedipus could have done to avoid the fate which overtakes him and, if he can find no such preventive step indicated, he feels that Oedipus is simply a passive, helpless victim of fate. The modern reader may also share a closely related feeling, that Oedipus is not a "guilty" man — does not deserve his fate. At least one modern classical

scholar has recently put this view forcefully.

These possible objections relate to two very important elements in tragedy. As we have said (pp. 110, 312–13), the protagonist must not be "a virtuous man brought from prosperity to adversity" (see Aristotle's *Poetics* 12, Appendix [1]). The nature of Oedipus's guilt has already been canvassed somewhat. But a final account of it depends upon our disposition of the other objection, that Oedipus is a "passive" character.

The Question of Focus. In the first place it is important to see that Sophocles might have written his play so as to have put the principal focus on some decisive act by which the protagonist causes his own ruin. Ibsen's *Ghosts,* for example, has such a focus. In that play Mrs. Alving, though her husband is a libertine and she feels that she ought to leave him, has yielded to the

1. This is taken from Chapter 13 of the *Poetics.*

pressures of conventional society and, with the best of motives, has gone back to him and borne him a son. As the play opens, the son, now a young man, returns home, and the now widowed mother gradually learns with horror that her hopes for her carefully nurtured son have been wrecked. He has inherited his father's disease and, as the play ends, goes mad before her eyes. He is only a victim, a pathetic figure. The tragedy is Mrs. Alving's. She had chosen with good intentions, but she had chosen unwisely, and she now suffers the consequence of her choice.

One can conceive of Sophocles' play worked out in somewhat the same way, becoming, instead of *Oedipus the King,* a sort of *Jocasta the Queen.* Jocasta, though she knew what the oracle had prophesied, would, in our supposed play, have gone on to bear Laius's child, and then have attempted, with Laius, to try to get around the consequences. She has even been willing to kill the child to forestall the horror of what he may do. She makes her decision — she commits herself to a course of action — which brings her doom upon her. So focused, the play would have an active /580/ protagonist and a decisive act. If it be objected that such a play would, by centering the play on Jocasta, turn Oedipus, like Ibsen's Oswald, into an essentially pathetic, not a tragic, figure, one must certainly agree.

But this play Sophocles chose not to write; instead he preferred to give us the play as it stands, which may seem a play which lacks a specific focus on some decisive act, the well-intentioned but disastrous commitment to a course of action. For though we can argue, if we like, that Oedipus actually performed such an act when he ventured to kill Laius and another such act when he married Jocasta (if he had believed the oracle fully he would have dared kill no man, dared marry no woman), still, these events took place long before the action of the play. They are brought into focus only late in the play. Is *Oedipus the King,* then, a play which lacks emphasis on some decisive act committed by the protagonist, and which presents us, consequently, with what is essentially a passive, suffering protagonist?

The " Action " of the Play. As Sophocles has actually focused the play, the " action " consists in Oedipus's struggle for knowledge — a struggle first for knowledge of the evil that besets the state, but ultimately a struggle for self-knowledge. This knowledge does not overwhelm a passive Oedipus. He has to strive actively for it — against recalcitrant witnesses and against the pleas of well-wishers who try to dissuade him from the quest. The oracle does not simply " announce " that Oedipus is the murderer. Even the specific accusation made by Teiresias as the instrument of the god is qualified by the obvious anger in which it is spoken. The accusation does not convince the Theban elders, for instance; it does not constitute " proof." Oedipus has demanded proof. We must not forget that it is Oedipus, more than any other person in the play, who manages to get together this proof which damns him.

It may be helpful at this point to remind ourselves that whereas in many stories there is a decisive change in the fortunes of the protagonist (he wins his battle or he is killed), still, in many other stories, what " happens " to the protagonist is not some overt change, but an inner one: the protagonist comes to a new knowledge of himself — he comes to understand himself as he did not before. The outer event and the inner event may be intimately connected with each other: in *Oedipus the King,* for example, the intellectual illumination has tremendous repercussions in the field of overt action. Oedipus can no longer reign in Thebes; moreover, he cannot bear any longer to look at the world about him. He puts out his eyes and begs for banishment. But the inner change, even when not connected with a decisive overt action, can be as meaningful as the first, and it can be as " dramatic." To take an example from one of the plays in this book, something of the greatest importance has happened to Lear, even if he should come at the end to be restored to his throne and kingdom. He has gained — and this is also true of Faustus [2] — a kind of knowledge which makes him a different man from the man whom we see at the beginning of the play.

Knowing as Action. Knowing, then, is a form of action. The gaining of /581/ knowledge can be the most important thing which happens to a character, and like other happenings it may either be stumbled upon by the weak and essentially passive character or it may be striven for heroically and tragically. Oedipus strives actively

2. in *Doctor Faustus* (*ca.* 1590), a tragedy by Christopher Marlowe.

for the damning knowledge; he does not bury his head in the sand. It is his glory that he *must* know. But if his striving for knowledge is his glory, it is also his weakness. He is not only confident of his own powers to unriddle what is obscure: he cannot conceive what the implications of full knowledge of any event may be for the human being. Life for the successful Oedipus is rational and has no mysteries that lurk in dark corners. Oedipus cannot comprehend, as indeed few human beings ever can (Faustus, we have seen, is another example), that human eyes may be dazzled and blinded by a *complete* illumination of even those things which seem best known and most familiar.

The speeches and actions of Oedipus in this play represent thoroughly those traits which manifested themselves in his leaving Corinth, his killing of Laius, and his acceptance of Jocasta and the crown — the mixture of nobility, pride, calculation, self-confidence, and impetuosity. We see in action here the man who took these actions years before, and since Oedipus has realized, not evaded, his true nature, we can understand how he came to the decisions that he did; that is, we can see from Oedipus's present conduct that those earlier actions were " in character." But by presenting the Oedipus of years later, Sophocles has been able to focus attention, not so much on the problem of action, as on that of knowledge. That is, Sophocles has chosen for primary emphasis the ironic discrepancy between full knowledge and man's partial knowledge. Oedipus is dramatized for us primarily as thinker rather than as actor, though of course his past actions are necessarily involved.

Like Rosmer in Ibsen's play[3] (or like Lear) Oedipus comes at the end to understand himself — and, again like them, only through the revelation of the superficiality of his former knowledge. We can go further and say that his final understanding is the product not of " success " but of suffering. It is a wisdom that contains and extends beyond mere rationalism, for it involves a deep-seated awareness of the limitations of rationalism.

Poetic Justice. What shall we say then to the reader who feels that Oedipus's punishment does not fit his crime? We may well take the line that Sophocles himself has the Chorus take

[3.] in *Rosmersholm* (1886), a tragedy by Henrik Ibsen.

at the end of the play. The appeal is to the facts. As a matter of fact, do the best-laid plans of mice and men often " gang a-gley," and do men incur penalties from life out of all proportion to their conscious infraction of the laws of life? The question is not: What is desirable or ideal human experience? but, What is general human experience?

Oedipus's punishment can scarcely be made to square with poetic justice — with getting his deserts — but that is just the point of the tragedy: that men do not actually experience poetic justice. Life does not follow the course that men think it will follow or ought to follow. The outcome of *Oedipus the King,* we may say, does not rest upon some thesis that /582/ Sophocles thought ought to be true, but on what Sophocles observed to be the actual state of affairs.

6. The Universality of Oedipus the King

Lest the reader feel that this is too dark and saturnine an account of the human situation, at least as it exists today, one needs only to appeal again to the facts. One need not read this play as a tract for the times of the atom bomb in order to suggest that the play has still something to say to our times — that it deals with a universal problem.

Our own age is one which has taken with the utmost seriousness the Faustian dictum that knowledge is power. We have sought knowledge passionately, and with remarkable success. Part of our motive has been the desire for power, but it would be unfair to deny that there has been a noble side to our motivation. We have been happy to garner even " useless " knowledge as somehow good in itself. We could not, we felt, have too many facts. We could not have too much knowledge. That is still the passionate faith of a great many of us, even at a time when the amount of knowledge which we have gained has become embarrassing to us.

It *has* become embarrassing — this is the testimony of the scientists themselves. And knowledge, as we are coming to see, is not the same thing as wisdom. At the moment when man has come to his fullest knowledge of how to manipulate the world of things — and his fellows, considered as objects of manipulation, considered as things — at just this moment he has come to see how little he knows himself, how nonlogical, how irrational the human mind itself is. To say all this is not to plunge into an obscurantism of despair. (A careful reading of Sophocles will indicate that Sophocles himself has offered no counsel of despair.) But we may actually be in a better position than recent generations have been to appreciate the general critique of rationalism which Sophocles offers us, for we have had the easy myth of automatic progress shaken for us as it was not shaken for them, and we have had a rather naïve faith in rationalism seriously questioned. /583/

from SOPHOCLES: A STUDY OF HEROIC HUMANISM by Cedric H. Whitman

These passages are taken from Whitman's Sophocles: A Study of Heroic Humanism *(Cambridge: Harvard University Press, 1951), Chapter 7, "Irrational Evil: Oedipus Rex." Some of Whitman's footnotes have been omitted, and those which appear here are followed by his name and their original number. All notes not followed by Whitman's name are the present editor's.*

From the prologue alone we can recognize /126/ Oedipus for what he is. Aristotle to the contrary, he is "of superior virtue"; the people regard him nearly as a god for his intelligence, and Oedipus himself recognizes his birthright at once and his responsibility when he accepts the challenge to act in the face of a *daimonion* — a "divine" affliction.

One of the most striking features of Sophoclean dramaturgy is the symbolic appropriateness of the prologue to the drama as a whole. As scene upon scene unfolds, Oedipus adheres, with ever rising intensity, to the heroic moral purpose which he declared in the opening tableau. And as the consequences loom larger and darker, Oedipus is the more confirmed in his consistent loftiness of character. Foreknowledge of the end of the story tends to prejudice the reader's opinion of him, and must have done so even in antiquity. But as Sophocles wrote his text, there is no evidence of moral delinquency in the hero. It is the myth, not the play, which raises such questions as, "Was Oedipus wrong to slay or marry anybody after hearing the prophecy?" Or, "If Laius believed the oracle, why did he have children, and if he did not believe it, why did he bother to expose Oedipus?" It is almost as irrelevant to criticize the play in the light of these questions as it would be to analyze the *Iliad* on the basis of the justice of the Trojan War.

Nevertheless, these questions continually recur. The moralist, seeing a man destroyed, assumes that he somehow deserved destruction, and the fact that Sophocles never directly says so — in fact, never even hints so — ought to have caused greater embarrassment than it has. True, the *Oedipus* does not accuse the gods as explicitly as does the *Trachiniae*. But the whole action, insofar as it is subtler, and the character of the hero, in that it is determined by a more conscious and uncompromising moral fibre, constitute what is perhaps more forceful than even the passionate lines which close the *Trachiniae* [1] — in short, a detailed picture of the irrational and unjustifiable evil inwrought in the texture of life, against which the greatest natural and moral endowments struggle in vain. The lack of any real counterpoise between sin and punishment, such as Aeschylus believed in, has made the play bewildering, but that is exactly Sophocles' purpose. . . . /127/

Oedipus Rex is, by this time, buried under so many layers of critical acumen, that anyone who dares believe in the innocence of Oedipus must answer formidable philologists and prove his mettle. Indeed, to those who consider Oedipus morally guilty of parricide and incest, there is little that can be said, for of course he committed these crimes, however unwittingly. Although Aristotle, who distinguishes carefully

1. Whitman believes that Sophocles wrote the *Trachiniae* about 435 B.C., a few years before *Oedipus Rex*. (He groups them together as "the two middle plays" of Sophocles — see p. 142.) In the final lines of this play Hyllus, the son of Heracles, blames the gods for the death of his father and bitterly attacks them for their cruelty.

between the willful act and the unconscious act,[2] would surely disagree, it might be urged that Oedipus' crimes are more in the religious than the purely legal or moral context, and that therefore, whatever his motivating intention, Oedipus himself is just as "hateful to the gods" — in the eyes, at least, of the ancient chthonian religion, with its blood-for-blood law, defended and exalted by daemonic hosts of Furies, with their attendant spirits, the *Alastores* and *Miastores*. But although this old religious attitude may have still prevailed among most Greeks of the time, it is doubtful how far and how simply Sophocles could have believed in the shadowy /128/ bloodhounds of murder in the middle of the Periclean age of reason. In 458, the Athenian public had witnessed the trial scene of the *Eumenides*,[3] and had seen Orestes acquitted in the final court of appeal; and if Orestes, why not Oedipus? But there was no orthodox creed in these matters. Even if the gods themselves were supposed to hold Oedipus guilty (and apparently they did), Sophocles was free to differ. In fact, it was the office of the tragic poet to hold his own values and to use these, not the plastic figures of the gods, as his moral standard. That perhaps is the crux of the problem: in popular belief the gods were supposed to hate and punish Oedipus for what he actually did; Sophocles, on the contrary, has painted him as a man willfully innocent, passionately honest in motive, and full of heroic arete.[4] And if he did so, he must have thought so, and he could not have concurred with the judgment of the gods.

It is precisely this difference of opinion between the gods and the poet, corresponding as it does to the disproportionate disposal of sin and punishment in the myth, which has made it so hard to adjust the apparent piety of Sophocles to the unmitigated pessimism inherent in the action of the *Oedipus*. To try to reconcile these opposites and draw therefrom a salutory lesson in sophrosyne[5] is likely to lead to self-contradiction.[6] The gods cannot be just, if Oedipus is morally innocent. Yet, as the hero's character stands, this seems to be the case. The implications are so gloomy, and so different from the traditional picture of Sophocles, that it has been proposed that Sophocles must have had some compensating thought in mind, and that the play must be a treatise on either the nothingness of man, the necessity of religion, or sometimes both.

Two other ways out of the dilemma have been suggested: predestination and the hamartia theory.[7] To lift the burden of guilt from Oedipus, however, by saying that his fall was predestined by the gods is to destroy his innocence as well. He becomes a cipher, and falls back into the theory of the nothingness of man. Besides, there is no evidence that such extreme fatalism ever existed among the Greeks until Stoic times. The subtle interplay of divine and human character in the Homeric poems cannot be summed up as predestination; for throughout all classical Greek literature possession by a daimon indicates, as in the case of the Atlas Metope,[8] not the /129/ annihilation but the illumination of individuality and moral responsibility.

On the other hand, the theory of the tragic

---

2. in his *Nicomachean Ethics*, III, i–v; V, viii.

3. the third play in Aeschylus' trilogy, the *Oresteia*. In the first play (*Agamemnon*), Agamemnon is murdered by his wife Clytemnestra and her lover Aegisthus. In the second play (*The Choephori*), Agamemnon's children, Orestes and Electra, avenge his death by killing their mother and Aegisthus. In the final play Orestes is acquitted of the crime of matricide, and the Furies (deities of retribution) who have been pursuing him are pacified.

4. Whitman sees *arete* as an almost superhuman quality, an inner impulse toward greatness, which makes a man a hero and drives him to expend himself in order to realize his internal "law." As the subtitle of his book indicates, Whitman regards this as a basic concern of Sophoclean tragedy.

5. *Sophrosyne* means temperance or self-restraint, a quality which Whitman sees as opposed to, and inferior to, *arete* in Sophocles' moral scheme.

6. For instance, compare some of Bowra's conclusions: Oedipus is morally and legally innocent, since he acted in ignorance (*Soph. Trag.*, p. 168); he is capable of a frenzy of pride (p. 165), which, however, has nothing to do with his fall (p. 175), except that it is the instrument by which the gods, who have predestined his fall, destroy him (pp. 192 ff., 209); at the same time, he is the victim of his own curse, which was an act of free will (pp. 172 ff.); he is also guilty of living in a "private universe" out of which the real "common universe" of the gods rouses him (p. 209). Bowra verges on the puzzling theory advanced long ago by Sudhaus, *König Oedipus' Schuld*, pp. 12 ff., that Oedipus was guilty of hybris, but that hybris had nothing to do with his fall. [Whitman's footnote 13. *Hybris* means overweening pride or arrogance. Ed.]

7. *Hamartia* is the term in Aristotle's formula for the best kind of tragic hero (*Poetics* xiii) which Bywater translates as "error of judgment," and which is often translated as "tragic flaw." In the second chapter of his book Whitman argued that Aristotle and later critics have illegitimately imposed the hamartia theory upon Sophocles' tragedies, "in spite of the fact that the steady search for hamartiae has all but taken the life out of Sophocles' vital works, and in spite of the difficulty that no hamartia has ever yet been found to fit the facts" (p. 36).

8. part of a sculptured frieze in the temple of Zeus at Olympia, where, Whitman pointed out earlier, "Heracles strains every muscle to uphold the sky, while Athena, the image of divine repose, with one graceful and relaxed arm makes the miracle possible" (p. 61).

flaw, it is usually taken for granted, seems especially applicable to this play. Yet, whenever it is applied, the familiar difficulties appear: one finds either too much or too little wrong with Oedipus. If he is wrong to have killed or married anybody, then his "error" or "failing" is hardly a trifling one, considering whom he killed and married; he becomes a considerable sinner. But if his only real failing is a hot temper, which no one could possibly call criminal, the degree of calamity to which it leads is as repellent as if Oedipus were entirely innocent. Either way, there is little moral satisfaction.

As was stated earlier, Oedipus was proverbial for sagacity and misfortune — for a fatal disequilibrium between inner gifts and outer circumstance. The effort to explain the latter by means of a tragic flaw has even led some critics to deny the sagacity of Oedipus. It has been said, for instance, that a god may have helped solve the riddle of the Sphinx and that if so Oedipus was not so clever as he thought.[9] But to a Greek, to say that a god helped him was only a way of saying that he was superhumanly wise; and that is exactly what the prologue symbolizes. Similarly, there seem to be no grounds for saying that, in dealing with the question of Laius' murder, Oedipus gets all the wrong answers.[10] To his sorrow, Oedipus gets all the right answers, and cannot be deterred from seeking them.

Yet his dominating characteristic is supposed to be a fiery spirit which corrupts his mind and destroys him.[11] Indeed, the character of Oedipus is complex, highly so; it involves extremes of gentleness or ferocity typical of heroic ages. Yet the fierce intensity of Oedipus must not be mistaken for mere rash violence. In the scene with Teiresias, the blind man of insight enters the stage at the king's summons and declares under pressure that Oedipus himself is guilty of Laius' blood. Oedipus instantly suspects a plot between the prophet and Creon to overthrow his rule, and the wrathful accusations which follow are incisive and violent.

Now in the *Antigone* it was observed that Creon's hasty suspicion of corruption was symptomatic of a tyrant. Oedipus too is a *tyrannos,* and the heat of his anger and his dire threats

may do him little credit. But he is not therefore mentally corrupt. Why should he believe this /*130*/ preposterous statement about himself? Teiresias offered no proof for what he said, but based it simply upon his prophetic art, which is not sufficient in this case to convince even the naïve chorus. The suspicion which rises in Oedipus, though wrong, is in no sense unnatural. The state was suffering from a curse, a religious pollution, which provided adequate opportunity for disorder and revolution. If Creon had wished to assume the controls, he could have chosen no better time, and no better instrument than Teiresias to break the reputation of Oedipus, whose power was not hereditary but rested on his arete. Destroy his glory, and his rule is destroyed. No better conspiracy could have been formed; even the reluctance of Teiresias to speak could be interpreted as a conducive subtlety. From the king's standpoint, since he had as yet seen no real evidence for connecting himself with the crime, it was clearly a case of collusion.

Granted, however, that easy access of suspicion is in the character of the tyrant, Oedipus shows no other tyrannical features, as Creon does in the *Antigone.* He can be wonderfully gentle, and the people are devoted to him. His deep respect for Jocasta is completely untyrannical. He never once, as Creon does when pressed, identifies the state with himself but, quite the opposite, pledges himself as a responsible and god-fearing ruler to its aid. One of the proofs of the skillful dramatist is the ability to show the tension between the habitual behavior of a character and the unexpected traits which he betrays under the strain of the dramatic moment. Although Sophocles conceives Oedipus throughout as capable of considerable ferocity, the extreme outbursts at Teiresias and Creon are exceptions to his usual behavior. No one in the play ever generalizes about the king's dangerous temper. If the suspicion which causes these outbursts is a shade tyrannical, it is even more in keeping with clearheadedness and shrewdness. . . . /*131*/

The famous hamartia in actuality is a part of Oedipus' central virtue, as Ajax' pride and Antigone's stubbornness are parts of their virtue. These are not defects of their qualities, but evidence of their qualities, and the way in which they differ from other men. The very fact that they are different, and are meant to be, necessi-

9. Bowra, p. 190. [Whitman's footnote 21]
10. *ibid.* [Whitman's footnote 22]
11. Cf. *ibid.*, p. 192, on the subject of Oedipus' θυμός. [Whitman's footnote 23]

tates a certain degree of misunderstanding. They will not always ingratiate themselves as polite society would have them do. The hero is always a little difficult to live with. If a man is a law unto himself, society will probably conclude that he has no law. And that is sometimes true. But it is also true that the usual standard of man in general is not primarily law but living; and if the hero cares nothing for the rules of living, he is never able to make his inner law comprehensible to those who do. . . . /132/

The quest for knowledge is only tangential to the tragic action of the *Trachiniae*, but in the figure of Oedipus, the man of supreme insight, or *gnome*, the quest for knowledge is itself the tragic action. Hence the wonderful unity of the *Oedipus*. Knowledge about the situation becomes, in time, the hero's knowledge about himself, and, by implication, man's knowledge of himself. For Oedipus is Everyman; but unlike his medieval counterpart Oedipus remains an individual. But every man is an individual, a point which the Middle Ages forgot; to Sophocles man was heroic man, and the hero is above all an /138/ individual. In the figure of Oedipus we see once more that exquisite balance between the general and the particular, the norm and the variant, which lies behind so much Greek art, whether it be the Homeric epics, or fifth-century sculpture, or the formal, but stoutly independent little men of the vase painter Cleitias. As the scenes of *Oedipus* unfold, the hero also becomes aware that he is really in quest of himself and that the quest is dangerous. But then he is only the more confirmed in it. The blaze of fury with which he repulses the accusation of Teiresias is no more intense than the terrible determination with which he pursues the truth after Jocasta mentions the three ways, and he realizes he may be guilty. It was perfectly possible for him to abandon the search then and there, by seizing on the fact that Laius was supposed to have been murdered by a group of robbers. The only eyewitness had said so, and " he said so in public, so he cannot take it back," as Jocasta points out. Oedipus had every right, it may be supposed, to take Jocasta's word for it, and be safe. But the honesty of Oedipus is heroic, and the hero's law is his arete and his place in history (*kleos*). How could he, the great solver of riddles, abandon the greatest riddle, or trust to any hearsay? He was not instructed in the case of the Sphinx, and he will not be now. He must find out himself, and so he chooses action again, though rather grimly, and insists that this eyewitness be sent for.

The attainment of true self-knowledge may be the most difficult and lonely of all forms of heroism. Certainly the *Oedipus Rex* contains the bitterest findings in all Sophocles' search for the meaning of humanity. . . . /139/

But what really functions is the mind of man, and its success reveals its failure. The failure has been emphasized, in terms of human nothingness, the folly of human wisdom, the gap between man and the gods, the emptiness of human good fortune. But these facts were all well known before Sophocles. Rather the essential interest lies in the strength of Oedipus, the keenness of human wisdom which can find out its own secret, the function of a divine necessity within man which makes a standard of its own and holds the standard to be worth more than empty good fortune. The darkness and discouragement of the play, on the other hand, come from the bitterness of the truth itself, and the fact that the arete of Oedipus brings him no praise for the victory over his own mystery and no reward for his courage and intellectual integrity. The gods within man are at work, but such is the circumstance of man's being that they bring him no glory.

The action of the play itself, therefore, is motivated by the free will of the hero, which culminates in the act of self-blinding. Bowra tries to show that it is his daimon which drives him to this deed, in order to fulfill the will of the gods; [12] but there is no will of the gods, so far as Oedipus is concerned, except insofar as his own will possesses a divine force. The Olympians have not willed his fall; they have foretold it. To say that the gods are responsible, as Oedipus does,[13] means at most that they permit life to be as it turns out to be. The gods in the *Trachiniae* and *Oedipus* seem little more than the animated power of circumstance and symbols of the fatal nexus of limitations within which man acts and suffers. When Oedipus cries, " Apollo has accomplished these evils," he is referring to the whole concatenation of events, including the oracle that symbolizes his total fate. The inelucta-

12. *Soph. Trag.*, pp. 177–85. [Whitman's footnote 73]
13. *Oed. Rex*, 1329 f. [Whitman's footnote 74; ll. 1287–89 in the Fitts-Fitzgerald version]

ble element is not a mysterious, far-off, causal Fate, /141/ or the will of Apollo, but life itself. Within the predestined necessity of living in this world, Oedipus has acted with a free will: " My own hand struck the blow," and he gives his own reasons.[14] He still has reasons, and he is free to treat himself as he will.

Oedipus is crushed by what he learns, yet his learning is a kind of victory — a Pyrrhic one, of course, in which the victor suffers most. But in the moral sphere, a Pyrrhic victory is surely the greatest. Oedipus hoped the answer would be more cheerful, as Ajax hoped to win the arms. But ultimately Ajax strove to keep his honor unstained, at any price; with equal fervor Oedipus strove for clear sight. And in the end he has it; Ajax cries, " darkness my light " — and Oedipus says to his eyes, " in dark hereafter . . . see." For both a veil has fallen. It is hard to say why Oedipus blinds himself, but the answer is not self-punishment. As Ajax seeks to manifest his true self by death, Oedipus seeks to know his true self by shutting out the deceptions of the outer world, which he has completely seen through. He is still seeking knowledge, as the dying Ajax sought honor. He would even stuff up his ears that he might contemplate the more relentlessly the evil truth he has found. If his confidence about learning was overweening, he certainly does not repent, but rather, like Don

14. *Oed. Rex*, 1331 ff. [Whitman's footnote 75; ll. 1290 ff. in the Fitts-Fitzgerald version]

Giovanni,[15] he goes to hell affirming his life principle. He swore to know himself and in the end he stands by that knowledge.

The kind of tragedy with which we have been dealing in the two middle plays must, if viewed squarely, give the death blow to the time-honored classicist conception of the simple, pious Sophocles. No amount of preconception can drive these two gloomy pieces into a shape consistent with a religious attitude of faithful trust in the justice of the gods. The chorus maintains its ground-bass of casuistical, popular morality, but the active and suffering souls play tragic variations upon it; and insofar as the gods appear or are mentioned at all, they contrive evil. But the gods as personages are not in the plays; they do nothing that life could not do. Whatever divinity meant to Sophocles, it was not summed up in the public religion of Athens; nor does the disillusion and sorrow of these two plays center around a fear that Zeus, Athena, or Apollo may not be perfectly just and well-disposed toward man. The gods — witness Athena in the *Ajax* — could be for Sophocles bleak symbols indeed. The fear is rather that human /142/ excellence, which has its own divinity, may not be sufficient to assert itself in the face of the irrational evil which descends without plan or justice, and whence no one knows. /143/

15. in Mozart's opera of that name.

from THE QUINTESSENCE OF IBSENISM
by George Bernard Shaw

The Quintessence of Ibsenism *grew out of a lecture which Shaw delivered in London to the Fabian Society (a socialist club) on July 18, 1890, and was published in 1891, shortly after the first production of* Ghosts *in England. A revised and enlarged second edition was published in 1913, with the phrase* Now Completed to the Death of Ibsen *added to the title; and a third edition (unchanged except for a new preface by Shaw) came out in 1922. The following passages are taken from the Dramabook reprint of the third edition (N.Y.: Hill & Wang, 1957). The foot-*

notes which appear here are the present editor's.

These passages will be more meaningful to the reader if he understands their place in the general plan of Shaw's book. In his first three sections (" The Two Pioneers," " Ideals and Idealists," " The Womanly Woman ") Shaw develops his central thesis, that Ibsen is a great " moral teacher " and " social pioneer " because he champions human freedom by attacking the vicious " tyranny of idealism," particularly the conventional " ideal of womanliness " which prescribes that a woman must sacrifice her own individuality and happiness by submitting to society's conception of her " duty " to her husband and children. Shaw then proceeds to demonstrate this thesis by examining Ibsen's plays, stating at the outset that he will avoid being " swept into an eddy of mere literary criticism, a matter altogether beside the purpose of this book, which is to distil the quintessence of Ibsen's message to his age " (pp. 59–60). He takes the plays up chronologically (beginning with Brand), *in three sections which he believes mark the stages of Ibsen's development: " The Autobiographical Anti-Idealist Extravaganzas," 1866–1873; " The Objective Anti-Idealist Plays," 1877–1890 (the beginning of this section is included here, as is most of the discussion of* Ghosts)*; and " The Four Last Plays," 1892– 1900. This is followed by four concluding sections: " The Lesson of the Plays," " What Is the New Element in the Norwegian School? " " The Technical Novelty in Ibsen's Plays " (portions of this are reprinted here), and " Needed: An Ibsen Theatre."*

The Objective Anti-Idealist Plays

Ibsen had now written three immense dramas, all dealing with the effect of idealism on individual egotists of exceptional imaginative excitability.[1] This he was able to do whilst his intellectual consciousness of his theme was yet incomplete, by simply portraying sides of himself. . . . having at last completed his intellectual analysis of idealism, he could now construct methodical illustrations of its social working, instead of, as before, blindly projecting imaginary personal experiences which he himself had not yet succeeded in interpreting. Further, now that he understood the matter, he could /79/ see plainly the effect of idealism as a social force on people quite unlike himself: that is to say, on everyday people in everyday life: on shipbuilders, bank managers, parsons, and doctors, as well as on saints, romantic adventurers, and emperors.

With his eyes thus opened, instances of the mischief of idealism crowded upon him so rapidly that he began deliberately to inculcate their lesson by writing realistic prose plays of modern life, abandoning all production of art for art's

sake. His skill as a playwright and his genius as an artist were thenceforth used only to secure attention and effectiveness for his detailed attack on idealism. No more verse, no more tragedy for the sake of tears or comedy for the sake of laughter, no more seeking to produce specimens of art forms in order that literary critics might fill the public belly with the east wind. The critics, it is true, soon declared that he had ceased to be an artist; but he, having something else to do with his talent than to fulfil critics' definitions, took no notice of them, not thinking their ideal sufficiently important to write a play about. . . . /80/

In his next play, Ibsen returned to the charge with such an uncompromising and outspoken attack on marriage as a useless sacrifice of human beings to an /86/ ideal, that his meaning was obscured by its very obviousness. *Ghosts*, as it is called, is the story of a woman who has faithfully acted as a model wife and mother, sacrificing herself at every point with selfless thoroughness. Her husband is a man with a huge capacity and appetite for sensuous enjoyment. Society, prescribing ideal duties and not enjoyment for him, drives him to enjoy himself in underhand and illicit ways. When he marries his model wife, her devotion to duty only makes life harder for him; and he at last takes refuge in the caresses of an undutiful but pleasure-loving housemaid, and leaves his wife to satisfy her conscience by managing his business affairs whilst he satisfies his cravings as best he can by reading novels, drinking, and flirting, as aforesaid, with the servants. At this point even those who are most indignant with Nora Helmer for walking out of the doll's house[2] must admit that Mrs. Alving would be justified in walking out of *her* house. But Ibsen is determined to show you what comes of the scrupulous line of conduct you were so angry with Nora for not pursuing. Mrs. Alving feels that her place is by her husband for better for worse, and by her child. Now the ideal of wifely and womanly duty which demands this from her also demands that she shall regard herself as an outraged wife, and her husband as a scoundrel. And the family

---

1. discussed in the preceding section ("The Autobiographical Anti-Idealist Extravaganzas"): *Brand* (1866), *Peer Gynt* (1867), *Emperor and Galilean* (1873).

2. *A Doll's House* (1879) was the play Ibsen wrote just before *Ghosts*. In the final act Nora walks out on her husband, Torvald Helmer, and their children, because, as she says, she is no longer willing to remain a submissive and helpless "doll-wife," and wants to "learn to face reality" and to "become a real person."

ideal calls upon her to suffer in silence lest she shatter her innocent son's faith in the purity of home life by letting him know the disreputable truth about his father. It is her duty to conceal that truth from the world and from him. In this she falters for one moment only. Her marriage has not been a love match: she has, in pursuance of her duty as a daughter, contracted it for the sake of her family, although her heart inclined to a highly respectable clergyman, a professor of her own idealism, named Manders. In the humiliation of her first discovery of her husband's infidelity, she leaves the house and takes refuge with Manders; /87/ but he at once leads her back to the path of duty, from which she does not again swerve. With the utmost devotion she now carries out an elaborate scheme of lying and imposture. She so manages her husband's affairs and so shields his good name that everybody believes him to be a public-spirited citizen of the strictest conformity to current ideals of respectability and family life. She sits up of nights listening to his lewd and silly conversation, and even drinking with him, to keep him from going into the streets and being detected by the neighbors in what she considers his vices. She provides for the servant he has seduced, and brings up his illegitimate daughter as a maid in her own household. And, as a crowning sacrifice, she sends her son away to Paris to be educated there, knowing that if he stays at home the shattering of his ideals must come sooner or later.

Her work is crowned with success. She gains the esteem of her old love the clergyman, who is never tired of holding up her household as a beautiful realization of the Christian ideal of marriage. Her own martyrdom is brought to an end at last by the death of her husband in the odor of a most sanctified reputation, leaving her free to recall her son from Paris and enjoy his society, and his love and gratitude, in the flower of his early manhood.

But when her son comes home, the facts refuse as obstinately as ever to correspond to her ideals. Oswald has inherited his father's love of enjoyment; and when, in dull rainy weather, he returns from Paris to the solemn strictly ordered house where virtue and duty have had their temple for so many years, his mother sees him show the unmistakable signs of boredom with which she is so miserably familiar from of old; then

sit after dinning killing time over the bottle; and finally — the climax of anguish — begin to flirt with the maid who, as his mother alone knows, is his own father's daughter. But there is this worldwide difference in /88/ her insight to the cases of the father and the son. She did not love the father: she loves the son with the intensity of a heart-starved woman who has nothing else left to love. Instead of recoiling from him with pious disgust and Pharisaical consciousness of moral superiority, she sees at once that he has a right to be happy in his own way, and that she has no right to force him to be dutiful and wretched in hers. She sees, too, her injustice to the unfortunate father, and the cowardice of the monstrous fabric of lies and false appearances she has wasted her life in manufacturing. She resolves that the son's life shall not be sacrificed to ideals which are to him joyless and unnatural. But she finds that the work of the ideals is not to be undone quite so easily. In driving the father to steal his pleasures in secrecy and squalor, they had brought upon him the diseases bred by such conditions; and her son now tells her that those diseases have left their mark on him, and that he carries poison in his pocket against the time, foretold to him by a Parisian surgeon, when general paralysis of the insane may destroy his faculties. In desperation she undertakes to rescue him from this horrible apprehension by making his life happy. The house shall be made as bright as Paris for him: he shall have as much champagne as he wishes until he is no longer driven to that dangerous resource by the dulness of his life with her: if he loves the girl he shall marry her if she were fifty times his half-sister. But the half-sister, on learning the state of his health, leaves the house; for she, too, is her father's daughter, and is not going to sacrifice her life in devotion to an invalid. When the mother and son are left alone in their dreary home, with the rain still falling outside, all she can do for him is to promise that if his doom overtakes him before he can poison himself, she will make a final sacrifice of her natural feelings by performing that dreadful duty, the first of all her duties that has any real basis. Then the weather clears up at /89/ last; and the sun, which the young man has so longed to see, appears. He asks her to give it to him to play with; and a glance at him shows her that the ideals have claimed their victim, and that the time has come for her to save him from a real horror by sending him from her out of the world, just as she saved him from an imaginary one years before by sending him out of Norway.

The last scene of *Ghosts* is so appallingly tragic that the emotions it excites prevent the meaning of the play from being seized and discussed like that of *A Doll's House*. In England nobody, as far as I know, seems to have perceived that *Ghosts* is to *A Doll's House* what the late Sir Walter Besant [3] intended his own sequel to that play to be. Besant attempted to show what might come of Nora's repudiation of that idealism of which he was one of the most popular professors. But the effect made on Besant by *A Doll's House* was very faint compared to that produced on the English critics by the first performance of *Ghosts* in this country. In the earlier part of this essay I have shown that since Mrs. Alving's early conceptions of duty are as valid to ordinary critics as to Pastor /90/ Manders, who must appear to them as an admirable man, endowed with Helmer's good sense without Helmer's selfishness, a pretty general disapproval of the moral of the play was inevitable. Fortunately, the newspaper press went to such bedlamite lengths on this occasion that Mr. William Archer, the well-known dramatic critic and translator of Ibsen, was able to put the whole body of hostile criticism out of court by simply quoting its excesses in an article entitled "Ghosts and Gibberings," which appeared in *The Pall Mall Gazette* of the 8th of April 1891. Mr. Archer's extracts, which he offers as a nucleus for a Dictionary of Abuse modelled upon the Wagner *Schimpf-Lexicon*,[4] are worth reprinting here as samples of contemporary idealist criticism of the drama.[5]

"Ibsen's positively abominable play entitled *Ghosts* . . . This disgusting representation . . . Reprobation due to such as aim at infecting the modern theatre with poison after desperately inoculating themselves and others . . . An open drain; a loathsome sore unbandaged; a dirty act done publicly . . . *** Ibsen's melancholy and malodorous world . . . Absolutely loathsome and fetid . . . Gross, almost putrid indecorum . . . Literary carrion. . . Crapulous stuff . . . Novel and perilous nuisance." *Daily Telegraph [leading article].* "This mass of vulgarity, egotism, coarseness, and absurdity." *Daily Telegraph [criticism].* "Unutterably offensive . . . *** Abominable piece . . . Scandalous." *Standard.* "Naked loathsomeness . . . Most dismal and repulsive production." *Daily News.* "Revoltingly suggestive and blasphemous /91/ . . . Characters either contradictory in themselves, uninteresting or abhorrent." *Daily Chronicle.* "A repulsive and degrading work." *Queen.* "Morbid, unhealthy, unwholesome and disgusting story . . . A piece to bring the stage into disrepute and dishonour with every right-thinking man and woman." *Lloyd's.* "Merely dull dirt long drawn out." *Hawk.* "Morbid horrors of the hideous tale . . . Ponderous dulness of the didactic talk . . . If any repetition of this outrage be attempted, the authorities will doubtless wake from their lethargy." *Sporting and Dramatic News.* "Just a wicked nightmare." *The Gentlewoman.* "Lugubrious diagnosis of sordid impropriety . . . Characters are prigs, pedants, and profligates . . . Morbid caricatures . . . *** It is no more of a play than an average Gaiety burlesque." *Black and White.* "Most loathsome of all Ibsen's plays . . . Garbage and offal." *Truth.* "Ibsen's putrid play called *Ghosts* . . . So loathsome an enterprise." *Academy.* "As foul and filthy a concoction as has ever been allowed to disgrace the boards of an English theatre . . . Dull and disgusting . . . Nastiness and malodorousness laid on thickly as with a trowel." *Era.* . . . /92/

The Technical Novelty in Ibsen's Plays

It is a striking and melancholy example of the preoccupation of critics with phrases and formulas to which they have given life by taking them into the tissue of their own living minds, and which therefore seem and feel vital and important to them whilst they are to everybody else the deadest and dreariest rubbish (this is the great secret of academic dryasdust), that to this day they remain blind to a new technical factor in the art of popular stage-play making which

---

3. an English novelist and literary figure (1836–1901). His sequel, published in 1890, is designed to show how Nora's desertion ultimately results in the destruction of her husband and their daughter.

4. (*German*) dictionary of insult or abuse. Wilhelm Tappert, a music scholar and great admirer of Wagner, published a collection of bitter anti-Wagner reviews under the title *Ein Wagner-Lexikon* (Leipzig, 1877), and an enlarged second edition entitled *Richard Wagner im Spiegel der Kritik* (*Richard Wagner As Viewed in Criticism*) (Leipzig, 1903).

5. The ellipses in this quotation are Shaw's; the asterisks indicate editorial cuts.

every considerable playwright has been thrusting under their noses night after night for a whole generation. This technical factor in the play is the discussion. Formerly you had in what was called a well made play an exposition in the first act, a situation in the second, and unravelling in the third. Now you have exposition, situation, and discussion; and the discussion is the test of the playwright. The critics protest in vain. They declare that discussions are not dramatic, and that art should not be didactic. Neither the playwrights nor the public take the smallest notice of them. The discussion conquered Europe in Ibsen's *Doll's House;* and now the serious playwright recognizes in the discussion not only the main test of his highest powers, but also the real centre of his play's interest. . . . /171/

In the new plays, the drama arises through a conflict of unsettled ideals rather than through vulgar attachments, rapacities, generosities, resentments, ambitions, misunderstandings, oddities and so forth as to which no moral question is raised. The conflict is not between clear right and wrong: the villain is as conscientious as the hero, if not more so: in fact, the question which makes the play interesting (when it *is* interesting) is which is the villain and which the hero. Or, to put it another way, there are no villains and no heroes. This strikes the critics mainly as a departure from dramatic art; but it is really the inevitable return to nature which ends all the merely technical fashions. Now the natural is mainly the everyday; and its climaxes must be, if not everyday, at least everylife, if they are to have any importance for the spectator. Crimes, fights, big legacies, /176/ fires, shipwrecks, battles, and thunderbolts are mistakes in a play, even when they can be effectively simulated. No doubt they may acquire dramatic interest by putting a character through the test of an emergency; but the test is likely to be too obviously theatrical, because, as the playwright cannot in the nature of things have much experience of such catastrophes, he is forced to substitute a set of conventions or conjectures for the feelings they really produce.

In short, pure accidents are not dramatic: they are only anecdotic. They may be sensational, impressive, provocative, ruinous, curious, or a dozen other things; but they have no specifically dramatic interest. There is no drama in being knocked down or run over. The catastrophe in *Hamlet* would not be in the least dramatic had Polonius fallen downstairs and broken his neck, Claudius succumbed to delirium tremens, Hamlet forgotten to breathe in the intensity of his philosophic speculation, Ophelia died of Danish measles, Laertes been shot by the palace sentry, and Rosencrantz and Guildenstern drowned in the North Sea. Even as it is, the Queen, who poisons herself by accident, has an air of being polished off to get her out of the way: her death is the one dramatic failure of the piece. Bushels of good paper have been inked in vain by writers who imagined they could produce a tragedy by killing everyone in the last act accidentally. As a matter of fact no accident, however sanguinary, can produce a moment of real drama, though a difference of opinion between husband and wife as to living in town or country might be the beginning of an appalling tragedy or a capital comedy.

It may be said that everything is an accident: that Othello's character is an accident, Iago's character another accident, and the fact that they happened to come together in the Venetian service an even more accidental accident. Also that Torvald Helmer might just as likely have married Mrs. Nickleby [6] as Nora. Granting /177/ this trifling for what it is worth, the fact remains that marriage is no more an accident than birth or death: that is, it is expected to happen to everybody. And if every man has a good deal of Torvald Helmer in him, and every woman a good deal of Nora, neither their characters nor their meeting and marrying are accidents. *Othello,* though entertaining, pitiful, and resonant with the thrills a master of language can produce by mere artistic sonority, is certainly much more accidental than *A Doll's House;* but it is correspondingly less important and interesting to us. It has been kept alive, not by its manufactured misunderstandings and stolen handkerchiefs and the like, nor even by its orchestral verse, but by its exhibition and discussion of human nature, marriage, and jealousy; and it would be a prodigiously better play if it were a serious discussion of the highly interesting problem of how a simple Moorish soldier would get on with a "supersubtle" Venetian lady of fash-

6. the hero's mother in Charles Dickens' novel, *Nicholas Nickleby* (1838–1839), a woman whose character is in many respects almost the opposite of Nora's.

ion if he married her. As it is, the play turns on a mistake; and though a mistake can produce a murder, which is the vulgar substitute for a tragedy, it cannot produce a real tragedy in the modern sense. Reflective people are not more interested in the Chamber of Horrors than in their own homes, nor in murderers, victims, and villains than in themselves; and the moment a man has acquired sufficient reflective power to cease gaping at waxworks, he is on his way to losing interest in Othello, Desdemona, and Iago exactly to the extent to which they become interesting to the police. Cassio's weakness for drink comes much nearer home to most of us than Othello's strangling and throat cutting, or Iago's theatrical confidence trick. . . . /178/

The drama was born of old from the union of two desires: the desire to have a dance and the desire to hear a story. The dance became a rant: the story became a situation. When Ibsen began to make plays, the art of the dramatist had shrunk into the art of contriving a situation. And it was held that the stranger the situation, the better the play. Ibsen saw that, on the contrary, the more familiar the situation, the more interesting the play. Shakespear had put ourselves on the stage but not our situations. Our uncles seldom murder our fathers, and cannot legally marry our mothers; we do not meet witches; our kings are not as a rule stabbed and succeeded by their stabbers; and when we raise money by bills we do not promise to pay pounds of our flesh. Ibsen supplies the want left by Shakespear. He gives us not only ourselves, but ourselves in our own situations. The things that happen to his stage figures are things that happen to us. One consequence is that his plays are much more important to us than Shakespear's. Another is that they are capable both of hurting us cruelly and of filling us with excited hopes of escape from idealistic tyrannies, and with visions of intenser life in the future.

Changes in technique follow inevitably from these changes in the subject matter of the play. When a dramatic poet can give you hopes and visions, such old maxims as that stage-craft is the art of preparation become boyish, and may be left to those unfortunate playwrights who, being unable to make anything really interesting happen on the stage, have to acquire the art of continually persuading the audience that it is going to happen presently. When he can stab

people to the heart by showing them the meanness or cruelty of something they did yesterday and intend to do tomorrow, all the old tricks to catch and hold their attention /182/ become the silliest of superfluities. The play called *The Murder of Gonzago,* which Hamlet makes the players act before his uncle, is artlessly constructed; but it produces a greater effect on Claudius than the *Oedipus* of Sophocles, because it is about himself. The writer who practises the art of Ibsen therefore discards all the old tricks of preparation, catastrophe, *dénouement,* and so forth without thinking about it, just as a modern rifleman never dreams of providing himself with powder horns, percussion caps, and wads: indeed he does not know the use of them. Ibsen substituted a terrible art of sharpshooting at the audience, trapping them, fencing with them, aiming always at the sorest spot in their consciences. Never mislead an audience, was an old rule. But the new school will trick the spectator into forming a meanly false judgment, and then convict him of it in the next act, often to his grievous mortification. When you despise something you ought to take off your hat to, or admire and imitate something you ought to loathe, you cannot resist the dramatist who knows how to touch these morbid spots in you and make you see that they are morbid. The dramatist knows that as long as he is teaching and saving his audience, he is as sure of their strained attention as a dentist is, or the Angel of the Annunciation. And though he may use all the magic of art to make you forget the pain he causes you or to enhance the joy of the hope and courage he awakens, he is never occupied in the old work of manufacturing interest and expectation with materials that have neither novelty, significance, nor relevance to the experience or prospects of the spectators.

Hence a cry has arisen that the post-Ibsen play is not a play, and that its technique, not being the technique described by Aristotle, is not a technique at all. I will not enlarge on this: the fun poked at my friend Mr. A. B. Walkley in the prologue of *Fanny's First Play* [7] need not be

7. Alfred Bingham Walkley was dramatic critic for the London *Times,* 1900–1926. In the Induction to *Fanny's First Play* (1911), Shaw caricatured him as Mr. Trotter, a critic who insists that "the definition of a play has been settled exactly and scientifically for two thousand two hundred and sixty years " by Aristotle, and delivers the following speech on the sort of drama that Shaw writes: "I say they are not plays. Dialogues, if you will. Exhibitions of character, perhaps: especially the character of the author.

repeated here. But I may remind him that /183/ the new technique is new only on the modern stage. It has been used by preachers and orators ever since speech was invented. It is the technique of playing upon the human conscience; and it has been practised by the playwright whenever the playwright has been capable of it. Rhetoric, irony, argument, paradox, epigram, parable, the rearrangement of haphazard facts

into orderly and intelligent situations: these are both the oldest and the newest arts of the drama; and your plot construction and art of preparation are only the tricks of theatrical talent and the shifts of moral sterility, not the weapons of dramatic genius. In the theatre of Ibsen we are not flattered spectators killing an idle hour with an ingenious and amusing entertainment: we are " guilty creatures sitting at a play ";[8] and the technique of pastime is no more applicable than at a murder trial. /184/

8. See *Hamlet,* II.ii.617–21.

Fictions, possibly. . . . But plays, no. I say NO. Not plays. If you will not concede this point I can't continue our conversation. I take this seriously. It's a matter of principle."

---

from INTRODUCTION TO GHOSTS by William Archer

These are the last two paragraphs of Archer's Introduction (first published in 1906), taken from the Viking Edition of The Works of Henrik Ibsen *(N.Y.: Scribner's, 1917), Vol. VII. The footnotes which appear here are the present editor's.*

In an interview, published immediately after Ibsen's death, Björnstjerne Björnson,[1] questioned as to what he held to be his brother-poet's greatest work, replied, without a moment's hesitation, *Gengangere.* This dictum can scarcely, I think, be accepted without some qualification. Even confining our attention to the modern plays, and leaving out of comparison *The Pretenders, Brand,* and *Peer Gynt,* we can scarcely call *Ghosts* Ibsen's richest or most human play, and certainly not his profoundest or most poetical. If some omnipotent Censorship decreed the annihilation of all his works save one, few people, I imagine, would vote that that one should be /203/ *Ghosts.* Even if half a dozen works were to be saved from the wreck, I doubt whether I, for my part, would include *Ghosts* in the list. It is, in my judgment, a little bare, hard, austere. It is the first work in which Ibsen applies his new technical method — evolved, as I have suggested, during the composition of *A Doll's House* — and he applies it with something of fanaticism. He is under the sway of a prosaic ideal — confessed in the phrase, " My object was to make the reader feel that he was

going through a piece of real experience "[2] — and he is putting some constraint upon the poet within him. The action moves a little stiffly, and all in one rhythm. It lacks variety and suppleness. Moreover, the play affords some slight excuse for the criticism which persists in regarding Ibsen as a preacher rather than as a creator — an author who cares more for ideas and doctrines than for human beings. Though Mrs. Alving, Engstrand and Regina are rounded and breathing characters, it cannot be denied that Manders strikes one as a clerical type rather than an individual, while even Oswald might not quite unfairly be described as simply and solely his father's son, an object-lesson in heredity. We cannot be said to know him, individually and intimately, as we know Helmer or Stockmann, Hialmar Ekdal or Gregers Werle.[3] Then, again, there are one or two curious flaws in the play. The question whether Oswald's " case " is one which actually presents itself in the medical books seems to me of very trifling moment. It is typically true, even if it be not true in detail. The suddenness of the catastrophe may possibly be exaggerated, its premonitions, and even its essential nature, may be misdescribed. On the /204/ other hand, I conceive it probable that the poet had documents to found upon, which may be unknown to his critics. I

1. a Norwegian novelist, poet, and dramatist (1832–1910).

2. taken from his letter to Schandorph, which is reprinted in Part Two.

3. Torvald Helmer is in *A Doll's House* (1879), Dr. Stockmann in *An Enemy of the People* (1882), and Hialmar Ekdal and Gregers Werle in *The Wild Duck* (1884).

have never taken any pains to satisfy myself upon the point, which seems to me quite immaterial. There is not the slightest doubt that the life-history of a Captain Alving may, and often does, entail upon posterity consequences quite as tragic as those which ensue in Oswald's case, and far more widespreading. That being so, the artistic justification of the poet's presentment of the case is certainly not dependent on its absolute scientific accuracy. The flaws above alluded to are of another nature. One of them is the prominence given to the fact that the Asylum is uninsured. No doubt there is some symbolical purport in the circumstance; but I cannot think that it is either sufficiently clear or sufficiently important to justify the emphasis thrown upon it at the end of the second act. Another dubious point is Oswald's argument in the first act as to the expensiveness of marriage as compared with free union. Since the parties to free union, as he describes it, accept all the responsibilities of marriage, and only pretermit the ceremony, the difference of expense, one would suppose, must be neither more nor less than the actual marriage fee. I have never seen this remark of Oswald's adequately explained, either as a matter of economic fact, or as a trait of character. Another blemish, of somewhat greater moment, is the inconceivable facility with which, in the third act, Manders suffers himself to be victimized by Engstrand. All these little things, taken together, detract, as it seems to me, from the artistic completeness of the play, and impair its claim to rank as the poet's masterpiece. Even in prose /205/ drama, his greatest and most consummate achievements were yet to come.

Must we, then, wholly dissent from Björnson's judgment? I think not. In a historical, if not in an aesthetic, sense, *Ghosts* may well rank as Ibsen's greatest work. It was the play which first gave the full measure of his technical and spiritual originality and daring. It has done far more than any other of his plays to "move boundary-posts." [4] It has advanced the frontiers of dramatic art and implanted new ideals, both technical and intellectual, in the minds of a whole generation of playwrights. It ranks with *Hernani* and *La Dame aux Camélias* [5] among the epoch-making plays of the nineteenth century, while in point of essential originality it towers above them. We cannot, I think, get nearer to the truth than Georg Brandes [6] did in the above-quoted phrase from his first notice of the play, describing it as not, perhaps, the poet's greatest work, but certainly his noblest deed. In another essay, Brandes has pointed to it, with equal justice, as marking Ibsen's final breach with his early — one might almost say his hereditary — romanticism. He here becomes, at last, "the most modern of the moderns." "This, I am convinced," says the Danish critic, "is his imperishable glory, and will give lasting life to his works." /206/

4. In a letter to Otto Borchsenius, a Danish journalist, written shortly after the publication of *Ghosts*, Ibsen said, "It may well be that the play is in several respects rather daring. But it seemed to me that the time had come for moving some boundary-posts."

5. Victor Hugo's *Hernani* was produced in 1830; *La Dame aux Camélias*, by Alexandre Dumas the younger (Dumas *fils*), in 1852.

6. a very influential Danish critic and aesthetician (1842–1927), who was one of the early defenders of Ibsen's work.

from INTRODUCTION TO IBSEN'S PLAYS
by Henry Louis Mencken

These passages are taken from H. L. Mencken's Introduction (dated 1917) to an early Modern Library edition of Ibsen's plays (N.Y.: Boni and Liveright, n.d.). The footnotes which appear here are the present editor's.

Ibsen, like Wagner and Manet, has lived down his commentators, and is now ready to be examined and enjoyed for what he actually was, namely, a first-rate journeyman dramatist, perhaps the best that ever lived. Twenty years ago he was hymned and damned as anything and everything else: symbolist, seer, prophet, necromancer, maker of riddles, rabble-rouser, cheap shocker, pornographer, spinner of gossamer nothings. Fools belabored him and fools defended him; he was near to being suffocated and done for in the fog of balderdash. I know of no sure cure for all the sorrows of the world, social, political or aesthetic, that was not credited to him, read into him, forced into his baggage. And I know of no crime against virtue, good order and the revelation of God that he was not accused of. The product of all this pawing and bawling was the Ibsen legend, that fabulous picture of a fabulous monster, half Nietzsche and half Dr. Frank Crane, drenching the world with scandalous platitudes from a watch-tower in the chilblained North. The righteous heard of him with creepy shudders; there was bold talk of denying him the use of the mails; he was the Gog and the Magog, the Heliogabalus, nay, the downright Kaiser, of that distant and pious era.[1]

No such Ibsen, of course, ever really existed. The genuine Ibsen was anything but the Anti-Christ thus conjured up by imprudent partisans and terrified opponents. On the contrary, he was a man whose salient quality was precisely his distrust of, and disdain for, any and all such facile heresies; a highly respectable gentleman of the middle class, /v/ well-barbered, ease-loving and careful in mind; a very skilful practitioner of a very exacting and lucrative trade; a safe and sane exponent of order, efficiency, honesty and common sense. From end to end of his life there is no record that Ibsen ever wrote a single word or formulated a single idea that might not have been exposed in a newspaper editorial. He believed in all the things that the normal, law-abiding citizen of Christendom believes in, from democracy to romantic love, and from the obligations of duty to the value of virtue, and he always gave them the best of it in his plays. And whenever, mistaking his position, someone charged him with flouting these things or with advocating some notion that stood in opposition to them, he invariably called the plaintiff to book, and denied vehe-

mently that he was guilty, and protested bitterly that it was outrageous to fasten any such wild and naughty stuff upon a reputable man. . . . /vi/

All this must be plain to anyone who goes through his so-called social dramas today, despite the confusing memory of all the gabble that went about in the high days of the Ibsen uproar. What ideas does one actually find in them? Such ideas, first and last, as even a Harvard professor might evolve without bursting his brain — for example, that it is unpleasant and degrading for a wife to be treated as a mere mistress and empty-head; that professional patriots and town boomers are frauds; that success in business usually involves doing things that a self-respecting man hesitates to do; that a woman who continues to cohabit with a syphilitic husband may expect to have defective children; that a joint sorrow tends to dampen passion in husband and wife, and so bring them together upon a more secure basis; that a neurotic and lascivious woman is apt to be horrified when she finds that she is pregnant; that a man of 55 or 60 is an ass to fall in love with a flapper of 17; that the world is barbarously cruel to a woman who has violated the Seventh Commandment or a man who has violated the Eighth. If you are discontented with these summaries, then turn to summaries that Ibsen made himself — that is, turn to his notes for his social dramas in his *Nachgelassene Schriften.*[2] Here you will find precisely what he was trying to say. Here you will find, in plain words, the ideas that he started from. They are, without exception, ideas of the utmost simplicity. There is nothing mysterious in them; there is not even anything new in them. Above all, /vii/ there is no idiotic symbolism in them. They mean just what they say.

As I have said, Ibsen himself was under no delusions about his dramas of ideas. He was a hard-working dramatist and a man of sense: he never allowed the grotesque guesses and fantasies of his advocates to corrupt the clarity of his own purpose. Down to the time he lost his mind — he was then at work on "John Gabriel Borkman" — he never wrote a line that had any significance save the obvious one, and he

---

1. Wilhelm Friedrich Nietzsche (1844–1900) was a German philosopher who vigorously attacked Christian morality. Dr. Frank Crane (1861–1928) was an American minister who wrote a very popular series of daily inspirational messages (syndicated in many newspapers and periodicals) noted for their sentimental platitudes and facile, homely optimism. Gog and Magog are Biblical representations of the nations that are to war against the kingdom of God under the leadership of Satan (Rev. 20:8); Heliogabalus (204–222 A.D.) was one of the most profligate of the Roman emperors; and the Kaiser is Wilhelm II, who was regarded in America, during World War I, as a brutal monster.

2. (German) posthumous writings, what we would call his "literary remains." These include the notes or memoranda on *Ghosts* reprinted in Part Two of this book.

never forgot for an instant that he was writing, not tracts, but stage-plays. When the sentimental German middle classes mistook "A Doll's House" for a revolutionary document against monogamy, and began grouping him with the preachers of free love, he was as indignant as only a respectable family man can be, and even agreed to write a new ending for the play in order to shut off that nonsense. A year later he wrote "Ghosts" to raise a laugh against the alarmed moralists who had swallowed the free lovers' error. . . .

Ibsen's chief interest, from the beginning to the end of his career as a dramatist, was not with the propagation of ethical ideas, but with the solution of aesthetic problems. He was, in brief, not a preacher, but an artist, and not the /viii/ moony artist of popular legend, but the alert and competent artist of fact, intent upon the technical difficulties of his business. He gave infinitely more thought to questions of practical dramaturgy — to getting his characters on and off the stage, to building up climaxes, to calculating effects — than he ever gave to the ideational content of his dramas. Almost any idea was good enough, so long as it could be converted into a conflict, and the conflict could be worked out straightforwardly and effectively. Read his letters and you will find him tremendously concerned, from the start, with technical difficulties and expedients — and never mentioning morals, lesson, symbols and that sort of thing at all. So early as the time he wrote "The League of Youth" you will find him discussing the details of dramatic machinery with Dr. Georg Brandes, and laying stress on the fact, with no little vanity, that he has "accomplished the feat of doing without a single monologue, in fact, without a single aside." A bit later he began developing the stage direction; go through his plays and observe how he gradually increased its importance, until in the end it almost overshadowed the dialogue. And if you would get, in brief, the full measure of his contribution to the art of the drama, give hard study to "A Doll's House." Here, for the first time, his new technique was in full working. Here he deposed Scribe [3] and company at one blow, and founded an entirely new order of dramaturgy. Other dramatists, long before him, had concocted dramas of ideas — and good ones. The idea in Augier's "Le Mariage d'Olympe" was quite as sound and interesting as that in "A Doll's House"; the idea in Augier's "Les Effrontés" perhaps exceeded it in both ways. But Ibsen got into "A Doll's House" something that Augier and Feuillet and Dumas *fils* and all that crowd of Empire dramatists [4] had never been able to get into their plays, and that was an air of utter and absolute reality, an overwhelming conviction, a complete concealment of the dramatic machinery. /ix/

And how did he conceal it? Simply by leaving it out. Scribe had built up an inordinately complex dramaturgy. His plays were elaborate and beautiful mechanisms, but still always mechanisms. He had to sacrifice everything else — reason, probability, human nature — to make the machine run. And Augier, Feuillet and Dumas, better men all, followed docilely in his tracks. They were better observers; they were more keenly interested in the actual life about them; they managed, despite the artificiality of their technique, to get some genuine human beings into their plays. But that technique still hung around their necks; they never quite got rid of it. But Ibsen did. In "A Doll's House" he threw it overboard for all time. Instead of a complicated plot, working beautifully toward a foreordained climax, he presented a few related scenes in the life of a husband and wife. Instead of a finely wrought fabric of suspense and emotion nicely balanced, neatly hanging together, he hit upon an action that was all suspense and all emotion. And instead of carefully calculated explanations, involving the orthodox couriers and prattling chambermaids, he let the story tell itself. The result, as William Archer has said, "was a new order of experience in the theatre." The audience that came to be pleasantly diverted by the old, old tricks found its nerves racked by a glimpse through a terrifying keyhole. This thing was not a stage-play, but a scandal. It didn't caress and soothe; it arrested and shocked. It didn't stay discreetly on the stage; it leaped out over the footlights.

---

3. Eugène Scribe (1791–1861), a prolific French dramatist, usually thought of as the originator of the "well-made play" (see the following paragraph).

4. French dramatists who flourished during the reign of Napoleon III, usually called the Second Empire (1852–1870). Among the most prominent were Émile Augier (1820–1889), Octave Feuillet (1821–1890), and Alexandre Dumas the younger (Dumas *fils*, 1824–1895).

The audience gasped and went out gabbling, and the result was the Ibsen madness, with its twenty years of folderol. But there were dramatists in the house who, with professional eye, saw more clearly what was afoot, and these dramatists, once they could shake off the Scribe tradition, began to imitate Ibsen — Jones and Pinero and later Shaw in England; Hauptmann and Sudermann in Germany; Gorki and many another in Russia; Hervieu, Brieux and their like /x/ in France; a swarm of lesser ones in Italy, Scandinavia and Austria. Ibsen, in brief, completely overthrew the well-made play of Scribe, and set up the play that was a direct imitation of reality. He showed that the illusion was not only not helped by the elaborate machinery of Scribe, but that it was actually hindered — that the way to sure and tremendous effects was by the route of simplicity, naturalness, ingenuousness. In "A Doll's House" he abandoned all of the old tricks save two or three; in "Ghosts" he made away with the rest of them, and even managed to do without a plot; by the time he got to "Little Eyolf" there was nothing left of the traditional dramaturgy save the act divisions. /xi/

from IBSEN'S DRAMATIC TECHNIQUE
by Peter F. D. Tennant

This passage is taken from the Introduction to Tennant's Ibsen's Dramatic Technique *(Cambridge, Eng.: Bowes & Bowes, 1948). The footnotes which appear here are the present editor's.*

Ibsen's realism, which gave the great impulse to the realistic drama of modern times, always remained only an approximation to contemporary life, and never descended to the unpoetic drabness of the naturalistic school and that of his own numerous imitators. We need only turn to one of Ibsen's most "realistic" plays, *Ghosts,* to see how conventional and unrealistic the play actually is, though it created an illusion of everyday life for Ibsen's contemporaries. This he did by the use of contemporary characters, contemporary dialogue, a contemporary indoor setting and an adherence to the conventions of the unities. How unrealistic and romantic is the fate *motif* which dominates the play. Coincidences are skilfully given the appearance of consequences. The sins of the fathers are visited on the children in the most irrational manner. /14/ Regine, who is Osvald's sister, has opportunely escaped inheriting the venereal disease from which Osvald suffers. The incestuous love of brother and sister is a time-honoured ingredient of romantic fate-tragedy, and the rest of the devices are equally traditional. In the same room, in the same circumstances as her mother with Osvald's father, Regine reproves Osvald for his advances with identically the same words. Nothing could finally be more unrealistic than Osvald's sudden physical decomposition in the last act, a feature which was defended tooth and nail by Ibsen's contemporaries against the sceptical disquisitions of doctors in Germany and Scandinavia, who seriously considered it worth while to disprove the possibility of such an occurrence in real life, and thereby hoped they had diminished the value of the play as a work of art.

Ibsen was furious at these interpretations, and his anger knew no bounds when his previous play, *A Doll's House,* was appreciated not as a drama but as a *cause célèbre,*[1] putting him into the false position of an agitator for women's rights, while lawyers seriously discussed the pros and cons of Nora's legal position. The acceptance of Ibsen's plays as reality and not as drama has enriched theatrical history with innumerable incidents which far surpass such apocryphal stories as that of the indignant American officer who shot Iago from the auditorium, of the old lady who warned Polonius behind the arras, or of the farmer who offered Richard III a horse for a far lower price than

1. (*French*) a celebrated legal case or controversy.

he was prepared to pay.[2] Ibsen's contemporaries, and many of his critics and commentators, failed to observe the ritual of handing over their identity with their coats in the cloakroom as they came to the theatre, and walked in, bringing with them the conventions and prejudices of ordinary life, not adopting those of the stage.

The failure of Ibsen's contemporaries to distinguish between fact and fiction was due to Ibsen's skill in letting his plays centre round the burning moral or social problems of the day.

---

2. In *Hamlet*, III.iv, Polonius hides behind the arras (tapestry hangings) in the Queen's chamber to eavesdrop on her interview with Hamlet. Hamlet, hearing a noise, runs his sword through the arras and kills him. In the climactic battle scene in *Richard III*, Richard's horse is killed and he exclaims, "A horse! A horse! My kingdom for a horse!" (V.iv.13).

This at least is true as far as his earlier modern plays are concerned. But nowadays the perspective of time makes it easier to consider Ibsen as a dramatist and artist and not as a moralist. His ideas have not stood the test of time as well as the characters which enunciate them, but the dramatic effect of his technique is as fresh as ever. He was not an original thinker, but he had the faculty for presenting second-hand ideas as human problems, in a /15/ dramatic form which gives his conflicts an illusion of depth and appears to endue his characters with flesh and blood. It is Ibsen's dramatic form, and not his ideas, which constitutes his great contribution to the theatre. From his earliest days he insisted on illusion and not reality as the basis of art. . . . /16/

from THE LIFE OF IBSEN by Halvdan Koht

This passage is taken from Koht's The Life of Ibsen, *translated by Ruth L. McMahon and Hanna A. Larsen (N.Y.: Norton, 1931), Vol. II.*

The professor of Greek at the University of Oslo wrote in a review: "Of all that we have read in modern dramatic literature, *Ghosts* is the play which comes closest to the ancient drama. . . . The tragedy of antiquity is called the fate- or family-drama, the tragic fate being inherited in the family. Here, too, we have a family tragedy, but it is also a social drama — the ancient tragedy resurrected on modern soil."

The Greek nature of this drama lies not only in the mighty principle of responsibility or nemesis which runs through it, but perhaps just as much in the severe artistic form. Plot and characters are drawn in firm and clear strokes; everything inconsequential and irrelevant is shorn away. Here, as in *A Doll's House*, the number of characters has been limited to five, and this time Ibsen has even managed to get along without so much as a servant girl or a messenger — we meet no one except those who have a place in the main action itself. In this way an atmosphere of austere grandeur is given to the whole drama.

This, however, was not the general feeling at the time of publication. On the contrary, it had an effect as if it were the climax of crass naturalism, and Ibsen was put in a class with Émile Zola. For ten years Zola had been publishing volume upon volume of his great novel-series about the /171/ Rougon-Macquart family, and had drawn in crude colors all the revolting vice and immorality which throve among the citizens — last of all and most crudely of all in *Nana* (1880), a picture of sheer sexual lust.

Hardly anything could so irritate Ibsen as to be classed with an author of this kind. It is true, he himself aimed to be a realist, to depict life with absolute fidelity, without ulterior considerations; but he resembled Flaubert more than he did Zola. He was a romanticist who had become realist — a man who thought romantically, but wrote realistically. He did not wish — did not even wish to seem — merely to study society in all the forms and consequences of vice and lust. The thing which filled his mind was the individual man, and he measured the worth of a community according as it helped or hindered a man in being himself. He had an ideal standard which he placed upon the community, and it was from this measuring that his social criticism proceeded. /172/

from THE IDEA OF A THEATER by Francis Fergusson

These passages are taken from the fifth chapter of Fergusson's The Idea of a Theater *(Princeton: Princeton University Press, 1949). The section headings have been retained, even where the complete section has not been reprinted. The footnotes which appear here are the present editor's.*

The Plot of Ghosts: Thesis, Thriller, and Tragedy

Ghosts is not Ibsen's best play, but it serves my purpose, which is to study the foundations of modern realism, just because of its imperfections. Its power, and the poetry of some of its effects, are evident; yet a contemporary audience may be bored with its old-fashioned iconoclasm and offended by the clatter of its too-obviously well-made plot. On the surface it is a *drame à thèse*,[1] of the kind Brieux was to develop to its logical conclusion twenty years later: it proves the hollowness of the conventional bourgeois marriage. At the same time it is a thriller with all the tricks of the Boulevard entertainment: Ibsen was a student of Scribe in his middle period. But underneath this superficial form of thesis-thriller — the play which Ibsen started /*148*/ to write, the angry diatribe as he first conceived it — there is another form, the shape of the underlying action, which Ibsen gradually made out in the course of his two-years' labor upon the play, in obedience to his scruple of truthfulness, his profound attention to the reality of his fictive characters' lives. The form of the play is understood according to two conceptions of plot, which Ibsen himself did not at this point clearly distinguish: the rationalized concatenation of events with a univocal moral, and the plot as the "soul" or first actualization of the directly perceived action.

Halvdan Koht, in his excellent study *Henrik Ibsen*, has explained the circumstances under which *Ghosts* was written. It was first planned as an attack upon marriage, in answer to the critics of *A Doll's House*. The story of the play

1. (*French*) drama advancing a thesis, a "problem play." Eugène Brieux (1858–1932) was a French dramatist, most of whose plays were pleas for the amelioration of various social evils.

is perfectly coherent as the demonstration and illustration of this thesis. When the play opens, Captain Alving has just died, his son Oswald is back from Paris where he had been studying painting, and his wife is straightening out the estate. The Captain had been accepted locally as a pillar of society but was in secret a drunkard and debauchee. He had seduced his wife's maid, and had a child by her; and this child, Regina, is now in her turn Mrs. Alving's maid. Mrs. Alving had concealed all this for something like twenty years. She was following the advice of the conventional Pastor Manders and endeavoring to save Oswald from the horrors of the household: it was for this reason she had sent him away to school. But now, with her husband's death, she proposes to get rid of the Alving heritage in all its forms, in order to free herself and Oswald for the innocent, unconventional "joy of life." She wants to endow an orphanage with the Captain's money, both to quiet any rumors there may be of his sinful life and to get rid of the remains of his power over her. She encounters this power, however, in many forms, through the Pastor's timidity and through the attempt by Engstrand (a local carpenter who was bribed to pretend to be Regina's father) to blackmail her. Oswald wants to marry Regina and has to be told the whole story. At last he reveals that he has inherited syphilis from his father — the dead hand of the past in its most sensationally ugly form — and when his brain softens at /*149*/ the end, Mrs. Alving's whole plan collapses in unrelieved horror. It is "proved" that she should have left home twenty years before, like Nora in *A Doll's House;* and that conventional marriage is therefore an evil tyranny.

In accordance with the principles of the thesis play, *Ghosts* is plotted as a series of debates on conventional morality, between Mrs. Alving and the Pastor, the Pastor and Oswald, and Oswald and his mother. It may also be read as a perfect well-made thriller. The story is presented with immediate clarity, with mounting and controlled suspense; each act ends with an exciting curtain which reaffirms the issues and promises important new developments. In this play, as in so many others, one may observe that the conception of dramatic form underlying the thesis play and the machine-made Boulevard entertainment is the same: the logically concatenated series of events (intriguing thesis or logical intrigue) which the characters and their relationships merely illustrate. And it was this view of *Ghosts* which made it an immediate scandal and success.

But Ibsen himself protested that he was not a reformer but a poet. He was often led to write by anger and he compared the process of composition to his pet scorpion's emptying of poison; Ibsen kept a piece of soft fruit in his cage for the scorpion to sting when the spirit moved him. But Ibsen's own spirit was not satisfied by the mere discharge of venom; and one may see, in *Ghosts,* behind the surfaces of the savage story, a partially realized tragic form of really poetic scope, the result of Ibsen's more serious and disinterested brooding upon the human condition in general, where it underlies the myopic rebellions and empty clichés of the time.

In order to see the tragedy behind the thesis, it is necessary to return to the distinction between plot and action, and to the distinction between the plot as the rationalized series of events, and the plot as " the soul of the tragedy." The action of the play is " to control the Alving heritage for my own life." Most of the characters want some material or social advantage from it — Engstrand money, for instance, and the Pastor the security of conventional respectability. But Mrs. Alving is seeking a true /150/ and free human life itself — for her son, and through him, for herself. Mrs. Alving sometimes puts this quest in terms of the iconoclasms of the time, but her spiritual life, as Ibsen gradually discovered it, is at a deeper level; she tests everything — Oswald, the Pastor, Regina, her own moves — in the light of her extremely strict if unsophisticated moral sensibility: by direct perception and not by ideas at all. She is tragically seeking; she suffers a series of pathoses and new insights in the course of the play; and this rhythm of will, feeling, and insight underneath the machinery of the plot is the form of the life of the play, the soul of the tragedy.[2]

The similarity between *Ghosts* and Greek

tragedy, with its single fated action moving to an unmistakable catastrophe, has been felt by many critics of Ibsen. Mrs. Alving, like Oedipus, is engaged in a quest for her true human condition; and Ibsen, like Sophocles, shows onstage only the end of this quest, when the past is being brought up again in the light of the present action and its fated outcome. From this point of view Ibsen is a plot-maker in the first sense: by means of his selection and arrangement of incidents he defines an action underlying many particular events and realized in various modes of intelligible purpose, of suffering, and of new insight. What Mrs. Alving sees changes in the course of the play, just as what Oedipus sees changes as one veil after another is removed from the past and the present. The underlying form of *Ghosts* is that of the tragic rhythm as one finds it in *Oedipus Rex.*

But this judgment needs to be qualified in several respects: because of the theater for which Ibsen wrote, the tragic form which Sophocles could develop to the full, and with every theatrical resource, is hidden beneath the clichés of plot and the surfaces " evident to the most commonplace mind."[3] At the end of the play the tragic rhythm of Mrs. Alving's quest is not so much completed as brutally truncated, in obedience to the requirements of the thesis and the thriller. Oswald's collapse, before our eyes, with his mother's screaming, makes the intrigue end with a bang, and hammers home the thesis. But from the point of view of Mrs. Alving's tragic quest as we have seen it develop through the rest of the play, this conclusion concludes /151/ nothing: it is merely sensational. . . .

Mrs. Alving and Oswald: The Tragic Rhythm in a Small Figure

As Ibsen was fighting to present his poetic vision within the narrow theater admitted by modern realism, so his protagonist Mrs. Alving is fighting to realize her sense of human life in

---

2. Fergusson earlier (p. 18) described the basic " tragic rhythm of action" as a sequence, or series of sequences, moving from Purpose (will) to Passion (feeling, suffering, pathos) and then to Perception (insight, awareness, epiphany). See the following paragraph and footnote 2 on page 356 of Sewall's essay.

3. T. S. Eliot, " Four Elizabethan Dramatists, A Preface to an Unwritten Book " (1924). On page 143 Fergusson quoted the sentence from which this phrase is taken: " In one play, *Everyman,* and perhaps in that one play only, we have a drama within the limitations of art; since Kyd, since *Arden of Feversham,* since *The Yorkshire Tragedy,* there has been no form to arrest, so to speak, the flow of spirit at any particular point before it expands and ends its course in the desert of exact likeness to the reality which is perceived by the most commonplace mind." The passage can be found in Eliot's *Selected Essays, 1917-1932* (N.Y.: Harcourt, Brace, 1932), p. 93.

the blank photograph of her own stuffy parlor. She discovers there no means, no terms, and no nourishment; that is the truncated tragedy which underlies the savage thesis of the play. But she does find her son Oswald, and she makes of him the symbol of all she is seeking: freedom, innocence, joy, and truth. At the level of the life of the play, where Ibsen warms his characters into extraordinary human reality, they all have moral and emotional meanings for each other; and the pattern of their related actions, their partially blind struggle for the Alving heritage, is consistent and very complex. In this structure, Mrs. Alving's changing relation to Oswald is only one strand, though an important one. I wish to consider it as a sample of Ibsen's rediscovery, through modern realism, of the tragic rhythm.

Oswald is of course not only a symbol for his mother, but a person in his own right, with his own quest for freedom and release, and his own anomalous stake in the Alving heritage. He is also a symbol for Pastor Manders of what he wants from Captain Alving's estate: the stability and continuity of the /152/ bourgeois conventions. In the economy of the play as a whole, Oswald is the hidden reality of the whole situation, like Oedipus' actual status as son-husband: the hidden fatality which, revealed in a series of tragic and ironic steps, brings the final peripety [4] of the action. To see how this works, the reader is asked to consider Oswald's role in Act I and the beginning of Act II.

The main part of Act I (after a prologue between Regina and Engstrand) is a debate, or rather agon,[5] between Mrs. Alving and the Pastor. The Pastor has come to settle the details of Mrs. Alving's bequest of her husband's money to the orphanage. They at once disagree about the purpose and handling of the bequest; and this disagreement soon broadens into the whole issue of Mrs. Alving's emancipation versus the Pastor's conventionality. The question of Oswald is at the center. The Pastor wants to think of him, and to make of him, a pillar of society such as the Captain was supposed to have been, while Mrs. Alving wants him to be her masterpiece of liberation. At this point Oswald himself

wanders in, the actual but still mysterious truth underlying the dispute between his mother and the Pastor. His appearance produces what the Greeks would have called a complex recognition scene, with an implied peripety for both Mrs. Alving and the Pastor, which will not be realized by them until the end of the act. But this tragic development is written to be acted; it is to be found, not so much in the actual words of the characters, as in their moral-emotional responses and changing relationships to one another.

The Pastor has not seen Oswald since he grew up; and seeing him now he is startled as though by a real ghost; he recognizes him as the very reincarnation of his father: the same physique, the same mannerisms, even the same kind of pipe. Mrs. Alving with equal confidence recognizes him as her own son, and she notes that his mouth-mannerism is like the Pastor's. (She had been in love with the Pastor during the early years of her marriage, when she wanted to leave the Captain.) As for Oswald himself, the mention of the pipe gives him a Proustian intermittence of the heart: he suddenly recalls a childhood scene when his father had given him his own pipe to smoke. He feels /153/ again the nausea and the cold sweat, and hears the Captain's hearty laughter. Thus in effect he recognizes himself as his father's, in the sense of his father's *victim;* a premonition of the ugly scene at the end of the play. But at this point no one is prepared to accept the full import of these insights. The whole scene is, on the surface, light and conventional, an accurate report of a passage of provincial politeness. Oswald wanders off for a walk before dinner, and the Pastor and his mother are left to bring their struggle more into the open.

Oswald's brief scene marks the end of the first round of the fight, and serves as prologue for the second round, much as the intervention of the chorus in the agon between Oedipus and Tiresias punctuates their struggle, and hints at an unexpected outcome on a new level of awareness. As soon as Oswald has gone, the Pastor launches an attack in form upon Mrs. Alving's entire emancipated way of life, with the question of Oswald, his role in the community, his upbringing and his future, always at the center of the attack. Mrs. Alving replies with her whole rebellious philosophy, illustrated by a detailed

4. See *Poetics*, Chapters 10–11, on peripety, and on complex recognition (Bywater translates it "discovery") in the next paragraph.

5. Agon means contest or conflict, which Fergusson relates to the first stage (purpose, will) of the "tragic rhythm."

account of her tormented life with the Captain, none of which the Pastor had known (or been willing to recognize) before. Mrs. Alving proves on the basis of this evidence that her new freedom is right; that her long secret rebellion was justified; and that she is now about to complete Oswald's emancipation, and thereby her own, from the swarming ghosts of the past. If the issue were merely on this rationalistic level, and between her and the Pastor, she would triumph at this point. But the real truth of her situation (as Oswald's appearance led us to suppose) does not fit either her rationalization or the Pastor's.

Oswald passes through the parlor again on his way to the dining room to get a drink before dinner, and his mother watches him in pride and pleasure. But from behind the door we hear the affected squealing of Regina. It is now Mrs. Alving's turn for an intermittence of the heart: it is as though she heard again her husband with Regina's mother. The insight which she had rejected before now reaches her in full strength, bringing the promised pathos and peripety; she sees Oswald, not as her masterpiece of liberation, but as the sinister, tyrannical, and /154/ continuing life of the past itself. The basis of her rationalization is gone; she suffers the breakdown of the moral being which she had built upon her now exploded view of Oswald.

At this point Ibsen brings down the curtain in obedience to the principles of the well-made play. The effect is to raise the suspense by stimulating our curiosity about the facts of the rest of the story. What will Mrs. Alving do now? What will the Pastor do — for Oswald and Regina are half-brother and sister; can we prevent the scandal from coming out? So the suspense is raised, but the attention of the audience is diverted from Mrs. Alving's tragic quest to the most literal, newspaper version of the facts.

The second act (which occurs immediately after dinner) is ostensibly concerned only with these gossipy facts. The Pastor and Mrs. Alving debate ways of handling the threatened scandal. But this is only the literal surface: Ibsen has his eye upon Mrs. Alving's shaken psyche, and the actual dramatic form of this scene, under the discussion which Mrs. Alving keeps up, is her pathos which the Act I curtain broke off. Mrs. Alving is suffering the blow in courage and faith; and she is rewarded with her deepest insight: [*Fergusson quotes here, in another translation, her speech beginning,* "You know, Manders, the longer I live the more convinced I am that we're all haunted," *which appears on page 74 of this book*.] . . . /155/ From the point of view of the underlying form of the play — the form as "the soul" of the tragedy — this scene completes the sequence which began with the debate in Act I: it is the pathos-and-epiphany following that agon.

It is evident, I think, that insofar as Ibsen was able to obey his realistic scruple, his need for the disinterested perception of human life beneath the clichés of custom and rationalization, he rediscovered the perennial basis of tragedy. The poetry of *Ghosts* is under the words, in the detail of action, where Ibsen accurately sensed the tragic rhythm of human life in a thousand small figures. And these little "movements of the psyche" are composed in a complex rhythm like music, a formal development sustained (beneath the sensational story and the angry thesis) until the very end. But the action is not completed: Mrs. Alving is left screaming with the raw impact of the calamity. The music is broken off, the dissonance unresolved — or, in more properly dramatic terms, the acceptance of the catastrophe, leading to the final vision or epiphany which should correspond to the insight Mrs. Alving gains in Act II, is lacking. The action of the play is neither completed nor placed in the wider context of meanings which the disinterested or contemplative purposes of poetry demand.

The unsatisfactory end of *Ghosts* may be understood in several ways. Thinking of the relation between Mrs. Alving and Oswald, one might say that she had romantically loaded more symbolic values upon her son than a human being can carry; hence his collapse proves too much — more than Mrs. Alving or the audience can digest. One may say that, at the end, Ibsen himself could not quite dissociate himself from his rebellious protagonist and see her action in the round, and so broke off in anger, losing his tragic vision in the satisfaction of reducing the bourgeois parlor to a nightmare, and proving the hollowness of a society which sees human life in such myopic and dishonest terms. . . . /156/ The most general way to understand the unsatisfactory end of *Ghosts* is to say that Ibsen could not find a way to represent the action of his protagonist, with all its moral and intellectual depth, within the terms of modern realism. In the attempt he truncated this action, and revealed as in a brilliant light the limitations of the bourgeois parlor as the scene of human life.

The End of Ghosts: The Tasteless Parlor and the Stage of Europe

Oswald is the chief symbol of what Mrs. Alving is seeking, and his collapse ends her quest in a horrifying catastrophe. But in the complex life of the play, all of the persons and things acquire emotional and moral significance for Mrs. Alving; and at the end, to throw as much light as possible upon the catastrophe, Ibsen brings all of the elements of his composition together in their highest symbolic valency. The orphanage has burned to the ground; the Pastor has promised Engstrand money for his

" Sailor's Home " which he plans as a brothel; Regina departs, to follow her mother in the search for pleasure and money. In these eventualities the conventional morality of the Alving heritage is revealed as lewdness and dishonesty, quickly consumed in the fires of lust and greed, as Oswald himself (the central symbol) was consumed even before his birth. But what does this wreckage mean? Where are we to place it in human experience? Ibsen can only place it in the literal parlor, with lamplight giving place to daylight, and sunrise on the empty, stimulating, virginal snow-peaks out the window. The emotional force of this complicated effect is very great; it has the searching intimacy of nightmare. But it is also as disquieting as a nightmare from which we are suddenly awakened; it is incomplete, and the contradiction between the inner power of dream and the literal appearances of the daylight world is unresolved. */157/*

Suggestions for Written Assignments

Before preparing his written assignments, the student would do well to review the section of his composition text dealing with the particular rhetorical structures he will use. While many of the following questions involve more than one method of analysis, he will find it especially helpful to review *definition* for such questions as 22 and 44, *division and classification* for 15 and 26, *exemplification* for 36, *comparison and contrast* for 7, 10, 19, and many others, *cause-and-effect analysis* for 4 and 20, *argumentation* for 33, 37, 41, and 42, *description of character* for 2 and 5, and *narration* for 1 and 6.

SHORT PAPERS ON THE INDIVIDUAL PLAYS

1. Narrate the sequence of events from the beginning to the end of *Oedipus Rex,* making clear the causal connections between them.

2. Write a character sketch of Othello, citing evidence for each of the traits you ascribe to him.

3. Explain the significance of the title of *Ghosts*.

4. Describe the action in one scene of *The Hairy Ape* where the treatment is clearly nonrealistic, and explain the effect that is produced.

5. Demonstrate that Oedipus does, or does not, undergo a real change in character during the course of *Oedipus Rex*.

6. Trace the changes in Othello's state of mind from his discovery of Desdemona's innocence to his suicide, particularly as these are revealed in the contrast between ll. 259–82 and ll. 338–56 in Act V, Scene ii.

7. Contrast the "philosophies of life" of Manders and Osvald, and explain where Mrs. Alving stands with respect to their views.

8. Explain the function of Paddy (Kreon, Roderigo, Engstrand).

9. Discuss the extent to which Oedipus is responsible for his tragedy, and the extent to which it is the result of forces external to him.

10. Compare and account for the different feelings evoked by the fates of Desdemona, Othello, and Iago.

11. Develop a hypothesis, in terms of Ibsen's purpose, to account for the fact that the most admirable characters in *Ghosts* end so much more wretchedly than the least admirable characters (making use of Ibsen's working notes on the play where these seem relevant).

12. Explicate Yank's final speech, distinguishing the alternative ways of life that are mentioned there and discussing how these relate to the preceding action and to the plight of modern man (making use of O'Neill's comments on the play where these seem relevant).

SHORT PAPERS ON THE INDIVIDUAL CRITICAL ESSAYS

13. Trace the logical sequence by which Aristotle moves from his definition of art in Chapter 1 to his definition of tragedy in Chapter 6.

14. Explain Aristotle's conception of the relationship between history, poetry, and philosophy (see especially Chap. 9) to account for his statement, "For the purposes of poetry a convincing impossibility is preferable to an unconvincing possibility" (Chap. 25, par. 5; see also Chap. 24, par. 6).

15. Analyze the organization of Bradley's essay, accounting for the division into five major sections.

16. Explain Bradley's distinction between "substance" and "form" (or "construction"), and show how this distinction affects his approach to tragedy.

17. Discuss the principal pairs of "opposites" which, according to Sewall, the tragic form holds in "precarious balance."

18. Show how Sewall's conception of the problems of critical method, stated in his preliminary section, affects his procedure in the remainder of the essay.

MEDIUM–LENGTH PAPERS INVOLVING
COMPARISONS BETWEEN THE PLAYS

19. Compare the roles of Desdemona and Osvald, particularly with regard to the feelings evoked by their unhappy fates and to the consequent effect upon our attitudes toward the protagonists (Othello and Mrs. Alving).

20. Oedipus, Othello, Mrs. Alving, and Yank can be placed on a descending social scale. Compare two or more of the plays in these terms, showing what effect the protagonist's social status has upon our response (or arguing that it has no significant effect).

21. Two of the plays are in verse and two are in prose. Compare two or more of the plays, showing what effect the verse or prose form has upon our response (or arguing that it has no significant effect).

22. The construction of these plays is usually thought of as involving four distinctly different dramatic styles: *Oedipus Rex* would be called classical, *Othello* romantic, *Ghosts* realistic, and *The Hairy Ape* expressionistic. Compare two or more of the plays, defining the styles involved and showing what effect they have upon our response (or arguing that they have no significant effect).

23. *Othello* and *The Hairy Ape* might each be seen as the tragedy of an innocent and relatively simple alien destroyed by a sophisticated and corrupt society. Compare the plays in these terms, and discuss whether this is an adequate formulation of them.

24. *Oedipus Rex* and *Ghosts* might each be seen as the tragedy of a protagonist trying to learn the real meaning of his past life in order to find his "true human condition" (as Fergusson suggests). Compare the plays in these terms, and discuss whether this is an adequate formulation of them.

25. All four plays might be called tragedies of discovery, in that each protagonist makes very important discoveries — about himself and his relationship to the world about him — that bring about his catastrophe. Compare two or more of the plays in these terms, explaining what each protagonist learns and discussing how this knowledge relates to the action of the play and to its effect upon us (e.g., is what we learn—about the action of the play, and perhaps about life in general—the same as what the protagonist learns?).

MEDIUM–LENGTH PAPERS INVOLVING
COMPARISONS BETWEEN THE CRITICAL ESSAYS

26. Classify the theories of tragedy (and the criticisms of the plays) in terms of some consistent principle, showing which critics share similar points of view.

27. Compare two or more of the critics in terms of their views on the effect of tragedy, and relate these views to their basic conceptions of tragedy.

28. Compare two or more of the critics in terms of their views on the best kind of tragic hero, and relate these views to their basic conceptions of tragedy.

29. Miller's essay can be seen (whether he intended this or not) as an answer to Krutch. Compare their two theories of tragedy, explaining their opposite positions on the possibility of tragedy in the modern world.

30. Krutch states that tragedy does "justify the ways of God to men," which Bradley denies. Compare their two theories of tragedy (and their two interpretations of this phrase) in such a way as to explain this opposition.

31. Discuss whether Sewall's objection to the treatment of tragedy in terms of "textbook categories" applies to Aristotle, Hume, and Bradley.

32. Aristotle (with his concept of "form" or "soul"), Bradley (with his "substance"), Sewall (with his "theoretic form"), and Fergusson (with his "life or soul of the play") are all trying to get at the essence of tragedy. Compare two or more of these critics in terms of their different conceptions of this essence, explaining why they therefore concentrate upon different aspects of the drama.

33. Demonstrate that Marjorie Barstow's article is, or is not, a proper application of the position of the *Poetics*.

34. Select two of the critics in Part Four (other than Marjorie Barstow) who seem to be applying — whether consciously or not — two different theories of tragedy included in Part Three, and demonstrate this relationship.

35. Compare Archer's opinion of those who object to *Ghosts* because Ibsen's portrayal of Osvald's disease is scientifically inaccurate with Aristotle's opinions on this general subject.

MEDIUM–LENGTH PAPERS INVOLVING
APPLICATIONS OF THE CRITICAL ESSAYS TO THE PLAYS

36. Discuss the protagonists of two or more of the plays in terms of one critic's conception of the best kind of tragic hero.

37. Demonstrate that Sophocles' play is, or is not, superior to Seneca's, in terms of the standards developed by one of the critics.

38. Justify the major alterations that Shakespeare made in Cinthio's story, in terms of the standards developed by one of the critics.

39. Discuss Sophocles' decision to begin his play at the point where he did (rather than earlier or later in Oedipus' career), in terms of Aristotle's conception of an artistic " whole."

40. Discuss the " probability," in Aristotle's terms, of Iago's success in persuading Othello of Desdemona's infidelity.

41. Bowra and Whitman disagree sharply in their interpretations of the following points in *Oedipus Rex*. Show how their disagreement on one or more of these points results from differences in their basic conceptions of the play, and argue in favor of one

interpretation (or of a combination of the two, or of a third alternative) on the basis of your own reading of the play.

  a. Oedipus' quarrel with Kreon.
  b. Oedipus' self-blinding.
  c. Oedipus' speech, ll. 1287–90.

42. Shaw, Mencken, and Tennant disagree sharply on what constitutes the real value of Ibsen's plays in general, or of *Ghosts* in particular. Explain this disagreement, and argue in favor of one of these views (or of a combination of them, or of some fourth alternative) on the basis of your own reading of *Ghosts*.

43. Aristotle's theory is derived from an examination of Greek tragedy, and Bradley's almost wholly from an examination of Shakespeare's tragedies. Discuss to what extent their theories are limited to the particular bodies of drama from which they were derived, and to what extent they are of more universal significance, using the four plays in Part One as representative examples of the different types.

TOPICS FOR LONG RESEARCH PAPERS

In preparing one of the following long research papers, the student will make his own selection of materials from the sources provided in this book. He should, however, be sure to draw both from the tragedies themselves and from the writings of the critics. The questions in parentheses will suggest some of the ideas that might be considered under each general topic.

44. Define tragedy. (Should the definition be primarily in terms of a kind of protagonist, a plot, an effect on the audience, an attitude toward life, or something else? Should it be limited to the drama or even to literature? Has it changed from the time of the Greeks to the present day?)

45. Describe the best kind of tragic hero. (Should he belong to a certain social class, exhibit a certain kind of character, believe in a certain philosophy, possess a certain kind of tragic flaw? Why should he have these characteristics?)

46. Discuss the role of fate in tragedy. (Is fate a primary element in tragedy? Is it even necessary? Is it more " tragic " to have the catastrophe brought about by fate, or by the protagonist's own failings, or by some combination of the two, or by some other cause?)

47. Explain the value of tragedy. (Why do men

write tragedies? Why do men enjoy them? Does great tragedy have a permanent effect upon its audience? upon society in general?)

48. Argue that tragedy is or is not possible in the modern world. (What social changes would seem to make it more or less difficult to write, or appreciate, tragedy today than in earlier times? Do *Ghosts* and *The Hairy Ape* seem as " tragic " as *Oedipus Rex* and *Othello*? What is peculiarly " modern " about *Ghosts* and *The Hairy Ape*? Do the differences between these two tragedies and the two earlier ones have anything to do with current attitudes toward religion? democracy? realism?)

49. Discuss the standard of taste in literature. (Is there a fixed standard by which to judge literary works? If so, what is it based on? How can you account for differences in taste between different individuals or between different historical periods? What is the relationship between a man's general critical theory — e.g., his definition of tragedy — and his judgment of any particular work?)

50. Evaluate the tragedies in Part One in terms of one of the critical positions in Part Three or Four, or in terms of your own standards.

51. Evaluate the theories of tragedy in Part Three in terms of their applicability to the tragedies in Part One, or of some other standard.

TOPICS FOR LIBRARY RESEARCH

52. Write a brief paper on one of the following:
a. The Delphic oracle.
b. The worship of Dionysos in ancient Greece.
c. Venetian sea power.
d. Elizabethan attitudes toward the Moors.
e. Bohemian Paris in the 1880's.
f. Nineteenth-century attitudes toward venereal disease.
g. The Industrial Workers of the World.
h. Working conditions aboard the coal-burning steamships.

53. Show how the conditions of Athenian (Elizabethan) theatrical performances account for certain differences between *Oedipus Rex* (*Othello*) and *Ghosts* (or between the *Poetics* and a modern critical essay).

54. Show how one of the plays or critical essays reflects certain aspects of its author's life and character.

55. Describe the first two or three American productions of *Ghosts* (*The Hairy Ape*) and their reception.

56. Explain how the approximate date of *Oedipus Rex* (*Othello,* the *Poetics*) has been determined.

57. Cite the evidence for believing that Seneca's plays were not intended for the stage.

58. Compare the reputations of Sophocles and Seneca during the Renaissance.

59. Discuss the reputation of the *Poetics* from the Renaissance to the present.

60. Discuss the Expressionist movement in the theater.

Suggestions for Further Reading

The best advice that can be given the student who wishes to pursue the lines of inquiry introduced by this book is to read more tragedies, as many more as he can. He might first seek to broaden his experience with a widely scattered sampling of plays drawn from the whole range of tragedy, without any concern for their relationship to the works he just studied; or he might prefer to begin on more familiar ground by moving on, at least at first, to plays which he can easily relate to them.

He might well begin with Sophocles' other two tragedies dealing with the Oedipus legend, the *Antigone* and *Oedipus at Colonus,* and then go on to some of his four remaining works: *Ajax, Trachiniae, Electra,* and *Philoctetes.* There are three other extant Greek tragedies treating various aspects of the Oedipus story: Aeschylus' *Seven Against Thebes* and Euripides' *Suppliants* and his *Phoenissae.* And this line of study might conclude with one or two later dramatizations of this material, such as Pierre Corneille's *Oedipe,* John Dryden and Nathaniel Lee's *Oedipus,* or Jean Cocteau's *The Infernal Machine,* probably the most interesting modern treatment of the story.

There is no better way to follow up a reading of *Othello* than with the other major tragedies of Shakespeare: *Romeo and Juliet, Julius Caesar, Hamlet, King Lear, Macbeth, Antony and Cleopatra,* and *Coriolanus.* The student might also sample some of the attempts to "improve" on *Othello,* such as Philip Massinger's *The Duke of Milan,* Edward Young's *Revenge,* or Voltaire's *Zaïre,* although he will find that their chief value is to increase his admiration for the original (the same can be said for most of the later versions of *Oedipus Rex*).

A course of reading related to *Ghosts* might begin with *A Doll's House,* since many critics see *Ghosts* as a kind of sequel to that play, and then proceed to *An Enemy of the People,* which is thought to contain Ibsen's answer to the violent criticism that *Ghosts* aroused. Again, the student could continue reading more of Ibsen, with *Brand, Peer Gynt, The Wild Duck, Rosmersholm, Hedda Gabler, The Master Builder, John Gabriel Borkman,* and *When We Dead Awaken.* Or, if he wishes to proceed to other playwrights' works comparable to *Ghosts,* he has a very large field to choose from, since, as Fergusson points out, Ibsen's play is an ancestor of the whole genre of realistic "thesis" or "problem" drama that has become so prominent on the modern stage. After reading *Ghosts,* the student will find most of the plays of Maxim Gorky, Eugène Brieux,

John Galsworthy, and Clifford Odets (to name a few representative practitioners in this genre) familiar. If, out of this large group, he prefers to begin with plays treating the same sort of material as *Ghosts,* then Anton Chekhov's *The Three Sisters* or Federico García Lorca's *The House of Bernarda Alba* can be recommended.

O'Neill's *The Emperor Jones* is probably closest in theme and manner to *The Hairy Ape,* but the student should read some of the author's other important works as well: *Beyond the Horizon, Anna Christie, Desire Under the Elms, The Great God Brown, Strange Interlude, Mourning Becomes Electra, Days Without End, The Iceman Cometh, A Moon for the Misbegotten, Long Day's Journey into Night,* and *A Touch of the Poet.* Other plays that might fruitfully be compared to *The Hairy Ape* include Georg Kaiser's *From Morn to Midnight* and Elmer Rice's *The Adding Machine.*

Having read the selection by Arthur Miller, a practicing playwright, in the critical section of this book, the student may wish to read some of the tragedies in which Miller has put his ideas into practice. *All My Sons, Death of a Salesman, The Crucible,* and *A View from the Bridge* will offer a deeper insight into Miller's views of the common man as a tragic hero.

Two fine recordings also deserve to be mentioned here: one of *Oedipus Rex* (in the William Butler Yeats translation, which abridges portions of Sophocles), produced by the Stratford, Ontario, Shakespeare Festival Players and directed by Tyrone Guthrie (Caedmon TC 2012), and one of *Othello,* starring Paul Robeson and José Ferrer (Columbia SL 153). Students who enjoy music will also want to hear Igor Stravinsky's oratorio, *Oedipus Rex* (Columbia ML–4644, London A–4106), and Giuseppe Verdi's opera, *Otello* (RCA Victor LM–6107, London A–4312, Cetra 1252).

The student who wants to read further in the theory of tragedy also has a choice of broadening his field to take in new critical positions or of learning more about those represented in this book. Of the theories of tragedy not included here, the two which have probably been most influential in the history of criticism can be found in the final section of Wilhelm Friedrich Hegel's *The Philosophy of Fine Art* (translated by F. P. B. Osmaston, London: Bell, 1920), and in Friedrich Nietzsche's *The Birth of Tragedy* (translated by Francis Golffing, N. Y.: Doubleday, 1956). (A. C. Bradley's own theory is ultimately derived from Hegel's, as he explains in a lecture entitled " Hegel's Theory of Tragedy " in his *Oxford Lectures on Poetry* [London: Macmillan, 1909].) It would be impossible to list here all the other interesting theories; instead, the student can be referred to Barrett H. Clark's *European Theories of the Drama, with a Supplement on the American Drama* (N. Y.: Crown, 1947, rev. ed.) and to Richard B. Vowles' *Dramatic Theory: A Bibliography* (N. Y.: New York Public Library, 1956). A student primarily interested in recent theories of tragedy could construct a workable reading list from the citations in Richard Sewall's essay, or for a fuller bibliography he can consult Henry Popkin's article on the drama in *Contemporary Literary Scholarship, A Critical Review* (N. Y.: Appleton-Century-Crofts, 1958), edited by Lewis Leary for the National Council of Teachers of English.

If the student desires to inquire further into the theories of tragedy represented in this book, he might start with some of the interpretations of (and controversies about) the *Poetics* from the Renaissance commentators (Bernardino Daniello, Julius Caesar Scaliger, Antonio Minturno, Lodovico Castelvetro, and others) down to the present day. Most of this material is identified in the surveys listed above and can also be found in Lane Cooper and Alfred Gudeman's *A Bibliography of the* Poetics *of Aristotle* (New Haven: Yale University Press, 1928), supplemented by Gerald E. Else's " A Survey of Work on Aristotle's *Poetics,* 1940–1954," *Classical Weekly,* Vol. 48, No. 6 (February 14, 1955). He can continue his study of A. C. Bradley's theory by reading (in addition to the lecture on Hegel) the second chapter of *Shakespearean Tragedy,* "Construction in Shakespeare's Tragedies," and the two chapters on *Othello.* Joseph Wood Krutch's essay might be followed by his book, *The American Drama Since 1918* (N. Y.: Braziller, 1957, rev. ed.), which contains a criticism of O'Neill. Additional insight into Arthur Miller's conception of tragedy can be derived from two of his articles, " The Nature of Tragedy " (New York *Herald Tribune,* March 27, 1949), and " The *Salesman* Has a Birthday " (New York *Times,* February 5, 1950), as well as from his Introduction to *Arthur Miller's Collected Plays* (N. Y.: Viking, 1957). Richard Sewall's theory is developed in his book *The Vision of Tragedy* and applied

there in the analysis of several tragedies, including *Oedipus Rex.* Finally, the student is advised to read further in Francis Fergusson's *The Idea of a Theater* (particularly Chapter I on *Oedipus Rex*), since it works out another theory of tragedy quite different from any represented in Part Three.

Some suggestions can also be given the student who wishes to examine other critical treatments of the plays included here, although he might well begin with a more complete reading of the books which were excerpted in Part Four. He will find brief but very suggestive comments on *Oedipus Rex* in the works of Hegel and Nietzsche cited above, and still different approaches to the play in H. D. F. Kitto's *Greek Tragedy* (N.Y.: Doubleday, 1955), Chapters V–VII; Paul Goodman's *The Structure of Literature* (Chicago: University of Chicago Press, 1954), Chapter II; and Bernard Knox's *Oedipus at Thebes* (New Haven: Yale University Press, 1957), in addition to the books of Richard Sewall and Francis Fergusson already mentioned. The field of Shakespearean criticism is so vast that no adequate listing of studies of *Othello* can be attempted here; perhaps the three sharply conflicting interpretations of the play in the essays by Elmer E. Stoll, Robert B. Heilman, and Arthur Sewell, contained in Leonard Dean's *Shakespeare: Modern Essays in Criticism* (N. Y.: Oxford University Press, 1957), are as good a place as any to begin, and the student can follow up the leads for further reading that he finds there. For additional commentary on *Ghosts* he can turn to Hermann J. Weigand's *The Modern Ibsen* (N. Y.: Holt, 1925) and Muriel C. Bradbrook's *Ibsen, the Norwegian* (London: Chatto & Windus, 1948), among other works, and to the debate on the respective merits of *Ghosts* and *Oedipus Rex* in Edmund Wilson's " Mrs. Alving and Oedipus," in *Discordant Encounters* (N. Y.: Boni, 1927). A survey of criticism of *The Hairy Ape* might start with Barrett H. Clark's *Eugene O'Neill: The Man and His Plays* (N. Y.: Dover, 1947), Edwin Engel's *The Haunted Heroes of Eugene O'Neill* (Cambridge: Harvard University Press, 1953), and Doris Falk's *Eugene O'Neill and the Tragic Tension* (New Brunswick: Rutgers University Press, 1958), which also refer to other discussions of the play.